INTERNATIONAL
MANAGERIAL
FINANCE

THE IRWIN SERIES IN FINANCE

EDITORS

Myron J. Gordon
University of Toronto

Robert W. Johnson
Purdue University

COHEN & HAMMER (eds.)   *Analytical Methods in Banking*

DAVIDS (ed.)   *Money and Banking Casebook*

GIES & APILADO (eds.)   *Banking Markets and Financial Institutions*

MELNYK & BARNGROVER   *Cases in Business Finance*

QUIRIN   *The Capital Expenditure Decision*

SHADE   *Common Stocks: A Plan for Intelligent Investing*

SMITH   *Economics of Financial Institutions and Markets*

VAN HORNE (ed.)   *Foundations for Financial Management: A Book of Readings*

WESTON & SORGE   *International Managerial Finance*

WIDICUS & STITZEL   *Personal Investing*

INTERNATIONAL MANAGERIAL FINANCE

J. FRED WESTON
Professor of Business Economics and Finance
University of California at Los Angeles

BART W. SORGE
Professor of International Business and Finance
University of Southern California

 1972

RICHARD D. IRWIN, INC.   *Homewood, Illinois   60430*
IRWIN-DORSEY LIMITED   *Georgetown, Ontario*

First Printing, October 1972

ISBN 0–256–01390–X
Library of Congress Catalog Card No. 72–86619
Printed in the United States of America

To DMS and WRO

Preface

THE UNITED STATES and the world are in the midst of another historic upheaval in international financial relations. The events of recent years have amply demonstrated that business firms and individuals alike are greatly affected by the changes and adjustments in international financial and trade relationships. Some of the impacts are immediate and direct; other effects operate indirectly through their major influences on governmental policies and thus on the money supply, interest rates, taxation, and spending.

Most readers will acknowledge that the events of recent years took them by surprise. There has been widespread but belated recognition of how these changing circumstances have affected firms and individuals both directly and indirectly. We believe that this book provides a basis for understanding international financing developments. It will therefore provide a basis for increased understanding of the events taking place. But more importantly, we feel that this book will increase the ability of firms and individuals to forecast the even greater changes that, in our judgment, lie ahead.

We have seen how international developments have had a major influence on domestic prices and costs. In addition to these direct effects, the indirect effects are numerous and powerful. Firms and individuals who thought that they were not involved in international happenings found that the events of recent years have demonstrated the contrary. It is virtually impossible to be isolated from the impact of international developments.

For example, in the recent revaluation of the currencies of many countries, it was generally supposed that higher prices would be charged by foreign sellers and that this would help the firms with which their goods compete in the United States. But we found that other firms in the United States were sellers to these foreign firms, and they were adversely affected by the currency realignment, so that some U.S. firms were hurt to the same degree as their foreign customers. Other American firms used imported products as raw materials in goods that they were producing and selling in an economy with price controls in the United States. They found that some of the raw materials they were purchasing abroad were increasing in price at the same time that there were limitations on their own selling prices. Thus, in the complex web of world events, international financial developments that initially appeared to benefit all American firms turned out to help some, but hurt other American firms to the same or a greater degree. The relationships are complex, and for a clear understanding one has to have a clear picture of the fundamentals involved and the nature of the interrelations. This is a basic aim of the present book.

For years the subject of international business finance was neglected because it seemed remote. It was regarded as a subject only for those who were directly affected, or for specialists who were required to master a profound, complex, and esoteric subject. These assumptions have been demonstrated to be invalid. The subject is not remote. We are all affected. In addition, what has become the subject matter of daily newspaper articles cannot be beyond the understanding of the individual citizen as well as the responsible business managers.

The world is continuing to shrink in size by all practical criteria. Communication throughout the world now takes place within a matter of minutes or even seconds. All parts of the world are now linked by jet transportation within a matter of hours. International economic and financial mechanisms reflect changes throughout the world rapidly. New cultural patterns are seen to spread throughout the world in brief periods of time. Most business and governmental decisions are now affected by international considerations because world relationships have now become interwoven. It is only natural then that financial aspects of business operations increasingly take on important international dimensions.

Our aim—to convey both a foundation for understanding, and an illustration of how to apply the basic elements of international finance to managerial policies and decision making—has guided the basic organization of this book. Part One emphasizes the foundation, framework, and tools for decision making. Part Two emphasizes the application of these materials in the formulation of managerial policy and decisions. However, even in Part One, when we have presented examples, we have shown how the general international financial economy and its institutions and instruments relate to decision making. In Part Two, we have related the policies and decision making to the framework developed in Part One. Our aim, however, is that by an orderly presentation of the key framework material, we provide a clear body of ideas to enhance the understanding of international financial developments and show how these developments do, in fact, affect business firms and individuals in a number of important ways.

This book is directed to a variety of audiences. It is addressed primarily to the point of view of the executives of firms affected by international developments. In addition, it is hoped that students and others who aspire to be involved in business activities will also find the material in this volume a useful preparation for moving toward their goals. Finally, and perhaps most importantly, the interaction of international business finance with the broader economic and social issues of the day makes the subject matter of vital concern to all citizens. Indeed, during these times, in order to read the daily newspapers with understanding, many materials in this book are required as background.

A number of forces continue to cause internationalization of the location of business operations and the patterns of trade and investment. These include a broadened range of competition, divergent trends in domestic and foreign costs in different industries, rapid changes in the development and the diffusion of technology, and shifts in the location of raw materials and supplies. The increased involvement in international developments will therefore be required by business firms, by those concerned with vital governmental policy, and by individual citizens in a number of ways.

The managers of business firms, particularly, will find that international financial developments have increased impacts on their operations. The new uncertainties and the changed nature of prospects will therefore require increased study of the ramifications, difficulties, and special factors involved as increased international financial relationships develop. Business managers have increased obligations to their firms to familiarize themselves with the new international sources of financing. The opportunities and threats involved in new international investments also must be fully understood.

The authors come to the writing of this book with knowledge based on many years of direct experience. The first author began direct contact with international finance in working with the international banking departments of two major California banks during the 1950s. He was also involved in studies and publications analyzing opportunities for business firms on an international scope. The second author has been engaged for over 30 years in international business decisions as either the chief executive officer or as a member of the board of directors of firms with major international commitments.

We acknowledge the assistance of a number of persons who provided help and ideas. We appreciated the comments and suggestions of Professors Gerlof Homan, Arnold Sametz, David Eiteman, Eugene Brigham, and Robert Aubrey. Walter R. Oreamuno provided important ideas and practical suggestions. Yutaka Imai helped so much he deserves to be listed as a coauthor. Grace Marshall edited the materials most critically. Lynn Hickman, Marilyn McElroy, and Dorothea Sorge typed many drafts with patience and forbearance. Many officials and government agencies provided us with explanations as well as documentation. We take final responsibility for all the views expressed.

While we came to the subject matter with a background of prior experience and study, we have found it necessary to learn many new aspects. To analyze and interpret the international economic events of recent years has required studying and rethinking many old as well as new concepts. The subject matter continues to be in a state of rapid and continued changes. It is our hope, therefore, that the book will provide a foundation for continued study and increased understanding of the events taking place. An important aim is to anticipate the further changes that are, in our judgment, inevitable.

September 1972   J. Fred Weston
                                                   Bart W. Sorge

Contents

Part two
MANAGEMENT POLICIES AND DECISIONS

in project analysis. Working capital management in international enterprise. The multinational firm. International financial trends.

part one

THE FRAMEWORK AND TOOLS OF ANALYSIS

1

International business finance and its environment

INTERNATIONAL finance now affects the lives of all persons. Daily newspaper headlines deal with new government policies concerning international trade and finance and with changes and realignments in exchange rates. The major role accorded international economic policies in President Nixon's New Economic Policy speech of August 15, 1971 demonstrates the importance of international finance for domestic financial and economic developments as well as for its international implications. Hence, increasingly, international business finance is inextricably interwoven with domestic business finance.

THE IMPACT OF INTERNATIONAL
FINANCIAL DEVELOPMENTS

International financial concepts and events have important implications for business firms and their executives. Individual firms can be affected directly or indirectly by international financial developments even though the managers of the firms may not realize that such developments do in fact affect their firms. Some examples will illustrate this truth.

1. Your firm has been a supplier to firm A which imports some critical materials and parts from foreign sources. Firm A finds that the costs of these parts have risen due to the dollar devaluation and the revaluation of Western European currencies. Firm A's profit margins decline, and in addition its sales fall off because firms that had been using domestic sources have taken a larger market share. Your firm's sales to firm A fall off as a consequence.

2. Your firm has been a supplier to firm B which sells its products abroad. The effect of the New Economic Policy on its foreign customers has been to cause a downturn in the economies of the countries in which

3

firm B's customers are located. Firm B's sales and profits fall. Your firm's sales decline as a result.

3. Your firm has been a supplier directly to firms such as Volkswagen in Germany which in turn sell their final product abroad. The rise in the value of the Deutsche mark has decreased the profits of those German firms. Volkswagen says that the 9.3 percent upward revaluation of the Deutsche mark against other currencies in late 1969 cost the company $65.6 million in 1970—a major reason, along with rising production costs, for the profit decline that year. Every percentage point the Deutsche mark rises costs VW $19 million per year. Your firm's sales to its foreign customers drop sharply.

4. Your firm neither buys from nor sells to foreign firms. It is not involved in foreign trade. But the materials your firm buys from another supplier have a high percentage of foreign goods in their content. The costs of these foreign goods rise and the costs of the goods supplied to your firm rise, with the result that a profit squeeze for your firm may occur.

5. Your firm uses internationally traded raw materials in its products. As a result of the reduced international value of the dollar in relation to other major currencies, the prices of these raw materials rise for U.S. firms. But in Phase II, the price increase for your industry has been limited to 4 percent, which does not cover your cost increases.

6. Your firm has been producing an equipment item abroad because of lower labor costs. Inflationary trends abroad have been increasing your costs of production abroad. In addition, the product manufactured abroad does not qualify for the investment tax credit since the investment credit provisions of the 1971 tax law do not apply to goods produced abroad. The profitability of this division is sharply reduced.

The above examples show how many firms can be affected by recent international financial developments. Some firms may be helped; some will be hurt. One broad change is that Canada and Mexico, along with other Latin American nations, have been surprised and upset by recent U.S. policies. Therefore, in the future these countries will seek to reduce their trade relations with the United States in favor of Western European nations and Japan. Both opportunities and problems are created by changes in the financial and economic environment.

These examples of the impact of recent international financial developments dramatize their substantial influence on practically all business firms.

These international financial developments are of special significance to the financial decisions of business firms. It is the central purpose of this book to provide materials that will be useful to financial managers in carrying out their responsibilities. The remainder of this first chapter will set forth some dimensions of international trade and finance, make a comparison of international business finance with domestic business finance, describe the important environmental factors affecting international business, and outline the organization of the book.

SOME DIMENSIONS OF INTERNATIONAL TRADE AND FINANCE

The world gross product exceeds $2 trillion to support a world population in excess of 3 billion people. The world volume of international trade is more than $200 billion per annum. Of this the United States accounts for some $40 billion per year, the amount having doubled in the past 40 years. This sum, however, represents less than 5 percent of U.S. annual gross national product which exceeds $1 trillion per year. The volume of exports and imports of the United States is greater than that of any other single country in the world, but the percentages of exports and imports to the total GNP of other major countries are generally higher than those of the United States. For example, the exports and imports of West Germany, the United Kingdom, and Canada are in excess of 20 percent of the gross national product of those countries. For Norway, Belgium, and the Netherlands, the percentage ranges from one third to one half of the total economic activity which takes place in those countries. It is clear that international trade and finance are of great significance to all of the major countries of the world.

By 1970 the United States owned assets abroad totaling $158 billion. U.S. liabilities to foreigners were $91 billion. Thus, the net positive international investment position of the United States was $67 billion. However, a high percentage of U.S. assets abroad are in the form of long-term investments, while the liabilities are predominately short term. This can create liquidity problems in times of international instability. The nature and significance of these problems will be explored in later chapters.

The number of U.S. affiliates abroad has grown from about 10,000 in 1957 to an estimated 25,000 in 1970. The number of U.S. corporations which own foreign affiliates abroad has grown from 2,800 in 1957 to 3,500 in 1970.[1] Financing requirements excluding operating costs and expenses of American-owned affiliates incorporated in other countries have grown from $16 billion in 1965 to $25 billion in 1970. Thus, the absolute magnitudes of international trade and finance are of major dimensions and are increasing.

These foregoing numbers are large compared with the smaller net figure in the U.S. balance of payments, or in the "net foreign investment" item carried in U.S. gross national product accounts. But these net figures

---

[1] Chase Manhattan Bank, "Financing U.S. Multinational Enterprise," *Business in Brief*, August 1971, p. 2.

reflect much larger flows of goods and capital movements from and into the United States. Furthermore, regardless of the absolute magnitudes of the international trade and investment accounts, their influence pervades almost every aspect of U.S. domestic economic and financial policy. If this is true for the United States, with only 5 percent of its gross national product accounted for by imports and exports, the significance for governmental policies of international trade and finance in some other countries, for whom foreign trade is a much higher percentage of their total economic activity, must be substantially greater.

Reasons for the increased importance of international financial management to U.S. business firms include the following: (1) While exports as a percentage of total U.S. business activity remain at the 5 percent level, for some individual industries the percentage rises to over 50 percent. With the overall U.S. balance-of-payments problem a matter of increasing concern, anything a firm or industry can do to contribute appropriately to the nation's balance of payments is desirable. (2) The percentage of sales and net profit of many individual U.S. firms from foreign operations is quite high. Also, the profitable utilization of what would otherwise be less than full capacity is important. For example, it has been stated by a large number of firms that if as much as 25 percent of their sales can be made abroad, this will contribute more than 50 percent of their net income. (3) There has been increasing investment abroad by private U.S. enterprise. This has often represented the adjustment of U.S. firms to the integration of economies abroad, as characterized by the European Economic Community or the "Common Market." (4) Of overriding importance is that with increased international trade, a firm may have to be able to compete abroad in order to compete in its own domestic market. This may be necessary both to achieve requisite economies of scale and for defensive reasons vis-à-vis foreign firms that have by this tactic developed economies of scale. (5) New opportunities are opening for U.S. firms to obtain funds abroad. Particularly noteworthy is the Eurodollar market. Sources of financing are expanding, and financial markets are becoming increasingly international.

Therefore, both the responsibilities and opportunities of individual business firms in international trade and finance have increased. It is the aim of this book to help the managers of business firms conduct their international operations with improved effectiveness.

DOES INTERNATIONAL BUSINESS FINANCE DIFFER FROM DOMESTIC FINANCE?

A fundamental question posed is whether the principles of international business finance differ from those of domestic operations. The existing literature of international business finance demonstrates that the principles are not fundamentally different. What is different is that the factors to be considered in international business decisions are substantially broader in range. The nature of the variables is different, there are more variables, and their rate of change has accelerated. Thus, while the decision-model techniques are not changed, the content and application of the models are altered.

The basic principles of domestic business finance are broadly and generally applicable. But the success of business decisions and their social effects are greatly influenced by implementation considerations. While the basic principles of domestic finance are the same as those of international business finance, the subject requires separate treatment for a number of reasons. A wider range of stimuli are involved. Important differences are involved in the application of the principles. New variables must be considered in international business financial decisions. These include a number of important aspects of environmental complexity and diversity, including:

1. New cultural-institutional factors.
2. Legal-political constraints.
3. More diverse labor laws and requirements.
4. The proliferation of regulations and requirements.
5. Differential rates of inflation in selling prices and costs.
6. New and increased risks from:
    a) Change in exchange rates and devaluation.
    b) Exchange controls.
    c) Restrictions on the flow of funds.
    d) Expropriation risks.

As a fundamental background for sound decisions in international business finance, this first chapter will now describe some important aspects of the international business environment which are basic to sound financial policies.

ENVIRONMENTAL FACTORS AFFECTING INTERNATIONAL BUSINESS

Successful international operations require that multinational firms be adequately informed about the environmental factors that affect business operations in foreign countries. In conducting a business operation in a foreign country it is not advisable to apply U.S. methods and techniques without regard to the customs, attitudes, and habits prevailing in the country of operation. It may be argued that these problems are not the concern of the financial vice president of a multinational firm. However, many of the environmental factors affecting foreign business operations strongly influence the financial outcome of business and commercial activities. The financial vice president of a multinational firm must be aware particularly of those environmental factors which influence his firm's operations from a financial point of view, so that he may make calculations of the financial consequences of business decisions.

The successful operation of a business venture requires the cooperation of many individuals. Therefore, it is of utmost importance that managements understand the attitudes, customs, and habits of the people in foreign countries from which their work force is or will be recruited. Managers must also understand the institutional arrangements that exist in a country of planned operations in regard to education, social welfare, and the legal system. The attitudes and policies of the foreign government applying to the initiation, operation, and liquidation of a foreign-owned business entity within its borders must be studied. The multinational manager must also have knowledge of taxes; government controls over the movement and use of capital funds; import, export, and price controls; and the rationing of goods and materials that might affect the operation of a foreign venture. Social legislation and its financial costs, as well as the foreign government's past and present fiscal and monetary policies, must be understood. A new foreign-owned business venture is also affected by local business customs and procedures, many not formalized but nevertheless observed by the local business community.

The historical behavior and the future expected trends of the foreign exchange value of the local currency in the foreign country are important in evaluating the profitability of a planned venture. Is the local currency readily convertible into other currencies, or is it restricted? Is its value constant in terms of gold or other foreign currencies? Does the country have a developed capital fund market? Is money available, and at what cost? What protections, if any, are available to avoid foreign exchange losses? All of these questions will affect the potential profitability of a foreign venture.

Demographic factors

In most countries of the world, foreign-owned business enterprises are required to employ a high percentage of nationals of the country in their business organization. Therefore, it is essential that the multinational firm be knowledgeable about the potential sources of its employees. Is the population uniform, or does it include groupings, as in many countries, where a large percentage of the population is native, a smaller percentage foreign immigrants, and an intermediate group a mixture of the two? What are the skills, education, and potential capability of each of the population groups?

The behavior and performance of people in a business organization are strongly influenced by their customs, habits, and attitudes toward work. In many foreign countries certain business activity is considered degrading even though in other countries this same activity is highly respected. A recent example of the effect of this attitude is the present difficulty in the Carribean area affecting the tourist industries. The native population considers service to others downgrading, a form of servitude, whereas in most European countries such a stigma is not attached to this activity.

The social stratification of the population often strongly influences the workers' behavior in job situations. Members of certain groups will refuse to work under the direction of people whom they consider from a lower strata than their own. For this reason in many countries vertical mobility of employees is very low or nonexistent. This means that under these conditions it is extremely difficult to hire a person from one of the lower strata of the population, train him, and advance him to a more important management position.

In many countries leaders are picked only from a certain small segment of the population. Often an employee in a leadership position must have attended a particular educational institution. When multinational firms have placed local employees in positions of importance without regard to these traditional qualifications from a local point of view, their effectiveness was greatly handicapped, sometimes seriously affecting the welfare of the foreign venture.

In many countries it is nearly impossible to advance a person without the proper "social" qualifications from one position to another of more responsibility. In our experience this applied even to U.S. and other foreign citizens working in a particular foreign country. There have been numerous instances where skilled North American or European employees had to be removed from a certain country and advanced in position in another part of the world before they could be returned to the original country several years later in a position of higher responsibility. Advancement in status within the country was not otherwise possible, due to local customs and attitudes.

The social structure of the population can also strongly affect the usefulness of local labor to the foreign employer. In countries where the basic social unit is the tribe rather than the family, the horizontal mobility of the population is severely restricted. Under these conditions there is little freedom on the part of the work force to move from one part of the country to another. Often a member of one tribe will not agree to shift his place of employment with an employer's needs into an area dominated by another tribe, due to fear for his own personal safety. Also the attitude of people toward work and the earning of a livelihood varies greatly from country to country.

Fortunately for the multinational firm, workers recruited from the local population in most countries show a sense of responsibility in carrying out their assigned duties. However, we have encountered exceptions to this in a number of developing countries. In our experience it has not been unusual to engage a native to carry needed supplies from one place to another, only to find upon his arrival at the destination that to lighten his burden most of the load he was carrying was dissipated and lost during transit by means of a small hole purposely punctured in the container. The fact that this made the whole operation useless from the employer's point of view made absolutely no impression on the native hired for the purpose. This is an attitude which may affect the performance of a wide range of tasks.

The education and potential skills of a work force are extremely important to the foreign employer. In the instance of developing countries it is often quite difficult to train a native to perform more than one simple operation. Therefore, an activity that normally can be carried out by 1 or 2 people in a developed country requires the hiring of 12 to 15 people each trained to do one particular, simple thing. Fortunately, however, over time these handicaps can be overcome by observation, experience, and systematic training to build up the skills of the native work force.

Due to general undernourishment of the native population in many countries it is also advisable for the foreign employer to feed his employees—their own diet, but on a regular and adequate basis. This results in much better performance and stamina on the part of the native employees. When in some developing countries the native population is too primitive in knowledge, attitude, and ability to fit into advanced production methods, it becomes necessary for the foreign employer to hire immigrants or their native-born descendants in order to obtain the required help. In many developing countries the descendants of Indian or Chinese immigrants are a valuable source of labor.

Other institutional and legal factors

The existing educational system and its requirements strongly influence the competence of a local work force. In many countries only members of certain population groups are privileged to receive higher level education. A separation in the kind of education children may receive takes place at the age of 9 or 10 in some countries, and there is no opportunity for later change once a child's educational progress is governed by the educational institution to which he has been assigned. It is very important for the foreign employer to realize that in most countries it is not possible to hire a person with a higher level of education and expect this individual to work under the direction of a person not so privileged. This makes it difficult to take a person educated within the lower echelons of the educational system, train him to greater competence, and have him become effective in the management of the business venture.

The foreign employer should also be aware of existing systems of social responsibility for the aged, the sick, or the unemployed. Institutional arrangements to take care of the needs of these people exist or are developing in most countries.

One must also understand the basis for the legal system of the intended country of operation. In general, most countries' legal systems are either based on the common law system of English origin, as in the United States, or are based on the civil law system of Latin origin, found largely in European countries and their former colonies. In some less developed countries one often finds a legal system that is based in part on either the common law or the civil law system, but is strongly influenced by local religious codes and attitudes.

Governmental factors

The attitude of a foreign government toward business, particularly foreign-owned business, is extremely important. When a national government is friendly toward private enterprise and is encouraging private investment on the part of foreigners, this will go far toward assuring success of a foreign business venture. If, on the other hand, the attitude of government is unfriendly toward private enterprise (or if there has been a constant change of governments, each less friendly toward business than its predecessor, such as occurred in Chile in 1971), the multinational firm is well advised to tread with caution before making a sizable investment in that country. The governments of many developing countries are socialistically inclined. They firmly believe that the government can do more for the country and people than private enterprise can. Under these circumstances it becomes difficult to establish a private business venture in such a country and continue it successfully over an extended period of time.

One must also be familiar in detail with the laws, regulations, and procedures that have been established by foreign governments that affect the operations of private enterprises. Of particular importance to the multinational firm are those laws, regulations, and procedures that govern the initiation and/or liquidation of a business entity owned by foreign investors. In our experience we have encountered a number of countries where it was relatively easy to initiate a business venture, even on a 100 percent foreign-owned basis. But, it became extremely difficult to liquidate the business activity when it proved to be unprofitable. In some instances it required several years to liquidate a business operation in a foreign country and withdraw invested funds and equipment. This was due to the fact that established regulations and procedures governing liquidation and withdrawal proved to be very troublesome, particularly concerning the discharge of local employees.

The financial executive of a multinational firm must be thoroughly acquainted with all the details of taxation when operating in a foreign country. Taxes on income, property, value added, sales, and capital all will have an effect on the profitability of the foreign venture. In many countries some taxes will be similar to those encountered in the United States. However, the determination and levying of taxes often is completely different.

In some developing countries taxes are assessed on foreign-owned business enterprises based on estimates made by the taxing authority. These are usually 5 to 10 times greater in magnitude than they actually should be according to the tax laws of the foreign country. Once a tax bill has been prepared, lengthy negotiations are required to have these estimated assessments reduced to an acceptable level, say two or three times what they ought to be according to their tax codes. These negotiations are made difficult in many countries because they must be carried on in the native language of the country. This forces the multinational firm into complete dependence on local talent to represent it in negotiating with the foreign government's taxing authorities.

Of particular danger to a multinational firm are penalty provisions contained in the tax laws of some developing countries. These may, for example, provide for an assessment of severe penalties based on annual turnover (total annual sales) without regard to profitability, once it has been determined that a foreign-owned firm is in violation of some tax rule or regulation. In some countries the threat of this exposure to punitive taxation may be carried back as much as five years, requiring the establishment of contingency reserves for such eventualities. It is beyond the scope of this study to set forth in detail all of the tax problems in all countries. The subject of taxes from the point of view of the U.S. multinational firm is covered in more detail in Chapter 7.

The rules and regulations governing the payment of dividends, particularly to foreign owners of business entities, must be known. Many countries levy a withholding tax on dividends which represents added taxation that is not usually recovered entirely when dividends are reported as income in the home country. When a foreign exchange shortage exists, governments often adopt rules and regulations which prevent the transfer of dividends out of the country.

The laws, rules, and regulations affecting the movement of capital funds, imports, exports, competition, and prices are of importance to the foreign-owned firm. Under extreme conditions goods and materials in short supply may be rationed to business firms, depending upon the importance of the firm to the local economy. It is important to know all of the rules pertaining to the original investment, such as required registration, when the foreign funds are first invested. Unless all rules are followed it may prove difficult later on to repatriate some of these funds, because failure to adhere to all laws, rules, and regulations may create continuing legal problems.

Quite often it is possible to enter into an investment contract with a foreign government prior to making the initial investment. At times, however, the political instability of the governments of some foreign countries causes these contracts or agreements to be of short duration. When after a political upheaval a new government comes into power, one of its first acts usually involves the cancellation of all agreements made by the prior government. Persistent and lengthy negotiations are then required to reestablish the former contractual privileges in connection with the financial transfers resulting from business operations. The availability of foreign exchange also becomes a severe problem when there is a shortage of foreign exchange reserves in the country of operation.

Social legislation

In foreign business planning, one must take into account the costs of existing social legislation in the country of operation, since these costs can be considerably larger than they are in the United States. Social security taxes on employers run as high as 30 percent of payrolls in a number of foreign countries. Health insurance protection is offered by many foreign governments at a reasonable cost. Vacation requirements on an annual basis are much more formalized in many countries than they are in the United States. Employees are granted rights to annual vacations by government edict. A two-week vacation after one year of service is often the rule, with a three-week vacation annually beginning after five years of service.

Annual or semiannual bonus payments are required in many countries, irrespective of the profitability of the business, and are based on monthly salaries or wages. Severance indemnities are required by law in a large number of foreign countries. A severance payment is almost always required upon termination of employment unless a separation is for certain specified causes. A severance payment of 1 month's salary per year of service for the first 10 years and 2 months' salary per year for each year of service thereafter is not uncommon. Therefore, firms are required to establish reserves to cover these large future liabilities.

In a number of countries, where still permitted, business firms change the legal entity of their organization every 10 years in order to avoid the larger severance requirements of 2 months per year after 10 years of service. Under these reorganizations all employees are paid off by the former company and are then rehired by the new business entity that has been formed. This move in the past has not been unpopular among employees due to the fact they are given large cash severance payments while at the same time continuing at full employment. However, in many countries these reorganizations solely for purposes of avoiding the larger severance accumulations are no longer permitted. It is evident from the brief discussion above that the costs resulting from social legislation cannot be ignored by the multinational business firm, since their total amount can seriously affect the profitability of a foreign venture.

Business customs

A very strong influence on foreign business ventures is exerted by local business customs and procedures. Many of these are not spelled out clearly in writing but merely exist in a business community as a result of long years of observance. In many foreign countries, the aggressiveness or pressure under which business is conducted in the United States is completely missing. The multinational firm that fails to take into account local business customs is risking failure. In the majority of foreign countries it is impossible to apply high-pressure U.S. sales methods successfully.

In most foreign countries serious business negotiations are usually preceded by several casual visits, during which direct negotiation or bargaining is avoided. Long time-outs for lunch and usual foreign business hours will have to be observed wherever they prevail. In some countries early business hours are not customary, and a long lunch break does not usually begin before 2:00 P.M. Business is then resumed at about 4:00 P.M. and continues until past 7:00 P.M., a time when U.S. employees have usually been home about two hours. Inviting a foreign businessman to a dinner for social or business reasons requires observance of the local customs in the country of operation. Fashionable dining facilities may still be empty at 9:00 P.M. and begin to attract customers only after 10:00 P.M.

In many foreign countries business is conducted on a gentlemen's agreement basis. Representatives of firms within the same line of activity get together periodically, sometimes only annually, and divide up available markets among their companies. Even though this is done on a very informal basis, the arrangements agreed upon are adhered to by those participating. It should be evident that these gentlemen's agreements limit competition and are in violation of U.S. antitrust laws. In some countries the government or representatives of a government-owned corporation participate in these informal discussions.

In some instances these meetings are held once a year with government participation to determine who will do what business, and for how much, during the coming year. At these meetings a newly formed, foreign-owned organization may be frozen out completely from participating in the activities of a particular industry unless it meets certain demands. In many countries these private informal agreements among business organizations severely limit the freedom to compete and act as a handicap on a multi-national firm's ability to develop its market in a foreign country. There have been instances where newly formed, American-owned enterprises have refused to honor these informal agreements and have made an effort to obtain a desired share of the market by whatever business means necessary. These divergences from locally accepted business procedures have made such American subsidiaries extremely unpopular in some foreign countries.

Monetary and fiscal policies

Past and present fiscal and monetary policies of the foreign government in the country of present or proposed business operations must be studied in order to determine what these policies may be in the future. The economic growth of a foreign country is often strongly influenced by the existence of proper fiscal and monetary policies. The resulting stability of purchasing power of the local currency and the relatively constant growth of the local economy are needed to assure the success of a multinational business undertaking. In most instances governments that have successfully handled the economy in the past and have practiced proper fiscal and monetary policies are not likely to change these suddenly to the detriment of the local economy and of the multinational companies that have located there.

The quality and usefulness of the national currency in a country in which a firm is operating are very important. The quality largely depends on past and present monetary and fiscal policies practiced by the country's government. The stability of a currency's purchasing power, its ready convertibility into other foreign currencies, and its relative constancy of value in terms of gold or other foreign currencies are all characteristics of a desirable national currency. Unfortunately, not all of these characteristics are always present, not even in the United States. Therefore, the financial officer of a firm planning an operation in a particular country must study the characteristics of the currency involved and must determine the costs to the planned venture if this currency does not have all the specified ideal characteristics mentioned above. When a local currency deteriorates in value and quality over time, it becomes necessary to demand a higher rate of profitability of a business venture. This is necessary because the costs of the loss of purchasing power suffered when granting trade credit must be covered by profits.

Money and capital markets

The availability of business funds on a short-, medium-, or long-term basis is an important part of the successful planning of business operations in a foreign country. Availability of local funds will greatly enhance the desirability of initiating a business venture in a country. When loans can be readily obtained at a reasonable interest cost, the planning problems of the financial manager are greatly eased. The availability of adequate local funds will permit the practice of monetary balance, a protective device against foreign exchange rate risk, a topic which is discussed in Chapter 5.

The practices of granting trade credit also vary greatly from those prevalent in the United States. If a firm has to purchase its materials in a market where supplies are short and the number of suppliers few, it becomes very difficult to obtain trade credit on a normal basis. Under these circumstances the firm will usually be required to pay a monthly interest fee for the duration of the trade credit. If, on the other hand, a firm purchases its materials in a market where supplies are plentiful and the number of suppliers large, trade credit can be obtained for extended periods on a cost-free basis.

The same problems prevail in the granting of trade credit by the selling firm. If one is a seller in a market where supplies are short and the competitors few in number, one can insist on payment of interest on the trade credit granted. However, if a business firm sells products in a market where supplies are plentiful and the sellers many, trade credit must be granted on a free basis. These problems become particularly critical when one operates in a country with serious price inflation. Under this circumstance, when a business firm grants extended trade credit in order to effect the sale of its products, it may suffer considerable loss of purchasing power on the funds involved between the delivery of the goods to the customer and the time that payment is received. When establishing a business in a country under severe inflationary conditions, one must make certain that the output of the firm can be sold under market circumstances favorable to the seller.

The financial markets of many countries, including some of the developing countries, offer means of protection against commercial and political risks to business organizations that are active in the export sector of their economy. The availability of foreign credit insurance against commercial and political risks presents an opportunity to decrease these risks greatly when a firm is doing business with other foreign countries. Protection against change in the foreign exchange value of the local currency is obtainable through local banking facilities even though an international financial market does not exist in a particular country, because often the bank, through correspondents in the other country involved, can obtain the desired market protection.

If the foreign exchange problem is one of enabling a firm to purchase foreign imports, these arrangements can usually be effected between one's commercial bank and the foreign government or central bank. In countries where devaluation of the local currency is a constant problem, the availability and cost of currency swap facilities should also be known, since the obtaining of a foreign credit swap decreases the risk of loss due to foreign exchange rate change of locally invested funds. The details of these arrangements are discussed in greater detail in Chapter 5.

In this study we will address ourselves largely to the financial environmental factors that affect the operations of a foreign business venture. However, it was considered advisable at the beginning of the study to call attention to the various nonfinancial environmental factors that if ignored can have serious financial consequences to the new foreign undertaking. This book will, therefore, seek to set forth materials to provide financial managers with the essential knowledge required for sound international financial management decisions. Its organization, discussed in the following section, reflects the special aspects of international business finance outlined above.

ORGANIZATION OF THIS BOOK

This book is divided into two main parts. Part One sets forth the required institutional background which provides a framework. It also develops the required tools of analysis. Part Two applies the background and tools to important areas of decision making and to policy formation in international business finance.

In Chapter 1, we have described the new and important environmental factors affecting decisions in this field. In international business finance we face environmental complexity and diversity. Many factors that would be held constant in an analysis of the potential for a domestic investment must be taken into consideration and analyzed when planning a foreign direct investment. Not only are the environmental factors in developing cultures more complex and more diverse but they are subject to more rapid changes as well.

Chapter 2 presents the basic economic background required to provide a vocabulary and understanding of the central mechanisms of international finance. The concept of comparative advantage is set forth. The nature of exchange rates and foreign exchange markets is explained. The major types of international transactions and how they are reflected in the balance-of-payments statements are covered in detail. The use of the balance-of-payments statement as a tool of analysis is described.

We discuss the various risks faced by business firms engaged in international finance and trade in Chapter 3. It begins with a discussion of the nature of risk. We then describe the commercial risks encountered when selling in foreign countries, as well as the political risks that affect these same sales. The political risks which affect foreign investments as well as foreign operations will also be discussed. The ever-present foreign exchange rate risks, losses that occur as a result of a change in the value of one currency in relation to another, are considered in detail. In addition to discussing these various risks we evaluate their possible effect on the profitability of foreign transactions.

Since these business risks are the result of fundamental underlying conditions, we analyze developing trends to aid the international financial executive in anticipating or forecasting changes which could greatly affect the profitability of his firm. We will indicate economic and financial factors which may be used as leading indicators to foretell possible financial troubles. A study of these will be helpful in formulating decisions as to which protective measures to employ, since the cost of protection must always be less than the possible losses against which one desires protection. Many of these protective measures are equivalent to insurance, under which the known cost of the means of protection is exchanged for the uncertain and potentially much greater costs resulting from the exposure to risk.

In Chapter 4 we examine in detail the various protective measures for dealing with the risks described in the preceding chapter. We will explain commercial credit insurance available in various countries and will evaluate various forms of investment insurance and investment guarantees. In Chapter 5 the main forms of dealing with exchange rate risks are described. These are the use of forward contracts and foreign currency swaps and the achievement of monetary balance.

Whenever financial reporting takes place in a different currency from that used in the country of operation, numerous additional problems arise which require deviations from accounting practices that are considered normal by firms which operate entirely on a domestic basis. The modifications from these domestic accounting procedures and their development will be the topic of Chapter 6.

Chapter 7 begins with a discussion of the most important of the general government rules and regulations, both U.S. and foreign, that influence the financial outcome of foreign operations. We then turn to the more specific role of taxes. The effects of tax provisions are so far-reaching that no treatment of international finance would be complete without full consideration of the diverse laws of different countries.

With the framework and tools developed in Part One, we turn to the treatment of international financial management policies and decisions in Part Two. We begin with Chapter 8, which describes a wide range of financing institutions and instruments found in international trade and investment. The conventional sources of financing business are summarized. The international lending institutions, both public and private, are also described. The financing practices distinctive to international activities are explained.

The problems of commercial export sales to foreign countries will be the topic of Chapter 9. Included are not only the procedures for financing such sales but also the problems encountered when attempts are made to protect the seller against international financial risks. A number of protective measures are available to reduce the formidable risks of international operations.

The foreign investment decision is analyzed in Chapter 10. The general concepts of project evaluation are employed, but the format of computations requires consideration of some additional variables associated with foreign operations. Because of restrictions on the repatriation of earnings and other foreign exchange controls, one important focus of the analysis is on the present value of cash flows actually available to the parent firm.

Working capital management in the international environment is treated in Chapter 11. This begins a series of chapters that are integrative in nature. The subjects include financing under inflationary conditions and cash management on a worldwide basis.

Chapter 12 traces a number of stages in the increasing degree of involvement of a firm in international business operations. The requirements of a multinational viewpoint in order for a firm to achieve the maximum potential from international operations are described.

Chapter 13 summarizes important international economic and financial developments in recent years, indicating their important implications for financial managers. Recent trends in balance-of-payments relationships, trends in exchange rate relationships, and the outlook for the position of the U.S. dollar in relation to other currencies are also treated.

Finally, in Chapter 14 we seek to draw the materials together into an integrated framework. We show how the theory is used in practical decision making. In summarizing the topics of this book, we hope to provide useful guidelines of value to a firm operating on a multinational basis.

PROBLEM 1-1

Your firm is considering an investment in Slabovia. You have been asked to evaluate the strengths and weaknesses of the country's environmental factors as they may affect the new business venture.

1. The population is 40 percent native Indian, 30 percent Negroes, 20 percent cross between above and white immigrants, and 10 percent white immigrants and their descendants.
2. Almost all important positions in the country are held by the white population and those of part-white origin.
3. The literacy rate of the population above age 16 is 45 percent.
4. Social security, health benefit, bonus, vacation, and termination regulations exist.
5. The education system follows European lines.
6. The governments have been unstable for the last 30 years until a military government took over 5 years ago.
7. The military government is making considerable effort to attract foreign

investment by offering income tax holidays and guarantees of ability to remit home interest, return of principal, and dividend payments within reasonable limits.

8. Annual devaluation over the past 20 years has varied from 30 to 70 percent. It has varied between 10 and 20 percent the last 3 years.

9. Increases in price levels have been similar to the rate of devaluation.

10. The money supply is presently increasing at a 15 percent annual rate.

11. Real economic growth the last 3 years has averaged 8 percent per year.

12. The country taxes income only at the source.

13. Corporate tax rates peak at 40 percent of taxable income.

14. A nationwide sales tax is 5 percent.

15. Business executives are recruited largely from the educated part of the population.

16. Business in various industries is conducted under informal agreements among firms in the particular industry.

17. Long-term funds are difficult to obtain.

18. Short-term funds cost 15 to 25 percent per year.

19. Foreign exchange controls limit imports and exports except those favored by the government.

20. Export subsidies and incentives are offered local exporters.

A. Indicate whether the influence of each factor is favorable (+), unfavorable (−), or neutral (N), and explain briefly the reason for your rating.

B. Present an overall appraisal of the environment in Slabovia for making a long-term investment.

SELECTED BIBLIOGRAPHY

Basche, James R., Jr. *Integrating Foreign Subsidiaries into Host Countries.* New York: The Conference Board, 1970.

Blough, Roy. *International Business: Environment and Adaptation.* New York: McGraw-Hill Book Co., 1966.

Fayerweather, John. *The Executive Overseas.* Syracuse, N.Y.: Syracuse University Press, 1959.

Granick, David. *The European Executive.* New York: Doubleday & Co., Inc., 1962.

Meister, Irene W. "Current and Future Factors Affecting International Business," *Financial Executive,* Vol. 39, No. 6 (June 1971), pp. 16–20.

Stewart, Charles F. *The Global Businessman: Readings from "Fortune."* New York: Holt, Rinehart & Winston, Inc., 1966.

Thompson, Morley P. "Pitfalls in Foreign Operation," *Financial Executive,* Vol. 37, No. 1 (January 1969), pp. 53–56.

Vernon, Raymond. *Manager in the International Economy.* Englewood Cliffs, N.J.: Prentice-Hall, Inc., 1968.

2

International transactions and financial flows

THE BASIS FOR INTERNATIONAL TRADE

Two BASIC concepts have been stated as the rationale for international trade. One is absolute advantage; the other is comparative advantage. A country has an absolute advantage if it is able to produce a good at a lower cost than other countries can. Thus, some writers in recent years have argued that international free trade achieves economic gains only when an absolute advantage exists. They have argued that the free trade doctrine has validity only in a world in which industrialized nations sell manufactured goods to the underdeveloped countries and the less developed countries sell raw materials and the products of agriculture to the more developed countries.

But the fundamental basis for international trade is not absolute cost advantages but the principle of comparative advantage. The law of comparative advantage simply states that trade will be mutually advantageous if one country is relatively more efficient in producing some products and other countries are relatively more efficient in producing other products. A classic example is the surgeon who is a better typist than his secretary but hires her to type his records because his comparative advantage is in surgery. We shall not repeat the technical demonstrations of the proof of the law or principle of comparative advantage since it is well covered in materials on international economics.[1] Furthermore, we all practice in our daily lives the fundamental principle of comparative advantage since we do not ourselves produce the many goods that we consume each day. We do not provide for ourselves the many services we require. We buy most goods and services from specialists. Specialization and the resulting di-

---

[1] See, for example, Charles P. Kindleberger, *International Economics* (4th ed., Homewood, Ill.: Richard D. Irwin, Inc., 1968), chaps. 1–3.

21

vision of labor results in a higher standard of living, more jobs, and more income for everybody. This is the basic idea involved in the law of comparative advantage that is equally valid in domestic as in international trade.

EXCHANGE RATES

One of the fundamental differences between international business finance and domestic business finance is that transactions and investments are conducted in more than one currency. For example, when an American firm sells goods to a French firm, the American normally desires to be paid in dollars and the French importer or French firm normally expects to pay in French francs. The buyer can pay in one currency and the seller receive payment in another currency because of the existence of a foreign exchange market in which individual dealers and many banks trade.

Since two different currencies are involved, a link or rate of exchange must be established between them. The conversion relationship between two different currencies is expressed in terms of their price relationship, known as the exchange rate. Currency exchange transactions take place in what is referred to as a foreign exchange market consisting of intermediaries who facilitate transactions in which payment may be made in one currency and received in another currency. The foreign exchange market exists in an economic sense, not necessarily in the physical sense of a particular locality. A market in an economic sense means that transactions are conducted and a uniform price is established for a given product.

The foreign exchange market is represented primarily by a series of trades achieved through transactions conducted by telephone and teletype networks. The major portion of foreign exchange market transactions is conducted by banks and dealers on behalf of their customers and with other banks. Central banks operate mostly through other banks.[2] In addition, of course, central bank policies may have a considerable influence on foreign exchange market transactions through influence on the money supply and on interest rates.

If foreign exchange rates did not fluctuate, it would make no difference whether a businessman has dollars or any other currency. However, since exchange rates do fluctuate, a firm is subject to exchange rate fluctuation risks if it has a net asset or net liability position in a foreign currency. If net claims exceed liabilities in a foreign currency, the firm is said to be in a "long" position because it will benefit if the value of the foreign currency

---

[2] Paul Einzig, "Organization of the Market," *A Textbook on Foreign Exchange* (New York: St. Martin's Press, 1966), chap. 2.

rises. If the firm is in a net debtor position with regard to foreign currencies, it is said to be in a "short" position because the firm will gain if the foreign currency declines in value.

Because of the risks of exchange rate fluctuations, transactions in forward contracts have developed in a forward or futures foreign exchange market. The forward or futures market enables a firm to engage in hedging in the attempt to reduce risks of exchange rate fluctuations. Individuals also speculate by means of transactions on the forward market. Forward contracts are normally for a 30-, 60-, or 90-day period, though special contracts for longer periods can be arranged by negotiation.

The existence of the forward market makes it possible for speculators to establish positions on the basis of their expectations. If New York speculators think that the Swiss franc is going to rise in value, they will

TABLE 2–1

Examples of a set of spot and forward exchange rates

	September 1972			December 1972	
	LC units per U.S. $	Value of LC in U.S. $		LC units per U.S. $	Value of LC in U.S. $
Spot...........	LC 2.00	$0.50	Spot	LC 1.70	$0.59
90-day			90-day		
forward.......	LC 1.90	$0.53	forward.......	LC 1.50	$0.67

immediately buy a 90-day forward contract to purchase Swiss francs. This will specify that the foreign currency will be delivered to them in 90 days at a price established by the 90-day contract. (This has been referred to as the current futures price.) This will represent a profit if the spot price 90 days later of the local currency in U.S. dollars will have risen. Conversely, if the speculator expects the dollar value of the foreign currency to fall, he will enter a futures contract to deliver the foreign currency. Then, if the value of the foreign currency declines, he can cover his short sale by buying the foreign currency at its hoped-for lower price.

In Table 2–1, we illustrate a set of spot and forward exchange rates. We have set forth the spot rate and 90-day forward rate between a local currency unit (LC) and the U.S. dollar. We show a spot rate of LC 2.00 and a 90-day forward rate of LC 1.90. In the following column, we have expressed the same relationship in terms of the value of local currency units in dollars. The spot rate of the local currency unit is $0.50, and the future rate is $0.53.

We also illustrate a set of expected exchange rates three months later when the 90-day forward rate matures. As of September 1972, the future spot and forward rates are forecasts, projections, judgments, or expected values, reflecting the average of the expectations of knowledgeable persons in the financial community of both countries, or a probability distribution of a range of possible future exchange rates. Some business decisions made in September must implicitly or explicitly include a forecast of the future spot and forward prices as of December. But, we emphasize that inherently some risk will always be involved when present decisions are based on expectations of future prices which cannot be known with certainty. The expected values we have provided are purely illustrative.[3] They show the expectation of the continued relative decline in the value of the U.S. dollar.

An exchange rate can be expressed in terms of the number of local currency units required to obtain $1 or, alternatively, the number of dollars and cents required to purchase one local currency unit. The latter, of course, represents the value of one local currency unit in dollars. In this book we will generally develop our analysis using both relationships because both have commercial and financial application.

For some types of international operations, business firms think in terms of the number of local currency units required to make an investment or the number of local currency units that they will receive for performing a service or a function. They are thinking in terms of what they can receive or what they need to have available in local currency units. On the other hand, quotations found in the financial press, *Wall Street Journal*, the major U.S. newspapers, and *The Federal Reserve Bulletin* of the Board of Governors of the Federal Reserve System generally employ the second method.

The logic for the second method is from the point of view of an American business firm or an American bank that thinks in terms of the number of dollars that it will receive for each local currency unit that it obtains in a transaction. Thus, if an American firm receives 100,000 local currency units from making a foreign sale, that firm may wish to make comparisons with the dollar costs of producing the goods in the United States. From a mechanical standpoint, it boils down to whether you prefer to multiply or divide in making calculations. But, since both methods have practical applications and since looking at both aspects of the relationship simultaneously is clarifying, we shall frequently present both prices. Two currencies are always involved in an exchange rate, and the manager of a U.S. multinational firm should be able to view the transaction both from the position of the local currency and from that of the U.S. dollar.

---

[3] Many important decisions of domestic business finance are also made under uncertainty. A considerable body of literature based on analysis of the probability distributions of returns and costs or the mean and variance of such probability distributions has been developed. Such analysis is fully applicable to the decisions of international business finance.

INTERNATIONAL TRANSACTIONS, FINANCIAL FLOWS, AND THE BALANCE OF PAYMENTS

The balance of payments of a nation is a double-entry accounting statement of its international economic transactions for a designated period of time. Since it is a double-entry system, there are two sides to the account:

Favorable changes	Unfavorable changes
Credits	Debits
Receipts	Payments
Plus	Minus
Exports	Imports

The receipts or plus side is equivalent to exports. The payments or minus side is equivalent to imports.

The detailed nature of the U.S. balance of payments is set forth in Table 2–2. In concept the 54 items of Table 2–2 can be summarized into 10 categories. These are:

1. Merchandise, exports, and imports.
2. Services.
3. Investment income.
A. *Balance on goods and services.*
4. Remittances, pensions, and other transfers.
5. U.S. government grants.
B. *Balance on current account.*
6. Long-term private capital flows.
C. *Balance on current account and long-term capital.*
7. Nonliquid short-term private capital flows.
D. *Net liquidity balance.*
8. Liquid private capital flows.
E. *Official reserve transactions balance.*
9. Liabilities to foreign official agencies.
10. U.S. official reserve assets.

Exports and imports are the most readily understood forms of international transactions. Services are the returns from the sale of products that are not primarily tangible goods. Investment income represents the return on capital investment. The next two categories represent payments that are unilateral; nothing is immediately received in return. The balance of payments with respect to current transactions can be calculated at that point. Items 6 to 8 represent long- and short-term capital flows. Below that is the official reserve transactions balance. This represents the balance of payments calculated with respect to all current items plus capital flows. This balance will have to be exactly offset by the sum of transactions in the official (government) agency accounts and in the U.S. official reserve assets as will be illustrated in the example in the final part of this section.

TABLE 2-2

U.S. balance-of-payments summary (seasonally adjusted, millions of dollars)

Line	(Credits +; debits −)	Reference lines (table 2)	1970	1970 I	1970 II	1970 III	1970 IV	1971 I r	1971 II r	1971 III p	Change: 1971 II–III	Jan–Sep 1970	Jan–Sep 1971	Change 1970–71
1	Merchandise trade balance [1]		2,110	513	751	704	142	269	−1,040	−537	503	1,968	−1,308	−3,276
2	Exports	2	41,980	10,241	10,582	10,696	10,461	11,030	10,720	11,481	761	31,519	33,231	1,712
3	Imports	16	−39,870	−9,728	−9,831	−9,992	−10,319	−10,761	−11,760	12,018	−258	−29,551	−34,539	−4,988
4	Military transactions, net	3, 17	−3,371	−908	−808	−884	−770	−667	−669	−715	−46	−2,600	−2,051	549
5	Travel and transportation, net	4, 5, 6, 18, 19, 20.	−1,979	−448	−500	−553	−478	−427	−610	−601	9	−1,501	−1,638	−137
6	Investment income, net [2]		6,242	1,577	1,469	1,571	1,626	1,783	2,169	1,670	−499	4,617	5,622	1,005
7	U.S. direct investments abroad	10, 11	7,906	2,039	1,905	1,973	1,988	2,033	2,409	2,053	−356	5,917	6,495	578
8	Other U.S. investments abroad	12, 13	3,503	886	886	882	851	864	832	845	13	2,654	2,541	−113
9	Foreign investments in the United States	24, 25, 26, 27	−5,167	−1,348	−1,322	−1,284	−1,213	−1,114	−1,072	−1,228	−156	−3,954	−3,414	540
10	Other services, net	7, 8, 9, 21, 22, 23.	588	147	133	157	150	212	176	177	1	437	565	128
11	**Balance on goods and services [3]**		**3,592**	**881**	**1,045**	**995**	**670**	**1,170**	**26**	**−6**	**−32**	**2,921**	**1,190**	**−1,731**
12	Remittances, pensions and other transfers	31, 32	−1,410	−338	−362	−359	−351	−342	−355	−388	−33	−1,059	−1,085	−26
13	**Balance on goods, services and remittances**		**2,182**	**543**	**683**	**636**	**319**	**828**	**−329**	**−394**	**−65**	**1,862**	**105**	**−1,757**
14	U.S. Government grants (excluding military)	30	−1,739	−418	−391	−444	−485	−428	−483	−527	−44	−1,253	−1,438	−185
15	**Balance on current account [4]**		**444**	**125**	**292**	**192**	**−166**	**400**	**−812**	**−921**	**−109**	**609**	**−1,333**	**−1,942**
16	U.S. Government capital flows excluding nonscheduled repayments, net [5]	34, 35, 36.	−1,837	−511	−480	−396	−450	−602	−679	−428	251	−1,387	−1,709	−322
17	Nonscheduled repayments of U.S. Government assets	37	244	88	114	2	40	4	102	72	−30	204	178	−26
18	U.S. Government nonliquid liabilities to other than foreign official reserve agencies	55	−436	−30	−224	82	−263	−82	−53	−176	−123	−172	−311	−139
19	Long-term private capital flows, net		−1,453	−969	−272	−220	7	−1,003	−1,795	−1,648	147	−1,461	−4,446	−2,985
20	U.S. direct investments abroad	39	−4,445	−1,358	−1,257	−897	−934	−1,370	−1,393	−1,399	−6	−3,512	−4,162	−650
21	Foreign direct investments in the United States	48	969	486	105	218	160	92	−16	−319	−303	809	−243	−1,052
22	Foreign securities	40	−942	−210	93	488	−337	−353	−388	−224	164	−605	−965	−360
23	U.S. securities other than Treasury issues	49	2,199	304	374	720	792	559	196	564	368	1,398	1,319	−79
24	Other, reported by U.S. banks	41, 52	199	31	68	44	56	−121	−236	−289	−53	143	−646	−789
25	Other, reported by U.S. nonbanking concerns	44, 50	576	−222	345	183	270	190	42	19	−23	306	251	−55
26	**Balance on current account and long-term capital [5]**		**−3,038**	**−1,297**	**−570**	**−340**	**−832**	**−1,283**	**−3,237**	**−3,101**	**136**	**−2,207**	**−7,621**	**−5,414**
27	Nonliquid short-term private capital flows, net		−545	−115	−140	−115	−175	−384	−394	−1,167	−773	−370	−1,945	−1,575
28	Claims reported by U.S. banks	42	−1,015	−162	−268	−189	−396	−73	−171	−991	−820	−619	−1,235	−616
29	Claims reported by U.S. nonbanking concerns	45	−360	−116	−23	−50	−171	−125	−138	−248	−110	−189	−511	−322
30	Liabilities reported by U.S. nonbanking concerns	51	830	163	151	124	392	−186	−85	72	157	438	−199	−637
31	Allocations of special drawing rights (SDR) [4]	63	867	217								651		

Line	Item	Ref. lines												
33	**Net liquidity balance**		-3,821	-1,254	-868	-675	-1,024	-2,504	-5,782	-9,293	-3,511	-2,797	-17,579	-14,782
34	Liquid private capital flows, net		-6,000	-1,610	-536	-1,400	-2,454	-3,029	51	-2,828	-2,879	-3,546	-5,806	-2,260
35	Liquid claims		242	262	-160	-17	157	-315	90	-520	-610	85	-745	-830
36	Reported by U.S. banks	43	-119	140	-127	-53	-79	-90	35	-405	-440	125	-460	-420
37	Reported by U.S. nonbanking concerns	46	361	122	-33	36	236	-225	55	-115	-170		-285	-410
38	Liquid liabilities	56	-6,242	-1,872	-376	-1,383	-2,611	-2,714	-39	-2,308	-2,269	-3,619	-5,061	-1,430
39	To foreign commercial banks		-6,507	-1,863	-441	-1,315	-2,888	-3,065	-92	-2,092	-2,000	-3,619	-5,249	-1,630
40	To international and regional organizations		179	142	-124	82	79	279	198	155	-43	3,100	632	532
41	To other foreigners		96	-151	189	-150	198	72	-145	-371	-226	-112	-444	-332
42	**Official reserve transactions balance**		-9,821	-2,864	-1,404	-2,075	-3,478	-5,533	-5,731	-12,121	-6,390	-6,343	-23,385	-17,042
	Financed by changes in:													
43	Nonliquid liabilities to foreign official reserve agencies	54	535	-266	735	-12	77	-8	-8	-9	-1	457	-25	-482
44	Nonliquid liabilities to foreign official agencies reported by U.S. Government	53	-810	-154	-235	-233	-188	-202	-160	-173	-13	-622	-535	87
45	Liquid liabilities to foreign official agencies	57	7,619	3,020	99	1,736	2,765	5,061	5,240	11,109	5,869	4,855	21,410	16,555
46	U.S. official reserve assets, net	58	2,477	264	805	584	824	682	659	1,194	535	1,653	2,535	882
47	Gold	59	787	-44	14	395	422	109	456	300	-156	365	865	500
48	SDR	60	-851	-270	-254	-251	-76	-55	17	-29	-46	-775	-67	708
49	Convertible currencies	61	2,152	831	818	34	469	373	-66	72	138	1,683	379	-1,304
50	Gold tranche position in IMF	62	389	-253	227	406	9	255	252	851	599	380	1,358	978
	Memoranda:													
51	Transfers under military grant programs (excluded from lines 2, 4, and 14)		613	137	191	116	169	191	162	256	94	444	609	165
52	Reinvested earnings of foreign incorporated affiliates of U.S. firms (excluded from lines 7 and 20)		2,885	n.a.	n.a.	n.a.	n.a.	n.a.	n.a.	n.a.	n.a.	n.a.	n.a.	n.a.
53	Reinvested earnings of U.S. incorporated affiliates of foreign firms (excluded from lines 9 and 21)		434	n.a.	n.a.	n.a.	n.a.	n.a.	n.a.	n.a.	n.a.	n.a.	n.a.	n.a.
54	Liquidity Balance, excluding allocations of SDR	56,57,58,63	-4,721	-1,629	-745	-1,154	-1,194	-3,209	-6,039	-10,174	-4,135	-3,528	-19,422	-15,894

NOT SEASONALLY ADJUSTED

Line	Item													
55	Balance on goods and services		---	1,234	1,300	-291	1,349	1,513	228	-1,400	-1,628	2,243	341	-1,902
56	Balance on goods, services and remittances		---	913	925	-657	1,002	1,188	-140	-1,795	-1,655	1,181	-747	-1,928
57	Balance on current account		---	465	487	-1,060	552	732	-670	-2,282	-1,612	-108	-2,220	-2,112
58	Balance on current account and long-term capital [5]		---	-1,310	-899	-1,535	706	-1,256	-3,615	-4,428	-813	-3,744	-9,299	-5,555
59	Net liquidity balance		---	-1,510	-1,704	-1,454	-152	-1,843	-3,596	-10,112	-3,516	-3,668	-18,551	-14,883
60	Official reserve transactions balance		---	-1,965	-2,069	-2,612	-3,174	-4,718	-6,462	-12,679	-6,217	-6,646	-23,859	-17,213

r Revised. p Preliminary. *Less than $500,000 (±). n.a. Not available.

1. Adjusted to balance of payments basis; excludes exports under U.S. military agency sales contracts and imports of U.S. military agencies.

2. Includes fees and royalties from U.S. direct investments abroad or from foreign direct investments in the United States.

3. Equal to net imports of goods and services in national income and product accounts of the United States.

4. The sum of lines 15 and 31 is equal to "net foreign investment" in the national income and product accounts of the United States.

5. Includes some short-term U.S. Government assets.

NOTE.—Details may not add to totals because of rounding.
Source: U.S. Department of Commerce, Office of Business Economics.

From *Survey of Current Business*, December 1971, p. 41.

Transactions which give rise to entries in the balance-of-payments accounts have also been divided into two broad categories. The first, which results from purposeful action, is primary transactions. The second is balancing financial flows which are secondary, accommodating, or compensatory. Primary or autonomous transactions initiate behavior and are represented by (1) buying or selling of merchandise and services, (2) unilateral outflows—private or government, and (3) U.S. investments in foreign countries or foreign investments within the United States. These three major categories embrace the individual items listed in Table 2–3.

TABLE 2–3

Primary international transactions

1. *a)* Merchandise exports.
    b) Merchandise imports.
2. *a)* Travel and transportation.
    b) Unilateral private transfers.
    c) Government grants.
3. *a)* Long-term U.S. investments in foreign countries.
    b) Long-term foreign investment in the United States.
    c) Short-term U.S. investment in foreign countries.
    d) Short-term foreign investment in the United States.
    e) Investment income and expense.

The initiating or primary transaction in turn gives rise to secondary or accommodating transactions. The effect of primary transactions on the U.S. balance-of-payments position, as reflected in the financial or accommodating transactions, will be either to change the total of U.S. claims against foreigners or to change the total claims of foreigners on the United States.

These two categories in turn are broken down as shown in Table 2–4.

TABLE 2–4

Effect of primary transactions on U.S. balance-of-payments position

Total U.S. claims against foreigners	*Total claims of foreigners on the United States*
1. U.S. accounts (claims) at foreign banks.	3. Foreign accounts at U.S. banks (U.S. liabilities).
2. U.S. claims on foreign nonbanks.	4. Foreign claims on U.S. nonbanks (U.S. liabilities).

On the left-hand side of this table total U.S. claims against foreigners are broken into two items: (1) U.S. accounts at foreign banks and (2) U.S. claims on foreign nonbanks. The total claims of foreigners on the United States are also indicated in Table 2–4. These are: (3) foreign accounts at U.S. banks and (4) foreign claims on U.S. nonbanks.

The primary transaction account has either a favorable or an unfavorable influence on the U.S. balance of payments. There are four possible combinations of initial effects from primary transactions on the U.S. balance of payments and the related secondary or financial transaction counterparts. These are set forth in Table 2–5.

If for any period of time the net increase in U.S. claims on foreigners exceeds the net increase in foreign claims on the United States, the balancing item would be an increase and improvement in the U.S. reserve position. On the other hand, if for any period of time the net increase in U.S. claims on foreigners is less than the net increase of foreign claims on the United States, the result would represent a deterioration of the

TABLE 2–5

Overview of patterns of primary and accommodating transactions and their influence on the U.S. balance-of-payments position

Primary transactions	Accommodating transactions	
Effect on U.S. balance-of-payments position	U.S. claims on foreigners, 1 or 2*	Foreign claims on U.S., 3 or 4*
Plus, credit......Increase, plus, debit,		
Minus, debit.....Decrease, minus, credit		
Plus, credit......		Decrease, minus, debit
Minus, debit.....		Increase, plus, credit

º Numbers refer to items in Table 2–4.

U.S. reserve position. The negative balance must be made up by reserve transactions by an official U.S. agency. These reserve transactions represent a negative net worth change in the U.S. position.

For any transaction, there will be a change in an account for a primary transaction and also a change in an account for a financial or accommodating transaction. In the process of carrying out what was initiated as a primary transaction, such as export of goods, several financial transactions may result. Two or more of the total number of subsequent stages in a transaction might be purely financial transactions, brought into being by one primary transaction. Generally, the impact on the net position of the United States is determined by the first financial transaction. The subsequent financial transactions simply alter the form of the U.S. claim on foreigners or of foreign claims on the United States.

A possible confusion in this connection should be avoided. The generalization is sometimes made that all short-term financial flows are accommodating transactions. But, this is not an accurate statement. The initiation of a movement of funds by a bank or by a large corporation to

TABLE 2–6

Illustration of major items of entry to the U.S. balance of payments*

2.	Exports	A	$2,000					
3.	Imports	E	($500)					
5.	Travel and transportation, net							
6.	Investment income, net					D	($3,000)	
7.	U.S. direct investments abroad							
8.	Other U.S. investments abroad	J	$800					
9.	Foreign investments in the U.S.							
11.	**Balance on goods and services**		($700)					
12.	Remittances, pensions, and other transfers	F	($200)	G	($1,300)			
13.	**Balance on goods, services, and remittances**		($2,200)					
14.	U.S. government grants (excluding military)	H	($1,000,000)					
15.	**Balance on current account**		($1,002,200)					
16.	U.S. government capital flows excluding nonscheduled repayments, net							
19.	Long-term private capital flows, net							
20.	U.S. direct investments abroad							
21.	Foreign direct investments in the U.S.							
22.	Foreign securities							
23.	U.S. securities other than Treasury issues					I	($10,000,000)	
26.	**Balance on current account and long-term capital**		($11,002,200)					
27.	Nonliquid short-term private capital flows, net							
28.	Claims reported by U.S. banks	J	($800)	B	($2,000)	C		
29.	Claims reported by U.S. nonbanking concerns	A	($2,000)	B	$2,000	$2,000	D	$3,000
30.	Liabilities reported by U.S. nonbanking concerns							
33.	**Net liquidity balance**		($11,000,000)					

34.	Liquid private capital flows, net...				
35.	Liquid claims...	C	($2,000)		
36.	Reported by U.S. banks...				
37.	Reported by U.S. nonbanking concerns...				
38.	Liquid liabilities...	$200	G $1,300	K ($50,000,000)	I $10,000,000
39.	To foreign commercial banks...	F			
40.	To international and regional organizations...				
41.	To other foreigners...	$500			
42.	**Official reserve transactions balance**	E ($41,000,000)			

Financed by changes in:

43.	Nonliquid liabilities to foreign official reserve agencies reported by U.S. government...				M $60,000,000
44.	Nonliquid liabilities to foreign official agencies reported by U.S. banks...		K $50,000,000	L ($20,000,000)	M ($60,000,000)
45.	Liquid liabilities to foreign official agencies...	H $1,000,000			
46.	U.S. official reserve assets, net...			L $20,000,000	
47.	Gold...				
48.	SDR...				
49.	Convertible currencies...				
50.	Gold tranche position in IMF...				

* Numbering of items corresponds to the official U.S. balance-of-payments summary as reproduced in Table 2–2. Values shown in parentheses represent debits (outflows).

obtain higher interest rates on short-term funds in a foreign money market is a primary transaction. As is true of other primary transactions, it will give rise to related financial transactions, but the initial movement of these short-term funds represents a primary transaction.

These general principles will now be illustrated by analysis of individual transactions. A number of primary transactions will be analyzed to show how each enters into the actual balance of payments as reported by the U.S. Department of Commerce, reproduced in Table 2–2. This will facilitate the financial manager's use of the balance-of-payments statement as an analytical tool.

The nature of the transaction is first described. The illustrative transactions are chosen to cover the most important types of primary transactions and the nature of associated financial flows. The resulting entries to the balance-of-payments accounts are described and recorded in Table 2–6. Table 2–6 lists the accounts by the numbers as listed in Table 2–2, the U.S. balance-of-payments summary. Our aim is to achieve an understanding of the transactions that are reflected in a balance-of-payments statement and thus provide a clear picture of what the balance-of-payments accounts represent. We emphasize that the following journal entries are for the U.S. balance-of-payments accounts, not accounting entries for individual firms. In fact, our illustrations relate to a number of different firms in the examples which follow.

Journal entries for illustrative balance-of-payments accounts

A. The U.S. EX firm sells $2,000 worth of equipment to an importer in France. The importer in France obtains a letter of credit from his bank. The U.S. EX firm receives from the French importer the confirmed irrevocable letter of credit via an American bank which is a correspondent bank with the French bank. The U.S. EX firm then draws a 90-day bill of exchange on the bank of the French importer in the amount of $2,000.

Entry: Line 2, an increase in exports by $2,000; line 29, an increase in claims reported by U.S. nonbanking firms on foreign nonbanking concerns of $2,000. An extension of credit is an "outflow" of funds, hence is a debit.

A1. The U.S. EX firm sends the bill of exchange to the French bank which accepts it. This makes it a claim reported by a U.S. nonbanking firm against a foreign bank (rather than a foreign nonbanking concern). However, since in Table 2–2, the U.S. balance-of-payments summary, no distinction is made in line 29 as to whom the claim is on—banking versus nonbanking—no entry is made in the U.S. balance-of-payments accounts.

B. The U.S. exporter discounts the banker's acceptance with the exporter's bank, which in turn credits the demand deposit account of the exporter.

Entry: Line 29, decrease in short-term, nonliquid claims of U.S. nonbanking firms of $2,000; this is a credit or plus entry. Line 28, increase in short-term, nonliquid claims of U.S. banks on foreigners of $2,000; this is a debit or negative entry.

C. The 90-day banker's acceptance matures. Now the U.S. bank has a liquid claim. This can be expressed in two ways. It can be shown as an increase in the demand deposit account of the U.S. bank with the French bank, or the settlement could be reflected in a decrease in the demand deposits of the French bank on the U.S. bank. We will assume in this illustration that the settlement is made by increasing the demand deposit account of the U.S. bank in the French bank because this shows up more directly in the balance-of-payments summary. What occurs then is the following:

Entry: Line 35 (36), liquid claims reported by U.S. banks, is increased by $2,000; line 28, nonliquid claims reported by U.S. banks, is decreased by $2,000.

D. The IM firm imports $3,000 worth of TV sets from Japan. The U.S. importer makes an arrangement with his New York bank, which issues a letter of credit. The Japanese exporter issues a 90-day bill of exchange; it is sent to the New York bank and is accepted.

Entry: The debit entry would be line 3, an increase in imports of $3,000. This gives rise to a claim of a nonbanking foreigner on a New York bank. The credit entry is to line 28, claims reported by U.S. banks, a negative $3,000 (the negative to a debit account is a credit entry). Line 28 is a net figure; in the U.S. balance-of-payments summary table there is no account specifically showing claims of nonbanking foreigners on Americans.

D1. The banker's acceptance is discounted by the Japanese exporter with the Japanese bank. This transforms the claim from being against a nonbanking foreigner to one against a foreign bank. But line 28 is on a net basis and does not distinguish between claims of foreign banks and foreign nonbanking concerns. Hence, this would not be reflected in the summary listing of accounts in the U.S. balance of payments because it simply does not provide for that much detail.

E. An American tourist buys a $500 airline ticket from Scandanavian Airways System (SAS) for a trip to Europe. He pays for it by a check on his American bank. SAS deposits the check in its U.S. bank. This represents then an increase in a claim by a foreigner on a U.S. bank.

Entry: Line 5, a decrease or debt in the travel and transportation account by $500; line 38 (41), an increase or credit in liquid liabilities to other foreigners.

F.   Mr. Jones, age 70, resides in Cuernavaca, Mexico. He is in receipt of his monthly social security check from the U.S. government of $200. He deposits the check in a Mexican bank. When he spends the money, it is received by Mexicans and ultimately becomes increased deposits in Mexican banks who increase their deposit accounts in U.S. banks.

Entry: Line 12, remittances, pensions, and other transfers, a negative amount of $200 is reflected in this item; line 38 (39), liquid liabilities to foreign commercial banks, is increased or credited by the $200.

G.   The same U.S. pensioner living in Cuernavaca also receives $1,300 from an American insurance company. In this case the insurance company draws a check on its U.S. bank. The only difference from the previous example is that in the former case the check is drawn by the U.S. government on its American bank. The end result is the same, that a Mexican bank will increase its deposits with a U.S. bank. This increases the liability of the U.S. bank to a Mexican bank.

Entry: The same as in F, but for $1,300.

H.   The U.S. government makes a grant to the Turkish government of $1 million to control the planting and harvesting of poppy seeds.

Entry: Line 14, U.S. government grants, by a negative $1 million since the effect is the same as importing goods or services. Since the payment is by check on a U.S. bank, the other entry is to line 45, liquid liabilities to foreign official agencies.

I.   The DI firm establishes a subsidiary in Canada on an equity basis by an investment of $10 million. The funds are spent in Canada on machinery. The U.S. firm has raised the money in the United States and draws checks on demand deposits in banks in the United States. The DI firm deposits the checks in a Canadian bank to purchase Canadian dollars. At that point, from an international transactions standpoint there is no further interest. Either claims of U.S. banks on Canadian banks are decreased or claims of Canadian banks on U.S. banks are increased. When the money is spent, it may be received by Canadian nonbanking persons. They, in turn, spend it; and it is likely to increase Canadian bank deposits. But the subsequent movements of the funds are Canadian internal transactions.

Entry: Line 20, U.S. direct investment abroad, which has increased by $10 million, so this is a negative entry. Line 38 (39), liquid liabilities to foreign commercial banks, would increase by $10 million, which would represent a credit, represented by extension of credit to the United States. In principle, a long-term portfolio investment or short-term funds that flow abroad to seek higher interest rates have the same effect in terms of the financial or accommodating transactions involved. The primary transaction may involve a different line number, but in concept and in economic and financial effects there is no difference. What we have is the impact of the primary transaction and a resulting financial accommodation.

J. Dividends from a Canadian portfolio investment in the amount of Can $800 are received by a U.S. investor. We will assume that the check is deposited by the U.S. investor in his U.S. bank and that the U.S. bank will increase its claims on Canadian banks. The U.S. bank will credit the U.S. investor's account with the U.S. dollar equivalent of Can $800; it then takes the check and sends it through for collection. The result is that the account of the U.S. bank in the Canadian bank is increased, expressed in Canadian dollars.

Entry: Line 6 (8), investment income, other U.S. investments abroad, is increased by the U.S. equivalent of Can $800; line 27 (28), claims reported by U.S. banks, is increased (debit) by the same amount, Can $800.

K. A French bank with large claims on U.S. banks purchases French francs from the Central Bank of France and pays for them by a check drawn on its deposits in U.S. banks.

Entry: Line 38 (39), liquid liabilities to foreign commercial banks, would be decreased by $50 million, and line 45, liquid liabilities to foreign official agencies, would be increased by $50 million. (Since it represents an offset to an overall negative balance of the United States, it is entered as a positive amount.)

L. The French Central Bank receives gold from the United States in the amount of $20 million which it pays for by drawing a check against a U.S. bank to make payment.

Entry: Line 45, liquid liabilities to foreign official agencies, would be decreased by $20 million; line 47, gold, would be increased by $20 million.

M. The Central Bank of France buys 90-day Treasury bills on a direct issue by the U.S. Treasury by being a successful bidder on a Treasury bill auction, thus purchasing $60 million of Treasury bills.

Entry: Line 43, nonliquid liabilities to foreign official reserve agencies reported by U.S. government, would increase by $60 million; and line 45, liquid liabilities to foreign official agencies, would decrease.

This completes the list of items illustrating how individual transactions are reflected as entries in the balance-of-payments accounts. A wide range of options exists as to the treatment of almost any transaction. A given transaction might follow one of several alternative routes. For example, in connection with imports from a foreigner, (1) the deposits of U.S. banks abroad might decrease, (2) the claims of U.S. individual nonbanks abroad might decrease, (3) the claims of foreign banks against U.S. banks might increase, (4) the claims of the foreign exporter against U.S. banks might increase, or (5) there might be offsetting adjustments in claims held by one against another. So a wide range of alternatives is always feasible.

It is important to recognize also that many accounts in the U.S. balance-of-payments summary are expressed from the standpoint of the U.S. balance of payments—on a net basis. Hence, some items that logic would suggest be entered as an increase in claims of foreigners, or liabilities to foreigners, actually appear as a negative entry to claims of the United States on foreigners. In the above exercise we made a specific assumption to show specific effects by covering a range of different types of transactions. We hope the reader will obtain sufficient understanding so that for any alternative assumption he may encounter he can reason through to determine the appropriate accounts involved.

Another step in the analysis is useful for conveying the nature of the balance in the payments accounts. For each transaction there is always an equal credit and debit. Therefore, the balance of payments is always in balance as any double-entry bookkeeping system must be. But for any group of accounts, an analysis of the interim balance has some analytical significance. To assist in understanding the alternative designations of interim balances discussed in the following section, it is useful to calculate each "balance." The balance on goods and services (line 11) is ($700) since the export and investment income accounts fall short of the import and travel accounts. The pension transfers were both debit items so the unfavorable balance is increased in line 13, balance on goods, services, and remittances. The U.S. grants are also a debit entry so the unfavorable balance is increased to ($1,002,200) in line 15, balance on current account.

The long-term capital outlay of $10 million increases the unfavorable balance to ($11,002,200) in line 26, balance on current account and long-term capital. The sum of the nonliquid claims and liabilities is a positive $2,200. Therefore, line 33, net liquidity balance, is ($11,000,000). Liquid claims and liabilities on balance add an additional debit of $40 million, so line 42, the official reserve transactions balance, is an unfavorable $41 million.

Following is the principal concept of the ultimate required balance. The size of the official reserve transaction balance determines the magnitude of the official reserve transactions but is opposite in sign to make the balance of payments ultimately balance. Table 2–6 shows that the sum of the transactions in the final section of the table is a positive $41 million.

Thus the balance of payments is in equilibrium. Each balance conveys information on the types of commercial, investment, or government behavior that will be required for ultimate balance. It also importantly provides information on future trends in international financial markets which have practical significance to the financial manager.

The most important categories of transactions have been illustrated. By actually working out the main types of individual transactions affecting a nation's balance of payments, a financial manager can achieve a better understanding of how the balance-of-payments statement is developed. Now that the underlying logic of the relation between primary transactions, financial flows, and the balance-of-payments accounts has been developed, we next consider the balance-of-payments statement as a tool of analysis for the international financial manager.

BALANCE-OF-PAYMENTS CONCEPTS

Until after the mid-1960s the United States had a large surplus in the goods and services account which was offset by government and private capital flows. In the late 1960s, the United States surplus of goods and services sales began to shrink sharply. The steady worsening in the U.S. overall balance-of-payments position had to be offset by increased U.S. dollar holdings by foreign official agencies and by using up of U.S. official reserve assets. This gave rise to the question as to what the appropriate way of measuring the U.S. balance-of-payments position should be. Since the addition of all the accounts in the U.S. balance of payments adds up to zero, the question arises just how a surplus or deficit balance of payments is determined. It depends to a large extent on the views and interests of those examining the balance-of-payments statement.

Basic transaction concept

The basic transaction concept was used by the U.S. Department of Commerce in the late 1940s and was until recently favored by the U.S. Treasury and the Federal Reserve. This balance considers certain international transactions as "basic" and insists that these primary or autonomous transactions are largely responsible for the financial relationships between nations. Included in these basic transactions are the following:

1. Current account.
2. Remittances and pensions.
3. U.S. government grants and capital (except U.S. reserves).
4. Private long-term capital, United States and foreign:
   a) Direct investments.
   b) Other (except for holdings of U.S. government bonds and notes).

These are placed above the line and are considered responsible for all other transactions of a secondary or compensatory nature. The items below the line are:

1. Errors and omissions.
2. Private short-term capital, United States and foreign.
3. Foreign holdings of U.S. government bonds and notes.
4. Foreign official short-term capital.
5. U.S. reserves of gold and convertible currencies and IMF position.

The above considers errors and omissions as being due to unrecorded short-term financial transactions. It also considers all short-term transactions to be of a compensating nature.

Current account balance

A balance that has been much in the news is the current account balance. This is a balance not only of merchandise exports and imports but also of services which are rendered by the United States and its private citizens to foreigners and services rendered by foreigners to the United States and its citizens. The so-called imports and exports of

TABLE 2–7

Grouping of U.S. international transactions under three balance-of-payments concepts

Balance on current account and long-term capital	Net liquidity balance	Official reserve transactions balance
Goods and services	Goods and services	Goods and services
Remittances and pensions	Remittances and pensions	Remittances and pensions
U.S. government grants and capital movements	U.S. government grants and capital movements	U.S. government grants and capital movements
Private long-term capital, U.S. and foreign	Private long-term capital, U.S. and foreign	Private long-term capital, U.S. and foreign
Nonliquid short-term private capital	Nonliquid short-term private capital	Nonliquid short-term private capital
Allocations of special drawing rights	Allocations of special drawing rights	Allocations of special drawing rights
Errors and omissions	Errors and omissions	Errors and omissions
Liquid private capital, U.S. and foreign	Liquid private capital, U.S. and foreign	Liquid private capital, U.S. and foreign
Foreign official liquid and nonliquid dollar holdings in the U.S.	Foreign official liquid and nonliquid dollar holdings in the U.S.	Foreign official liquid and nonliquid dollar holdings in the U.S.
U.S. official reserve assets	U.S. official reserve assets	U.S. official reserve assets

Source: U.S. Department of Commerce. John Hein, "Measuring the U.S. Balance of Payments," *Conference Board Record*, September 1971, p. 36.

services are sometimes referred to as invisible imports and exports due to the fact that physical goods do not change hands.

Also included are remittances, pensions, and other transfers in and out of the United States, as well as U.S. government grants (excluding military). In June 1971, the U.S. Department of Commerce adopted a revised presentation of the balance-of-payments relationships.[4] Three fundamental groupings are employed, as shown in Table 2–7.

The first grouping, "Balance on current account and long-term capital," corresponds to what we have described above as the "basic transaction concept." The second grouping is a new liquidity concept. The net liquidity concept remedies an important weakness that had existed in the old system. The old concept treated short-term private liquid liabilities on an asymmetrical basis. Foreign short-term liquid claims against the United States were considered a threat to liquidity while private short-term liquid U.S. claims against foreigners were not taken into account. Movements of both U.S. and foreign short-term funds are now accorded the same treatment. A second difference has been well stated as follows:

A second difference between the old and the new liquidity concept lies in the treatment of certain nonliquid liabilities to foreign official institutions. Under the old concept, shifts of official funds from liquid to nonliquid assets (customarily called "special financial transactions") had had a favorable effect on the balance, even though these so-called nonliquid holdings had been fairly close to liquid. Under the new treatment, such holdings are shown below the line, as part of the financing items, and thus do not affect the balance. Because of these two shifts from above the line to the balancing items, the net liquidity balance is believed to better serve the purpose that the old liquidity balance originally had been intended to perform, i.e., to be "a broad indicator of potential pressures on the dollar resulting from changes in our liquidity position."[5]

Official reserve transactions balance

The third concept now employed is identical with the old "official settlements" definition. Under this concept, settlement items which are regarded as financing the balance on all other transactions are shown below the line. The settlement items include only "reserve transactions" and when appropriate, special intergovernmental transactions. The balance on all other transactions is thus the balance settled by official transactions.

Having reviewed the different ways of measuring our balance-of-payments position, we next consider which concept provides the best information on what is happening to the U.S. international financial position.

[4] David T. Devlin, "The U.S. Balance of Payments: Revised Presentation," *Survey of Current Business,* Vol. 51 (June 1971), pp. 24–32, 33–57.

[5] John Hein, "Measuring the U.S. Balance of Payments," *Conference Board Record,* September 1971, p. 35.

The answer is that no one measure is best by all criteria. What is most useful depends upon the nature of the important international financial transactions that are taking place. The fact that we now have three official measures indicates that the analysis of international economic and financial developments is becoming increasingly complex and sophisticated. The financial manager must study the balance-of-payments relationships in detail, and their trends as well, to determine their implications for exchange rates and for predicting government policies affecting the flow and convertibility of funds.

THE EURODOLLAR SYSTEM

A development of great significance in international business finance is rapid expansion of the Eurodollar system which has provided an international money market. An innovation in the early 1950s was the development of the practice of banks accepting interest-bearing deposits in currencies other than their own. Since this development occurred mostly among European banks and since the interest-bearing deposits were denominated in dollars, the system has been referred to as the "Eurodollar market." Probably no more than 70 percent of the market is represented by European banks and denominated in dollars. Japanese and other banks accept interest-bearing deposits in currencies other than their own. With the increasing strength of the West German mark and other currencies, the interest-bearing deposits are sometimes denominated in currencies other than the dollar. But the preponderance of practice justifies the term "Eurodollar market."

The development and growth of Eurodollar deposits

Eurodollars come into existence when an American or foreign owner of a deposit with a bank in the United States transfers funds to a foreign bank or to a foreign branch office of an American bank. Normally, transfers of funds into the Eurodollar market are prompted by the consideration that American dollars can be placed with banks abroad at higher rates of interest than can be earned on time deposits or other short-term investment outlets in the United States. Foreign banks accept the Eurodollar deposits because they can, in turn, lend them at higher rates.

The factors which gave rise to the growth of the Eurodollar market are diverse. Of considerable influence were government controls over their credit systems in some countries, particularly the United States, and the need of an international currency to facilitate the tremendous expansion in international trade that took place beginning in the 1950s.

Regulations applying to the U.S. credit system which stimulated the development of the Eurodollar market include Regulation Q, the Interest

Equalization Tax, and the controls exercised by the Office of Foreign Direct Investments (OFDI). Regulation Q sets maximum ceilings on the rate of interest that U.S. banks can pay on time deposits. Hence, when world money markets become such that short-term funds can receive higher interest rates by being deposited in banks abroad, money moves from the United States into foreign money markets. Since these funds are frequently held temporarily by corporations but are intended to be used in connection with international investment or international trade, the holders of such funds prefer to have them denominated in dollars rather than in local currencies because of the past general acceptability of the U.S. dollar as a medium for settling international balances.

As a further step in this effort to control the outflow of U.S. dollars to protect the U.S. balance-of-payments position, the U.S. government established in 1963 an Interest Equalization Tax. The Interest Equalization Tax placed a special levy on long-term borrowings by foreign issuers sold to U.S. residents. The net effect was to increase the interest costs to foreigners of borrowing in the United States by 1 percentage point.

The factors giving rise to the Eurodollar market have been described; it is useful now to understand its operations. The clearest exposition is provided in the concrete and numerical illustration provided in the presentation set forth by the Bankers Trust Company in 1964. The material is reproduced in the following section.

In February 1965, the United States instituted a voluntary foreign credit restraint program. U.S. corporations and banks were asked by the U.S. authorities to limit voluntarily their direct investment capital exports as a part of a program to arrest the drain on U.S. gold supplies. They were encouraged to borrow the required capital for their overseas investment programs in foreign markets. U.S. banks were asked to limit the amount of their foreign loans in relation to the level of foreign lending in which they had engaged during recent years.

The original regulations split the countries of the world into three schedules. Each company received a general authorization to invest in each schedule group up to a specified percentage of the average amount it had invested in the base years of 1965–66. Schedule A included the less developed countries, and the allowance was 110 percent of the base. Schedule B encompassed parts of the whole sterling block, the Middle East oil-producing countries, and Japan, providing an allowance of 65 percent of the base. Schedule C covered most of Continental Europe to which companies could not send any additional capital. However, in most cases they could reinvest earnings up to 35 percent of their average direct investment in the base period. These regulations were continued when the voluntary program was replaced by a more formal capital-control program in early 1968.

There are gaps in the regulations affecting direct investors. The OFDI

controls the amount of capital a company can export for direct investments or short-term money market investments. But a firm which makes a
time deposit or purchases a certificate of deposit from a foreign branch of
a U.S. bank simultaneously avoids both the Interest Equalization Tax and
the controls of the OFDI. Also, Canada is exempt from the Interest Equalization Tax and from the OFDI. Thus, U.S. investors may buy new issues
of Canadian stocks and bonds without penalty. Funds loaned by Americans to Canadians flow to the European dollar market where they are re-
loaned in part to U.S. companies.

Thus, a major factor in the growth of the Eurodollar market were these
artificial restrictions on money and capital flows from the United States
to Europe. Such restrictions are always avoided by the market in a number
of indirect ways. The development of the Eurodollar market and the rate
of its growth represented the avoidance of such restrictions.

On the other side, the growth of the Eurodollar market was also stimulated by the monetary authorities of individual European countries seeking to support their domestic policy goals. In the late 1950s, West Germany became concerned with its balance-of-payments surplus, the inflow
of capital, and the increase in domestic liquidity. The German Central
Bank offered spot dollars and simultaneously offered forward exchange
rates on terms which created an arbitrage incentive for German banks to
invest funds outside West Germany.

Thus, the stimulation to the Eurodollar market came in part from the
restrictions on capital outflows by the U.S. government and in part from
the effort by some of the European governments from time to time to
stimulate the capital outflows. Almost paradoxically, however, a vital factor in the growth of the Eurodollar market has been the strength of the
U.S. dollar as an international currency. The dollar is the world's leading
reserve currency, and a large portion of world trade is denominated in
dollars and calls for settlement in dollars. While some of the currencies of
European countries have in recent years achieved a strong position and
high confidence, they lacked a number of attributes necessary for an international currency. These deficiencies included the lack of a large supply, the lack of universal acceptability, and the lack of the breadth of the
market essential to the successful functioning of a money market on a
worldwide scale.

Accounting for the Eurodollar

The following is from a Bankers Trust Company pamphlet *The Eurodollar Market.*[6]

---

[6] This material is reproduced with permission from the Bankers Trust Company
from its pamphlet *The Euro-dollar Market* by Roy L. Reierson (New York: Bankers
Trust Company, 1964).

Euro-dollars come into existence when a bank located abroad accepts deposits denominated in dollars. These deposits are interest-bearing and have a stated maturity. They may be redeposited with a succession of banks before they are ultimately used to finance a business transaction. The following outline is intended to illustrate, with the help of "T" accounts, how Euro-dollar transactions may affect the assets and liabilities of American and foreign commercial banks and of ultimate borrowers of Euro-dollars abroad.

Before creation of the Euro-dollar. It shall be assumed that a Swiss bank holds a demand deposit with a New York bank, here designated as New York bank A. This is not a Euro-dollar deposit, since it is with a bank located in the United States. On the statements of condition of the two respective banks, this deposit appears as follows:

New York Bank A		**Swiss Bank**	
	Demand deposit due Swiss bank: $1	Demand balance with New York bank A: $1	

Creating the Euro-dollar. It shall now be postulated that the Swiss bank concludes that its demand deposit in New York is larger than required for working purposes. Instead of placing the funds on time deposit with an American bank, investing in Treasury bills or other money market instruments in New York, or converting into Swiss francs for use at home, the Swiss bank chooses to make a time deposit in dollars with a merchant bank in London, where a higher interest rate is obtainable than in the American market.

If it is assumed that the merchant bank in London keeps its account with New York bank B, New York bank A would be instructed by the Swiss bank to transfer its balance to New York bank B: such transfers in New York may be in Federal funds but are generally in Clearing House funds. These hypothetical transactions would involve the following entries on the books of the respective banks:

New York Bank A		**Swiss Bank**	
Reserves (transferred to New York bank B): −$1	Demand deposit due Swiss bank: −$1	Demand balance with New York bank A: −$1	
		Time balance with merchant bank, London: +$1	

New York Bank B		**Merchant Bank, London**	
Reserves (received from New York bank A): +$1	Demand deposit due merchant bank, London: +$1	Demand balance with New York bank B: +$1	Time deposit due Swiss bank: +$1

It is apparent that the total of deposits with banks in the United States has not changed but that deposit ownership has shifted from the Swiss bank to the merchant bank in London. At the same time, a new deposit liability, denominated in dollars, has been created outside the United States. This dollar liability assumed by the merchant bank in London constitutes a Euro-dollar deposit.

Links in the chain.   The chain of redepositing occurs if the merchant bank in London employs the dollar balance it holds in New York in the Euro-dollar market. It shall be assumed that this is done by lending the dollars to, or redepositing them with, a French bank, which in turn is presumed to hold its account in the United States with New York bank C. These transactions would involve the following net entries:

New York Bank B	
Reserves (transferred to New York bank C): −$1	Demand deposit due merchant bank, London: −$1

Merchant Bank, London	
Demand balance with New York bank B: −$1	
Time balance with French bank: +$1	

New York Bank C	
Reserves (received from New York bank B): +$1	Demand deposit due French bank: +$1

French Bank	
Demand balance with New York bank C: +$1	Time deposit due merchant bank, London: +$1

As a next step, the French bank shall be presumed to redeposit its Euro-dollar balance with an Italian bank which bids for dollar deposits in the market. If the latter has as its American correspondent New York bank D, the following applies:

New York Bank C	
Reserves (transferred to New York bank D): −$1	Demand deposit due French bank: −$1

French Bank	
Demand balance with New York bank C: −$1	
Time balance with Italian bank: +$1	

New York Bank D	
Reserves (received from New York bank C): +$1	Demand deposit due Italian bank: +$1

Italian Bank	
Demand balance with New York bank D: +$1	Time deposit due French bank: +$1

As the result of the foregoing transactions, the amount of demand deposits in New York remains unchanged at $1, but an additional $3 of deposit liabilities is now outstanding with banks outside the United States, with a corresponding increase in bank assets abroad. The position of all banks involved at this point appears as follows:

New York Bank D

	Demand deposit due Italian bank: $1

Swiss Bank

Time balance with merchant bank, London: $1	

Merchant Bank, London

Time balance with French bank: $1	Time deposit due Swiss bank: $1

French Bank

Time balance with Italian bank: $1	Time deposit due merchant bank, London: $1

Italian Bank

Demand balance with New York bank D: $1	Time deposit due French bank: $1

Eventually, it is assumed, the $1 held by the Italian bank is loaned to an Italian trader desiring to obtain United States dollars in order to pay for commodities purchased in world markets. The Italian bank makes its balance with New York bank D available to this borrower, who uses it to pay the commodity dealer, assumed to be banking with New York bank E. (If the seller banks elsewhere, e.g., in London or Paris, the chain of intermediary transactions would be lengthened, although the end result would not be altered.) Giving effect to these various debits and credits produces the following:

New York Bank D

Reserves (transferred to New York bank E): −$1	Demand deposit due Italian bank: −$1

Italian Bank

Demand balance with New York bank: D: −$1	
Loan to Italian trader: +$1	

New York Bank E

Reserves (received from New York bank D): +$1	Demand deposit due commodity dealer: +$1

Italian Trader

	Indebtedness to Italian bank: +$1
	Amount due commodity dealer: −$1

Liquidation of the Euro-dollar. To illustrate the process by which Euro-dollars may be extinguished, the next assumption is that the Italian trader subsequently repays his dollar indebtedness to the Italian bank out of dollars earned from exports or acquired in the foreign exchange market in the form of a claim on New York bank F, thereby restoring the Italian bank to the position prior to undertaking the foreign trade financing:

New York Bank F		Italian Trader	
Reserves (transferred to New York bank D): −$1	Demand deposit due Italian trader: −$1	Demand balance with New York bank F: −$1	Indebtedness to Italian bank: −$1

New York Bank D		Italian Bank	
Reserves (received from New York bank F): +$1	Demand deposit due Italian bank: +$1	Demand balance with New York bank D: +$1 ———————— Loan to foreign trader: −$1	

The Italian bank, it shall be postulated, has now consummated the financing for which it had obtained Euro-dollars from the French bank and, with no further profitable employment in immediate sight, uses its dollar receipts to meet its liability to the French bank upon maturity:

New York Bank D		Italian Bank	
Reserves (transferred to New York bank C): −$1	Demand deposit due Italian bank: −$1	Demand balance with New York bank D: −$1	Time deposit due French bank: −$1

New York Bank C		French Bank	
Reserves (received from New York bank D): +$1	Demand deposit due French bank: +$1	Time balance with Italian bank: −$1 ———————— Demand balance with New York bank C: +$1	

The Euro-dollar deposit liability of the Italian bank has thus been liquidated. As when the Euro-dollar first came into existence, the volume of bank deposits in the United States has not changed. If the French bank in turn uses its balance with its New York correspondent bank to repay the merchant bank in London, the latter liquidates its liability to the Swiss bank, and the Swiss bank, finally, decides not to reinvest elsewhere in the Euro-dollar market but instead to rebuild its demand deposit balance with its New York correspondent, all Euro-dollars involved in this hypothetical series of transactions will have been extinguished, leaving the situation as it was before the Euro-dollar was created:

New York Bank A	Swiss Bank
Demand deposit due Swiss bank: $1	Demand balance with New York bank A: $1

Summary.   The foregoing has illustrated the expansion of Euro-dollar deposits as they move from bank to bank abroad, and also the hypothetical liquidation of such deposits as the underlying transactions are closed out. The effect on total bank deposits, both in the United States and abroad, may thus be summarized in the following tabulation:

		Outstanding deposit liabilities of banks in New York	Outstanding Euro-dollar deposit liabilities of banks located abroad
(1)	Swiss bank holds deposit with New York bank	$1	—
(2)	Swiss bank deposits balance in Euro-dollar market with merchant bank in London	1	$1
(3)	Merchant bank in London places Euro-dollar deposit with French bank	1	2
(4)	French bank places Euro-dollar deposit with Italian bank	1	3
(5)	Italian bank makes Euro-dollar loan to Italian trader	1	3
(6)	Italian trader pays dollars to commodity dealer	1	3
(7)	Italian trader repays Euro-dollar loan to Italian bank	1	3
(8)	Italian bank repays Euro-dollar deposit to French bank	1	2
(9)	French bank repays Euro-dollar deposit to merchant bank in London	1	1
(10)	Merchant bank in London repays Euro-dollar deposit to Swiss bank	1	—

A final cautionary observation is imperative. The foregoing illustrations have been based on a fairly simple set of assumptions. In practice, there is obviously no clear segregation of bank assets between those representing funds acquired in the Euro-dollar market and those stemming from other sources. Funds received in the form of dollar deposits by a bank located outside the United States may be placed in various types of assets. The preceding illustrations assume they are redeposited with banks outside the United States or loaned to a foreign borrower. Alternatively, of course, the receiving bank may build up its demand or time deposits with banks in the United States or may invest the funds in the American money market, either in United States Treasury bills or in other open market paper.

The significance of the foregoing material may be briefly summarized. In the illustration, the outstanding Eurodollar deposit liabilities of banks located abroad increased by $3 as a result of moving one dollar of deposits of a New York bank into the Eurodollar market. While there is much argument over the nature and sources of the growth of the Eurodollar market, the principles explaining the magnitude of the Eurodollar multiplier are similar to those for the credit expansion multiplier for any fractional reserve banking system, domestic or international. For example, suppose that a million dollars moves from a New York bank into a Eurodollar market bank. Let us assume further that as a matter of prudence, the Eurodollar market bank holds a 10 percent reserve against its deposits. It then lends out $900,000. Suppose further that the proceeds of the loan are deposited in another Eurodollar bank. Suppose further that it holds a 10 percent reserve and reloans the 90 percent. If the process is continued and there is zero leakage of the loans and redeposits outside of the Eurodollar banking system, then the basic principles of the deposit expansion multiplier apply and the initial movement of a million dollars from a New York bank to the Eurodollar money market banking system would result in an expansion of the outstanding Eurodollar deposit liabilities of banks located in the Eurodollar banking system by $10 million.

If, on the other hand, the proceeds from the first loan by the first Eurodollar bank which received the shift of the million-dollar deposit from the New York bank to the Eurodollar system were used by the recipient to rebuild or create a desired level of balances to be held for working capital purposes in a New York City bank, then the leakage would be 100 percent. Hence, the outstanding Eurodollar deposit liabilities would have increased by only the amount of the switch of the New York bank to the European bank. In fact, when the loan is repaid to the European bank, the European bank extinguishes or repays the Eurodollar deposit to the other European bank which had switched the deposit in the first place. The change in the outstanding Eurodollar deposit liabilities of European banks would have been zero.

The multiplier effect of Eurodollar deposit creation depends upon the magnitude of leakage. Milton Friedman attributes a considerable portion of the increase in Eurodollars to this multiple expansion process: "their major source is a bookkeeper's pen."[7] Professor Machlup stressed the same phenomenon in an article whose title conveyed the same implication.[8] Without a Eurodollar deposit expansion multiplier of much greater than one, the Eurodollar market would not have grown by the magnitude that it has.

Referring to an estimate of an increase in Eurodollars of $30 billion,

[7] Milton Friedman, "The Eurodollar Market: Some First Principles," *Morgan Guaranty Survey*, October 1969, pp. 4–14.

[8] Fritz Machlup, "The Magicians and Their Rabbits," *Morgan Guaranty Survey*, May 1971, pp. 3–13.

Milton Friedman has argued that U.S. deficits during the 5-year period when Eurodollar deposits increased by $30 billion amounted to less than $9 billion. The magnitude of the intermediation of the holding of certificates of deposits in American banks and shifting them to the Eurodollar banks also would account for only a fraction of the $30 billion. Therefore, the difference, argues Friedman, must be accounted for by the Eurodollar deposit expansion multiplier.

The Eurodollar market is highly dynamic, transactions are intricate and diverse, and the market is continuously changing in response to new developments in the international financial economy. Some general characteristics of the Eurodollar market have been basic:

1. The movements of Eurodollar deposits and the magnitude of Eurodollar loans are characteristically in large amounts. The terms of Eurodollar deposits and loans are determined by market conditions rather than by consideration of customer relations. Funds are deposited and redeposited on an unsecured basis. This is a highly active market with narrow profit margins. The market has great breadth; it absorbs inflows of large amounts and meets substantial withdrawals.

2. The risks of moving funds to the Eurodollar market are not absent. First, the operation of the Eurodollar banking system is a fractional reserve system. The potential degree of pyramiding can rise to the reciprocal of the reserve ratio held by the Eurodollar banks. If this reserve ratio is 1/10, then the multiplier could potentially be 10. Second, there is evidence that a substantial proportion of Eurodollar deposits are loaned or invested at maturities longer than the maturities of the deposits. This may limit the ability of such European banks to carry a creditor if he runs into financial difficulties. A number of major failures among European corporations have occurred as a consequence. The bankruptcies have not yet been sufficiently widespread, however, to cause serious weaknesses in the Eurodollar market.

3. In addition, there are uncertain credit risks involved. While the placing of deposits in the Eurodollar market has characteristics of a long-term lending operation; some institutions behave as though these were short-term money market transactions without risk. Redeposits of Eurocurrency balances from bank to bank are on an unsecured basis. Assurances are not provided that funds are being advanced to finance a transaction which will be liquidated when the time deposit matures. Furthermore, the credit institution is unable to determine the total of foreign currency liabilities of the next bank in a chain. In general, the easy availability of liquid funds always provides some temptation for expansionary lending policies and relaxation of credit standards. The problem is aggravated by the lack of uniformity in financial statements among foreign borrowers and the lack of an active exchange of credit information among the financial institutions involved. Finally, unlike certificates of deposit issued by leading New

York banks, Eurodollar deposits are not negotiable instruments. Hence, they cannot be readily liquidated.

4. Somewhat paradoxically, the existence and growth of the Eurodollar market does not reduce the volume of credit available in the United States. This has been brought out by the illustration of the operation of the Eurodollar market described in the previous section. This may be an example of having one's cake and eating it too. The Eurodollar market makes it possible for foreign holders of dollar balances with American banks to transfer ownership of these deposits to European banks at a profit. As a consequence, there is a greater incentive to hold bank deposits in the United States. American bank deposits are reduced only when funds acquired in the Eurodollar market move to a central bank which uses them to purchase gold from the U.S. Treasury if the funds are used to liquidate a debt which is owed a bank in the United States.

Indeed, a potential problem is that a restrictive credit policy with rising rates in the United States may attract a large inflow of foreign currency deposits. Hence, the operation of the Eurodollar market may make it possible for banks and individual business firms to offset tighter national credit policies. Another potential source of monetary instability resulting from the operation of the Eurodollar market is in the relationship to exchange rates. Large volumes of funds move from country to country in response to interest rate differentials. Thus, the pattern of relative demand and supply for individual national currencies may be subject to wide swings. The large amount of liabilities expressed in foreign currencies that may grow within an individual nation is inherently a source of potential instability. Large demands for a national currency or large disposals of a national currency may result in substantial and varying shifts in the demand for or supply of a national currency versus a foreign currency commitment. Pressures on exchange rates may result.

SUMMARY

This chapter has sought to present the basic international framework for understanding the most frequently used terminology and mechanisms involved in developing managerial policies in international business finance. It began with a summary of the ideas associated with the law of comparative advantage in international trade. Comparative advantage simply represents an extension of the widespread practice in the domestic economy of using the economies and gains from the division of labor and obtaining the benefits of specialization through trade.

The existence of different foreign currencies gives rise to the necessity of expressing the price relationship among them, which is the concept of exchange rates. An exchange rate of LC 2 to $1 represents the value of the dollar in terms of the number of LCs it demands. Alternatively, the relationship can be expressed as $0.50 which indicates the value in dollars of LC 1. Both ways of expressing exchange rates are useful for appropriate purposes. Because exchange rates fluctuate over time, the development of forward contracts or forward foreign exchange markets was described. The use of forward foreign exchange markets by both hedgers and speculators was briefly indicated as a basis for further development in subsequent chapters.

The major types of primary transactions in international trade and commerce were set forth. The related financial transactions and flows were discussed in connection with a series of illustrative examples in which the major types of transactions and the major types of balance-of-payments accounts are affected. The aim was to obtain a better understanding of how international transactions are reflected in the balance-of-payments accounts. The summary of balance-of-payments transactions is provided by the balance-of-payments statement. It is used as a tool for planning, policy formation, and decision making over a number of important areas that will be discussed in subsequent chapters. What the relevant balance is in the balance-of-payments statement depends on the nature of the individual problem or opportunity facing the financial manager.

Finally, the nature of the Eurodollar market as a part of a developing international financial system was described. The balance-of-payments mechanism and the Eurodollar market are both important mechanisms used in analysis of international economic developments by financial managers. Their role will be developed in connection with the following discussion of problems and opportunities of international finance. We begin with a discussion of the nature of risks in international business and how they may effectively be managed.

PROBLEM 2–1

A. Suppose that the official exchange ratio between dollars and the foreign local currency is $2 = LC 1, but that at a point in time the following discrepancy exists:

    In New York: $2.00 = LC 1 or $1.00 = LC 0.50
    In foreign: $1.95 = LC 1 or $1.00 = LC 0.513

Questions:
1. The New York dollar price of the LC is too high or too low?
2. The foreign dollar price of the LC is too high or too low?
3. The foreign LC price of the dollar is too high or too low?
4. The New York LC price of the dollar is too high or too low?
5. What arbitrage action would take place in New York?
6. What arbitrage action would take place in the foreign country?

B. Now assume that the exchange ratio between the dollar and the franc is $0.25 = Fr 1 or $1 = Fr 4. Then the consistent cross rate between the LC and the franc would be LC 0.50 = Fr 4, since both equal $1 and LC 1 would equal Fr 8 or LC 0.125 = Fr 1. If the actual rate were LC 0.111 = Fr 1, what arbitrage action by Americans would be profitable, that is, what would be the nature of the triangular movement of funds in the arbitrage activity?

PROBLEM 2–2

For the following transactions (1) make journal entries using the U.S. balance-of-payments accounts items shown in Table 2–2; and (2) calculate the balances of lines 11, 13, 15, 26, 33, and 42 and discuss their relationships for the transactions listed.

A. The U.S. USM firm sells $8,000 worth of merchandise to an importer in Germany. The importer in Germany obtains a letter of credit from his bank. The American USM firm received from the German importer the confirmed irrevocable letter of credit via an American bank which is a correspondent bank with the German bank. The U.S. USM firm then draws a 90-day bill of exchange on the bank of the German importer in the amount of $8,000.

A1. The U.S. USM firm sends the bill of exchange to the German bank which accepts it.

B. The U.S. USM firm discounts the banker's acceptance with the exporter's bank that in turn credits the demand deposit account of the exporter.

C. The 90-day banker's acceptance matures, resulting in an increase in the demand deposit account of the U.S. bank with the German bank.

D. The U.S. TRIM firm imports $9,000 worth of radios from Korea. TRIM makes an arrangement with its New York bank which issues a letter of credit. The Korean exporter issues a 90-day bill of exchange; it is sent to the New York bank and is accepted.

E. An American tourist buys a $500 airline ticket from KLM, the Dutch airline company, for a trip to Europe. He pays for it by a check on his American bank. KLM deposits the check in its U.S. bank.

F. Mr. Smith, aged 68, resides in Kingston, Jamaica. He receives his monthly social security check of $100 from the U.S. government. He deposits the check in a Jamaican bank which increases its deposits in U.S. banks.

G. Smith also receives $200 from an American automobile company. The automobile company draws a check on its U.S. bank.

H. The U.S. government makes a grant to the Korean government of $1 million to control the planting and harvesting of poppy seeds.

I. The U.S. USDI firm establishes a subsidiary in France on an equity basis by an investment of $2 million. The USDI firm has raised the money in the United States and draws a check on demand deposits in banks in the United States. The USDI firm deposits the check in a French bank to purchase francs.

J. Dividends from a U.S. portfolio investment in West Germany in the amount of $1,000 is received by a U.S. investor. The check is deposited by the U.S. investor in his U.S. bank, and the U.S. bank will increase its claims on West German banks.

K. A German bank with large claims on U.S. banks purchases Deutsche marks from the Central Bank of Germany and pays for them by a $10 million check drawn on its deposits in U.S. banks.

L. The German Central Bank receives gold from the United States in the amount of $10 million which it pays for by drawing a check against a U.S. bank to make payment.

M. The Central Bank of Austria is a bidder on a 90-day Treasury bill auction and becomes a purchaser of $3 million of Treasury bills, buying from the U.S. Treasury.

PROBLEM 2–3

A. Make the appropriate T-account entries to illustrate the operations of the Eurodollar market for the transactions which follow. (Key your entries by the letters of the transaction, (a), (b), etc. Follow the pattern as presented in the chapter.)

B. Make up a table recording (1) the outstanding deposit liabilities of banks in New York and (2) the total outstanding Eurodollar deposit liabilities of banks located abroad as of the end of each of the transactions (a) through (i). Comment on the implications of your table.

Transactions to be recorded in T-accounts:

a) A German bank uses its demand deposits of $100,000 at New York bank A to make a time deposit in an Italian bank which has a demand deposit in New York bank B.

b) The Italian bank uses its demand deposit of $100,000 at New York bank B to make a time deposit in a British bank which has a demand deposit account in New York bank C.

c) The British bank uses its demand deposit of $100,000 at New York bank C to make a time deposit in a Swiss bank which has an account in the New York bank D.

d) The Swiss bank uses its demand deposit of $100,000 at New York bank D to make a loan to a Swiss importer who pays by check the New York commodity seller who deposits it in his account at New York bank E.

e) The Swiss trader sells the goods and repays the $100,000 loan to the Swiss bank.

f) The Swiss bank meets its $100,000 liability to the British bank at maturity.

g) The British bank meets its liability to the Italian bank at maturity.

h) The Italian bank meets its liability to the German bank at maturity.

i) The German bank rebuilds its $100,000 deposit at New York bank A.

SELECTED BIBLIOGRAPHY

Aliber, Robert Z.   "Counter-Speculation and the Forward Exchange Market," *Journal of Political Economy*, December 1962, pp. 609–13.

————. "Exchange Risk, Yield Curves and the Pattern of Capital Flows," *The Journal of Finance*, May 1969, p. 361.

Arndt, Sven W.   "International Short-Term Capital Movements," *Econometrica*, January 1968, p. 59.

Auten, John H.   "Counter-Speculation and the Forward Exchange Market," *Journal of Political Economy*, February 1961, pp. 49–55.

Balassa, Bela (ed.).   *Changing Patterns in Foreign Trade and Payments*. Series on Problems of the Modern Economy. New York: W. W. Norton & Co., Inc., 1964.

Brehmer, Ekhard.   "Official Forward Exchange Operations," *IMF Staff Papers*, November 1964, pp. 389–412.

Coombs, Charles A.   "Treasury and Federal Reserve Foreign Exchange Speculations," *Federal Reserve Bank of New York Monthly Review*, September 1964, pp. 162–72.

Devlin, David T.   "The U.S. Balance of Payments: Revised Presentation," *Survey of Current Business*, Vol. 51 (June 1971), pp. 24–57.

Dudley, L., and Passell, P.   "The War in Vietnam and the United States Balance of Payments," *Review of Economics and Statistics*, November 1968, p. 437.

Einzig, Paul.   *The Euro-dollar System*. 3d ed. New York: St. Martin's Press, Inc., 1965.

————. *Foreign Exchange Crises*. New York: St. Martin's Press, Inc., 1968.

————. "Organization of the Market," *A Textbook on Foreign Exchange*, chap. 2. New York: St. Martin's Press, Inc., 1966.

Friedman, Milton.   "The Euro-dollar Market: Some First Principles," *Morgan Guaranty Survey*, October 1969, pp. 4–14.

Friedmann, Wolfgang P., and Béguin, Jean-Pierre.   *Joint International Business Ventures in Developing Countries*. Case Studies and Analysis of Recent Trends. New York: Columbia University Press, 1971.

Hagemann, Helmut A.   "Reserve Policies of Central Banks and Their Implications for U.S. Balance of Payments Policy," *The American Economic Review*, March 1969, p. 62.

Hein, John.   "Measuring the U.S. Balance of Payments," *Conference Board Record*, September 1971, p. 35, 36.

Hynning, C. J.   "Balance of Payments Controls by the United States," *The International Lawyer*, April 1966, p. 400.

International Economic Policy Association.   *The United States Balance of Payments*. Washington, D.C., 1966, 1968.

Kindleberger, Charles P.   *International Economics*, chaps. 1–3. 4th ed. Homewood, Ill.: Richard D. Irwin, Inc., 1968.

Klopstock, Fred H.   *The Euro-dollar Market: Some Unresolved Issues. Essays in International Finance, No. 65.* Princeton, N.J.: Princeton University, Department of Economics, 1968.

Machlup, Fritz. "The Magicians and Their Rabbits," *Morgan Guaranty Survey,* May 1971, pp. 3–13.

Swoboda, A. K. *The Euro-dollar Market: An Interpretation. Essays in International Finance, No. 64.* Princeton, N.J.: Princeton University, Department of Economics, 1968.

3

The risks of international financial
management

THE NATURE OF THE RISKS

THE RISKS of foreign operations differ both in degree and kind from the risks of domestic activity. The differential rates of inflation abroad may have a severe impact on goods manufactured abroad and sold in a number of other foreign countries. Changes in foreign exchange rates and devaluation may also have a number of effects. The financial position of foreign operations will be greatly influenced by the U.S. value of monetary assets held abroad. In addition, the ability of foreign manufacturing operations to make sales in countries with differing amounts of foreign exchange rate change will be affected. Exchange controls will also have an impact. Finally, the commitment of investment funds abroad makes a firm subject to the political and legal environment of the host country.

Thus, risks in foreign operations differ in degree and kind from those associated with domestic production and sales. Exchange rate risks are different and are great. The restrictions on currency and investment transfers do not occur in domestic transactions but foreign restrictions are substantial. Expropriation risks are much greater. The requirements for adjusting to local institutions and law are much larger. How do we appraise these risks in analytical terms?

Risk analysis involves consideration of the probability distributions of revenues and costs—comparison is made of expected returns and the statistical dispersion of expected returns as measured by the variance or standard deviation of alternative outcomes. The risk-return relations are likely to be different for foreign activities than for domestic operations. Domestic operations are likely to offer prospects of lower expected returns and lower standard deviations; foreign investments may offer higher expected returns and higher standard deviations of returns. The need to utilize decision models for investment under uncertainty takes on increased practical importance.[1]

---

[1] See any modern textbook in business finance for an exposition of these concepts. They are also summarized in Appendix C to this book.

Another aspect of investment decisions under uncertainty becomes of increased importance in analysis of foreign investment decisions. The variance or standard deviation of returns includes both diversifiable and nondiversifiable risk. While the standard deviation of returns from foreign investments may be large, a portion of this risk may be diversified away by the firm by forming a portfolio of foreign investments or by combining domestic and foreign investments.

The nondiversifiable risk is the covariance of investment returns with the "market returns." The economic characteristics of foreign markets are likely to be more different from those affecting other investments in the United States than is the case for domestic investments. This is because the performance of most industries in the United States is dominated by general economic conditions as reflected in movements in gross national product. But the diversity of characteristics among individual countries is greater than among different industries in a given country. Levy and Sarnat found that the correlation coefficient among returns for nine countries was either negative or below 0.25 in 27 out of 45 possible observations.[2] Thus the risks of foreign investments as measured by the dispersion of their returns or the probability of loss may be greater than for domestic investments. However, their negative covariance with domestic investments *may improve* the overall risk-return relations for the total "portfolio" of the firm which includes foreign investments in its activities.

THE RISKS ASSOCIATED WITH FOREIGN ACTIVITY

A systematic treatment of the risks of international operations is now set forth. The international operations of business firms are exposed to three types of risks: commercial risks, political risks, and foreign exchange rate risks. Table 3–1 indicates our judgment of the relative magnitude of risks in different types of foreign business operations.

TABLE 3–1
Risks of foreign business activity

	Type of risk		
Type of action	Commercial	Political	Exchange rate
Selling................	10	2	5
Portfolio investments...........	7	4	10
Direct investments and manufacturing operations.......	2	10	8

Scale: 10 high; 5, medium; 1, low.

---

[2] H. Levy and M. Sarnat, "International Diversification of Investment Portfolios," *American Economic Review*, Vol. 60 (September 1970), p. 672.

Commercial risks

Commercial risks are encountered when sales are made to foreign buyers on a credit basis. Losses can occur due to protracted delay in payment on the part of the buyer (when not due to political conditions within his country), the failure or refusal of the buyer to accept and pay for goods or services when not due to a failure or fault on the part of the seller, and the insolvency of the buyer.

Political risks

All foreign business actions are affected by political risks. Losses from political risks may occur due to governmental action which interferes with the completion of contractual obligations between parties of two countries. This interference may be due to restrictions placed on the transfer of funds from the foreign country to the United States. The enactment of new laws, decrees, orders, or regulations putting into effect quotas, embargoes, or discriminatory increases in tariff rates can also interfere with normal business activity. Cancellation of export or import licenses already issued, or only partial renewal of these licenses, can cause financial losses. Requisition, expropriation, or confiscation of property by a foreign government, or the occurrence of war or hostile warlike action, including civil war, revolution, rebellion or insurrection, or civil strife in time of peace or war, can cause losses.

Since no private insurance organization, or combination of insurance agencies, would have at its disposal a sufficiently large amount of funds to cover the uncertain and potentially large losses due to political risks, this insurance is written by the Export-Import Bank and the Overseas Private Investment Corporation, both U.S. government corporations. For short-term sales transactions, insurance is available through the Foreign Credit Insurance Association. Insurance for medium-term sales transactions can be obtained either through the Foreign Credit Insurance Association or directly from the Export-Import Bank. The Overseas Private Investment Corporation (OPIC), successor to the Agency for International Development (AID), is concerned solely with the insurance of investments.

Exchange rate risks

Losses due to exchange rate risks occur whenever the value of the national currency of one party to a business transaction changes unfavorably in relation to the value of the national currency of the other party.

Exchange rate risks affect selling transactions where such sales are made in terms of a foreign currency. Until payment is made and converted into the home currency, the seller is never certain of the value of the receipts. A downward adjustment, or devaluation, of the foreign currency results in a decrease in the purchasing value of receipts. Exchange rate risks also affect portfolio and direct investments in a foreign country when these investments are made in terms of the currency of that country.

Particularly sensitive to foreign exchange rate risks are portfolio investments in debt instruments which promise to return a fixed number of units of the foreign currency at the end of the investment period. Portfolio type equity investments and direct investments are not as exposed to exchange rate risks since real assets associated with these investments increase in value in terms of the devalued foreign currency. However, profits from foreign investments are always affected by changes in the value relationship between two national currencies. Therefore, possible currency devaluations strongly affect the estimated net profitability of foreign investments.

Efforts to minimize financial losses from foreign operations always involve costs as well as benefits. But the competitive nature of international business requires avoidance of unnecessary costs. Careful study of expected future events that may affect a planned business venture can help determine whether the potential benefits from protective actions would outweigh the associated costs.

THE FOREIGN ENVIRONMENT AND RISKS

All three of the risks—commercial, political, and foreign exchange rate —are strongly influenced by environmental factors, political, social, and economic in nature, that are present in the country of an existing or intended foreign business transaction or activity.

Sources of political risks

Studies agree that political stability is the most important requisite for orderly economic development and growth of a nation. A government politically stable on a solid foundation of public support is more likely over time than a less-stable government to be able to take those actions which will minimize the risks that concern the multinational firm. Some firms make systematic analyses of the political outlook in different countries as a basis for choosing some countries and rejecting others for making investments based on the short- and long-term outlook for political stability. A number of questions and indicators can be employed to judge future political stability:

1. If it had formerly been a colony, how much experience in self-government was provided by the controlling nation? The quality of experience in self-government provided while a country was a colony will

greatly influence its future political stability. Without prior experience in self-government, a nation may expect some political difficulties.

2. How long has the country been an independent nation? If a nation has not been independent for a long period of time, political upheavals may be a part of the learning process.

3. How strong were traditional tribal and regional ties before a national government was established? Where tribal or regional loyalties were strong, much more time is required to develop allegiance to the national government. Also party rivalries may be more bitter.

4. How much unemployment exists in the economy? A large pool of unemployment breeds discontent. Poverty makes the people susceptible to revolutionary change because they feel they have little to lose.

5. Is there great inequality in income distribution? Great inequality in income distribution may lead to a feeling that the existing system is unjust and lead to mass support for its overthrow.

6. Is there some start toward industrialization in the economy to balance agriculture? A country entirely dependent on agriculture is likely to have a deficit in its balance of payments, have slow economic growth, and consequently have underemployment. All of these contribute to dissatisfaction with the prevailing government.

7. Are there social and political constraints which limit the ability of a person to move up in the social, economic, or political hierarchy? If a person with ability cannot move up the social, economic, or political scale, he may seek an alternative form of society in which he has greater opportunities.

8. Is there a splintering of political parties? The existence of a large number of splinter political parties may lead to the inability to achieve a clear majority or continuity in political administrations and policies.

The above eight factors are but a sample of the kinds of characteristics of a country that can be studied. Such analysis provides a basis for scientific predictions of the future stability or instability of its political institutions.

Political risks arise from the actions of national governments which interfere with or prevent international business transactions, or change the terms of agreements, or cause the confiscation of wholly or partly foreign-owned business property. Massive risks are also associated with the occurrence of hostile or warlike action, including civil war, revolution, rebellion, or civil strife, which also would interfere with foreign business ventures. A government resting on a stable political base and enjoying a steady growth of its economy is less likely to interfere with foreign business transactions or engage in the confiscation or nationalization of foreign-owned private property. Such a government is also less likely to be involved in revolution, rebellion, and civil strife within its borders. External wars between nations are, of course, always possible. However, these usually do not occur without a prior series of events and indicators. The alert multinational firm, continuously atuned to developments throughout the world, will usually be forewarned.

Sources of commercial risks

Commercial risk arises from the inability of the foreign buyer to meet his financial obligations, or due to his inability to purchase the foreign currency in terms of which his obligation was contracted. A growing and prospering economy will reduce commercial risk, since prosperous businesses are not likely to default on their business obligations. Also, governments supported by a growing and prospering economy are usually not the ones that would increase commercial risk by making it impossible for the local buyer to obtain the necessary foreign currency to meet his financial obligations to foreign firms.

In addition to the above, of prime importance in the prevention of commercial risk is the application of sound credit appraisal and judgment. The seller must have available adequate information on the credit worthiness of the buyer. Such information can be obtained from banks and credit organizations in the country of the buyer or in some instances from U.S. commercial banks. Both the Export-Import Bank of the United States and the Foreign Credit Insurance Association have been accumulating over the years extensive files on foreign buyers of U.S. products and services.

Sources of foreign exchange rate risks

Foreign exchange rate risk materializes when the foreign exchange value of a national currency in terms of which business transactions or obligations are expressed changes in relation to the home currency of the internationally operating enterprise. Even though the decrease in the foreign exchange value of a national currency is directly responsible for foreign exchange rate losses, devaluation is *not* the basic cause. It is merely the end product of a chain of events which if not interrupted by purposeful government actions eventually results in currency devaluation. An awareness of these events, especially in developing countries, can serve as advance warning of impending devaluations.

A number of factors are critical in forecasting exchange rate fluctuations. We shall briefly summarize 10:

1. Sound money supply growth.
2. Appropriate fiscal policy.
3. Effective coordination of national economic policies.
4. Trends in price levels and costs of production.

5. Labor union strength and aggressiveness.
6. Size and rate of growth of welfare expenditures.
7. Character of foreign diplomatic and military commitments.
8. Balance-of-payments surplus or deficit.
9. Foreign exchange reserve position.
10. Investment versus liquidity position.

Each of these will be explained:

1. For price level stability a necessary condition is balance between the rate of growth of the money supply and the rate of growth in real output in the economy. The principle is simple to enunciate, but its implementation may be quite difficult for the monetary authorities. But if the money supply growth exceeds the rate of real growth in the nation's output of goods and services, an increase in the price level will take place to bring the rate of growth in gross national product in money terms to equality with the rate of growth in the money supply.

2. The guideline for fiscal policy is for the government deficit or surplus to be related to the needs for stimulation or dampening of expansion in the remainder of the economy. If the economy is operating at less than full employment, fiscal policy has an appropriate role of stimulating the economy. If the demands on the economy are already in excess of what its real growth in output can satisfy, the need is for a fiscal surplus (or a decrease in the deficit) to restore balance.

3. Especially critical is the need to coordinate monetary and fiscal policy to the nation's deficit or surplus in its balance of payments. A nation such as West Germany which has been running a balance-of-payments surplus should seek to offset the inflow of funds by a tight (surplus) fiscal policy while avoiding a tight monetary policy which would raise interest rates so high as to attract an additional flow of capital from abroad for the high yields. A nation such as the United States, running a persistent balance-of-payments deficit, should pursue an expansionary fiscal policy to offset the outflow of purchasing power while not easing monetary policy to the point that low interest rates will cause funds to flow abroad seeking higher yields. In recent years, both West Germany and the United States have *not* fully coordinated their monetary and fiscal policies to their balance-of-payments trends.

4. Another symptom of a broader range of economic problems, along with balance-of-payments trends, are trends in price levels and in the cost of production. If monetary and fiscal policy are inflationary, price levels will rise and so will costs of production. These symptoms of the disease have to be attacked at their source. Otherwise, unfavorable comparative trends in price levels and costs of production will aggravate the balance-of-payments problems.

5. When labor unions are strong and determined to match or exceed

increases in the costs of living with wage increases, inflationary conditions are aggravated. If wage increases exceed productivity increases on the average, the difference will be made up by price level increases. Hence, if the cost of living has been rising due to excess aggregate demand and labor unions obtain contracts providing for wage increases related to past cost-of-living increases, this will add a cost-push element to the causes of inflation.

6. Along with huge outlays in connection with hostilities in Southeast Asia, the United States made large increases in welfare expenditures in 1966. Without evaluating the long-run merits of the welfare program, these are expenditures which increase spending power in the short run without a corresponding increase in the current output of goods and services to absorb such increases in spending power. Thus, these U.S. outlays have also been inflationary since 1966. Similarly, in other countries the outlays for public welfare may be large in relation to the size or productivity of the national economic output. Inflationary effects will likewise be predictable.

7. Large government expenditures abroad will represent outflows in the balance of payments. For example, expenditures of the United States in connection with the hostilities in Southeast Asia have been an important contributor to the domestic fiscal deficit and to deficits in the balance of payments which cause unfavorable exchange relationships.

8. The balance-of-payments accounts have five main sections: (*a*) goods and services; (*b*) remittances, transportation, and travel; (*c*) long-term capital flows; (*d*) short-term capital flows; and (*e*) foreign exchange and gold flow adjustment transactions. If a nation experiences a persistent deficit and adverse trends in its goods and services account, the other accounts may move unfavorably as well. A deficit in the balance of payments is a reflection of a number of problems in other areas of the type discussed in the previous seven items.

9. A nation with a large foreign exchange surplus can stave off the consequences of balance-of-payments deficits for a time. This was true for the United States. But a declining foreign exchange position is an indicator that a foreign exchange adjustment will be required. If the increase in the domestic price level is not reversed, *a trade deficit* results from the country's commercial relations with other nations, involving the sale and purchase of goods and services. If this condition persists, it has an eventual *adverse effect on the country's foreign exchange reserves,* since these reserves are spent in meeting foreign obligations. Declining foreign exchange reserves and rising liquid liabilities to foreigners are likely to result in *the devaluation of the country's currency* by government action in order to seek to restore balance in its trade with other countries.

10. Some nations such as the United States may have a strong creditor position with regard to their overall investments abroad and still experi-

ence balance-of-payments problems. The foreign direct investments improve the long-term asset position of the United States but, as described in Chapter 2, increase the short-term liabilities. The increase in short-term claims on the United States are potentially claims on U.S. dollars. This, therefore, puts pressure on the exchange value of the U.S. dollar.

Analysis of the above 10 basic economic factors can provide a basis for prediction of exchange rate adjustments. Some people had argued that such leading indicators did not apply to the United States. The declines in the foreign exchange values of the U.S. dollar and the formal announcement of the de facto devaluation by President Nixon on September 15, 1971 have underscored the validity of the above framework for analysis.

SUMMARY OF FACTORS AFFECTING RISKS IN INTERNATIONAL TRADE

The risk factors discussed in this chapter are outlined in Table 3–2. The environmental factors affecting the three types of risks of inter-

TABLE 3–2
Summary of environmental factors affecting risks

Commercial risks:
Credit worthiness of the foreign buyer
Political stability of buyer's government
Level and growth of buyer's national economy
Level and trend of activity in buyer's industry
Foreign exchange resources of buyer's government
Spot and forward quotations of the buyer's currency in terms of the currency of the seller

Political and foreign exchange rate risks:
Political stability of government of host country
International relations of host country
Level and growth of foreign economy
Foreign exchange reserves of host country
International trade surplus or deficit of each country
International balance-of-payments position of countries
Growth of quantity of money in domestic circulation in each country
Comparative position and trends in domestic costs of production and price levels of export goods
International investment position of countries involved
Soundness of fiscal policies of host country

national operations are set forth. It will be noted that the factors affecting political risks and exchange rate risks overlap, so they are grouped together.

One of the most important of the environmental factors affecting business transactions with or operations in foreign countries is the political stability of governments. The management of the multinational firm must continuously study the outcomes of national, state, and at times even local elections in the countries in which it is interested. It must analyze the trends in these elections in order to be aware of the increasing influence of political parties which if in a controlling position could cause shifts in government policies hostile to private enterprise in general and foreign-owned enterprises in particular. A recent example of this is Chile, where a gradual political change has taken place during the last 10 years culminating in a communist-oriented government after the elections of 1969, followed by nationalization of foreign-owned copper properties in 1971.

Along with the study of political conditions within countries, managers of the multinational firm must be aware of evolving commercial relationships between the countries of the world. They must pay particular attention to these relationships in parts of the world in which their firm is operating. Competitive trade relationships among nations must be studied since these may lead to political rivalries.

The magnitude and growth rate of the national economies of countries with which, or in which, a firm is doing business must be regularly analyzed. Where available, the level of activity in particular industries of interest must be noted, since sometimes their economic trends may be at variance with those of the national economy. The export and import patterns as well as the volume of foreign exchange reserves must be studied. Government monetary and fiscal policies and particularly sudden changes in these must be noted. Price level indicators as well as the quantity of money in circulation in each country must be observed. A study of foreign exchange quotations on a spot as well as a forward basis will be helpful. Of particular importance are the discounts or premiums in relation to the spot rate that are quoted on forward contracts. These premiums or discounts represent the forward expectations of knowledgeable people in the financial communities of the two countries whose currencies are involved in the forward contract.

PROBLEM 3–1

You are an analyst in the credit department of your firm. A foreign customer from Redulia wishes to purchase $30,000 of producer's goods on a 3-year open account basis with a 10 percent down payment. You are asked to investigate and make recommendations based on the following facts:

1. Economic activity of the country has grown 6 percent annually.
2. The industry of the applicant has grown at a 10 percent rate annually.
3. The foreign firm's share of the volume of business in its industry has increased annually by 15 percent.
4. The current and quick ratios of the applicant have decreased 5 percent per year the last 3 years. The current ratio is presently 1.9:1, and the quick ratio is 1.2:1.

5. The applicant's debt to equity ratio is ½, and it has been decreasing at a rate of 5 percent annually during the last few years.
6. The country of the applicant is rated by the FCIA in the next to highest category.
7. The country's money supply has grown at an annual rate of 10 percent.
8. The country is running a 10 percent trade deficit.
9. Twenty percent of the country's economic activity is connected with the tourist industry which has been growing 15 percent annually.
10. The government has been stable over the last five years.

A. Briefly comment on each of the above factors as an influence on the credit risk involved in making the sale.

B. Present an overall appraisal of the credit risk involved in making the sale.

PROBLEM 3–2

In Chapter 3 indicators were set forth that would provide barometers giving advance indications to financial managers of prospective depreciation or appreciation of a nation's currency. Utilize data on as many of these given on the following list as can readily be obtained for a devaluating or revaluating currency. The German appreciation of its currency in 1969 and 1971 or the U.S. depreciation and devaluation of its currency in late 1971 may be used. The best single source of monthly data is *International Financial Statistics* published by the International Monetary Fund, Washington, D.C.

1. Budget.
2. Money supply.
3. Price level.
4. Merchandise trade—surplus or deficit.
5. Balance of payments—surplus or deficit.
6. Gold and foreign exchange position.
7. Premium or discount of the 30-day forward market rate as compared with the foreign exchange market spot rates.

A. Assemble tables for as many of the above series as can conveniently be obtained on a quarterly basis for at least eight quarters prior to the appreciation or depreciation of the currency.

B. Discuss the extent to which the data you have assembled provides lead time suggesting that the change in currency value would take place.

PROBLEM 3–3

An exporter is comparing the sale of goods on extended credit to a buyer in Country A with a buyer in Country B. The probabilities of devaluation in the two countries are shown below. In which country is the risk of devaluation greater?

States	Probabilities of devaluation	Percentage devaluation Country A	Country B
1...............	.2	0	10
2...............	.5	16	18
3...............	.3	40	30

SELECTED BIBLIOGRAPHY

Alenmann, Roberto T. "Monetary Stabilization in Latin America," *Journal of Finance*, May 1961, pp. 167–75.

Baer, Werner, and Kerstenetzky, Isaac (eds.). *Inflation and Growth in Latin America*. Homewood, Ill.: Richard D. Irwin, Inc., 1964.

deVries, M. "Exchange Depreciation in Developing Countries," IMF *Staff Papers*, November 1968, p. 560.

de Vries, Margaret. "The Magnitudes of Exchange Devaluation," *Finance and Development*, Vol. 4. International Monetary Fund and IBRD, 1968.

Levy, H., and Sarnat, M. "International Diversification of Investment Portfolios," *American Economic Review*, Vol. 60 (September 1970), p. 672.

Whitman, Marina von Neuman. *Government Risk-Sharing in Foreign Investment*. Princeton, N.J.: Princeton University Press, 1965.

4

Insurance and guarantee programs for foreign operations

EFFORTS to minimize financial losses from foreign operations always involve costs as well as benefits. The ever-increasing competitive nature of international business demands that increases in economic costs should never be undertaken lightly, not even for the prevention of possible financial losses in foreign operations. Careful study and estimation of expected future events that may affect a planned business venture can help determine whether the potential benefits from protective action would outweigh the associated costs.

In this chapter, we analyze the costs and benefits of a range of forms of insurance and guarantee programs available. In the following chapter, we describe methods for achieving exchange risk protection.

This chapter is basically divided into two broad parts. One part covers export sales, and the second part covers investments. The primary agency involved in insurance of export sales is the Foreign Credit Insurance Association (FCIA). The Export-Import Bank (Eximbank) performs a cooperative and facilitating role with FCIA. However, the range of responsibilities of the Eximbank is much broader than insurance of export sales. Indeed, one reason for the ambiguity in its role with regard to export sales is that it apparently regards itself as an agency of last resort in cooperating on insurance for such sales to the extent required by the needs of the country, and to the extent those needs are not being met in practice by the FCIA and its related activities. So the FCIA and the Eximbank are both involved with insurance programs of a variety of forms which we will describe in connection with sales. The second part of the chapter focuses on investments. Here, the major agency is the Overseas Private Investment Corporation (OPIC), the successor to the Agency for International Development (AID), although AID continues with a residual of activities. Both insurance and guarantee programs are involved in connection with investment as contrasted with just insurance programs in connection with export sales.

FOREIGN CREDIT INSURANCE

Insurance policies are available from the Foreign Credit Insurance Association for short-term credit sales of up to six months, and occasionally to one year, covering the sale of consumer goods and for medium-term transactions of from 181 days to normally five years involving transactions in capital or producer's goods. Terms up to seven years are available in order to meet foreign competition, particularly for aircraft and marine sales. Overall insurance policies combining short- as well as medium-term sales are also available.

All of these policies may be obtained either on a comprehensive basis covering both commercial and political risks or on a political-risk-only basis. Further modifications are possible to protect manufacturers during the production period of specialty goods which are constructed according to the specifications of the foreign buyer. Modifications are also possible to protect American goods while in inventory on foreign shores when these inventories have been established in order to facilitate the foreign sales of U.S. merchandise.

The insurance policies available from FCIA are made possible by cooperation between the Export-Import Bank of the United States and FCIA. Since no private insurance company, or even all the member firms of the FCIA, has sufficient assets to insure the potentially huge political risks of major political upheavals, the political risk coverage of the FCIA policies is underwritten by Eximbank. Also, in case of large commercial-risk policies, Eximbank reinsures the commercial risks above a maximum amount.

In addition to this cooperation with FCIA, Eximbank also issues medium-term comprehensive and political-risk-only policies to U.S. exporters on a case-by-case basis.

The cost of foreign credit insurance varies with the country of destination of the goods covered, the length of the credit term, and the security offered, if any (such as a letter of credit). Premiums do not vary with the credit worthiness of the individual foreign buyer. It is assumed that all foreign buyers accepted for credit coverage are good credit risks. For premium purposes, countries of foreign buyers are divided into four groups: A, B, C, and D. The most stable, and therefore the safest countries, are grouped in A; and the least stable, or risky countries, in D. The shorter the credit terms or the stronger the guarantees of eventual payment, the lower the premiums.

The cost of insurance for a transaction which has been negotiated on a sight draft basis, which means that the amount due will be paid immediately upon presentation of the proper shipping documents, will be lower than a transaction granting credit over an extended period. In a similar manner the cost of insurance for a transaction which is covered by a confirmed letter of credit will be less costly than that for a transaction where the guarantee of payment rests only on the credit worthiness of the foreign buyer. As is explained in greater detail in Chapter 9, a confirmed letter of credit reduces the risk of nonpayment to negligible proportions, since the U.S. confirming bank, as well as the foreign bank issuing the letter of credit, guarantees that payment will eventually be made to the U.S. exporter.

Protection is not available for 100 percent of the value of the goods sold to a foreign buyer. Until May 1966, in the case of medium-term transactions, the foreign buyer was required to make a minimum down payment of 20 percent. Since then a down payment of 10 percent has been permitted in A and B countries. However, 20 percent is still preferred. There are no down payment requirements for short-term transactions. In the case of a short-term comprehensive policy the seller is required to carry 10 percent of the commercial risk and 5 percent of the political risk of the gross invoice value of his sale at his own risk. In the instance of a political-risk-only policy this retention is reduced to 5 percent. Even though the Foreign Credit Insurance Association and the Export-Import Bank will cover up to 90 percent of the financed amount for comprehensive policies in A and B countries, in some higher risk C and D countries, the seller may be required to carry a larger percentage of the risk for his own account.

Short-term policies

At present, comprehensive short-term premiums average 0.46 percent of the insured value for all countries. The lowest premiums are 0.09 percent for 30 days for A countries, but the premiums for D countries run as high as 2.14 percent for 180 days. The lowest premium of 0.09 percent for a 30-day transaction covered by a confirmed letter of credit with an A-rated country is available only to exporters whose export mix covered by their FCIA policy is heavily weighted in favor of A- and B-rated countries. An exporter whose export mix is largely to C- and D-rated countries might pay as much as 0.14 percent on the confirmed letter of credit 30-day transaction.

To show the effect of a credit guarantee on the part of a confirming U.S. commercial bank for a longer period, let us consider the cost of comprehensive policies in countries with varied degrees of risk. The lowest premium for a 180-day transaction to a D country with a bank guarantee is 0.37 percent. In comparison, a 180-day transaction to an A country on an open account basis carries a lowest premium of 0.36 percent of the insured amount, while the same transaction to a D country can require a premium as high as 2.14 percent. If it is desired that political risk only be covered in these transactions, the premiums are approximately 75 percent of those charged on a comprehensive basis.

Examples of the cost of insurance for various short-term risks

1. The Smith Company has made an export sale of $10,000 to an A country firm, with a confirmed 30-day letter of credit. Its export sales are largely to A- and B-rated countries. The premium is 0.09 percent.

The insured part of the transaction and its cost would be determined as follows:

$$
\begin{array}{ll}
\text{Amount of sale} & \$10,000 \\
\text{Less exporter's risk, } 10\% & 1,000 \\
\hline
\text{Insured amount} & \$\ 9,000 \\
\text{Premium} = \$9,000 \times 0.0009 = \$8.10
\end{array}
$$

Since the protection is for 30 days or $\frac{1}{12}$ of a year, the annual premium rate would be 0.09 percent $\times$ 12 = 1.08 percent.

2. The Jones Company has made an export sale of $20,000 to a D country company on a six-month open account basis. It will assume 10 percent of the risk.

The insured part of the transaction and its cost would be determined:

$$
\begin{array}{ll}
\text{Amount of sale} & \$20,000 \\
\text{Less } 10\% \text{ exporter's risk} & 2,000 \\
\hline
\text{Insured amount} & \$18,000 \\
\text{Premium} = \$18,000 \times 0.0214 = \$385.20
\end{array}
$$

On an annual basis the cost would be 2.14 percent $\times$ 12/6 = 4.28 percent.

3. The Smith Company also makes a $20,000 sale to a D country firm on a six-month basis but receives a confirmed letter of credit.

Its premium would be computed as follows:

$$
\begin{array}{ll}
\text{Amount of sale} & \$20,000 \\
\text{Less } 10\% \text{ exporter's risk} & 2,000 \\
\hline
\text{Insurable amount} & \$18,000 \\
\text{Premium} = \$18,000 \times 0.0037 = \$66.60
\end{array}
$$

On an annual percentage basis this would be 0.37 percent $\times$ 12/6 = 0.74 percent.

In this case it might be argued that it is not worthwhile to insure a confirmed letter of credit transaction. However, it must be kept in mind that the letter of credit protects only against commercial risk. Since the policy is a comprehensive policy protecting against political risk as well, insuring such a transaction with the FCIA is advantageous.

Medium-term policies

Medium-term comprehensive premiums vary from 0.46 percent of the financed portion of the sale for a one-year term in an A market to 6.62 percent for a five-year term in a D market. When the foreign buyer has made a 10 percent down payment and the U.S. exporter assumes 10 percent of the risk, a transaction with a firm in an A country may have a premium as low as 0.46 percent for a one-year term and 1.68 percent for a five-year term. In the instance of a D country company under the same circumstances, the premiums would vary from 1.82 percent for a one-year term to 6.62 percent for a five-year term. As in the case of short-term policies, the premiums for medium-term political-risk-only policies are approximately 75 percent of that for comprehensive policies. Where protection during the manufacturing period is desired, a small charge is added to the premium. When it is desired to protect goods in foreign inventory, consignment coverage for political risk only is available for 50 percent of the normal premium fee covering the goods during the shipping and storage periods in the foreign inventory. However, full premiums apply as soon as the goods are sold on a credit basis. In the case of medium-term transactions having a final maturity of three years or more, if the first half of the installments have been paid promptly, FCIA will consider increasing the insured coverage to 100 percent providing the exporter was not required to assume more than 10 percent of the risk for his own account.

Examples of the cost of insurance for various medium-term risks

1. The Apex Company has sold a $50,000 tractor on a five-year open account basis to a buyer in an A country. It receives a 10 percent down payment and carries 10 percent of the remaining risk.
   The premium would be calculated as follows:

$$
\begin{array}{lr}
\text{Value of sale} & \$50,000 \\
\text{Less } 10\% \text{ down payment} & 5,000 \\ \hline
\text{Remainder} & \$45,000 \\
\text{Less } 10\% \text{ risk assumed by seller} & 4,500 \\ \hline
\text{Amount to be insured} & \$40,500 \\
\end{array}
$$

Premium = $40,500 \times 0.0168 = \$680.40$

The cost of insurance on an annual percentage basis is 1.68 percent $\times$ $1/5 = 0.336$ percent.

2. The General Aviation Company has sold an aircraft engine of a value of $90,000 to a buyer in a D country. The terms are the same as in Example 1.
   The insurance premium would be calculated as follows:

$$
\begin{array}{lr}
\text{Value of sale} & \$90,000 \\
\text{Less } 10\% \text{ down payment} & 9,000 \\ \hline
\text{Remainder} & \$81,000 \\
\text{Less } 10\% \text{ of risk carried by seller} & 8,100 \\ \hline
\text{Amount to be insured} & \$72,900 \\
\end{array}
$$

Premium = $72,900 \times 0.0662 = \$4,825.98$

The premium cost on an annual percentage basis would be 6.62 percent $\times$ $1/5 = 1.324$ percent.

3. The Williams Company has sold a tractor and several trailers to a

buyer in a D country for the sum of $150,000. The FCIA requires for that particular D country that the seller carry 30 percent of the risk for his own account. The company will receive a 10 percent down payment and grant open account credit on the balance.

The premium calculations would be as follows:

Amount of sale......................	$150,000
Less 10% down payment..............	15,000
Remainder.....................	$135,000
Less 30% seller's risk................	40,500
Amount to be insured............	$ 94,500

Premium cost = $94,500 × 0.0662 = $6,255.90

On an annual percentage basis the cost of the premium itself is the same as in Example 2 above, namely 6.62 percent × 1/5 = 1.324 percent. However, in this instance the seller's total cost on a percentage basis is likely to be higher than that of the firm in Example 2, since the Williams Company's financing costs on the uninsured portion of the sale will be higher due to greater risk.

In the case of losses, payments are made to the insured, and the insurers then make an effort to recover the amounts paid. Benefits under Foreign Credit Insurance Association policies depend upon actual losses incurred and cannot exceed the face value of the policy.

The foregoing is a general outline of the FCIA's premium and policy structure as well as its requirements as to down payment for medium-term policies only and the assumption of risk on the part of the seller. These structures and requirements are not quite as inflexible as they may appear. In practice, the FCIA's criteria for judgments as to insurability are not at all fixed. The needs of the individual insured are considered in detail, and every effort is made to serve his needs.

In addition to the above policies the FCIA has introduced several additional policies and liberalized others during 1970 to make the U.S. exporter more competitive.

Catastrophe policy

There is a policy designed for catastrophic political upheavals to cover high-volume, low-profit exporters; it is a political-risk-only policy. Premium rates are as low as 0.1 percent of the insured value and will cover all of an exporter's short- as well as medium-term sales. Under this policy the exporter retains 30 percent of the risk and there is a nine-month waiting period for currency transfer risks—the risk of the foreign importer not being able to get the exporter's currency to pay his bill before settlement is due. However, other political risks are handled on a normal basis. For medium-term transactions an exporter may obtain commercial-risk coverage on an individual sale basis.

Comprehensive master policy

A comprehensive master policy has been designed to cover all of the export sales of an exporter, both short and medium term. It is worldwide in scope. Buyer limits and premiums are set and reviewed annually. Coverage on medium-term sales will stay intact for the term of the credit granted provided the insured renews the master policy; otherwise full premiums will apply from the date of the policy's expiration to the end of the credit term.

This policy permits the coverage on an overall basis or to be split on a buyer-by-buyer, or obligation-by-obligation basis *if* different financial institutions are involved. Usually the coverage of all eligible sales is required and the insured takes all commercial losses below an agreed-upon percentage. As with automobile collision insurance, the greater the deductibility the lower the premium. Political losses due to transfer risks (nonconvertibility risks) under this policy also require a longer waiting period than the regular policies before they are paid. Under the comprehensive master policy the FCIA may assign the insured firm a discretionary credit limit per customer that applies to both short-term and medium-term transactions. Under this arrangement the insured may initiate sales to customers up to the level of the discretionary limit without having to make special applications for approval by FCIA. In order to be of greatest service to its insured, FCIA attempts to set the discretionary limit at a level that would take care of the insured's needs for sales to the majority of his customers. The exercise of sound credit judgment on the part of the insured firm will be rewarded by higher discretionary limits and at times lower premiums. This policy places greater emphasis on the credit judgment of the exporter, a procedure that we have long advocated.[1]

Small business policy

A policy for small businesses is designed for firms new to the export business which export less than $200,000 per year. It provides them with commercial- and political-risk coverage on short-term as well as medium-term export sales. Record keeping and other procedures are kept to a minimum to assist the new exporter.

Agricultural coverage

In the case of agricultural exports where profit margins are extremely small, it is now possible to obtain coverage for up to 98 percent of the

---

[1] J. Fred Weston and Bart W. Sorge, "Export Insurance—Why U.S. Lags," *Columbia Journal of World Business,* Vol. 2, No. 5 (September–October 1967), pp. 67–76.

financed portion of the sale. Warehousing coverage has been extended by lengthening the repayment period from six months to one year. Another important recent change permits short-term sales in a foreign currency to be insured for comprehensive as well as political-risk coverage.

Foreign credit insurance systems compared

Foreign credit insurance has been available abroad since the 1920s. A comparison between three systems is provided in Table 4–1. The United

TABLE 4–1

Summary comparison of three foreign credit systems, 1971

United States	*United Kingdom*	*Germany*
1. Choice of short-term policies: Comprehensive or political-risk-only—not both.	1. Choice of short-term policies: Comprehensive and political-risk-only to subsidiaries.	1. Choice of short-term policies: Large selection of policies as desired.
2. Exclusions under short-term policies: Cash or fully secured sales. Added exclusions by negotiation.	2. Exclusions under short-term policies: None.	2. Exclusions unders hort-term policies: Specific short-term policies permitted. Single-buyer revolving policies available. Blanket policy—exclusion of small sales. Global policy—exclusion prepaid and letter of credit sales.
3. Premium rates: Short term— Letter of credit...... 0.09%–0.37% Short term— 180 days... 0.36 –2.14 Average short term....... 0.46 Small exporter policy...... — — Medium term, 1 year..... 0.46 –1.82 Medium term, 5 years..... 1.65 –6.62 Pol.-risk-only.... 75% of comp. risk	3. Premium rates: NA NA 0.25 0.575 NA 1.25–3.25 NA	3. Premium rates: 0.75% 1.5 NA — — (1.5% plus 0.1% per three months over six months). 0.5%
4. National currency requirements: U.S. dollars only except short term transactions.	4. National currency requirements: Buyer or third country currencies permitted.	4. National currency requirements: Buyer or third country currencies permitted.
5. Credit terms: 10% down payment on medium term, 20% preferred.	5. Credit terms: Normally 20% preferred and 5% cash with order.	5. Credit terms: At least 15% to be paid by the time producer's good are put into operation.
6. Shipping requirements: U.S. ports only, up to 50% foreign content on an exception basis.	6. Shipping requirements: 30% foreign ports permitted on reciprocal agreement basis.	6. Shipping requirements: 30% foreign ports permitted.
7. Small exporter policy: Available.	7. Small exporter policy: Available.	7. Small exporter policy: None.
8. Sales effort: Good.	8. Sales effort: Excellent.	8. Sales effort: Not known.

Source: International Exports Credit Institute, *Insurance Systems in International Finance* (New York, 1971).
NA = not available.

States did not provide protection comparable to that of the other two countries until its changes in 1962.

EXIMBANK[2]

The Export-Import Bank of the United States, formerly known as the Export-Import Bank of Washington, is directly active in the export promotion effort by offering:

1. Guarantees (mostly to U.S. commercial banks which finance on a without-recourse basis) of medium-term credits granted by U.S. exporters to foreign buyers.
2. Guarantees to U.S. firms on goods consigned or leased abroad or exhibited at overseas trade fairs.
3. Guarantees on engineering, planning, and feasibility studies and technical, constructional, etc., services performed abroad.
4. Long-term loans to foreign buyers of U.S. capital or producer's goods.
5. Guarantees to banks which provide funds to foreign buyers of U.S. capital goods on terms up to 12 years.
6. Loans to U.S. commercial banks against their portfolio holdings of export debt obligations.

INVESTMENT INSURANCE FROM OPIC

Protection against losses resulting from foreign investments has been available since the early 1950s from the Investment Guarantees Division of the Agency for International Development (AID), U.S. Department of State, and predecessor agencies.[3] In December 1969, Congress created the Overseas Private Investment Corporation, a new, independent U.S. government corporation, when amending the Foreign Assistance Act of 1961. The purpose of this corporation was to mobilize and facilitate the participation of U.S. private capital and skills in the economic and social progress of less developed friendly countries and areas, thereby complementing the development assistance objectives of the United States. OPIC is governed by a board of directors which includes high-ranking government officials and a majority of private citizens knowledgeable in international business.

OPIC is presently offering the following:

---

[2] More details on the operations of the Export-Import Bank are set forth in Chapter 8.

[3] For details as to the predecessor agencies, see Barthold W. Sorge, "United States Foreign Investment Guarantees," *Report to Management No. 14* (Los Angeles: Graduate School of Business Administration, University of Southern California, July 1966).

1. Incentives to investors, including insurance against loss due to specific political risks of currency inconvertibility, expropriation and war, revolution or insurrection. (The investment insurance program of OPIC is a successor to the specific political risk program previously offered by AID.)
2. Financial assistance through (a) guarantees against loss from commercial as well as political risk; (b) direct loans in dollars or foreign currencies; and (c) preinvestment information, counseling, and cost sharing.

OPIC-assisted investments must be financially sound, new investments, or expansions of existing projects in lower income countries. They must be competitive and welcome in the foreign country, and must contribute to the social and economic progress of the people.

Insurability

To be insurable, the investment must be intended to remain in the foreign enterprise for a period of three years or more. The maximum insurance period is 20 years. A firm commitment to invest must not have taken place. The country of the investment must have entered into an investment insurance contract with the U.S. government. Ample funds to successfully complete the project must be available, and earnings from the project must be able to meet the interest and repayment schedules. The majority ownership of the project must also be in private hands. However, should a foreign government be the majority owner, control over the project must be in private hands. In the case of particularly large investments, or projects in countries where OPIC's total risk exposure is already unusually large, or when investments are in sensitive project areas, insurance coverage will have to be negotiated on an individual basis which will take into account the higher risks involved. Negotiations of the more limited coverage in these areas represent a change from the previous insurance policies in force.

Grounds for ineligibility of investments for insurance

Investments of a short-term nature do not qualify for investment insurance by OPIC. A foreign investment of a U.S. citizen in which a foreign government is the majority participant will not qualify for investment insurance because one of the purposes of the investment insurance program was to encourage the development of the private sector of the host country's economy.

Investments are not eligible for coverage if they involve:

1. Short-term investments.
2. Majority foreign government ownership or control.

3. Manufacturing of ammunitions.
4. Gambling facilities.
5. Production of alcoholic beverages.
6. Sports stadiums, amusement parks, golf courses, etc.
7. Production of surplus commodities.

In spite of the fact that strict rules of eligibility based on U.S. procurement have applied to all OPIC-insured investments. these rules were relaxed in September 1970. However, OPIC will continue to be concerned with the long- and short-term effects of U.S. investment abroad on the U.S. balance of payments.

The investment insurance program does not offer insurance against such risks as the devaluation of a foreign currency or the default of a buyer in paying for purchases. It does not cover the failure of a buyer to repay due to commercial losses or protection against other business risks. Protection is not available for existing investments or for investments which have been irrevocably committed before application has been filed with OPIC. Prior to becoming committed the investor must apply for and receive a registration letter, the issuance of which allows the investor to continue with investment plans without prejudice to an ultimate determination of insurance eligibility on other grounds.

The maximum insured amount under ordinary rules may be 200 percent of the original insured investment in the case of equity investments, plus an amount equal to the principal and interest on insured loan investments. At the time of entering into an insurance contract with OPIC the insured must state a maximum insured amount and a current insured amount. The maximum insured amount is governed by the limits as stated above. The current insured amount is the volume of the exposed risks in dollars during the current insurance year. The difference between the two is referred to as a standby amount.

Forms of eligible investments

Foreign investments of U.S. persons may be of different forms or categories and yet be eligible for insurance coverage. A discussion of several types follows:

Equity investments. Foreign equity investments include the acquisition of all or part of the shares of a foreign enterprise, the establishment of a foreign branch operation, or proprietary investment in a business entity established under local laws. These investments may be made in several forms:

Cash. Insurance coverage is available for investments made in U.S. dollars, or credits for U.S. dollars, or foreign currency purchased with U.S. dollars for the purpose of making the investment.

Retained earnings. With a few exceptions, the reinvestment of earnings of a foreign enterprise in connection with a new project, or of expansion, modernization, or development of an existing business, is eligible for insurance coverage if the funds invested in the project could have been repatriated to the United States under exchange control regulations.

Materials and equipment. Both new and used materials and equipment are eligible for insurance as investment contributions.

Patents, processes, and techniques. Investments in the form of contributions of patents, processes, and industrial techniques or licenses are eligible for convertibility insurance only to encourage the spread of advanced technological methods. Trade names, trademarks, or goodwill, even though closely associated with licensing of patents, processes, and techniques are not eligible for coverage.

Services. Contributions of engineering and management services will be eligible for insurance when contributed for an equity interest or on a long-term loan basis.

Loan guarantees. A commercial guarantee of the repayment obligations of a foreign enterprise to a third party, such as a bank or other local institution, will be eligible for coverage if the loan guaranteed is eligible under the investment insurance program criteria.

Loans. A loan to a foreign enterprise evidenced by any type of loan instrument expressed in dollars or any other convertible currency, either secured or unsecured, is eligible for insurance. However, the date of repayment must be at least three years or longer. The refinancing of existing indebtedness is ordinarily not insurable. However, a new loan which is arranged for the purpose of refinancing an existing debt of a foreign enterprise to other than the investor may be insured providing the new loan has a term of at least six years and the debt being refinanced has either already matured or will mature within one year of the date of making the new loan.

Insurable proceeds. Proceeds from the licensing of patents, processes, or techniques and technical managerial assistance agreements are insurable for nonconvertibility only providing these investments are intended to extend for at least five years.

Construction contracts. OPIC provides this insurance but strongly recommends that investors contact the Export-Import Bank to insure equipment at risk or liabilities incurred in connection with construction contracts or contracted services. OPIC will not insure a contractor when a construction contract is with a foreign government unless the foreign exchange is provided for the project by the Agency for International Development, International Finance Corporation, International Development Association, or any other U.S. government or international agency lender, or if the end product of the contract has an intended life of less than three years.

Long-term supplier's credit. The extension of long-term credit by a supplier of equipment or commodities may under certain conditions be eligible for insurance when the extension of credit is tantamount to the making of a loan and the sale of the goods has a significant development impact. Insurance will not ordinarily be issued when substantially equivalent protection is available from the Export-Import Bank or from the Foreign Credit Insurance Association.

Lender's contracts. Special contracts of insurance have been developed to encourage greater participation in overseas development by institutional lenders, such as banks, insurance companies, and pension funds.

Thus a wide range of equity and debt forms of investment are eligible for the insurance coverages provided by OPIC. The nature of the insurance coverages is next discussed.

Convertibility insurance

Insurance of convertibility is applicable in three situations: (1) when the U.S. investor is prevented from converting his local currency into U.S. dollars for a period of 30 days by the direct operation of a law, decree, or regulation, or an affirmative administrative act; (2) when the investor is prevented from converting his local currency into dollars for a specified number of days, not less than 60, or the failure of the applicable government authorities to act upon a duly submitted application for transfer; (3) when an investor is permitted to convert his local currency into U.S. dollars, but only at a discriminatory rate of exchange—less than 99 percent of the rate of exchange that would be used to convert such local currency under the insurance. Under the above conditions, as long as the local currency is not retained by the investor for more than 18 months, the U.S. government will pay the investor in dollars a sum equal to 99 percent of the dollar equivalent of his inconvertible local currency. When foreign government action prevents an investor from effectively receiving, as well as converting, local currency, this risk must be provided against by expropriation or war coverage.

Expropriation insurance

Protection against expropriation is principally available to investment in equities and loans. Protection is not absolute; it varies with the substance of the foreign government's action. For this reason, OPIC contract provisions should be carefully examined.

Equities. It is assumed that the expropriation of equity investments has occurred if the foreign government prevents the following:

1. The investor from receiving dividends that have been declared by the foreign firm;
2. The investor from exercising the rights that are fundamentally his resulting from his ownership of an equity interest in the firm;
3. The investor from selling his equity shares, or losing effective control over dividends received, or if he is unable to withdraw from the foreign country dividends and liquidation payments that he has received from the firm in which he has an interest, or the proceeds from the sale of any of his shares;
4. The foreign firm from exercising effective control over a major portion of its properties or from continuing the operation of the insured project.

OPIC does not normally insure an investor against breach of a concession agreement granted by the foreign government unless this breach amounts to an expropriation. Not insured also is the failure of the foreign government to pay for goods or services delivered to it, or failure of the foreign government to live up to its promises of a commercial nature such as not delivering promised electrical power.

Loans. In the case of a loan investment, expropriation is assumed to have occurred if:

1. The investor is prevented from receiving principle or interest when due, or is prevented from withdrawing received funds from the foreign country;
2. The investor is prevented from disposing of his debt instrument or is prevented from withdrawing the proceeds of its sale from the foreign country;
3. If the borrowing foreign enterprise is prevented from exercising effective control over a substantial portion of its properties or is prevented from continuing the operation of the project for which the loan was obtained.

Coverage is also granted if the foreign government imposes on the foreign firm regulation or taxation that is discriminatory against the investor or other nonnationals, particularly if such regulation or taxation is very much in excess of that applied to nationals of the country. Protection is not provided against action of a foreign government if such action takes place as a result of a voluntary agreement between the government, the investor, or the foreign firm, or if the investor or the foreign firm have provoked the government into taking confiscatory action. Specifically the investor will not be protected against bona fide foreign exchange control actions on the part of the government.

War, revolution, and insurrection insurance

Damages resulting from the hostile acts of internationally or nationally organized forces or organized revolutionary or insurrectionary forces, including acts of sabotage by such forces, are covered by another kind of insurance. Also covered is injury to tangible property that results directly from actions taken in hindering, combating, or defending against such hostile acts during war, revolution, or insurrection.

The insurance does not cover damages to the physical property of the firm that is caused by civil strife of a lesser degree than revolution or insurrection. Neither does the policy cover intangible property such as accounts, bills, currency, deeds, evidence of debt, money, securities, etc. Coverage will also not be granted if it can be shown that the investor or the foreign firm were negligent in taking reasonable precautions to prevent damage to the firm's properties.

Insurance fees charged by OPIC and their computation

Fees for insurance are assessed on an annual basis and must be paid in advance. The cost of convertibility insurance is $3/10$ of 1 percent of the current insured amount. Insurance against the risk of expropriation is $6/10$ of 1 percent of the current insured amount. Insurance against the risks of war, revolution, and insurrection is also $6/10$ of 1 percent of the current insured amount. In addition, $1/4$ of 1 percent is charged annually on the standby amount for each coverage. This permits the insured to determine each year for each specific risk the current amount of coverage. When this has been determined, it also determines the standby amount, since it is the difference between the maximum amount and the current amount. The examples below illustrate the computation of the fees for each of the three types of coverages.

Illustration of computation of fees for convertibility insurance[4]

The U.S. Company, an eligible investor, invests $50,000 in equity shares in a new foreign enterprise, the LDC Corporation, doing business in a less developed country; the U.S. Company is issued convertibility insurance with a maximum insured amount of $100,000. For the first contract period, the U.S. Company estimates that only $5,000 of local currency earnings from the LDC Corporation will be paid as dividends; it therefore requests only $5,000 of current coverage for year one. The other $95,000 of the maximum $100,000 of coverage will be kept on a standby

---

[4] The illustrations are based on materials provided by OPIC.

basis for possible use in later years. The U.S. Company's fee for year one
is computed as follows:

	Amount	Rate	Fee
Current insured amount...................	$ 5,000	$\frac{3}{10}\%$	$ 15.00
Amount by which the maximum insured amount exceeds the current insured amount (the "standby" amount)................	95,000	$\frac{1}{4}\%$	237.50
Fee for year one.........................			$252.50

In year 10, the U.S. Company decides that in year 11 it will plan to sell
its shares in LDC Corporation to a businessman in the foreign country and
convert the proceeds into dollars. Because of the profitable nature of the
business and the reinvestment of its earnings, the U.S. Company's equity
investment in the LDC Corporation has risen to $100,000. The U.S. Com-
pany elects $100,000 as the current insured amount at the next annual
election date. The fee is computed as follows:

	Amount	Rate	Fee
Current insured amount for year 11........	$100,000	$\frac{3}{10}\%$	$300.00
Standby amount........................	0	$\frac{1}{4}\%$	0
Fee for year 11.........................			$300.00

This example shows the order of magnitude of costs to obtain convertibility insurance coverage. It will be noted that moving the $95,000 from
standby to actual insurance coverage costs an additional $47.50.

Illustration of fee computation for war and expropriation coverage

A U.S. citizen makes an investment of $20,000,000 in a new foreign
manufacturing enterprise, of which half ($10,000,000) is in the form of
stock in the foreign enterprise, consisting of 50 percent of its shares, and
the other half is in the form of a 10-year loan at 5 percent interest per annum on the outstanding principal, repayable in five equal annual installments beginning in year three. The enterprise is expected to have $3,500,-
000 of long-term liabilities from other sources and a profit of $1,000,000 in
the first year. During the first year as much as $24,000,000 of the assets of
the foreign enterprise will be in the form of project-connected tangible
property.

The amounts of expropriation and war coverage and the fees payable
in the first year will normally be as follows:

Expropriation coverage

Equity:

Maximum.........	$20,000,000[a]			
Current..........	10,500,000[b]	@ 6/10% =	$ 63,000	
Standby.........	9,500,000	@ 1/4% =	23,750	
		Subtotal.........	$ 86,750	

Loan:

Maximum.........	$12,000,000[c]			
Current..........	10,500,000[d]	@ 6/10% =	$ 63,000	
Standby.........	1,500,000	@ 1/4% =	3,750	
		Subtotal.........	$ 66,750	
		Total............	$153,500	

War, revolution, and insurrection coverage

Equity:

Maximum.........	$20,000,000[a]			
Current..........	7,200,000[e]	@ 6/10% =	$ 43,200	
Standby.........	12,800,000	@ 1/4% =	32,000	
		Subtotal.........	$ 75,200	

Loan:

Maximum.........	$12,000,000[c]			
Current..........	7,200,000[f]	@ 6/10% =	$ 43,200	
Standby.........	4,800,000	@ 1/4% =	12,000	
		Subtotal.........	$ 55,200	
		Total............	$130,400	

[a] 200 percent of the equity investment of $10,000,000.

[b] $10,000,000 equity investment plus anticipated $500,000 in profits attributable to the investor's shares in year one. No capital repatriation is contemplated.

[c] $10,000,000 loan plus $500,000 interest accruable in year one; $500,000 in year two; $400,000, year three; $300,000, year four; 200,000, year five; $100,000, year six.

[d] $10,000,000 loan plus $500,000 interest accruable in year one. Long-term liabilities are equal to this amount plus $3,500,000 long-term liabilities from other sources.

[e] The investor's equity-based share in the tangible property, since book value figures are not available for year one, is computed as follows:

$$\frac{\underset{\$10,000,000}{(Equity)} + \underset{\$500,000}{(Profits)}}{\underset{\$20,000,000}{(Total\ equity\ capital)} + \underset{\$1,000,000}{(Surplus)} + \underset{\$14,000,000}{(Long\text{-}term\ liabilities)}} = \frac{\$10,500,000}{\$35,000,000} = 3/10 \,.$$

Where covered property is $24,000,000, the current insured amount should be:

$$\$24,000,000 \times 3/10 = \$7,200,000 \,.$$

[f] The investor's loan-based share in the tangible property in the example is:

$$\frac{\underset{\$10,000,000}{(Principal)} + \underset{\$500,000}{\underset{interest)}{(Unpaid\ accrued}}}{\underset{\$20,000,000}{(Total\ equity\ capital)} + \underset{\$1,000,000}{(Surplus)} + \underset{\$14,000,000}{(Long\text{-}term\ liabilities)}} = \frac{\$10,500,000}{\$35,000,000} = 3/10 \,.$$

The current insured amount should therefore be:

$$\$24,000,000 \times 3/10 = \$7,200,000 \,.$$

INVESTMENT GUARANTEES

Investment guarantees are presently offered by the Overseas Private Investment Corporation, a U.S. government owned corporation, for portfolio investments in foreign developing countries and by the Agency for International Development, U.S. Department of State, for Latin American housing projects. Both of these programs stand ready to protect the U.S. investor in the case of investment projects which are acceptable to the guarantors. In contrast to the three types of risk insurance protecting direct investments discussed above, the investment guarantees protect the investor against all risks.

Investment guarantees are available only for countries that have entered into investment guarantee agreements with the U.S. government. These agreements specify the rights of the U.S. government should an investment guarantee become effective and the United States become owner of the investment in jeopardy and make efforts to salvage it. Investment guarantees are issued only if a designated agency in the host country has certified that the investment to be guaranteed is in the best interests of the host country's economic development. It is this latter requirement that seriously limits the availability of investment guarantees in numerous countries.

Investment guarantees offered by OPIC

OPIC participates in the financing of foreign investment projects in two ways. It makes loans from its own resources[5] or it guarantees portfolio investments on the part of U.S. persons. The project, to be eligible for guarantees, must have the consent of the local government and must be a new venture or an appreciable expansion or modernization of an existing successful enterprise. (By making these investment guarantees, OPIC shares with the projects owners the risks associated with the project—agricultural or commercial operation in developing countries.)

OPIC issues loan guarantees only to U.S. individuals, corporations, partnerships, or lending institutions, and only if a corporation, partnership, or institution is at least 50 percent owned by U.S. persons. Foreign corporations or lending institutions are eligible if they are wholly owned by one or more U.S. persons with the provision that 5 percent of the holding shares may be owned by non-U.S. citizens in order to meet local requirements for the local ownership of qualifying shares.

To be eligible for protection the project must include manufacturing, processing, storage, agribusinesses, utilities, transportation, commercial hotels, or tourist facilities and must result in sustained profitable operations.

---

[5] The lending activity of OPIC is discussed in Chapter 8.

The percentage of U.S. participation in the financing of the undertaking, as well as participation in management and the value of the goods that will be purchased from the United States and developing countries, will influence the desirability of the project from OPIC's point of view. At least 51 percent of the equity interest of the investment must be in the hands of private persons. Under unusual conditions it is at times permitted to cover portfolio investments in an enterprise in which majority ownership is by foreigners. However, under these circumstances, the management control over the project must be in private hands. Furthermore, 25 percent of the equity interest is then required to be in U.S. hands. The project must be amply financed to assure its financial and economic success. The profits derived from the investment must be sufficient to maintain an approved and acceptable loan repayment and interest schedule.

At the present time projects ineligible are those which (1) are related to the production of munitions; (2) are facilities for gambling; (3) involve runaway manufacturing, replacing existing U.S. facilities; (4) are subject to unreasonable restrictions of trade; (5) are a monopoly not in the best interests of the United States or the local country; (6) have a significant adverse affect on the local country's balance-of-payments problem; (7) produce agricultural commodities in direct competition with the export of U.S. surplus commodities; (8) have a detrimental influence on the balance-of-payments position of the United States due to the effect of the dollar investment under the guarantee.

Proceeds from loans guaranteed by OPIC may be used for the procurement of goods and services in developing countries, the United States, and from other free world nations. However, when the procurement schedule calls for the obtaining of capital equipment, in part from other developed nations, OPIC requires that those nations participate in the financing of the project.

The fees for OPIC investment guarantees will vary with OPIC's initial assessment of the risks involved as well as the ultimate rate of profitability of the project and its impact on the developing country. The minimum fee charged by OPIC for investment guarantees is 1.75 percent per year on the outstanding guaranteed principal amount. It is OPIC's practice to negotiate a fee agreement providing for reasonable increases in the fee based on the profitability of the enterprise.

OPIC will guarantee the full amount of the balance of loans still due. To encourage U.S. firms to participate in projects in developing countries on an equity investment basis, OPIC will guarantee these investments but will normally not guarantee more than 50 percent of each equity investor's loss in the event the project is unsuccessful. The fee for such a guarantee will vary from case to case depending on the risk for coverage, not to exceed 10 years.

Investment guarantees offered by AID

The housing investment guarantee program is administered by the Agency for International Development (AID) of the U.S. Department of State. Investments eligible for such guarantees are those which make a material contribution to the solution of existing housing and urban development problems. A negotiated program is offered to all nonprofit sponsors, contrasted with competitive housing investment guarantee proposals submitted by private investors. The purpose of the housing investment guarantees is to aid or make possible the participation by private enterprise in the development of the economic resources and productive capabilities of developing friendly countries. Loan guarantees may also be obtained for loans to thrift and credit institutions that are engaged in the financing of the construction of homes or housing projects. Preferred projects are those in American republics which are of a self-liquidating nature which aid the local housing problems. In Latin America this includes housing projects desired to provide housing for lower income families. The costs of these projects are under strict controls in order to make low sale prices possible. AID operates its loan investment guarantee program under the Foreign Assistance Act of 1969 which replaced the former act of 1961. This act specifies that the objectives of its worldwide program are as follows:

1. To facilitate and increase the participation of private enterprise in furthering the development of the economic resources and productive capacities of less developed friendly countries and areas.

2. To promote the development of thrift and credit institutions engaged in programs of mobilizing local savings for financing the construction of self-liquidating housing projects and related community facilities.

The participation of local capital is strongly encouraged. The statutes require that 25 percent of the financing be obtained from local sources. Projects where a larger percentage of the needed funds is obtained from local sources will be favored by AID. A project to be eligible must be sponsored by a host country sponsor, citizen or firm, at least 50 percent beneficially owned by host country persons. Furthermore, the project must be a bona fide joint venture between the host country sponsor and the U.S. participant who must be a U.S. citizen or entity more than 50 percent beneficially owned by a U.S. person. The investment must be in the form of long-term 15- to 20-year dollar loans to provide mortgage financing. Interest on these loans shall not exceed normal rates considering money market conditions and the risks involved. An AID guarantee for any one project is presently limited to a maximum of $3 million per project with a minimum of $1 million unless the given country has established other limits.

AID charges an application fee of $1,000 and an acceptance fee of $2 per thousand of the amount of the guarantee. The AID guarantee fee that AID charges is based on the unpaid principal balance of the guaranteed loan investment and is paid periodically as follows: (1) 0.5 percent per annum where repayment of the loan in U.S. dollars has been guaranteed by the government of the host country; (2) 1 percent per annum where mortgages are insured in local currency by a government mortgage insurance institution, housing agency, or other public or private institution acceptable to AID; and (3) 2 percent annum in all other cases where AID has decided to extend a loan gaurantee.

Unless a devaluation risk is guaranteed for instance by the host government, AID will require a devaluation insurance fee to cover the risk of devaluation. The fee, which is not refundable, will be set for each particular country at the time guarantees are issued.[6]

SUMMARY

In this chapter we have described the costs and benefits of a range of forms of insurance guarantee programs. Insurance policies are available from FCIA for credit sales to foreigners. Loans and guarantees to promote exports are available from the Eximbank. Investment insurance policies and guarantees are available from OPIC and AID.

Foreign credit insurance policies come either on a comprehensive basis or on a political-risk-only basis. They are for short-term credit sales of consumer's goods and medium-term credit sales of producer's goods to foreign customers. The premium depends on the country of destination, length of credit term, and the security. Foreign buyers are required to make 10 to 20 percent minimum down payment on medium-term transactions, depending upon the risk category of their country. The U.S. seller can then insure 90 percent of the financed portion of his sales if the policy is on a comprehensive basis and 95 percent on a political-risk-only basis.

Additional types of policies were introduced in 1970. They are a catastrophe policy, comprehensive master policy, small business policy, and agricultural policy. The catastrophe insurance is a political-risk-only policy for high-volume, low-profit exporters. The comprehensive master policy covers all of the export sales of an exporter. The characteristic of this policy is that FCIA may assign the insured firm a discretionary credit line per customer so that the exporter has to exercise sound credit judgment of his customers. The small business policy is designed for firms new to the export business. Political- and commercial-risk coverage is available for

---

[6] This represents a distinct departure from previous practice. This is the only source to our knowledge of insurance against devaluation except for the use of the forward foreign exchange markets as described in the following chapter.

short- and medium-term sales. The agricultural policy covers up to 98 percent of the financed portion of the sale of agricultural products.

Guarantees are available from the Eximbank to U.S. firms on goods consigned or leased abroad or exhibited at overseas trade fairs, and on various services performed abroad.

Investment insurance policies are available from OPIC on private direct investments in developing countries. These investments must offer acceptable risks to OPIC, contribute to the economic and social progress of the private sector of the host country, and be of a long-term nature. The objects of coverage include equity investments, proceeds from the licensing of patents and technical-managerial knowhow, construction contracts, long-term supplier's credit, lender's contracts, and branch bank contracts. The insurance policies offer protection against specific political risks such as (1) inconvertibility of currency; (2) expropriation; and (3) damages resulting from war, revolution, and insurrection.

The investment guarantee program of OPIC applies to portfolio investments in projects with high priority in the host country's development program. AID's investment guarantees apply largely to South American pilot housing programs and the development of housing financial institutions. Investment guarantees are available only in countries that have entered into investment guarantee agreements with the U.S. government.

APPENDIX

OVERSEAS PRIVATE INVESTMENT CORPORATION

(An Agency of the U.S. Government)

Country List: Investment Insurance and Investment Guaranty Program†
(February 1, 1971)

The OPIC Investment Insurance and Investment Guaranty Programs are available, *as of this date*, in the following listed less developed countries and semi-independent states, as noted.

1. *Investment insurance*			2. *Investment*
Convertibility	*Expropriation*	*War, revolution, and insurrection*	*guaranties (extended risk)*
Afghanistan	Afghanistan	Afghanistan (war only)	—
Antigua	Antigua	Antigua	Antigua
Argentina	—	—	—
Barbados	Barbados	Barbados	Barbados
Botswana	Botswana	Botswana	Botswana
Brazil	Brazil	Brazil	Brazil
British Honduras	British Honduras	British Honduras	British Honduras
Burundi	Burundi	Burundi	Burundi
Cameroon	Cameroon	Cameroon	Cameroon
Central African Rep.	Central African Rep.	Central African Rep.	Central African Rep.
Ceylon	Ceylon	Ceylon	Ceylon
Chad	Chad	Chad	Chad
China, Rep. of	China, Rep. of	China, Rep. of	China, Rep. of
Colombia	Colombia	Colombia	Colombia
Congo (Kinshasa)	Congo (Kinshasa)	Congo (Kinshasa)	Congo (Kinshasa)
Costa Rica	Costa Rica	Costa Rica	Costa Rica
*Cyprus	*Cyrpus	*Cyprus	*Cyprus
Dahomey	Dahomey	Dahomey	Dahomey
Dominica	Dominica	Dominica	Dominica
Dominican Republic	Dominican Republic	Dominican Republic	Dominican Republic
Ecuador	Ecuador	Ecuador	Ecuador
El Salvador	El Salvador	—	—
Ethiopia	Ethiopia	Ethiopia	Ethiopia
Gabon	Gabon	Gabon	Gabon
Gambia	Gambia	Gambia	Gambia
Ghana	Ghana	Ghana	Ghana
Greece	Greece	Greece	Greece
Grenada	Grenada	Grenada	Grenada
*Guatemala	*Guatemala	*Guatemala	*Guatemala
Guinea	Guinea	Guinea	Guinea
Guyana	Guyana	Guyana	Guyana
Haiti	Haiti	Haiti	Haiti
Honduras	Honduras	Honduras	Honduras
India	India	India	India
Indonesia	Indonesia	Indonesia	Indonesia
Iran	Iran	Iran	Iran

† Economically developed countries are excluded from the OPIC Investment Incentive programs. Investment insurance against inconvertibility and expropriation only may be available for some of the underdeveloped dependencies of France, the Netherlands, Portugal, and the United Kingdom.
* Program currently inoperative for legal or administrative reasons.
Source: Overseas Private Investment Corporation, circular (Washington, D.C.: 1971).

1. Investment insurance			2. Investment guaranties (extended risk)
Convertibility	Expropriation	War, revolution, and insurrection	
Israel	Israel	Israel	Israel
Ivory Coast	Ivory Coast	Ivory Coast	Ivory Coast
Jamaica	Jamaica	Jamaica	Jamaica
Jordan	Jordan	Jordan	Jordan
Kenya	Kenya	Kenya	Kenya
Korea	Korea	Korea	Korea
Laos	Laos	Laos	Laos
Lesotho	Lesotho	Lesotho	Lesotho
Liberia	Liberia	Liberia	Liberia
Malagasy	Malagasy	Malagasy	Malagasy
Malawi	Malawi	Malawi	Malawi
Malaysia	Malaysia	Malaysia	Malaysia
Mali	Mali	Mali	Mali
*Malta	*Malta	*Malta	*Malta
*Mauritania	*Mauritania	*Mauritania	*Mauritania
Morocco	Morocco	Morocco	Morocco
Nepal	Nepal	Nepal	Nepal
Nicaragua	Nicaragua	Nicaragua	Nicaragua
Niger	Niger	Niger	Niger
Nigeria	Nigeria	—	—
Pakistan	Pakistan	Pakistan	Pakistan
Panama	Panama	Panama	Panama
Paraguay	Paraguay	Paraguay	Paraguay
Philippines	Philippines	Philippines	Philippines
Rwanda	Rwanda	Rwanda	Rwanda
St. Christ.-Nevis-Ang.	St. Christ.-Nevis-Ang.	St. Christ.-Nevis-Ang.	St. Christ.-Nevis-Ang.
St. Lucia	St. Lucia	St. Lucia	St. Lucia
Senegal	Senegal	Senegal	Senegal
Sierra Leone	Sierra Leone	Sierra Leone	Sierra Leone
Singapore	Singapore	Singapore	Singapore
*Somali Rep.	*Somali Rep.	*Somali Rep.	*Somali Rep.
*Sudan	*Sudan	*Sudan	*Sudan
Swaziland	Swaziland	Swaziland	Swaziland
Tanzania (excl. Zanzibar)	Tanzania (excl. Zanzibar)	Tanzania (excl. Zanzibar)	Tanzania (excl. Zanzibar)
Thailand	Thailand	Thailand	Thailand
Togo	Togo	Togo	Togo
Trinidad-Tobago	Trinidad-Tobago	Trinidad-Tobago	Trinidad-Tobago
Tunisia	Tunisia	Tunisia	Tunisia
Turkey	Turkey	Turkey	Turkey
*U.A.R. (Egypt)	*U.A.R. (Egypt)	*U.A.R. (Egypt)	*U.A.R. (Egypt)
Uganda	Uganda	Uganda	Uganda
Upper Volta	Upper Volta	Upper Volta	Upper Volta
Venezuela	Venezuela	Venezuela	Venezuela
Vietnam	Vietnam	Vietnam	Vietnam
Western Somoa	Western Somoa	Western Somoa	Western Somoa
*Yugoslavia	*Yugoslavia	*Yugoslavia	*Yugoslavia
Zambia	Zambia	Zambia	Zambia

PROBLEM 4-1

Your firm is considering a sale of tractors to Sudania on a five-year basis. Your customer has a good standing in his business community. Sudania is rated C by the FCIA, which requires that you carry 20 percent of the financed portion of the $100,000 transaction at your own risk. Your customer is proposing a 10 percent down payment, which is acceptable to the FCIA. The FCIA's premium on the transaction will be 4 percent of the financed portion of the sale. Your own cost of financing not guaranteed by the FCIA is 12 percent per year and on the portion guaranteed is 7 percent. The profit on your sale is 8 percent after taxes but before insurance expenses. Your business is operating at 75 percent capacity. The buyer will pay you 10 percent interest on any unpaid balance.

A. Should you make the sale on the basis that the buyer makes the entire payment at the end of the fifth year? Make the comparison for the full five years.

B. Should you make the sale on the basis that the buyer makes repayments of $18,000 each year? Present the analysis for the fifth year on the assumption that the FCIA charge and the profit on the sale are prorated over each of the five years.

PROBLEM 4-2

Multinat is contemplating a shipment of production machinery to one of its foreign subsidiaries. The country of destination has been rated C. A normal 10 percent down payment and the assumption on the part of the seller of 10 percent of the financed portion are still permitted. The value of the shipment is $100,000, and the subsidiary has requested permission to pay for this shipment over a five-year period. The cost of FCIA comprehensive coverage for this shipment would be $3.85 per hundred of the financed portion of the shipment. The rate for political-risk-only coverage would be $2.90 per hundred.

Successive governments in the country of the subsidiary have become more and more socialistic. New national elections are pending during the proposed credit period of the transaction. The country of the sub has also signed an investment guarantee treaty with the U.S. government, and investment insurance is available from OPIC at regular rates. The after-tax benefit resulting from the use of the new equipment is estimated to equal the equivalent of $20,000 per year. Should Multinat insure via the FCIA or purchase investment insurance from OPIC?

PROBLEM 4-3

The Johnson Company is considering the sale of a diesel tractor for $60,000 to a firm in Seaboria, a country rated D by the FCIA. The FCIA requires the seller to carry 30 percent of the insured portion for his own account. The foreign buyer has agreed to make a 10 percent down payment, make uniform payments at the end of each of five years, and pay 6 percent interest on the outstanding balance on the purchase. The insurance premium on a five-year open account sale is 6.62 percent of the insured portion of the sale. With FCIA insurance coverage the Johnson Company can finance its exports by loans from its commercial bank at a rate of 8 percent per year. Without the guarantee of the FCIA policy, the company would be forced to approach private sources to handle the financing at an annual rate of 10 percent.

Should the Johnson Company go to the expense of purchasing FCIA insurance?

SELECTED BIBLIOGRAPHY

Agency for International Development. *Housing Investment Guaranty Program—Information for Applicants.* Washington, D.C., 1971.

————. Office of Private Resources. *Investment Survey Handbook.* Washington, D.C., 1968.

————. *Worldwide Housing Guaranty Program—Price Investment Survey— Scope of Work.* Washington, D.C., 1971.

Hollis, Stanley E. *Guide to Export Credit Insurance.* New York: Foreign Credit Insurance Association, 1971.

International Exports Credit Institute. *Insurance Systems in International Finance.* New York, 1971.

Overseas Private Investment Corporation. *An Introduction to OPIC.* Washington, D.C., 1972.

————. *Annual Report Fiscal 1971.* Washington, D.C., 1971.

————. *General Terms and Conditions.* Washington, D.C., 1961.

————. *Guaranties of Loans.* Washington, D.C., 1971.

————. *Incentive Handbook.* Washington, D.C., 1972.

————. *Incentive Handbook for Financial Institutions.* Washington, D.C., 1972.

————. *Incentive Handbook—Investment Insurance.* Washington, D.C., 1972.

————. *Incentive Handbook—Investment Financing.* Washington, D.C., 1972.

Sorge, Barthold W. "United States Foreign Investment Guarantees," *Report to Management No. 14.* Los Angeles: Graduate School of Business Administration, University of Southern California, July 1966.

Weston, J. Fred and Sorge, Bart W. "Export Insurance: Why the U.S. Lags," *Columbia Journal of World Business,* Vol. 2, No. 5 (September-October 1967), pp. 67–76.

5

Exchange rate risk protection in foreign operations

Exchange rate risk protection can be effected by three different means: (1) It can be obtained by the purchase of forward contracts for the sale or purchase of foreign currencies in terms of U.S. dollars. (2) Where available, foreign currency swaps can be consummated with central banks or commercial banks in countries of planned investment or operation. (3) Foreign exchange risk losses can be minimized by making certain that the foreign branches or subsidiaries are operated on a monetary balance basis where monetary assets equal monetary liabilities.

THE FORWARD MARKET

A purchase of a forward contract permits the exchange of one currency for another at a fixed ratio and at a specified time. As a result, the forward contract substitutes a known and usually smaller cost for the uncertain and usually larger cost due to foreign exchange rate risk caused by the possible devaluation of one currency in terms of another. The obtaining of a forward contract, however, does not always assure the lowest cost due to foreign exchange rate change. It merely fixes this cost at a predetermined level. Should the actual devaluation turn out to be less than the expected magnitude, the cost of the forward contract may turn out to be higher than the amount of loss that would have resulted from devaluation. Therefore, the forward contract does not eliminate all uncertainty and risk. There is always the chance of paying more for the elimination of risk than the loss that actually would have occurred.

The forward foreign exchange market is a part of the general foreign exchange market in which foreign currencies are bought and sold to satisfy the needs of international transactions. These markets are located in most of the major trading centers of the world. In New York City the foreign exchange market consists of the foreign departments of about a

94

dozen commercial banks and a number of independent foreign exchange dealers all doing business with each other by telephone and teletype. The foreign exchange and forward contract needs of U.S. business are normally forwarded to New York for execution.

Forward quotations are given in two ways. The forward quotations are given in terms of the cost of a unit of foreign exchange in dollars. For instance, *The Wall Street Journal* prints daily quotations of the cost of various foreign currency units ready for transmittal to a foreign destination. This is the so-called asked price. In *The Wall Street Journal* of August 16, 1971 appeared the following quotations as of August 13, 1971 for the British pound in terms of U.S. dollars:

	Friday	*Previous day*
Spot rate	2.4199	2.4200
Thirty-day futures	2.4219	2.4213
Ninety-day futures	2.4209	2.4196

Quotations obtained from the International Department of the Bank of America also for August 13, 1971 were as follows:

	Bid rate	*Asked rate*
Spot rate	2.4195	2.4197½
Thirty-day rate	2.4220	2.4237½
Ninety-day rate	2.4205	2.4217½

For the same period, *International Reports' Statistical Market Letter* gave the following quotations:

IR guidance rates for foreign exchange futures (against U.S. dollars)

	Bid rate	*Asked rate*
One-month futures	P 0.75	P 1.25
Three-month futures	P 0.25	P 0.75
Six-month futures	P 0.25	P 0.25
Twelve-month futures	D 0.63	D 0.38

Notice that the *International Reports* quotations were given on an annual percentage basis designated either by P, premium, or D, discount. The information used by IR and the commercial banks is the same. IR merely converts the information on an annual percentage basis for the benefit of its subscribers.

Converting the Bank of America quotations to an annual percentage basis results in the following:

Thirty-day bid rate:

$$\text{Percent change from spot rate} = \frac{2.4220 - 2.4195}{2.4195}\left(\frac{360}{30}\right)$$

$$= \frac{0.0025}{2.4195}\left(\frac{12}{1}\right) = \frac{0.0300}{2.4195} = P\ 1.23\%$$

Calculating the other quotations in similar manner would change the bank's quotations as follows:

	Bid rate	Asked rate
Thirty-day futures..............	P 1.23%	P 1.98%
Ninety-day futures..............	P 0.17%	P 0.33%

Following President Nixon's pronouncements on new international fiscal policies the international money markets were sufficiently disturbed so that no foreign exchange market quotations appeared in *The Wall Street Journal* until the issue of August 24, 1971, giving quotations for August 23, 1971. They were as follows:

	Monday	Previous day
Spot rate......................	2.4450	2.4700
Thirty-day futures..............	2.4483	—
Ninety-day futures..............	2.4455	—

Quotations obtained from the Foreign Department of the Bank of America also for August 23, 1971 were as follows:

	Bid rate	Asked rate
Spot rate*.....................	2.4475	2.4525
Thirty-day rate.................	2.4487	2.4548
Ninety-day rate.................	2.4469	2.4536
Bank buy-sell rate†.............	2.4100	2.4600

* Average of all the rates in the Los Angeles market that day.
† The bank buy-sell rate is the actual cost to the buyer or seller that day.

Contracts to purchase or sell a foreign currency on a forward basis in terms of the U.S. dollar can be obtained for all developed countries and a number of the more stable developing countries. Use of the forward market is beneficial since forward contracts fix a definite dollar value for foreign currency payments or receipts that are scheduled to take place at the end of the forward contract period. Forward contracts are usually available on a 30-, 60-, 90-, or 180-day basis. Under special conditions it is sometimes possible to negotiate forward contracts on a longer basis, up to two years.

The cost of this protection is the premium or discount that is required over the spot rate—the exchange ratio in effect when the forward contract is purchased. The premium or discount required varies from 0 to 2 or 3 percent per annum for currencies that are considered reasonably stable. For currencies undergoing devaluation in excess of 4 to 5 percent per year, discounts required may be as high as 15 to 20 percent per year. When the risk of future devaluation exceeds 20 percent per year, forward contracts are usually no longer available.

The magnitude of the premium or discount required depends upon the forward expectations of the financial communities of the two countries involved and upon the supply and demand conditions in the foreign exchange market. Since members of the financial communities in the two countries are usually well informed as to the future expectancy of the forward exchange value of their respective currencies, the premiums or discounts quoted are very closely related to the probable occurrence of changes in the exchange rates. As a result, the forward market is chiefly used as protection against unexpected changes in the foreign exchange value of a currency.

Example of how the forward market works

On August 23, 1971, the British subsidiary of Multinat sold a large merchandise order to a British customer on a 90-day basis in terms of British pounds. It also wished to transfer funds to its parent organization in the United States. The amount of the sale was 500,000 UK pounds. From the above-shown quotations of the Bank of America one can see that the bid rate for UK pounds on a 90-day forward basis was 2.4469 dollars per pound, a small discount (0.098 percent) from the spot rate quotation of the same date. The firm has several choices: (1) It can take 500,000 pounds from working capital, if not needed, exchange them on the basis of the day's spot rate, and send the funds to Multinat. This would result in a transfer of dollars to the United States of 500,000 times 2.4475 less commissions and transfer charges, or about $1,223,000. (2) If the subsidiary has no idle funds, it can borrow the money in pounds and send the funds in dollars to the United States. (3) It can purchase a 90-day forward contract to sell the pounds and then transfer the funds to Multinat. If this were done, the U.S. dollars received by Multinat in 90 days would be $1,223,450, or $1,222,750 after commissions and transfer charges.

Which action is best for the firm in this example depends on relative borrowing rates as well as relative opportunity costs of the funds in both countries, since the spot and 90-day forward rates are very close. If the British lending rate is higher or the profitability of investments available to the subsidiary is higher than in the United States, the funds should be kept in the United Kingdom. The funds should be transferred to the U.S. immediately if the rates are higher in the United States.

One other important item enters into this decision: What are the forward expectations of the Multinat financial management? If they disagree sharply from those expressed by the forward rates, these expectations should influence the decision.

A second example emphasizes the influence of expectations on decisions with regard to the use of the forward exchange markets. This illustration will compare the pattern characteristic of Latin American countries in past years with patterns characteristic of selected Western European countries in recent years. We start with the basic situation that the USP Company will receive LC 380,000 in December 1972. The USP Company incurred costs in dollars and wishes to know the definite amount of dollars it will receive in December 1972. It is considering three alternatives to avoid the risk of exchange rate fluctuations.

The first alternative is to buy a forward contract which provides for the sale of LCs for dollars at the 90-day forward rate quoted in September. The USP Company will utilize the LC 380,000 it receives in December to pay for the dollars it has contracted to buy at the 90-day forward rate. Under this arrangement the USP Company does not receive the dollars until December.

The second alternative is to borrow from a bank the amount the USP Company will be receiving in December. By borrowing, the USP Company receives the LC 380,000 immediately and can immediately purchase dollars with the LCs received at the September spot rate. When the USP Company receives the LC 380,000 in December, it may use the funds to liquidate the loan it has incurred in September.

The third alternative is to make no attempt to cover the exchange risk involved in waiting the three months for receipt of the LC 380,000. Under the third alternative the USP Company will convert the LC 380,000 into dollars at the spot rate in December.

Which of these alternatives is better will depend upon the pattern of relationships between the spot rate and the 90-day forward rate in September and in December. To illustrate this, the three alternatives will be analyzed under a pattern of spot and forward rates as of actual rates of September and a set of expected rates of December 1972. First we shall consider the pattern of rates that was characteristic of Latin American countries in past years. The basic facts are set forth in the following tabulation:

	September 1972		December 1972	
	Value of $ in LC	*Value of LC in $*	*Value of $ in LC*	*Value of LC in $*
Spot rate..................	LC 1.90	$0.53	LC 2.10	$0.48
Ninety-day forward rate.....	LC 2.00	$0.50	LC 2.20	$0.45

We can now analyze the three alternatives. The first alternative involves the purchase of a December future's contract in which the USP Company agrees to pay LC 380,000 to receive dollars at the September 90-day forward rate which is LC 2.00. Therefore, under the first alternative the USP Company has contracted to receive definitely $190,000. However, it will not have use of that money for 90 days. Typically the customer would arrange this with his bank or a trader with whom he has conducted operations in the past so that he is known to them. The fee charged by the bank is already reflected in the exchange rate. For example, if the expected spot rate in the future is as indicated, LC 2.10, then the applicable exchange rate for the September 90-day forward rate would be lower by the amount of the fee built in. If the normal difference between the September forward rate and the December spot rate were 0.07, the spread of 0.10 that we have illustrated here might represent an additional 0.03 as compensation to the bank or the foreign exchange trader.

Under alternative two the USP Company borrows LC 380,000 divided by 1.90, or $200,000. Of course, an interest factor will be involved because the USP Company will have to pay interest on the loan which it has obtained from the foreign bank. On the other hand, the USP Company will have the funds three months earlier and can invest those funds at its opportunity cost. Since in this example we are focusing on the influence of different patterns of spot and forward exchange rates, we will assume that the relationship between the borrowing cost in the foreign country and the firm's opportunity cost on the use of the funds is such that the profitability and the interest factor cancel out.

Under the third alternative, in December 1972, the LC 380,000 would be converted into dollars at the spot rate then in effect. This would represent LC 380,000 divided by 2.10, or $180,000. This result depends upon whether the expectations with regard to the exchange rates in December 1972 are actually realized. Under alternative three the $180,000 represents an expected amount to be received in December 1972.

Among the three alternatives the largest number of dollars is received under alternative two in which the LC 380,000 were borrowed and $200,-000 is received. This is definitely better than the $190,000 received under alternative one. Compared with alternative three we cannot be certain. The expected spot rate for December 1972 represents a decline of the local currency unit in dollars from $0.50 at the spot rate of September 1972 to $0.48 at the spot rate in December 1972. However, if the December spot rate turned out to be exactly the same as the September spot rate or if the value of LCs in dollars actually rose, alternative three could become the best of the three alternatives. In general, if a management is almost certain that the value of the local currency will decline over time, the logic is to make the arrangements to convert the local currency into the domestic currency as soon as possible. This is achieved by using either alternative one or two which enables the USP Company to protect the value of its sales volume.

Now we turn to the alternative type situation characteristic of the relationship between the United States and Western European countries in recent years. This is the pattern in which the value of the local currency unit is expected to be rising in relationship to the U.S. dollar as time goes on. Such a pattern is illustrated in the table that follows:

	September 1972		December 1972	
	Value of $ in LC	*Value of LC in $*	*Value of $ in LC*	*Value of LC in $*
Spot rate..................	LC 2.00	$0.50	LC 1.70	$0.59
Ninety-day forward rate.....	LC 1.90	$0.53	LC 1.50	$0.67

The same three alternatives are assumed to be available to the USP Company, but the pattern of analysis for the three alternatives will be different. Under alternative one the USP Company obtains LC 380,000 divided by the 90-day forward rate of LC 1.90, or $200,000.

Under alternative two the USP Company borrows LC 380,000 and buys dollars immediately. The spot rate is LC 2.00 so that the USP Company receives $190,000. Again we will assume the relationship between the interest cost and the opportunity profit rate is such that they will exactly cancel out.

Under alternative three where no action has been taken the conversion will take place at the LC 1.70 spot rate expected to exist in December. The USP Company will, therefore, receive LC 380,000 divided by LC 1.70, or $223,600.

Among the three alternatives, using the numbers given in the illustration, alternative three is better than alternative one which is better than alternative two. This result obtains because the number of LC units to buy $1 is expected to drop over time, which is to say that the value of one LC in dollars is rising over time. But this result is based on the expectations being close to reality. Again it could very well be for any period of time that instead of the spot rate in December representing a smaller number of LCs required per dollar, if international monetary conditions change, the spot rate in December might actually be above the spot rate in September. If the spot rate in December resulted in an LC rate equal to or higher than the spot rate in September, the third alternative would be the worst rather than the best of three possible actions. Alternative one would then be the best because it yields $200,000 as compared to receiving $190,000 under alternative two.

In summary, among the alternatives available in seeking to protect a firm's exchange rate position an unequivocal choice cannot be made. The answer is dependent upon judgments about what future exchange rates will be in comparison with current exchange rates. Choice among the alternatives depends upon the relationship between the current forward rate and the future spot rate as well as the relative opportunity cost of money in two countries. The decision is basically a businessman's judgment which heavily depends upon a forecast of future foreign exchange rates. This is the reason why we emphasize in Chapter 2 an understanding of the basic mechanisms involved. Also, in Chapter 3 we focus on a number of forecasting considerations for making judgments about what the pattern of future exchange rate relationships will be.

But if one takes the expectations as a basis for the decisions, a strong generalization can be made. In dealings with firms in countries whose currencies show greater strength than the domestic currency, the firm should delay conversion from the foreign currency into the weaker domestic currency as long as possible. In that way benefit will be gained from the rising value of the stronger currency so that the largest number of dollars will be received. Conversely, when the foreign currency unit is in a strong downward trend in value in relation to the domestic currency unit, it is better to utilize arrangements that will enable conversion from the foreign currency unit to the domestic currency unit as soon as possible. When currency patterns are in strong trend movements, the generalizations provide firm guidance. However, when exchange rate movements are not so pronounced, the choice among the alternatives involves uncertainty and a businessman's risk will be involved.

Measuring the percentage of devaluation or of revaluation

From the standpoint of the United States we are accustomed to expressing the value of foreign currencies in dollars. When the British devalued the pound in 1967, the value of the pound in dollars was changed from $2.80 to $2.40. This was generally referred to as a devaluation of the

British pound by 14.3 percent—a decline in the value of the British pound in dollars by 14.3 percent. However, as we pointed out in Chapter 2, there are two ways of expressing exchange rates. One is in terms of the number of dollars that the foreign currency unit is worth or alternatively the number of foreign currency units required to buy $1 or to be worth $1.

From the standpoint of a U.S. financial manager, he must consider both formulations. Viewing worldwide operations translated into dollars, he expresses every foreign currency in terms of its dollar value because that is the common denominator for him. However, he and his managers of operations conducted in foreign countries are also confronted by problems posed in terms of the number of foreign (local) currency units required to conduct the business of the firm.

The logic for calculating the percentage of devaluation is straightforward. The percentage change is always calculated by taking the new minus the old, divided by the old. When devaluation is expressed in terms of the number of foreign currency units, the formula is:

$$\frac{X_1 - X_0}{X_0} = \text{percentage increase in number of foreign currency units required; this is also the percentage devaluation of the foreign currency.}$$

When currency values are expressed in terms of their dollar values, we are dividing the number of foreign currency units into $1. Therefore, the formula becomes:

$$\frac{\frac{1}{X_1} - \frac{1}{X_0}}{\frac{1}{X_0}} = \frac{X_0}{X_1} - 1 = \frac{X_0 - X_1}{X_1} = \text{percentage decline in the dollar value of the foreign currency.}$$

These general expressions can now be illustrated. For example, suppose that a currency has been devalued from 400 pesos to the dollar to 500 pesos to the dollar. What is the percent devaluation? From the standpoint of the number of pesos required per dollar, a 25 percent change or devaluation has taken place. In symbols this is $(X_1 - X_0) / X_0$ or $(500-400) / 400$, equals 25 percent. From the standpoint of the value of the pesos in dollars, the peso has declined in value from .25¢ to .20¢, a devaluation of 20 percent. Using the formula this is $(X_0 - X_1) / X_1$ or $(400-500) / 500$, equals 20 percent. Thus it is equally correct to state that a 25% or a 20% devaluation of the currency has taken place. It depends upon the problem under analysis.

The principle is similar in connection with foreign currency revaluations upward in relation to the dollar as has occurred in the early 1970s. Suppose the franc has risen in value from $.20 to $.25. What percentage revaluation does this represent? The change also represents a decrease from 5 to 4 in the number of francs that may be obtained per dollar. From the standpoint of the manager of foreign operations, his franc financing requirements in relation to dollars have decreased by 20 percent: (4–5) / 5, equals −20 percent. From the standpoint of the cost of acquiring francs with U.S. dollars, the U.S. dollar requirements have increased by 25 percent: (5–4) / 4, equals 25 percent.

It is necessary to keep both points of view in mind to avoid confusion. The U.S. financial manager must become accustomed to looking at currency values from both points of view. Considerable misunderstanding might develop if the U.S. financial officer receives communication from the financial manager of a foreign subsidiary who refers to a devaluation expressed in the percentage of the number of local currency units required to conduct local operations. If the American financial manager interprets this percentage devaluation as a decline in the dollar value of the foreign currency unit, there will be confusion because these are not the same percentages. Therefore, in this book we purposely have expressed the devaluation relationships both ways—sometimes one way and sometimes the other—for the purpose of focusing the attention of the American financial manager, particularly, on the necessity for reorganizing both points of view. Both views are perfectly appropriate depending upon the point of reference that is being employed. When we have stated a percentage devaluation, we have attempted to make clear in each instance the point of reference for expressing the percentage that is being used.

Therefore, we shall be using the word devaluation from both the standpoints we have described. When we use the expression, "devaluation of a foreign currency," we shall be referring to the percentage change in the number of foreign currency units required to purchase one dollar:

$$\frac{X_1 - X_0}{X_0}$$

When we use the expression, "the percentage change in the dollar value" of a foreign (local) currency unit, the percentage devaluation will be computed from the following:

$$\frac{X_0 - X_1}{X_1}$$

THE FOREIGN CURRENCY SWAP

When exchange rates are subject to extremely wide fluctuations, the risks of forward market positions are so great that trading in the forward markets will cease to take place. In such circumstances, swap arrangements may be made available by governments or private traders to encourage international transactions involving their countries. The swap arrangements are used to protect the value of export sales as well as the value of original investments in a foreign country. In what follows we focus our attention on the use of the swap to protect the value of original investments. The use of the swap in export sales is given an extensive treatment in Chapter 9.

When investments are made in a foreign country in terms of its local currency and under conditions of intermediate or severe currency devaluation, the foreign currency swap presents an effective hedge against losses from foreign exchange rate risks due to unfavorable changes in the foreign exchange rate. The currency swap can prevent the erosion of the dollar value of the invested funds during the swap period. It also presents an advantageous alternative to the borrowing of local currency funds by a foreign subsidiary of a firm headquartered in a country with comparatively stable currency, since interest rates in countries of unstable currencies are usually very high.

The history of currency swapping

Following World War I, several central European countries, including Austria, Czechoslovakia, and Hungary, engaged in currency swapping in order to obtain much-needed foreign exchange.[1] In 1929 the Bank of France did a brisk and profitable business swapping francs for dollars and sterling with private French banks so as to maintain its own discount rate at a high level while it was experiencing a plethora of funds.[2] In 1927 and 1928 the Italian National Institute of Exchange actively engaged in swap operations in the leading foreign exchange markets in order to regulate the international movement of funds. Between 1928 and 1932 Spain used foreign exchange swap operations to protect its dwindling stock of gold.[3]

Commercial banks engaged in international banking frequently swap currencies in order to meet temporary needs for funds. Since World War II the treasuries and central banks of all major trading nations have been very active in swapping currencies with their foreign counterparts in order to stabilize their own currencies. The Federal Reserve Bank of New York actively participates in foreign currency swapping operations on behalf of the Treasury of the United States whenever it is necessary to support the U.S. dollar on a temporary basis in various international financial markets.

Foreign currency swap transactions between business organizations and foreign commercial and central banks are an innovation of the 1950s and have been largely confined to "soft currency" countries in South

---

[1] Paul Einzig, *A Dynamic Theory of Forward Exchange* (London: Macmillan & Co., Ltd., 1961), p. 427.

[2] Claude McMillan, "The Swap as a Hedge in Foreign Exchange," *California Management Review*, Vol. 4, No. 4 (Summer 1962), p. 59.

[3] Einzig, *Dynamic Theory*, pp. 455, 459.

America.[4] These countries have had great need for foreign exchange to meet their international obligations. The Bank of Brazil, a private bank acting as fiscal agent for the Brazilian government, until recently has been most active in this type of swap transaction.

The nature of currency swapping

The currency swap involves the exchange of one currency into another at an agreed-upon ratio, the swap rate, with the exchange being reversed at exactly the same ratio at the end of the swap contract period. In the case of the credit swap, currency swapping actually consists of an exchange of a credit in one currency for a credit in another with both credits being repaid at the end of the swap period. In effect, the currency swap involves a simultaneous spot and futures contract for an exchange of one currency with another with the spot and future rates being equal in value.

The cost of the currency swap to the U.S. investor is the larger number of dollars required to obtain a given value of foreign currency due to the swap discount than would be required if this same value were obtained by an exchange at the free market spot rate. An additional cost is the interest rate (r_F) which the foreign bank charges on the local currency obtained, and which is not offset by interest paid on the dollars involved in the swap transaction, since the foreign bank usually refuses to pay such interest.

The advantage of the currency swap to the investor consists of the protection against a decrease in the dollar value of the invested funds resulting from possible future local currency devaluations. This protection against future currency devaluation does not, however, extend to the profits from an investment. The decision as to whether a business should employ the currency swap requires an evaluation of the costs as compared with the potential losses. Should inflation continue in the foreign country, the resulting deterioration in the foreign exchange value of the local currency would be of concern. Another factor influencing the currency swap decision is the importance of the investment outcome to the firm. If the amount of invested funds is large in relation to the investor's financial capability, the currency swap should be employed; if the invested funds are relatively small, the risks of future currency devaluation may be more readily assumed.

Currency swapping is encouraged by the increasing need for foreign currencies on the part of foreign subsidiaries, particularly those engaged in manufacturing or engineering service activities. This need for foreign currencies is further increased by the usual economic growth of the host

---

[4] *Financing Foreign Operations* (New York: Business International, Inc., October 1961), pp. 18, 19, 102, 103.

countries. Foreign subsidiaries, once established, desire to maintain or increase their share of the market and as a result will increase their investments on a local currency basis. For the same reason, additional investments may often be made even when the expected rate of profitability is equal to or less than the anticipated percentage of devaluation. It is under these circumstances that the foreign currency swap should be employed in order to avoid financial losses.

The greatest stimulant to foreign currency swapping is the serious and persistent need for convertible foreign exchange on the part of the host country, a need which arises out of its surplus of imports over exports. Shortages cannot always be covered by loans from the International Monetary Fund or other international financial agencies.

Difficulties are usually not encountered in the determination of a mutually acceptable swap discount. Agreement on this percentage decrease of the swap rate in relation to the spot rate is due to the opposite forward expectations of the swapping partners. A foreign government usually expects the future deterioration of the foreign exchange value of its national currency to be less than it actually becomes. Therefore, the foreign government being in severe need of foreign exchange is most likely to be satisfied with a relatively small swap discount when the swap contract is made. A business organization operating or investing in a foreign country, on the other hand, usually expects the future currency devaluation to be as great as or greater than in the recent past and for this reason is usually willing to accept a greater swap discount than would otherwise be the case. During periods of intermediate or extreme devaluation, the relatively low interest rate of 2 to 5 percent on the foreign currency charged by the foreign central bank is usually of little significance.

Currency swapping can be divided into two general classes: official swaps and private swaps.

Official swaps

An official currency swap is one consummated between a private investor and a foreign government, one of its agencies or a fiscal agent. In this case the transaction is backed by the credit and trustworthiness of the foreign government. The writers know of no instance where performance under an official swap contract has been defaulted, no matter how serious the need for convertible currency. Official swaps are of three kinds: credit, financial, and export.

The credit swap.   In the large majority of instances where currency swapping is engaged in between central banks and private business, the swapping involves an exchange of a credit in one currency for a credit in the other. The multinational firm engaged in currency swapping through its commercial bank makes a dollar credit available to the foreign central bank. The foreign central bank, in turn, makes a local currency credit available in its country to a subsidiary or other business organization as determined by the owner of the dollars.

The financial swap.   Under the financial swap the foreign investor, through his commercial bank, makes an amount of dollars available to a foreign central bank which, in turn, gives to his designated representative as partial payment an amount of local currency as determined by the existing swap rate. At the end of the swap period the foreign central bank completes the transaction by giving the representative additional local currency in an amount equal to the difference between the spot rate then in effect and the swap rate used initially.

Occasionally the financial swap agreement may contain provisions for partial liquidations of the swap before the end of the contract period, such as a 50 percent liquidation after 180 days, a further 25 percent liquidation after 270 days, etc. The spot rate in effect at the end of each of these partial liquidation periods determines the added amount of foreign local currency to be paid by the foreign central bank.

Export swaps.   When a government wishes to boost its country's exports, its central bank may make export swaps available to its exporters, foreign-owned subsidiaries included. Under this procedure, for example, an Argentinian exporter borrows, on the basis of his sales contract, convertible foreign currency in the country of destination of his exports to be repaid with the proceeds from the exports. This convertible currency is then delivered to the Argentina Central Bank for conversion into local currency. The Argentinian exporter thus has local funds to procure raw materials and cover the expenditures of manufacturing or procurement of the goods to be exported. After the export transaction has been completed he liquidates his foreign currency loan, pays a relatively low rate of interest on the local funds advanced him by his central bank, and receives additional local currency depending upon the relationship between the then-existing spot rate and the original swap rate. The payment of the additional local currency completes the contract for the acquisition of the much-needed foreign exchange on the part of the central bank.

The export swap and the financial swap, discussed above, amount to an advance delivery of convertible currency and a delayed payment on the part of the foreign central bank. The advantage to the foreign central bank is that it obtains much-needed foreign currency sooner, and the advantage to the exporter is that he does not suffer a decrease in real value receipts during the period of preparation, delivery, and collection.

Private swaps

Private currency swaps are swaps executed between foreign investors and commercial banks. In contrast to official swaps, private swaps usually do not exceed one year in length and are costlier to the foreign investor. The interest rate on local-currency funds is often as high as 30 percent, which makes the employment of a currency swap advisable only when a high rate of future devaluation is expected. Moreover, currency swapping on a private basis is not likely to prove as profitable as swapping with official government agencies, since the expectations of the swapping partners in regard to further devaluation are not as different. Private swaps are presently available in Argentina, Brazil, and Columbia.[5]

General considerations

The advantages of the currency swap as exchange rate risk protection to a business organization are not limited to initial investments in a foreign country. Swap transactions are also beneficial when subsequent investments are made in foreign operations. The reversal of a swap at the end of a swap contract removes uncertainty in connection with the receipt of interest payments, dividends, or reduction of principal payments from the foreign subsidiary, thus greatly aiding the corporate financial planning of the parent organization. Foreign currency swapping can be an advantage to any organization that is regularly required to obtain foreign local currencies in exchange for its dollars. In fact, foreign currency swapping can even be an advantage to speculators providing such currency swaps are available to them.

The advantages of the introduction of the currency swap into the investment process can be demonstrated by the use of several investment evaluation methods. The comparative profitability of swap over no-swap investments as well as the advantages of the swap over the no-swap investment can be determined to aid the financial planning of the multinational firm.

The simplest method of evaluation, ignoring the time value of money, can be carried out either on a single- or multiple-time-period basis. When the time value of money is recognized, three methods of evaluation are possible: the net present value, the profitability index, and the net present value per dollar invested. All three of these methods incorporate the discounting of future net cash receipts and expenditures to determine their present value.

Investing without the currency swap

Under normal circumstances a business organization making a local currency investment (F_0) in a foreign country purchases such currency with dollars (V_0) on the open market at the so-called free market spot

---

rate (X_0), whenever this is permitted by the country's foreign exchange laws. Toward the end of the investment period, or whenever the original investment, profits, or interest are to be remitted home, the foreign subsidiary converts its local currency into dollars on the free market at the spot rate (X_1) existing at that time. Under these circumstances all of the funds—original investment, profits, interest, and dividends—are fully exposed to exchange rate risk.

The profit from such a dollar investment (V_0) on a single period basis is given by the following expression:

$$Pr_{NS} = V_0\left(\frac{X_0}{X_1}(1 + g_F) - (1 + r_{US})\right)$$

where g_F is the profitability of the foreign investment and r_{US} represents the opportunity or borrowing cost of the U.S. investment funds (V_0). On a percentage basis the profit equals:

$$Pr_{NS} = \frac{X_0}{X_1}(1 + g_F) - (1 + r_{US}) .$$

For the investment to be profitable $X_0 / X_1 (1 + g_F)$ must be greater than $(1 + r_{US})$ from which one can obtain that $(g_F - r_{US}) X_1 / X_0$ must be greater than $X_1 - X_0 / X_0$. If this is not the case, the investment will not even return the originally invested funds.

Assume that the profitability of a foreign investment (g_F) is 30 percent, the expected rate of devaluation 20 percent, the spot rate at the time of investment 200 LC per dollar, the U.S. investment funds \$5,000, and the opportunity or borrowing cost of these funds 10 percent, then:

$$(g_F - r_{US})X_1/X_0$$

$$= 0.3 - 0.1\left(\frac{240}{200}\right) = 0.18 ,$$

which is less than 0.2, the expected rate of devaluation. This means that the investment would result in a loss:

$$Pr_{NS} = V_0\left(\frac{X_0}{X_1}(1 + g_F) - (1 + r_{US})\right)$$

$$= 5,000\left(\frac{200}{240}(1 + 0.3) - (1 + 0.1)\right)$$

$$= 5,000(-0.0167)$$

$$= -\$83.50 , \text{ a loss.}$$

Investing with the currency swap

The exchange rate risk can be decreased materially when the foreign currency swap is introduced into the investment process. Under this procedure an investing multinational firm makes available through its commercial bank a hard currency credit (V_0^S) whose opportunity or borrowing cost is r_{US} and its foreign subsidiary, in turn, receives a local currency credit (F_0) on which it pays an interest rate (r_F). The amount of the local currency received is equal to the dollars (V_0^S) times the swap rate (S_0), which always represents a discount from the spot rate. It thus is an added cost to the investing firm, since a larger number of dollars will be required to obtain the needed local currency funds (F_0). Since the amount of local currency funds is the same whether a swap is used or not, $V_0^S S_0$ is equal to $V_0 X_0$. Due to this equality, one can determine the dollars required for the investment via the following:

$$V_0^S = V_0 \frac{X_1}{S_0} \; ;$$

also the swap discount on a percentage basis is:

$$\text{Swap discount} = \frac{X_0 - S_0}{X_0} \, .$$

The profitability of a foreign investment on a swap basis is given by the following expression:

$$Pr_S = V_0^S\left(\frac{S_0}{X_1}(g_F - r_F) + 1 - (1 + r_{US})\right) = V_0^S\left(\frac{S_0}{X_1}(g_F - r_F) - r_{US}\right)$$

and on a percentage basis the profit is

$$Pr_S = \frac{S_0}{X_1} (g_F - r_F) - r_{US} \, ,$$

for profit (g_F) must be larger than

$$r_F + \frac{X_0}{S_0} r_{US} \, .$$

Making the same assumptions as in the case of the no-swap investment above and specifying in addition that the swap discount will be 20 percent and that the interest rate on the local currency funds will be 5 percent, the percentage profitability of the investment via the swap will be:

$$Pr_S = \frac{S_0}{X_1} (g_F - r_F) - r_{US} = \frac{160}{240} (0.3 - 0.05) - 0.1 = 0.0667 \, .$$

This is acceptable, since the 6.67 percent profit is in excess of the firm's opportunity cost.

Under the swap arrangement the original investment funds are no longer jeopardized by fluctuations in the exchange value of the foreign currency. The amount originally invested (V_0^S) is returned to the foreign investor at the end of the swap contract when the swap is reversed. Profits resulting from the investment, however, are still subject to the effects of the exchange rate deterioration; and for this reason foreign currency swap-ping is a helpful but not a complete means of protection. This handicap can be overcome if the investing firm obtains a greater amount of foreign currency than is needed for the investment and converts the excess, where permitted, back into dollars on the free market on the basis of the spot rate (X_0). The cost of this added protection is the greater number of dol-lars tied up during the swap period.

Comparing the swap with the no-swap investment

When comparing the two procedures of investment it is evident that the principal additional cost of the swap arrangement is that of requiring more funds than would be necessary if the swap arrangement were not used. The availability of these additional funds depends on the investing firm's supply and demand for investment capital. The cost of these addi-tional funds may be considered the opportunity cost, that is, the profita-bility foregone by not investing these same funds in other business oppor-tunities.

The introduction of the currency swap into the investment process as an exchange rate risk protection device is an advantage whenever the profit per dollar invested is greater with swap than the profit per dollar if the investment were made without the employment of the currency swap, namely,

$$\frac{Pr_S}{V_0{}^S} > \frac{Pr_{NS}}{V_0} \, .$$

$$\frac{S_0}{X_1} (g_F - r_F) - r_{US} > \frac{X_0}{X_1} (1 + g_F) - (1 + r_{US}) \, .$$

From the above relationship can be developed expressions for the mini-mum magnitude of the percentage devaluation during the swap contract that must take place for a given foreign rate of interest (r_F) and a given swap discount (SD) as demanded by the swapping partner. An expression can also be derived which indicates the maximum swap discount that can be accepted, given a foreign rate of interest and the percentage of devalu-ation (RD), in order for the use of the currency swap to be advantageous. The cost of the U.S. funds cancels out of the above expressions.

$$RD > SD g_F + (1 - SD) r_F$$

or

$$RD = \frac{X_1 - X_0}{X_0} \, ,$$

$$RD > g_F - (1 - SD)(g_F - r_F) \, ,$$

and

$$SD < \frac{RD - r_F}{g_F - r_F} \, .$$

Applying the financial details of the foregoing example we find the following:

RD must be larger than $SD(g_F) + (1 - SD)r_F$
20% is larger than 20% (0.3) + (1 − 0.2)(0.5%)
$$= 6\% + 4\% = 10\% \, .$$
RD must be larger than $g_F - (1 - SD)(g_F - r_F)$
20% is larger than 30% − (1 − 0.2)(30% − 5%)
$$= 30\% - 20\% = 10\% \, .$$
SD must be smaller than $\dfrac{RD - r_F}{g_F - r_F}$
20% is smaller than $\dfrac{20\% - 5\%}{30\% - 5\%} = \dfrac{15\%}{25\%} = 60\% \, .$

It should be noted that the formula developed above assumes that the anticipated percentage devaluation is actually realized. But, since it is probable that the actual rate of devaluation is greater than the anticipated value, a cautious manager should consider the employment of the currency swap even when the profit rate with the swap is slightly lower than the anticipated profit rate without the swap.

The foreign currency swap enables the multinational firm to make foreign currency investments in its subsidiaries with greater safety than when it is not used, since it protects the dollar value of the investment funds during the swap contract period. Even though earnings from swap investments are not protected, the employment of the currency swap makes possible low-profit investments that often must be made for nonfinancial reasons. Only when the investment itself is unprofitable will there be a loss to the investing firm. In comparison, investments made without the currency swap result in a loss whenever their rate of profitability compounded during the investment period is less than the percentage of devaluation over this same time span.

Financial managements of firms investing in "soft currency" countries must carefully evaluate the economic costs of the currency swap to make certain that these are not greater than the anticipated benefits of its protection against exchange rate risk. Careful estimation of the expected percentage of devaluation over the investment period is required, since the benefits of the currency swap are directly related to it. The employment of the currency swap in the foreign investment process can make a firm's foreign investments more competitive with its other investment opportunities; therefore, its use, where available, should always be seriously considered.

A comparison of methods of swap analysis

Other writers have formulated analyses of the decision to use or not to use a swap arrangement. Different formulas have been employed. They can be shown to be equivalent to ours.

Such a reconciliation is provided in Table 5–1 with reference to a presentation by Claude McMillan. Table 5–1(a) presents McMillan's nota-

TABLE 5–1(a)

Comparison with alternative formulation of swap analysis

McMillan notation	Weston and Sorge notation
Percentage gain *without* a swap:	
$P_i(100\% - P_c) - P_c - I$ (I)	$Pr_{NS} = \dfrac{X_0}{X_1}(1 + g_F) - (1 + r_{US})$
Percentage gain *with* a swap:	
$P_i(100\% - P_c) - \dfrac{FI}{S}$ (II)	$Pr_S = \dfrac{S_0}{X_1}(g_F - r_S) - r_{US}$

	McMillan symbols	Weston and Sorge symbols
The number of cruzeiros required to buy one dollar on the free market at the beginning of the investment period..............	F	X_0
The number of cruzeiros required to buy one dollar on the free market at the end of the investment period...................	$F_1 = \dfrac{F}{100\% - P_c}$	X_1
The percentage *increase* in the cruzeiro value of the cruzeiro investment during the life of the investment......................	P_i	g_F
The percentage *decrease* in the dollar value of the cruzeiro on the free market during the life of the investment................	P_c	$\dfrac{X_0 - X_1}{X_1}$*
The annual rate of interest on the dollars employed to make the cruzeiro investment, in percentage.........................	I	r_{US}
The number of cruzeiros received from the Bank of Brazil for each dollar swapped....	S	S_0
Local currency credit....................		$V_0 S S_0 = F_o$
Interest rate on local currency credit.......		r_F

* This is $\dfrac{\dfrac{1}{X_1} - \dfrac{1}{X_0}}{\dfrac{1}{X_0}} = \dfrac{X_0}{X_1} - \dfrac{X_0}{X_0} = \dfrac{X_0}{X_1} - 1 = \dfrac{X_0 - X_1}{X_1}$

Source: Claude McMillan, "The Swap as a Hedge in Foreign Exchange," *California Management Review*, Vol. 4, No. 4 (Summer 1962), pp. 60–61.

tions followed by ours. Then we show the symbols used by McMillan and those we use. In Table 5–1(b) we translate McMillan's notations and symbols into ours. We begin by taking McMillan's formula (I) for a percentage gain without employment of a swap and express this in our sym-

TABLE 5–1(b)

Reconciliation with alternative formulation of swap analysis

McMillan (I):

$$P_i(100\% - P_c) - P_c - I$$

Expressed in Weston and Sorge symbols:

$$Pr_{NS} = g_F\left(1 - \frac{X_1 - X_0}{X_1}\right) - \frac{X_1 - X_0}{X_1} - r_{US} \qquad (1)$$

$$= g_F\left(\frac{X_1 - X_1 + X_0}{X_1}\right) + 1 - \frac{X_1 - X_0}{X_1} - 1 - r_{US} \qquad (2)$$

$$= g_F\left(\frac{X_0}{X_1}\right) + \frac{X_0}{X_1} - (1 + r_{US}) \qquad (3)$$

$$Pr_{NS} = \frac{X_0}{X_1}(1 + g_F) - (1 + r_{US}) \qquad (4)$$

McMillan (II):

$$P_i(100\% - P_c) - \frac{FI}{S}$$

Expressed in Weston and Sorge symbols:

$$Pr_S = g_F\left(1 - \frac{X_1 - X_0}{X_1}\right) - \frac{X_0 r_{US}}{S_0} \qquad (5)$$

$$= g_F\left(\frac{X_0}{X_1}\right) - \frac{X_0}{S_0}(r_{US}) \qquad (6)$$

$$= \frac{X_0}{S_0}\left(\frac{S_0}{X_1}g_F - r_{US}\right) \qquad (7)$$

a) McMillan assumes investment of V_0, not V_0^S.

b) Since $V_0 X_0 = V_0^S S_0$, multiply (7) by $\dfrac{S_0}{X_0}$

$$Pr_S = \frac{S_0}{X_0}\left[\frac{X_0}{S_0}\left(\frac{S_0}{X_1}g_F - r_{US}\right)\right] \qquad (8)$$

$$= \frac{S_0}{X_1}g_F - r_{US} \qquad (9)$$

bols in equation (1). In equation (2) we add 1 and at the same time subtract 1 from the right-hand side. By rearranging terms we obtain our formula for the percentage profitability of a no-swap investment in equation (4).

McMillan's equation (II) for the calculation of the percentage gain using a swap is formulated on the assumption that a local currency credit is not involved. His formula is for V_0 instead of our V_0^S. We have pointed out that $V_0 X_0 = V_0^S S_0$ and $V_0 = V_0^S S_0/X_0$. Therefore, to obtain our equation, McMillan's equation would have to be multiplied by S_0/X_0. In addition, McMillan's equation differs from ours in that he does not have a term r_F representing the interest payment on the local currency credit involved.

MONETARY BALANCE

Monetary assets and liabilities are those items whose value, expressed in the local currency, does not change with devaluation. A partial listing follows:

Monetary assets	Monetary liabilities
Cash	Accounts payable
Marketable securities	Notes payable
Accounts receivable	Tax liability reserve
Tax refunds receivable	Bonds
Notes receivable	Preferred stock
Prepaid insurance	

Alchian and Kessel investigated the experience of a number of U.S. firms, both during inflationary and deflationary periods, and determined that business organizations that are net monetary debtors benefit from inflation whereas those that are net monetary creditors do not; the reverse of this is true in the case of deflation.[6]

As a general rule, branches and foreign subsidiaries of U.S. firms operating in foreign areas are monetary creditors. Among their assets are cash in the foreign currencies and accounts receivable from foreign customers. Indebtedness, if any, is usually owed the parent company in terms of U.S. dollars—debts which do not offset monetary assets in terms of the foreign currency. Therefore, the achievement of monetary balance requires the borrowing of foreign currency and the spending of these funds for business purposes. The cost of obtaining monetary balance and reducing exchange rate risk is the interest that must be paid on the borrowed funds.

Consider the dollar value of a foreign subsidiary at the present to be:

$$\text{Value}_0 = \frac{\text{Net real assets}}{X_0} + \frac{\text{Net monetary assets}}{X_0}$$

where X_0 is the present spot rate. A year later the value will be:

$$\text{Value}_1 = \frac{\text{Net real assets}}{X_0} + \frac{\text{Net monetary assets}}{X_1}$$

where X_1 is the spot rate one year hence. The change in dollar value during the year is given by:

$$\text{Value}_0 - \text{Value}_1 = \frac{\text{Net monetary assets}}{X_0} - \frac{\text{Net monetary assets}}{X_1}.$$

---

[6] Armen A. Alchian and Ruben A. Kessel, "Redistribution of Wealth through Inflation," *Science*, Vol. 130 (September 4, 1959), pp. 535–39.

This represents the loss in dollar value of the foreign subsidiary due to the change in the foreign exchange value of the local currency. In the above it is assumed that the real assets will not lose value and that their local currency value will increase with the decrease in the foreign exchange value of that currency.

Net monetary assets are defined as monetary assets minus monetary liabilities. If this value is equal to a quantity A, then the loss would be:

$$\text{Loss} = A\left(\frac{1}{X_0} - \frac{1}{X_1}\right).$$

If instead of taking this loss the subsidiary borrows an amount equal to A locally and spends this money on equipment or inventory, then the sub's net monetary position would be equal to zero and neither gain nor loss would result with changes in the foreign exchange value of the local currency. The cost of this protection is the interest that would have to be paid on the additionally borrowed funds to achieve monetary balance. This is given by:

$$\text{Cost}_r = \frac{r_F A}{X_1}$$

where r_F is the foreign borrowing rate, A equals the amount of loan, and X_1 is the spot rate at the end of the year, assuming that the interest is paid at the end of the year, at which time the then current spot rate is used to convert the cost into dollars.

For the net monetary position of zero to be of value, the cost, $r_F A/X_1$, must be less than the loss, $A(1/X_0 - 1/X_1)$.

$$\frac{r_F A}{X_1} < A\left(\frac{1}{X_0} - \frac{1}{X_1}\right).$$

From the above one can establish that the employment of monetary balance techniques is an advantage whenever $r_F < (X_1 - X_0)/X_0$, where $(X_1 - X_0)/X_0$ is the expected rate of devaluation during the year.

If local borrowing by the foreign subsidiary reduces borrowing in the United States, then the net cost of the foreign borrowing is reduced to the difference between the foreign rate of interest and the interest rate normally paid in the United States. Any time that this difference in interest rates is less than the expected rate of devaluation, borrowing to achieve monetary balance and thus avoiding exchange rate risk is advisable.

Borrow foreign if

$$r_F - r_{US} < \frac{X_1 - X_0}{X_0}$$

where r_{US} is the U.S. borrowing rate.

Assume that a foreign subsidiary of Multinat has LC 1,000,000 more monetary assets than monetary liabilities and that the existing spot rate is LC 200 equal $1 U.S.[7] If the devaluation of the local currency is expected to be 20 percent during the coming 12 months, Multinat's loss due to devaluation in U.S. dollars would be:

$$\text{Loss} = A\left(\frac{1}{X_0} - \frac{1}{X_1}\right) = 1,000,000\left(\frac{1}{200} - \frac{1}{240}\right)$$
$$= 1,000,000(0.000833) = \$833$$

The cost of avoiding this loss due to exchange rate risk would be the borrowing of LC 1,000,000 at an interest rate of 15 percent and paying this interest at the end of the year when the spot rate is expected to be LC 240 per U.S. dollar.

$$\text{Cost} = A\,\frac{r_F}{X_1} = 1,000,000\,\frac{0.15}{240} = \$625$$

This shows that the cost of protection is less than the expected loss, therefore a worthwhile move. It should also be noted that even when the cost of protection is slightly greater than the expected loss it may still be better to achieve monetary balance, because the *actual* loss could be greater than the cost of protection. Now if one assumes that the foreign subsidiary had need for this LC 1,000,000 and would have obtained it from Multinat via the existing spot rate and that the parent would have borrowed the amount from its bank at a rate of 10 percent per year, then the extra cost of the funds would have been

$$\text{Cost} = A\,\frac{r_{US}}{X_0} = 1,000,000\,\frac{0.10}{200} = \$500\;.$$

From this it can be seen that the differential cost of the protection, the difference between the two costs, was actually $625 - $500 = $125.

The benefits of monetary balance as an exchange risk protective device result from the fact that if there is any downward change in the value of the foreign currency in relation to the U.S. dollar, losses incurred due to the possession of monetary assets are balanced by profits resulting from the possession of an equal amount of monetary liabilities. U.S. firms are well advised to have their branches and subsidiaries operate on a monetary debtor basis in countries with a continuing inflationary bias.

SUMMARY

Three techniques may contribute to the reduction of the erosion of values due to exchange rate fluctuations: (1) use of the forward foreign exchange contract, (2) use of foreign currency swap arrangements, and (3) achieving monetary balance.

Use of the forward market is the protective device against foreign

---

[7] LC is used throughout this volume to mean "local currency."

exchange losses most often employed under ordinary conditions. It is beneficial because forward contracts fix a definite dollar value for foreign currency payments or receipts that are scheduled to take place at the end of the forward contract period, say in 90 days.

Foreign currency swapping is a device to protect particularly the value of investments in countries whose currencies are "soft." The likelihood of considerable devaluation is so high that forward markets may not even exist. There are two general classes: official swaps and private swaps. The former type involves a foreign government or its agents whereas the latter involves only private parties. Official swaps consist of the credit swap, the financial swap, and the export swap. The credit swap is most often employed. Moreover, official swaps are less expensive than are private swaps.

Monetary balance is a technique designed primarily to protect the value of the monetary assets of foreign subsidiaries (in terms of the currency of the parent's country) from devaluation of the foreign currency. If the foreign subsidiary is a net creditor in foreign currency (i.e., if its locally dominated monetary assets exceed its locally denominated monetary liabilities), it will suffer from the loss in purchasing power of its monetary assets (in terms of the currency of the parent firm's country). Therefore, to avoid this loss in purchasing power the foreign subsidiary may borrow locally and achieve a zero net monetary asset position. In this manner the subsidiary can shift the purchasing power loss of its locally denominated assets to the local debtor. The cost of achieving monetary balance is the interest that must be paid on the borrowed funds. The optimal net monetary asset position depends on the borrowing cost, the anticipated rate of devaluation, and its uncertainty.

The swap essentially involves a simultaneous spot and future contract with the same fixed spot and future rates at a discount from the current spot rate. The advantage of the currency swap is that it can protect the value of foreign investment from prospective further devaluation of the foreign currency. The cost of the swap includes the swap discount and the interest charged by foreign banks.

APPENDIX

List of symbols used in Chapter 5

F_0 = amount of local currency investment

F_1 = value of the investment in terms of the local currency at end of one period

V_0 = value of the dollar investment, without a swap

V_0^s = dollar investment required using a swap arrangement

X_0 = free market spot exchange rate at time of investment (expressed in the number of foreign currency units required to buy one dollar)

X_1 = free market exchange rate at the end of one period
S_0 = swap rate of exchange—number of local currency units for one dollar
Pr_{NS} = profit on the investment, if no swap (expressed either as an amount or as a rate of profit)
Pr_S = profit on the investment, when a swap is used (expressed either as an amount or as a rate of profit)
g_F = profit rate on the foreign investment (expressed in the local currency)
r_{US} = borrowing cost of U.S. funds
r_F = interest rate on foreign funds

PROBLEM 5–1

In September 1972, a U.S. parent company expects to receive LC 380,000 in December 1972 on a sale to a European subsidiary. The spot and forward rates for September and the anticipated rates for December 1972 expressed in LCs per U.S. dollar are:

September 1972	*December 1972*
Spot rate.............. LC 2.00	Spot rate.............. LC 1.70
90-day forward rate....... LC 1.90	90-day forward rate....... LC 1.50

Alternative 1: Sell a December local currency contract for $200,000. This December contract will be covered by the receipt of LC 380,000 in December.

Alternative 2: The European subsidiary borrows LC 380,000 with which it buys dollars at the September spot rate of LC 2.00. It receives $190,000 which it remits to the parent in September. In December the subsidiary repays the loan at a 12 percent interest rate and makes the repayment in local currency. A charge expressed in dollars is made to the U.S. parent company at this time.

Alternative 3: Accept exchange rate risk. The parent is paid at the spot rate in December 1972.

A. How much does U.S. parent receive under the three alternatives?

B. Which alternative should it select?

C. What factors would it consider before selecting among the three alternatives?

PROBLEM 5–2

In September 1972, U.S. parent expects to receive LC 380,000 in December 1972. The spot and forward rates for September and December of the given year are:

September 1972	*December 1972*
Spot rate.............. LC 1.90	Spot rate.............. LC 2.10
90-day forward rate...... LC 2.00	90-day forward rate....... LC 2.20

Alternative 1: Sell December contract for $190,000. Cover by receipt of LC 380,000 in December.

Alternative 2:   U.K. subsidiary borrows LC 380,000, buys spot September dollars at LC 1.90 and remits to parent. In December, subsidiary repays loan plus interest on loan at 12 percent and charges parent for the interest.

Alternative 3:   Accept exchange rate risk. The parent is paid at the spot rate in December 1972.

A. How much does U.S. parent receive under the three alternatives?

B. Which alternative should it select?

C. Before the fact, what factors would it consider before selecting among the three alternatives?

PROBLEM 5–3

The 10 leading countries of the world have reached a currency agreement on the devaluation of the dollar in terms of gold and an upward revision of the exchange rate for certain European countries plus Japan. Under these circumstances one would expect that no further deterioration in the exchange rate value of the dollar in terms of foreign currency units would take place. Why didn't speculation stop and dollars flow back to the United States?

PROBLEM 5–4

A. The Multinat Company has an investment opportunity requiring an outlay of 200 million cruzeiros. The exchange rate (X_0) at the time was 200 cruzeiros to the dollar. The percentage increase in the cruzeiro value of the cruzeiro investment during the one-year life of the investment (g_F) was expected to be 50 percent. The percentage decrease in the value of the cruzeiro $(X_1 - X_0)/X_0$ on the free market during the one-year period was expected to be 10 percent. The number of cruzeiros received from the Bank of Brazil for each dollar swapped (S_0) is 100.

Questions:
1.   What would Multinat's gain without a swap be?
2.   What would Multinat's gain with a swap be?

B. Assume that the percentage decrease in the value of the cruzeiro was 40 percent. Answer 1 and 2.

C. Assume the original conditions again except that the number of cruzeiros received from the Bank of Brazil for each dollar in the swap is 50. Answer 1 and 2.

PROBLEM 5–5

As a result of rapid expansion the Colombo subsidiary of Stewart Manufacturing finds itself with an excess of monetary assets such as cash and accounts receivable. The majority of the funds for the expansion have come from Stewart Manufacturing in the form of U.S. dollar loans since local currency funds are costly in Colombo due to a high rate of annual price level increases and currency devaluation averaging about 25 percent per year.

Presently, the subsidiary has a net monetary position, that is, an excess of monetary assets over monetary liabilities of LC 10 million. The exchange rate is presently LC 50 per U.S. dollar. The subsidiary needs more funds. As a last resort, Stewart Manufacturing will furnish additional sums which it has to borrow in the United States at an annual rate of 8 percent. Occasionally local currency funds can be obtained on a three-month discounted basis at an annual cost of 30 percent per year.

The financial vice president has been asked to make a recommendation in regard to the source of the added funds required.

SELECTED BIBLIOGRAPHY

Alchian, Armen A., and Kessel, Ruben A. "Redistribution of Wealth through Inflation," *Science*, Vol. 130 (September 4, 1959), 535–39.

Einzig, Paul. *A Dynamic Theory of Forward Exchange*. London: Macmillan Co., Ltd., 1961.

Financing Foreign Operations, pp. 18, 19, 102, 103. New York: Business International, Inc., October 1961.

Furlong, William L. "Minimizing Foreign Exchange Losses," *Accounting Review*, April 1966, pp. 244–52.

International Financial Statistics. Washington, D.C., International Monetary Fund, all issues.

McMillan, Claude. "The Swap as a Hedge in Foreign Exchange," *California Management Review*, Vol. 4, No. 4 (Summer 1962), pp. 57–65.

Reimann, Guenter, and Wigglesworth, Edwin F. (eds.) *The Challenge of International Finance*. New York: McGraw-Hill Book Co., 1966.

Sweeny, H. W. Allen. "Protective Measures against Devaluation," *Financial Executive*, Vol. 36, No. 1 (January 1968), pp. 28–37.

6

The accounting treatment of
foreign operations

THE ACCOUNTING problems of foreign operations generally divide into two classes: First are the accounting problems encountered within the country of operation, such as the revaluation of assets, etc., in the face of loss of purchasing power of the national currency. Second are the problems encountered when converting the accounting figures in a foreign currency into those of the parent organization.

It is generally recognized, even in the United States, that continuing large increases in price levels make normal accounting practices obsolete. Normal accounting practices are based on recovery of historical asset costs. With large price level increases, they do not provide the necessary funds for asset replacement. In the United States no general effort has been made so far to adjust for internal price level changes. In contrast to this, many foreign countries have permitted asset write-ups which create additional depreciation, resulting in moderating taxes on overstated reported profits. However the policies of various countries have not been at all uniform. Some permit the write-up of assets with price level changes but then deny that the added values may be used as depreciation to reduce income taxes.

Even in the United States specific efforts such as the shift from first-in, first-out (Fifo) to last-in, first-out (Lifo) inventory costing procedures have been used to avoid the distortions resulting from persistently rising price levels. When price levels are rising, current replacement or opportunity costs are higher than historical costs. The use of Fifo inventory costing understates costs recorded in the income statement to calculate net income. One example would be the use of parts purchased one month before for $10 each, but which now cost $12 because of a recent price increase. The use of historical costs (e.g., Fifo) results in an understatement of costs and a consequent overstatement of net income before taxes. One of the undesirable consequences is that the firm's income taxes based on its overstated profits are higher than they otherwise would be.

ASSET UPWARD REVALUATION AS A RESULT OF INFLATION

Some foreign countries have recognized the necessity of reflecting inflationary price rises in their accounting procedures. Among the countries permitting some price level adjustment in their accounting are Argentina, Brazil, Chile, Peru, Australia, Canada, Great Britain, France, and Germany. The details of the rules pertaining to asset revaluation vary from country to country. Australia, Canada, and Great Britain permit asset write-ups but do not require them. However, the asset write-up in those countries is not permitted to result in added depreciation allowances, thus saving its companies taxes. By contrast, Italy, Japan, Argentina, and Chile permit increased depreciation for tax purposes of the added balance sheet values created by asset revaluation. However, Brazil, one of the countries suffering most from continued inflation, permits asset write-up but does not permit this write-up to result in additional depreciation expenses for tax-deductibility purposes.

There is general agreement in most countries that fixed, long-term assets require upward revaluation as the upward trend of price levels continues. Such long-term fixed assets are real assets that tend to maintain their real value, in contrast with monetary assets which have fixed values. Such agreement, unfortunately, does not exist relative to the accounting treatment of inventory. Goods in inventory in many countries are treated as current assets; that is, their value is continued at the original production or purchase price. However, in actuality most business firms operating under inflationary conditions find that inventory costs increase as price level rises take place. To solve this problem many multinational firms convert local investing purchases into U.S. dollars using the spot rate on the date of purchase and then, later, determine the local selling price by the use of the spot rate in effect at that time.

When asset write-ups are made, an offsetting revaluation reserve is created on the net worth or capital side of the balance sheet. This increase in capital values is taxed by some countries and not by others. Argentina and Brazil permit the issuance of tax-free stock dividends to offset part of this revaluation reserve and tax only that portion that is not reflected in the issuance of additional common stock. Germany levies a small tax on revalued net worth, and France and Belgium tax only that part of the revaluation surplus which is eventually capitalized into common stock.

Example of the use of revaluation reserves for asset write-ups

Rio Cimento S.A. has been operating in a country with a high rate of inflation. Its balance sheet at the end of 1970 is as follows:

RIO CIMENTO S.A.
Balance Sheet as of December 31, 1970
(in thousands of LC)

Current assets...............	1,000	Current liabilities..............	500
Gross plant and equipment.....	10,000	Long-term debt...............	1,000
Reserve for depreciation.......	5,000	Common stock................	1,500
Net plant and equipment......	5,000	Revaluation reserve...........	0
		Retained earnings..............	3,000
		Total Liabilities	
Total Assets............	6,000	and Capital............	6,000

It was determined that a revaluation of the assets of 20 percent was appropriate because of a decline in the purchasing power of the local currency of 20 percent during 1970. The Net Plant and Equipment account is increased by 20 percent or LC 1,000,000 in this example. The revaluation reserve is credited by a like amount of LC 1,000,000. The new balance sheet is as follows:

RIO CIMENTO S.A.
Balance Sheet as of January 15, 1971
(in thousands of LC)

Current assets...............	1,000	Current liabilities..............	500
Gross plant and equipment.....	11,000	Long-term debt...............	1,000
Reserve for depreciation.......	5,000	Common stock................	1,500
Net plant and equipment......	6,000	Revaluation reserve...........	1,000
		Retained earnings..............	3,000
		Total Liabilities	
Total Assets............	7,000	and Capital............	7,000

The revaluation reserve is then debited by LC 1,000,000, the amount of the stock dividend. The Common Stock account is credited (increased) by a corresponding amount. In some countries the increase in the Gross Plant and Equipment account may be written off in tax-deductible depreciation. The book value of the shareholders' equity has increased only by the amount of the effect of inflation on the replacement cost of the firm's fixed assets. The new balance sheet after the stock dividend is as follows:

RIO CIMENTO S.A.
Balance Sheet as of January 15, 1971
(in thousands of LC)

Current assets...............	1,000	Current liabilities..............	500
Gross plant and equipment.....	11,000	Long-term debt...............	1,000
Reserve for depreciation.......	5,000	Common stock................	2,500
Net plant and equipment......	6,000	Revaluation reserve...........	0
		Retained earnings..............	3,000
		Total Liabilities	
Total Assets............	7,000	and Capital............	7,000

In Brazil and Chile asset revaluations are permitted on an annual basis. Shortly after the end of each calendar year the Economics Department of each government publishes a price level change indicator for use in revaluation of asset and capital accounts. For example, early in 1968 the Brazilian government published, as shown in Table 6–1, a set of coefficients extending back to 1938 that permitted companies to readjust the net asset value of long-term assets still in use at the end of 1967. These coefficients are multipliers that may be applied to the net asset value of long-term assets purchased during the year indicated. Since this policy was adopted in Brazil, business firms have made adjustments annually as soon as the multiplier for the year just completed is published by the Government Economic Office.

TABLE 6–1

Government price level change indicator for Brazil, 1938–67

Year	Coefficients	Year	Coefficients
1938	410.22	1953	70.23
1939	388.04	1954	55.43
1940	365.82	1955	48.04
1941	322.60	1956	40.65
1942	269.77	1957	36.96
1943	232.83	1958	31.41
1944	203.26	1959	22.91
1945	173.69	1960	17.38
1946	151.52	1961	12.57
1947	140.43	1962	8.13
1948	133.04	1963	3.69
1949	121.94	1964	2.12
1950	107.16	1965	1.67
1951	83.69	1966	1.22
1952	81.30	1967	1.00

Argentina has permitted the upward revaluation of assets only twice, once in 1960 and a second time in 1968. Chile permits a deduction from income subject to taxes based on the excess of amount by which 20 percent of the capital accounts exceeds the permitted price level adjustment write-up of the investment and fixed asset items. The amount of the deduction from income subject to taxes is limited to 20 percent of the initial taxable income amount.

Example of the effects of revaluation on measurement of taxable income

The Chilian subsidiary of Multinat had taxable income of E° 100,000 during 1968, a year in which there was an assumed increase of 20 percent in the cost of living and devaluation of 40 percent of the escudo in relation to the U.S. dollar. The subsidiary had purchased E° 200,000 worth of equipment (obligated in terms of U.S. dollars) and was carrying this long-term foreign debt on its balance sheet as a separate item.

UNIDAS INDUSTRIES S.A.
Balance Sheet as of December 31, 1968
(in thousands of escudos)

	Original	*Change*	*Final*
Current assets..........................	400	0	400
Investments............................	100	20	120
Fixed assets:			
Foreign-purchased fixed assets...........	200	80	280
Reserve for depreciation.................	10	0	10
Net foreign-purchased assets.............	190	80	270
Other plant and equipment*.............	2,000	160	2,160
Reserve for depreciation.................	1,200	0	1,200
Net other plant and equipment*..........	800	160	960
Total Assets.....................	1,490	260	1,750
Current liabilities.......................	100	0	100
Long-term foreign debt...................	200	80	280
Other long-term debt....................	100	0	100
Capital and reserves.....................	1,090	200–20	1,270
Total Liabilities and Capital.........	1,490	260	1,750

° The depreciated value of "other plant and equipment" is used.

The assets purchased by long-term debt in terms of U.S. dollars are increased by 40 percent as the local currency value of the foreign long-term debt increases by the same percentage. This increase can be depreciated in following years.

Investments, net other fixed assets, and the capital and reserves accounts are all increased by the cost-of-living increase multiplier of 20 percent. If there is an excess increase of the capital accounts over those on the asset side of the balance sheet, an amount equal to 20 percent of the firm's before-tax income may be used to reduce this item and thereby reduce income taxes. Any excess above that is lost and represents a decrease in the adjustment of the capital accounts.

In the above example, 20 percent of the capital accounts was E° 218,000. Investments were written up by E° 20,000, and net fixed assets by E° 160,000, the total being E° 180,000. Therefore, the potential deduction from taxable income is E° 48,000. But the limit is 20 percent of taxable income or E° 20,000. Hence E° 18,000 of the increase in the capital accounts is lost permanently as a reduction from taxable income.

The foregoing example illustrates the technical nature of regulations in foreign countries with regard to the upward revaluation of assets and its effects on tax liabilities. Practice varies greatly. In a world of continuing inflation, it is essential that the financial manager of a multinational firm study the rules and regulations for each foreign country in which his firm is now operating or planning to conduct operations.

FINANCIAL TRANSLATION—PREVAILING PRACTICES

Of greatest importance to the financial manager of a multinational firm are the practices and customs followed when converting financial results of foreign operations from the foreign balance sheet and profit and loss statement into U.S. dollars. The general practice is to carry long-term assets on the U.S. books of the parent corporation on the basis of their dollar value at the time of purchase, less applied depreciation, which is also figured on a dollar basis. This reflects the prevailing treatment of the parent company's own fixed assets. When long-term assets are finally disposed of or sold, their sale price is converted into dollars and compared with existing book values in dollars at the time of sale. Gains or losses are then recognized on a dollar basis.

Example of translating foreign subsidiary's value into U.S. dollars

On January 10, 1965, Multinat's foreign subsidiary purchased plant and equipment valued at LC 200 million. At the time of purchase the exchange rate between the local currency and the U.S. dollar was LC 100 per dollar. This purchase resulted in an entry in Multinat's books for this subsidiary of 200,000,000/100 = $2,000,000 for foreign plant and equipment added.

Depreciation on this equipment was scheduled over a 20-year period or $100,000 per year. The plant and equipment were sold early in 1971 at a price of LC 540 million. The spot rate at the time of sale was LC 300 per U.S. dollar. Therefore, the sale price in dollars of the plant and equipment was 540,000,000/300 = $1,800,000. The accounts for the plant and equipment at the time of sale were:

Foreign plant and equipment	2,000,000
Less: Reserve for depreciation	600,000
Net book value	1,400,000

The sale thus resulted in a gain of $400,000 ($1,800,000 − $1,400,000).

Practices with respect to the treatment of inventories are somewhat different. All inventory items purchased for a foreign subsidiary in terms of dollars are recorded at their dollar values on the books of the parent corporation. Those inventory items purchased in various foreign countries are converted to dollar prices at the spot rates then ruling and are kept in terms of dollars thereafter. When inventories are used in the manufacturing process, they are charged to the inventory account at their dollar values on the books of the parent corporation. When inventories are sold, the amount realized is expressed in dollars based on the current spot rate and charged to the inventory account on that basis.

In several countries where persistent increases in price levels take place, many multinational firms practice dual bookkeeping for inventory. Inventories are kept on the basis of the local national currency as well as in dollars. When items are finally sold or used out of inventory, the dollar prices are converted to local currency using the existing spot rate for the two currencies. The charge to the inventory account expressed in local currency units will not be greatly different from the inventory value expressed in local currency units since all but most recent exchange rate fluctuations will already have been reflected in the dual bookkeeping accounts.

Monetary assets and liabilities, financial items which do not change in value in terms of the local currency, are translated into dollars using the spot rate existing on the statement day. This represents a distinct change from practices prevalent 10 to 15 years ago. It was then considered proper that long-term monetary assets and liabilities should be stated at their dollar value at the time of their original acquisition. However, current practices permit the translation of local currency values of all monetary assets and liabilities, both short term and long term, into dollars using the spot rate on the date of translation.

With devaluation of the foreign currency, monetary liabilities decrease in dollar value, thereby resulting in a gain which should be recognized in a revaluation reserve account. Funds in this revaluation account can then be used to offset losses due to downward revaluation of monetary assets. Any time the local currency decreases in value in relation to the dollar, all monetary assets will drop in dollar value, causing a corresponding dollar loss. The reverse pattern occurs with upward revaluation of foreign currencies in relation to the dollar.

Example of accounting translation

The following is an example of the accounting treatment of balance sheet items by a foreign subsidiary and its multinational parent. First given are the subsidiary's and parent's balance sheets at the end of 1965. The last two are as of the end of 1966, a year later. At the end of 1965 the exchange rate was LC 5 per dollar; at the end of 1966 it was LC 6 per dollar. The subsidiary purchased LC 6,000,000 worth of fixed assets during 1966. Inventories are assumed to have been purchased during the year on the balance sheet date. There was no change in the long-term debt during the interval.

At the beginning of 1965 the net monetary assets (monetary assets minus monetary liabilities) of the subsidiary were $1,000 - (500 + 6,000)$ $= -$ LC 5,500,000. At the end of 1966 the net monetary assets were $1,400 - (700 + 6,000) = -$LC 5,300,000. The average of these two values is $-$ LC 5,400,000. Since during the year the change in the foreign exchange value of the local currency was from 5 per dollar to 6 per dollar,

Subsidiary's Balance Sheet as of December 31, 1965
(in thousands of LC)

Monetary assets	1,000	Current liabilities	500
Inventories	5,000	Long-term debt	6,000
Fixed assets	20,000	Net worth	15,500
Reserve for			
depreciation	4,000		
Net fixed assets	16,000	Total Liabilities	
Total Assets	22,000	and Capital	22,000

(in thousands of U.S. dollars)

Monetary assets	200	Current liabilities	100
Inventories	1,000	Long-term debt	1,200
Fixed assets*	6,000	Revaluation reserve	400
Reserve for		Net worth	4,400
depreciation†	1,100		
Net fixed assets	4,900	Total Liabilities	
Total Assets	6,100	and Capital	6,100

Subsidiary's Balance Sheet as of December 31, 1966
(in thousands of LC)

Monetary assets	1,400	Current liabilities	700
Inventories	6,000	Long-term debt	6,000
Fixed assets	26,000	Net worth	21,700
Reserve for depre-			
ciation	5,000		
Net fixed assets	21,000	Total Liabilities	
Total Assets	28,400	and Capital	28,400

(in thousands of U.S. dollars)

Monetary assets	233	Current liabilities	117
Inventories	1,000	Long-term debt	1,000
Fixed assets‡	7,000	Revaluation account	580
Reserve for		Net worth	4,136
depreciation§	1,400		
Net fixed assets	5,600	Total Liabilities	
Total Assets	6,833	and Capital	6,833

* The fixed assets shown are not in the relationship of 5 to 1 to those shown on the foreign balance sheet because the majority were purchased in prior years when the exchange ratio between the two currencies was lower.

† Depreciation write-off is over a period of 20 years.

‡ The LC 6,000,000 fixed assets purchased during the year are converted to U.S. dollars at the 6 to 1 rate and added to the fixed asset account.

§ One twentieth of LC 6,000,000 was added to the reserve for depreciation account.

the gain from this was 5,400 (1/5 − 1/6) or 5,400/30 = LC 180,000. This is the amount that has been added to the revaluation reserve on the books of the parent and will be used to offset future foreign exchange rate losses.

When operations take place in a foreign country suffering from persistent rapid increases in price levels, decreases in the foreign exchange value of the local currency take place at frequent intervals. It is then generally advisable to develop a monthly average exchange rate to convert monthly operating results into dollars. Where changes in the exchange rate are not particularly severe, two or three changes in the conversion rate may be sufficient during each year.

It should be obvious from the above discussion that in countries with a continuing inflationary bias, local management of subsidiaries should be encouraged to follow these policies:

1. Never have excessive idle cash on hand. If cash accumulates it should be used to purchase inventory or other real assets.
2. Attempt to avoid granting excessive trade credit or normal trade credit for extended periods. If accounts receivable cannot be avoided, an attempt should be made to charge interest high enough to compensate for the loss of purchasing power.
3. Avoid, wherever possible, giving advances in connection with purchase orders unless a rate of interest is paid by the seller on these advances from the time you, the buyer, pay them to the time of delivery, at a rate sufficient to cover the loss of purchasing power.
4. Borrow local currency funds from banks or other sources whenever these funds can be obtained at a rate of interest equal to or smaller than the anticipated rate of devaluation.
5. Make an effort to purchase materials and supplies locally in the country in which the foreign subsidiary is operating on a trade credit basis, extending the final date of payment as long as possible.

The principles involved in the above recommendations were discussed in Chapter 5 among the various means of avoiding foreign exchange rate losses.

FINANCIAL TRANSLATION—EMERGING PRINCIPLES AND PRACTICES

The general prevailing financial translation practices as described above represent a combination of the so-called current-noncurrent approach and the monetary-nonmonetary approach. The current-noncurrent approach assumes that fixed assets were acquired at the historical exchange rate and that any inflation in local currency has not changed the real value of the fixed assets. The current-noncurrent approach also assumes that inventories, since they are usually turned over from 8 to 10 times a year, will reflect current exchange rates if exchange rate changes do not occur more frequently than inventory turnover rates. On this basis, fixed assets are translated at the historical exchange rate as of date of purchase. Inventories are translated at current exchange rates on the assumption that these were the exchange rates in effect as of the date of purchase of the inventories. Inventories and fixed assets represent the real assets on the assets side of the balance sheet.

The current-noncurrent approach value called for translation of long-term debt at the old exchange rates. This appears to involve a logical error because the long-term debt obligation is expressed in local currency units. With the shift in exchange rates the current dollar value in relation to LCs has changed in relationship to the historical dollars received; therefore, a gain or loss has actually taken place.

Therefore, over a period of years modifications of the current-noncurrent approach took place. Practice has moved toward the monetary rule which provides that current exchange rates are applicable to the translation of all monetary assets and liabilities, while historical exchange rates are applicable to real assets. *APB Opinion*, No. 6, issued in 1965, recognized the monetary rule to be "appropriate in many circumstances." The preliminary draft of a new Accounting Principles Board ruling on financial translation indicates that it will follow the "so-called monetary rule that provides for restatement of all balance sheet items that have a specific dollar value."[1] The Accounting Principles Board is further recommending that after calculating a "loss" or "exchange adjustment" due to inflation and new exchange rates, firms should not charge the full amount in the year in which it is reported. The total of these "exchange adjustments" should be deferred over the life of the debt involved.

Since accounting opinion is moving toward the monetary rule, we shall illustrate its application and then contrast it with the prevailing practice we have already described. In the following example, we set forth the books of the United States Company covering a subsidiary operating in West Germany. In column 1 the subsidiary books are expressed in marks. In column 2 the subsidiary books are translated into dollars by the monetary rule. It is assumed that the old exchange rate was four marks to the dollar and that the new exchange rate is three marks to the dollar. All monetary assets and liabilities are translated at the new exchange rate while all real assets are translated at the appropriate historical exchange rate. Following this rule we can determine the effects of the firm's net monetary liability position. This is set forth in Memorandum Analysis No. 1. Effects of the new exchange rate on the net monetary asset or liability position of the subsidiary are shown on page 132.

Because the firm in the analysis is in a net monetary liability position and the value of the foreign currency has risen in relationship to the dollar, the new value of this net obligation expressed in the new exchange rate has increased by $300. This represents an increase in the foreign currency value of its debt obligations or a loss. It will be noted that when this $300 loss is entered into the books of the subsidiary as translated into

---

[1] Charles N. Stabler, "Accounting Panel, in Reversal Now Favors Deferring Losses in Dollar Cheapening," *The Wall Street Journal*, December 15, 1971, p. 2.

U.S. COMPANY
Balance Sheets for December 31, 1971

	(1) Subsidiary books in DM		Exchange rate	(2) Translated by the monetary rule	
Cash........................	DM 1,200		3/1	$ 400	
Receivables.................	2,400		3/1	800	
Inventories.................	3,600		4/1	900	
Current Assets..........		DM 7,200			$2,100
Gross plant and equipment...............	9,600				
Less: Reserve for depreciation.............	1,200				
Net plant and equipment......	8,400		4/1		2,100
Total Assets..........		DM 15,600			$4,200
Current payables............	2,400		3/1	800	
Long-term debt.............	4,800		3/1	1,600	
Total Debt.............		DM 7,200	3/1		$2,400
Capital stock.............	6,000		4/1		
Retained income............	2,400		4/1		
Exchange adjustment account..................					(300)
Revaluation account.........					
Net worth.................		8,400			2,100
Total Liabilities and Net Worth..........		DM 15,600			$4,200

Net monetary liabilities position...................... DM 3,600
Value in dollars at exchange rate of DM 4 to $1   900
Value in dollars at exchange rate of DM 3 to $1 1,200
Increase in net obligations (loss).................... ($ 300)

dollars, the balance sheet is in balance. This result is in contrast to the prevailing practice in which if inventories are translated at the current rate, the changes in the asset items will be out of balance with the exchange adjustment account calculated purely on the basis of the analysis of the net monetary position of the company.

In our judgment there are two arguments in support of the full application of the monetary rule that appears to be in process of being recommended by the Accounting Principles Board. The first is that if inflation has been taking place, there is a strong argument for using the last-in, first-out method of inventory costing as described earlier in this chapter. This provides that current operations are charged with current costs of inventory. The balance sheet implication of the Lifo method of inventory costing is to maintain the balance sheet value of the inventory at its historical acquired basis. This therefore provides a further justification for applying the historical exchange rate to inventories as well as to fixed assets. The second benefit is that there will be an internal consistency between the exchange adjustment account calculated by analysis of the net monetary asset or liabilities position of the firm and the change in the other balance sheet account.[2]

Thus it appears to us that if the prevailing accounting practice of valuing fixed assets at historical costs and of charging inventories at current cost using Lifo (which results in carrying inventories on the balance sheet at their historical cost), the application of the monetary rule for international financial translation will yield internally consistent and correct results.

SUMMARY

It is difficult to generalize as to the accounting treatment for inflation in individual countries. Our main emphasis would be on charging current operations with the current or opportunity costs of the use of both fixed assets and inventories. Not only is this conceptually correct, but it avoids erosion of the real physical quantities of assets required to conduct business. With regard to inventories this is accomplished by using the last-in, first-out (Lifo) method. This charges current operations with the most recent cost of inventories and leaves the balance sheet value of inventories at historical or acquisition costs which then provide the appropriate basis for the application of the net monetary rule in financial translation.

With regard to fixed assets, the application of the monetary rule requires that the fixed assets be carried at their original acquisition costs and then the historical exchange rate is applied in financial translation. However, in a number of countries provision is made for writing up the value of fixed assets by a government-provided index. This higher value is then used as a basis for reducing taxable income by making the depreciation charge to taxable income at a level that reflects the values of real assets as they would be expressed at current price level. This avoids applying taxation to overstated amounts of reported profits.

There are generally two methods of translating foreign corporate balance sheet and profit and loss statement items into terms of the home country currency of the parent organization. The existing free market spot rate between the two currencies is used in the translation of monetary assets and monetary liabilities. The historic foreign exchange rate, the

---

[2] Therefore, the argument by Zenoff and Zwick and others that the net monetary rule can be applied only when the rate of inflation is equal to the rate of devaluation in the subsidiary's country is invalid because it fails to recognize that the shift in the exchange rate reflects the combined effects of the rate of inflation in the local currency country and in the parent. D. B. Zenoff and J. Zwick, *International Financial Management* (Englewood Cliffs, N.J.: Prentice-Hall, Inc., 1969), pp. 485–510. The new exchange rate reflects the situation in the country of the subsidiary as well as in the country of the parent, as well as many other factors such as government official transactions, speculative activity which may be either stabilizing or destabilizing, cost trends in export goods versus cost trends in domestic goods, etc.

rate existing at the time of acquisition, governs the translation of the historical balance sheet values of fixed assets and inventories into dollars. If the above-discussed accounting procedures are followed, the gains and losses due to the foreign exchange rate value change of local currency are then recognized on the books of the parent corporation as gains and losses in terms of dollars and are accumulated or charged against a foreign exchange rate risk reserve account.

PROBLEM 6-1

Multinat plans to make an investment of LC 200 million in a South American subsidiary: 150 million on an equity and 50 million on a long-term debt basis. At the time of the investment the spot rate will be LC 100 per U.S. dollar. The LC 200 million will be spent on land, 200 million on plant and equipment, and 120 million (including the $300,000 value of equipment from the United States) to establish the subsidiary. The remainder of the funds will be invested in working capital including cash. To obtain some protection against devaluation, the subsidiary will borrow on a roll-over short-term basis LC 50 million at a cost of 15 percent per year. Its earnings before interest and taxes (EBIT) on total assets will average 30 percent per year after the second year. During the first year these same profits will be 10 percent and in the second, 20 percent. Calculate EBIT on the basis of total assets at the beginning of each period. Inventory investment at the beginning will be LC 10 million which is expected to grow in terms of the local currency at a rate of 30 percent per year. Accounts payable and other payables are expected to increase by LC 20 million per year for the first five years. The rate of devaluation during the first five years is expected to average 20 percent per year. The sub will use straight-line depreciation and will depreciate its plant and equipment over a 10-year period.

For the sake of simplification assume that the annual addition to inventory takes place at the end of each year. To protect its investment in the instance of the LC 50 million loan, Multinat arranged for a currency swap for a five-year term with a swap rate of LC 80 per U.S. dollar and interest of 6 percent on the local funds obtained. Multinat charges its subsidiary 10 percent interest on the dollars tied up to make the swap possible. No dividends will be paid. The subsidiary's income tax rate is 50 percent.

A. Develop the balance sheets for the subsidiary as of the date of its establishment and then for the end of each of the first three years. Express these in LC as well as in dollars.

B. Develop an income statement in LC for each of the first three years.

PROBLEM 6-2

This problem is based on the data given in Problem 1 in which Multinat utilizes a local currency swap. In this problem it is now assumed that Multinat does not utilize swap protection. The problem requires that the outcome be measured in terms of dollars and local currency under the following conditions:

A. Multinat makes a local currency loan to its subsidiary at a 15 percent interest rate without swap protection.

B. Multinat makes the loan to its subsidiary, but the obligation of the subsidiary will be in terms of dollars and bear an interest rate of 10 percent. Will the subsidiary realize enough on the transaction to repay the loan expressed in terms of dollars?

PROBLEM 6-3

A Chilean subsidiary has investments of E° 10 million and net plant and equipment of E° 50 million. In addition it has net E° 5 million of equipment that was foreign purchased on an external debt basis on which is still owed E° 6 million. The net worth of the firm is E° 90 million. During the year just passed, its income after taxes was E° 10 million. The local change in price levels during the previous year was 15 percent; and the drop in the value of the escudo, 20 percent. The firm's tax rate is 50 percent, current assets are E° 55 million, and current liabilities, E° 19 million.

Show the before and after adjustment balance sheets of this firm in escudos.

PROBLEM 6-4

Shown below is the balance sheet of Multinat's subsidiary operating in a country suffering from serious inflation:

Balance Sheet of Subsidiary as of December 31, 1971
(in thousands of LC)

Cash....................	1,200	Current payables..........	2,400
Receivables.............	2,400	Long-term debt...........	4,800
Inventories.............	5,400	Total Debt...........	7,200
Current Assets........	9,000	Common stock...........	6,000
		Retained earnings.........	8,400
Net plant and		Net worth...............	14,400
equipment............	12,600	Total Liabilities	
Total Assets........	21,600	and Net Worth...	21,600

A. When the assets of the subsidiary were acquired and its debt obligations incurred, the exchange rate was LC 4 for $1, and as of the new balance sheet date of December 31, 1971, the exchange rate was LC 5 per $1. How much in dollars is the change in the real net worth position of the subsidiary due to the devaluation of the local currency?

B. Translate the balance sheet of the subsidary into dollars applying the net monetary rule. Discuss your results.

PROBLEM 6-5

Assume the same facts as in Problem 4 except that the parent firm has another subsidiary, Superbo, Inc., and that the new exchange rate expressed as the number of LC units to a dollar is 3 to 1. This problem reflects the situation of a subsidiary operating in Western Europe.

A. When the real assets of the subsidiary were acquired and its debt obligations incurred, the exchange rate was LC 4 per $1. What is the gain or loss from financial translation reflecting the effects of the new rate?

B. Translate the balance sheet of the subsidiary applying the monetary rule. Discuss your results.

SELECTED BIBLIOGRAPHY

Basche, James R., Jr. *Measuring Profitability of Foreign Operations.* Managing International Business, Survey by the Conference Board, No. 7, 1970.

Berg, Kenneth B., Mueller, Gerhard G.; and Walker, Lauren M. (eds). *Readings in International Accounting.* Boston, Mass.: Houghton Mifflin Co., 1969.

Browne, Dudley. "Differences between U.S. and Foreign Reporting," *Financial Executive,* January 1963.

Hayes, Donald J. "Translating Foreign Currencies," *Harvard Business Review,* Vol. 50, No. 1 (January–February 1972), pp. 6–7, 11–15, 18, 158–59.

Keegan, Warren J. "Multinational Pricing: How Far Is Arm's Length?" *Columbia Journal of World Business,* Vol. 4, No. 3 (May–June 1969), pp. 57–66.

MacNeill, James H. "Accounting for Inflation Abroad," *Journal of Accountancy* (August 1961).

Zenoff, D. B., and Zwick, J. *International Financial Management.* Englewood Cliffs, N.J.: Prentice-Hall, Inc., 1969.

7

Government policies and rules
affecting international business

THE MAJORITY of government policies and regulations imposed on international businesses have their origin in international balance of payments or foreign exchange shortage problems. The initiation and adoption of these policies and rules have stemmed from government efforts to solve these two pressing problems. Most European countries and almost all developing countries have continuously imposed limitations and restrictions on capital flows related to international business activities. Until 1966 the United States was one of the few countries among the trading nations of the world that placed no restrictions on the flow of capital funds into or out of the country. Due to chronic U.S. balance-of-payments problems, which have continuously worsened since 1957, even the U.S. government has been forced to initiate policies and regulations which have affected both international trade and the flow of funds. These regulations have continued to become more severe with each passing year.

The purposes of the rules and controls adopted by various countries have been twofold: (1) to reduce the outflow of much-needed foreign exchange reserves by restricting capital flows, and (2) to increase the volume of exports of goods and services in order to earn additional foreign exchange to overcome the country's foreign exchange shortage. The government policies and rules designed to decrease the outflow of foreign exchange will be discussed first since the problems created by these rules are the most directly troublesome to the multinational firm in seeking to finance its overseas operations.

THE PRESERVATION OF FOREIGN
EXCHANGE RESERVES

As pointed out in Chapter 3, a continuing deterioration of a country's balance-of-payments position will cause a weakening of its foreign exchange reserve position. This means that as a given country spends more of its currency in the rest of the world than the rest of the world spends within that country, the rest of the world will build up a totality of claims against the given country which eventually must be satisfied. It is this process of satisfying the claims of foreigners which results in a shortage of foreign exchange reserves, since these reserves are used to settle foreign claims. It is when foreign exchange reserves are low and no additions are available that governments, including the United States, resort to measures to prevent a further deterioration of their foreign exchange reserve positions.

The first measure adopted is usually one of limiting the outflow of capital funds to other nations. In this connection the U.S. government in 1967 established the interest equalization tax which was designed to make the borrowing of long-term funds in the United States as expensive, or more so, than borrowing these same funds in other capital markets. When this proved insufficient, the U.S. government, at first on a voluntary basis, established certain limits governing the outflow of funds for foreign investment purposes on the part of U.S. multinational firms. The small number of firms at first involved in this "voluntary" program has grown in number over the years; and new policies and procedures have been developed by the Commerce Department, which was chosen to manage and oversee this capital-outflow-limitation program.

The restrictions on capital flows have become more severe over time. Today it is nearly impossible for a U.S. corporation to export additional capital funds for investment in developed countries. Even for semi- or underdeveloped countries it is sometimes difficult to obtain the required permissions to make investments of U.S. dollars for foreign business purposes. In defense of the actions of the U.S. government, it must be stated that the private sectors of other trading nations have never enjoyed the same relative freedom to make investment decisions without regard to their nation's foreign balance-of-payments position as has the U.S. private sector. Capital transfers on the part of firms as well as individuals have long been controlled by the majority of the nations of the world.

When foreign exchange controls are established, their principle purpose is to decrease the outflow of foreign exchange reserves. In addition to government rules prohibiting the export of capital funds, the limited foreign exchange reserves are rationed to permit payment for the most desired imports. Many governments establish a list of import priorities for which the expenditure of foreign exchange will be approved. These import controls are established to prevent import of goods considered unimportant to the development of the nation's economy. When foreign exchange reserve problems temporarily become very severe, a complete prohibition of any and all imports, no matter for what purpose, may result. Fortunately, these most severe conditions do not usually continue for long periods at a time.

However, a multinational firm attempting to operate one of its subsidiaries in a country under these severe restrictions may find it difficult to conduct its business on rational economic principles. Often very much-needed parts that are usually imported from the home country are required in order to keep manufacturing processes going on a normal basis. Since business control devices usually strain a government's administrative capability, delays and inflexibilities become characteristic in the handling of these programs. Offers by businesses to import much-needed goods without requiring eventual payment in foreign currencies go unheeded, since the complexities of seeking to substitute regulation for a price system do not afford time for analysis of individual situations. In our experience there have been numerous instances where the foreign government would have saved considerable sums if it had permitted the importation of a few needed parts so that service to one of the foreign government's own agencies could have been continued.

In addition to placing controls on the transfer of funds to pay for imports, governments often impose severe restrictions on the transfer of funds to pay dividends or interest to foreign owners, or even to permit the return of capital to foreign lenders. Export controls are established to make absolutely sure that no domestic business organization has the capability of secretly retaining foreign currencies which by law are required to be surrendered to the country's central bank as soon as received. These controls serve as a check so that the receipt of foreign exchange by export organizations can be anticipated in order to make certain that these funds are paid over to the country's central bank without delay.

One possible way for businesses to procure needed imports is for them to arrange two- or three-way barters with foreign exporters with government approval. Under this arrangement agreements are made between the importer and foreign importers and exporters to exchange certain domestic goods for foreign imports, without involving the exchange of currencies. Another solution sometimes possible is to propose to the local government various means of increasing overall exports. As an inducement for firms to engage in this desired activity, the government may grant permission for them to divert a small portion of the additional foreign exchange earned to purchase needed imports.

GOVERNMENT ACTIVITY TO INCREASE EXPORTS

Almost all nations of the world seek to stimulate the export of goods and services. The U.S. government has been involved in this activity since the establishment of the Export-Import Bank of Washington in 1933.

These export-promoting efforts may involve subsidies in the form of a reduction or refund of taxes that firms have previously paid on the exported goods. The reduction of taxes can make prices more competitive and serves as an inducement to greater export effort. Governments also provide assistance in planning and financial aids for developing new foreign markets for an exporter's products. In addition, governments furnish commercial- and political-risk export insurance at attractive rates to ease the financing of export trade by the exporting firms. This also serves as an inducement to greater export effort.

In the United States the recently formed Overseas Private Investment Corporation (OPIC) will assist U.S. exporters in launching commercial studies designed to increase the volume of exports of U.S. goods. Under certain conditions OPIC will even absorb part of the costs of such studies if the investigation turns out to be negative. Foreign investments that are required in connection with these export-promoting activities are readily approved and even insured for the lenders so that the needed funds may be readily procured. If it turns out that these investments are of a sufficiently long duration to satisfy the requirements of OPIC, the investments will even be insured under its investment insurance program which was detailed in Chapter 4. As was mentioned there, FCIA or Eximbank insurance of medium-term transactions in connection with export sales is limited to a maximum of seven years. However, under certain special circumstances in order to meet foreign competition, particularly that aided by foreign governments, U.S. authorities will consider insuring and assisting the financing of even longer-term transactions.

To further the development of exports from the United States, American export sales companies located outside the United States and formed for the purpose of export promotion activities are given special tax considerations by the Internal Revenue Service. Free zones are established by almost all countries in which foreign goods can be stored prior to import into the country or reexport to a third nation. Many countries have designated border areas in which they permit manufacturing facilities to be established that receive most of their supplies from foreign countries and which assemble the finished product for immediate export. Often these border industries are completely exempt from normal import limitations imposed on the remainder of the country.

Some governments pay their exporters direct subsidies to encourage an increase in the volume of exports. Others permit their exporters to retain a certain percentage of foreign exchange earned by previous exports and give them permission to spend this foreign exchange as they desire. Other countries refund any taxes that have been paid to the government at any stage of the production processes prior to export. Taxes paid on a "value-added" basis are also refunded to the exporting firm.

In an effort to stimulate further exports, many governments also grant special treatment to requests for needed imports by export-oriented industries. At times export-oriented industries are granted additional favors if a government practices multiple foreign exchange rates. The export industries are assigned a high rate of exchange which permits them to receive a relatively larger number of local currency units for foreign exchange when compared with those industries that are not so favored. Tax incentives are also used by governments to encourage the establishment of additional export-oriented industrial activities. These incentives may include complete tax exemption on profits from added exports for a specified number of years. Following an initial grace period, there is provision for a gradual increase of profit taxation over a specified period until finally taxes are levied on a normal basis.

Governments are broadening their efforts to encourage the increase of exports to earn additional foreign exchange. New devices and schemes are continuously being adopted in the various countries of the world. It is advisable, therefore, that an internationally operating multinational firm keep informed on the latest benefits and incentives that are offered by the governments of various foreign nations. These benefits should influence a management's choice of countries in which to conduct foreign-based operations.

THE INTERNATIONAL TAXATION OF INCOME

Almost all countries tax income at its source. The profits resulting from the operation of productive assets within a country are always taxed by its government. If taxation at the source were the sole concept of taxation, the tax problems of the multinational firm would be simple. Unfortunately, such is not the case.

General provisions relating to international taxation

In addition to taxation of income at the source, some governments levy taxes on the basis of the nationality or the domicile of the business entity. Some even levy taxes based on the location of control of the business venture. It is these different concepts of taxation that create difficulties in the form of multiple taxation of income for firms operating on an international basis.

The negative impact of multiple taxation on international business was recognized by the United States in the late eighteen hundreds. To remove this inequity the U.S. government entered into tax treaties with the governments of many trading nations of the world. These treaties spelled out the rights of their citizens and the taxes that they must pay as they conduct business in or with each other's countries. Tax treaties generally provide for domestic credits of foreign income taxes paid. A citizen who is taxed by his own country on the basis of nationality and is operating in a foreign country that taxes income at the source will receive credits by his government for the taxes that he was required to pay in the country of the tax-treaty partner. Tax treaties and conventions usually define the terms of residence, nationality, domicile, and control. They also usually limit the amount of taxes on unearned income such as dividends, royalties, and interest received.

There are variations in the rules that govern the manner in which these foreign taxes paid are applied or credited against domestic taxes due. Some taxing entities permit a percentage of the foreign taxes paid to be deducted from the foreign after-tax income, whereas other taxing entities insist that the full before-tax income be reported in the country of domicile or citizenship and that the foreign taxes paid then be deductible from the domestic taxes assessed.

To avoid multiple taxation on the basis of the location of control of a business venture, many British business firms located their managements abroad. Since this proved to be a disadvantage to the economy of Britain, the provisions of the United Kingdom Overseas Trading Act were changed in 1957, abandoning a concept of taxation that had been in effect since the early 1900s. When a country taxes income on the basis of residence of the shareholders and the location of management as well as the nationality of shareholders and place of incorporation, then international tax differentials may induce inefficiencies in the choice of nationality, place of incorporation, and location of management control as multinational firms plan their foreign operations.

Income resulting from sales to a foreign country is usually taxed only if the seller has a "permanent establishment" in the country of the buyer. It is for this reason that a multinational firm initiating business relationships with a particular country by the sales of its products is well advised to do this initially on a "nonestablishment" basis. This can be effected by travel of its personnel or by contractual relationships with foreign distributors who will handle all details as to sales and service during the initial period. In this way the many problems of taxation and other governmental rules can be avoided until it has been firmly established that there exists a sufficient demand for the company's products to warrant the establishment of a business organization in this foreign country. Income from royalties is normally not taxed by the country in which these are collected.

The United States taxes the income of U.S. citizens and corporations irrespective of where their income is earned or received, with few exceptions. The same applies even to U.S. noncitizen residents who have foreign-source incomes, even though they may have no income from within the United States.

Exceptions to general tax rules

Several exceptions are made to the general rules on taxation just set forth. One exception is made for earned foreign income in the case of U.S. citizens who live abroad.[1] Under these provisions a U.S. citizen who earns his livelihood and at the same time is a resident of a foreign country for a period in excess of 510 "full" days within an 18-month period is not taxed on the earned income obtained in the country of residence. The Internal Revenue Act of 1969 limited this exclusion to $20,000 per year during the first three years and $25,000 per year thereafter. However, such U.S. citizens residing in foreign areas must still report and pay taxes on all nonearned income such as royalties, dividends, and interest, whether of domestic or foreign origin.

Example of taxation of U.S. citizens living abroad. John Smith, a single U.S. citizen, is employed on a two-year contract by United Engineering in Brazil at a salary of $30,000 per year. At the same time he has dividend income from investments of $1,000 and long-term capital gains of $5,000. His taxable income before deductions would be calculated as follows:

Earned income	$30,000	
Less exclusion	20,000	$10,000
Dividend income	1,000	
Less dividend credit	100	900
50% of capital gain		2,500
Taxable income before deductions		$13,400

Income on investments in Puerto Rico and U.S. possessions. Some further exceptions are made in the case of income resulting from investments in U.S. possessions and Puerto Rico. If a U.S. corporation derives more than 80 percent of its gross income from sources within a U.S. possession or Puerto Rico for a three-year period and if for such period 50 percent or more of the gross income is derived from the active conduct of a trade or business within a possession of the United States, then such income is not subject to U.S. taxes until it is received within this country in the form of dividends. These provisions extend to U.S. corporations the tax deferral privileges in connection with their operations in a U.S. possession or Puerto Rico that are extended to U.S. firms operating in foreign countries under certain conditions. In fact, under these same laws, it is possible for a U.S. investor to incorporate and operate within a U.S. possession or Puerto Rico and thereby remove himself entirely from normal tax obligations to his government.

---

[1] Examples of earned income are wages and salaries, as well as the proceeds of personal-income contracts.

Western Hemisphere Trade Corporation. Another exception to normal methods of taxation is represented by the Western Hemisphere Trade Corporation. The Western Hemisphere Trade Corporation is defined as a domestic corporation that conducts all of its business in the western hemisphere, obtains 95 percent of its gross income from sources outside of the United States, and obtains 90 percent or more of its gross income from the active conduct of a trade or business venture. This business entity was created by the Revenue Act of 1942, which provides that the maximum marginal tax rate be 38 percent instead of the usual 48 percent. This decrease in taxation results from special credits against net income. This type of organization was created as a result of an effort on the part of the U.S. government to encourage trade with South America after World War II.

Domestic International Sales Corporations. The Revenue Act of 1971 permitted the establishment of Domestic International Sales Corporations (DISC) which are also afforded special treatment. The purpose of these U.S.-incorporated firms is the encouragement and expansion of U.S. exports. To induce greater export effort, the act provides for the deferral of one half of the taxes on the DISC's income related to export activity. The other half of the income is deemed to have been paid to the shareholders, and as such is taxable to them as dividends without the usual dividend exclusion made in the case of corporation shareholders. This means that the DISC does not pay any income taxes, that its shareholders pay its income tax for it, but only on one half of the qualified export-related income.

Most corporations incorporated in one of the 50 states can qualify as a DISC if the following conditions are met.

1. Ninety-five percent of its gross receipts must consist of qualified export receipts.[2]
2. Qualified export assets[3] must be 95 percent of total assets.

---

[2] Qualified export receipts are defined as follows:

a) Gross receipts from the sale, exchange, or other disposition of export property.

b) Gross receipts from the lease or rental of export property, if such property is used outside the United States.

c) Gross receipts from the sale, exchange, or other disposition of qualified export assets.

d) Gross receipts which are related and subsidiary to any qualified sale, exchange, or other disposition of qualified export assets.

e) Dividends with respect to stock of a related foreign export corporation.

f) Interest on any obligation which is a qualified export asset.

g) Gross receipts for engineering and architectural services for construction projects outside the United States.

h) Gross receipts for the performance of managerial services in furtherance of other qualified export receipts of a DISC.

[3] Qualified export assets are defined as follows:

a) Export property.

b) Assets used in connection with the sale, lease, rental, storage, handling, transportation, packaging, assembly, and servicing of export property. (cont.)

3. During the year in which it is treated as a DISC it must have only one class of stock, with a stated value of at least $2,500.
4. The corporation must have elected to be treated as a DISC.

A DISC may not make unlimited investments in foreign countries in connection with its export promotion activities. The amount of additional foreign investments is limited each year to the following:

1. The depreciation of the previous foreign investment.
2. Amount of capital raised abroad.
3. Fifty percent of the group's profits from foreign operations.
4. Fifty percent of the royalty payments received from foreign sources.

However, a DISC has the right, within specified limits, to invest in warehouses in foreign countries and to buy the securities of related export firms.

A DISC may make so-called producers' loans to firms producing export goods. However, there are definite limitations as to the magnitude of such loans that it can make to its parent. These limitations are as follows:

1. A loan plus the unpaid balances of all previous loans may not exceed the accumulated DISC income at the beginning of the month in which the loan is made.
2. The loan must be evidenced by a note or other evidence of indebtedness with a maturity not to exceed five years from the date of the loan.
3. The loan may be made only to a person who is engaged in the United States in manufacturing, production, growing, or extraction of export property.
4. The total of all unpaid loans may not exceed the borrower's investment in plant, machinery, and equipment plus the amount of property held for sale, lease, or rental plus the aggregate research and experimental expenditures, the total of this sum to be multiplied by the proportion of export sales to total sales during a prior three-year period.

To avoid profits being funneled arbitrarily by the parent to the DISC by transfer pricing, the following limitations are imposed on the profits that a DISC may make:

---

c) Accounts receivable and other evidences of indebtedness which arise out of export transactions.
d) Cash and other working capital funds.
e) Obligations arising out of producers' loans.
f) Stocks or securities of a related foreign export corporation.
g) Obligations issued, insured, or guaranteed by Eximbank or FCIA.
h) Obligations issued by domestic corporations organized for the purpose of financing export property.

1. Profits may be equal to 4½ percent of qualified export sales plus 10 percent of the DISC's export promotional expenditures.
2. DISC profits may be 50 percent of the profits of both the DISC and its parent that are export related plus 10 percent of the export promotional expenses.
3. DISCs may claim all of the profits related to all marginally produced export goods, that is, they may claim credit for all increases in export volume over previous levels.
4. DISCs may claim all of the profits on export sales of goods that have been transferred to it on an arm's length basis.

The Department of the Treasury is expected to issue administrative rules which will clarify limitations 3 and 4.

TABLE 7–1

Example of the tax saving of a DISC

Total sales of parent...................................		$2,000,000
Profits before taxes on these sales........................		$ 200,000
Income taxes at 50%...................................		100,000
Earnings after taxes....................................		$ 100,000
Assume that sales via the DISC are.....................		$ 500,000
Export promotion expenditures.........................		30,000
Permissible profit of DISC:		
4% of 500,000 + 10% of 30,000 =		
20,000 + 3,000 = 23,000		23,000

		DISC	*Parent*
Earnings before taxes...............		$23,000	$ 177,000
Taxes:			
DISC 25%.....................		5,750	
Parent 50%...................			88,500
Earnings after tax.................		$17,250	$ 88,500
Total earnings after tax.......................	$105,750		
Compared with before tax....................	100,000		
Deferred taxes............................	$ 5,750		

If a DISC pays a dividend from tax-deferred earnings, these are fully taxable without the usual dividend credit applying in the instance of corporate shareholders. See Table 7–1 for an example of the tax saving of a DISC.

Selection of the operating form from a tax standpoint

For operations outside of the United States, its possessions, or Puerto Rico, the multinational firm has a number of choices in the selection of an operating entity. The simplest to initiate and also the easiest to dissolve is a branch of the American multinational firm. From a tax point of view, operation by means of a branch has advantages but also disadvantages at times. Operation as a branch simplifies the U.S. tax problems on the part of the American firm. All of the branch's expenses and income are treated the same as any other income of the firm when it reports results of operations to the Internal Revenue Service. Branch losses are fully deductible; and, of course, profits are also fully taxed.

One serious drawback to the operation of a branch results from the fact that some countries establish an income relationship between the branch and the worldwide organization. Once this percentage relationship is established, the government will then tax the branch operating in its country on the basis of its predetermined percentage of worldwide income. This is no disadvantage as long as the firm's worldwide income and branch income in a particular country fluctuate together or that of the branch increases. However, should the profits of the branch drop while worldwide income increases, this obviously would result in higher than necessary local taxes until the profit relationship between this branch and worldwide operations is again reexamined, usually at two- to four-year intervals.

Example of potential disadvantages of branch operations. Worldwide Exploration operates a branch in a southern European country. The income before taxes of the branch has averaged $50,000 per year for the first two years. During the same period Worldwide's overall income has been $1 million before taxes. On this basis it is determined that the branch's before-tax income is 5 percent of that of the whole organization. Following this, 5 percent of Worldwide's overall before-tax profits are assessed by the southern European government against the branch for a number of years. If the before-tax profits of the branch drop sharply in the third year to $10,000 while the firm's overall profits increase to $2 million, the taxes payable to the foreign government are based on $100,000. This is 10 times higher than as though the taxes were computed on the basis of actual branch profits alone.

Another serious disadvantage of branch operations is caused by the fact that it exposes the parent organization to direct risks should unforeseen accidents occur. In addition, the worldwide organization must make disclosures of financial details of worldwide operations to the foreign government, a practice not considered desirable. These difficulties can be avoided by forming a wholly owned subsidiary in the United States (or in a foreign country that taxes income only at the source) and then having this corporate entity form the branch in the southern European country as its sole business activity.

Use of subsidiaries in foreign operations. Multinational firms most often decide to operate by means of subsidiaries in foreign areas. However, operating on a worldwide basis by means of foreign subsidiaries presents numerous problems which often have tax consequences. Prior to the passage of the Revenue Act of 1962, operating in a foreign area by means of a subsidiary provided certain distinct advantages in that income from the foreign operation was not regularly taxed by the United States until remitted to the parent organization in the form of dividends.

As a result of this potential deferment, most American multinational firms made use of subsidiaries located in so-called tax-haven countries that taxed their citizens and corporations only on income earned within the country of location. It was thus possible to avoid multiple taxation while operating in numerous countries irrespective of whether tax treaties existed between the United States and the country of operation, or the country of incorporation of the foreign subsidiary. However, the passage of the Revenue Act of 1962 has made operations on a worldwide basis by means of foreign subsidiaries much less attractive. Since the Revenue Act of 1962 has affected the foreign operations of American citizens and businesses profoundly, its requirements are next delineated.

THE U.S. REVENUE ACT OF 1962

Prior to the Revenue Act of 1962, income earned by U.S.-controlled foreign corporations (CFC) was not taxable to its U.S. owners until the income was remitted in the form of dividends. The Revenue Act of 1962 provided that certain income of the CFC is taxable to some shareholders even if the income has not yet been received in the form of dividends. The application of these provisions requires consideration first of the concept of control of a foreign corporation and second of the nature of the income of the foreign corporation and its taxation. Each will be discussed in turn.

Definition of control of a foreign corporation

A U.S.-controlled foreign corporation is any foreign corporation in which more than 50 percent of the total combined voting power is owned or deemed to be owned by U.S. shareholders, each owning 10 percent or more of the voting stock of such foreign corporation. Thus the Revenue Act of 1962 classifies American shareholders in foreign corporations into two groups: those holding less than a 10 percent interest, and those holding 10 percent or more of the outstanding shares of the corporation. Common shares of foreign corporations owned by other foreign corporations in which a U.S. shareholder has an interest are considered to be owned by him in proportion to his share of ownership of that other corporation's outstanding stock. In addition, constructive ownership rules provide that an individual is deemed to own stock owned directly or indirectly by his spouse, children, grandchildren, and parents.

A further complication arises since the control of a first foreign corporation is judged on the basis of percentage of ownership of its common shares, whereas the ownership of subsidiaries and sub-subsidiaries of this foreign corporation are judged on the basis of value of ownership. Under these provisions an American firm could own 49 percent of the voting stock and 95 percent of a nonvoting preferred stock of a foreign corporation where all of the voting stock represents 10 percent and the nonvoting preferred stock 90 percent of the equity value of the corporation. Under the rules, the foreign corporation is not a U.S. CFC because the U.S. percentage of voting ownership is only 49 percent. However, its percentage interest in the equity value of the foreign corporation is 90.4 percent (95 percent of 90 percent plus 49 percent of 10 percent). Therefore, any subsidiary of this foreign corporation will automatically be considered a U.S. CFC as long as the foreign corporation owns an interest exceeding 55.4 percent of the outstanding shares. Under the rules, the American firm is considered to be the holder of 90.4 percent of the ownership interest of the foreign corporation. Since 90.4 percent of 55.4 percent exceeds 50 percent, this would result in a determination that the sub-subsidiary is a U.S. CFC.

Example of determination of U.S. control of foreign corporations. The capital section of Multinat's Bahamian joint venture is as follows:

```
10,000 shares of 7% preferred stock..... $900,000
10,000 shares of common stock.........   100,000
```

Of the above shares, Multinat owns 9,500 shares of the preferred stock and 4,900 of the common shares. All other shares are owned by foreign entities in which no U.S. person has an interest.

Since 4,900 shares of common stock represent a minority interest, the minority-owned Bahamian subsidiary is not a U.S. CFC and Multinat does not have to pay U.S. taxes on its proportional part of the Bahamian firm's income.

If, now, the Bahamian firm forms a wholly owned subsidiary in Trinidad, this subsidiary is considered a U.S. CFC. On a value basis Multinat owns 95 percent of $900,000 and 49 percent of $100,000 of the equity value of the joint venture ($855,000 plus $49,000 or $904,000 out of a total of $1,000,000). This represents a 90.4 percent interest on an equity value basis, and thus the Trinidadian subsidiary is considered a U.S. CFC. Multinat must report 90.4 percent of the subsidiary's income on its U.S. tax returns irrespective of whether these sums have been received in the form of dividends.

Now assume that other foreigners own a 40 percent interest in the Trinidadian firm. It is still considered a U.S. CFC because 90.4 percent of 60 percent is still greater than 50 percent. Only when the foreign ownership interest exceeds 44.6 percent will the Trinidadian firm be a non-U.S.

CFC (because 90.4 percent of less than 55.4 percent is less than 50 percent).

The foregoing discussion of the Internal Revenue Service definition of "control" demonstrates that the concept is not simple. The financial manager must analyze carefully the nature of the ownership relations of all firms in which his firm has made investments because of the magnification potential in the determination of "control."

Income subject to taxation prior to the remission of dividends

If it has been determined upon the basis of the considerations described above that U.S. persons (this includes corporations, since corporations are treated as "persons" in law) control a foreign corporation, certain forms of income of the foreign corporation are subject to taxation to the U.S. person prior to the actual receipt of income from the CFC. Before the Revenue Act of 1962, a U.S. manufacturing company could sell its product to a foreign-based subsidiary in a tax-haven country and the transfer pricing would result in showing a high percentage of the profits to be realized by the foreign subsidiary. The U.S. taxes on such income could thereby be deferred until the income of the foreign subsidiary was returned to the U.S. company in the form of dividends. To avoid such tax deferment, the Revenue Act of 1962 identified certain forms of income regarded as characteristically involved in such foreign-based company devices for deferment of income realization. These types of income were discussed in a section of the Internal Revenue Code at paragraphs identified as "subpart F," so have been referred to as "subpart F income." Subpart F income has also been called "foreign-based company income." If a foreign corporation's subpart F income is less than 30 percent of its total income, it is not taxed as such. If the subpart F income is equal to or greater than 70 percent, all of the firm's income is considered subpart F income. Percentages in-between are taxed on the actual percent of subpart F income to the total.

The foreign-based company income which is subject to U.S. taxation before remission in the form of dividends consists of three main categories: (1) foreign personal holding company income, (2) foreign-based company sales income, and (3) foreign-based company service income. Each of these forms of income in the case of a U.S. CFC is defined in the tax code, the provisions of which are now briefly summarized.

Foreign personal holding company income. Foreign personal holding company income includes unearned income such as dividends, interest, oil lease rents, and gains from the sale or exchange of securities or from trades in commodity futures. It is mainly income from investments. A foreign corporation is a foreign personal holding company if more than

50 percent of its outstanding stock is owned directly or indirectly by or for not more than five individuals, U.S. citizens or permanent residents, or if at least 60 percent of its gross income in its first year and 50 percent in subsequent years constitutes foreign personal holding company income.

Foreign-based company sales income. Foreign-based company sales income includes profits, commissions, and other income derived in connection with the purchase of personal property from a related person and its sale to any person. Transactions in which a related (controlled) person (corporation) is not a party either at the buying or selling end are not covered by the subpart F provisions. Also not covered are sales of goods produced or manufactured in the country of incorporation or from its sale of goods of whatever origin to customers in the country of incorporation or the rendition of all kinds of services so long as they are performed in the country of incorporation. To take advantage of these latter exclusions, a multinational firm must establish subsidiaries in all countries in which it is planning to do business.

Foreign-based company service income. Service income of a CFC includes income derived in connection with the performance of technical, managerial, engineering, scientific, commercial, or similar services which are performed for or on behalf of a related person and are performed outside the CFC's country of incorporation. This income is also taxed before remission as dividends.

Exclusions from subpart F income

Excluded from reportable subpart F income are a number of categories. These reflect the aim of encouraging U.S. exports or income from foreign services and aiding developing countries. One exclusion from reportable subpart F income is represented by earnings from investments in a less developed country, providing that this income is reinvested in that country. Dividends, interest, and net gains from investments in less developed countries are not taken into account up to the amount of increase for the year in qualified investments in such countries. When later these investments are withdrawn, this previously excluded subpart F income becomes taxable to the shareholders.

Shipping income in connection with the use or chartering or leasing of ships or aircraft in foreign commerce, and income from services directly related to such use, need not be included in subpart F income. Export trade income derived from the sale of services connected with U.S.-produced property may also be excluded providing the CFC qualify as an export trade corporation. The foreign corporation can qualify as an export trade corporation if for a prescribed period 90 percent or more of its gross income is foreign income and 75 percent or more of this resulted from export trade, or 50 percent or more was derived from the sale of U.S.-grown agricultural products. There are limits on the amount of such export trade income that may be excluded. This limit is equal to 150 percent of export promotion expenses, or 10 percent of gross receipts, or the proportion of the increase in investments and total export trade assets for a year. This means in effect that export trade income must be reinvested in export operations if it is not to be taxed in a given year.

Certain items received from unrelated persons are not treated as subpart F income. These are rents and royalties derived in the active conduct of the business. Examples are rents received by a corporation in the real estate renting business; dividends, interest, and gains received by those in the banking and finance business; and dividends, interest, and gains received by an insurance company from investments of its reserves.

An increase in earnings of a U.S. CFC that is invested in U.S. property is taxable to the controlling shareholder as subpart F income. This is so taxable due to the fact that this increase has the practical effect of a

TABLE 7–2

Effective foreign tax rate versus required minimum distributions of earnings and profits

Effective range of foreign income tax	Required minimum distribution of earnings
0 to less than 10	90
10 to less than 20	86
20 to less than 28	82
28 to less than 34	75
34 to less than 39	68
39 to less than 42	55
42 to less than 44	40
44 to less than 46	27
46 to less than 47	14
Over 47	0

dividend payment to the controlling shareholders. U.S. property is defined as any tangible property acquired after 1962 in the United States; common shares of an investment corporation; obligations of a U.S. person; and the rights to use in the United States any patent, invention, or secret process acquired or developed by the controlled corporation for use in the United States. Not considered U.S. property in connection with this concept are obligations of the U.S. government; bank deposits and property purchased in the United States for export; business loans made in connection with the sale and processing of property, aircraft, rolling stock, vessels, motor vehicles, and containers used in foreign commerce; and certain reserves of insurance companies.

A U.S. corporate shareholder in a U.S.-controlled corporation may avoid an immediate tax on some part of income if the CFC distributes a required percentage of its earnings to its shareholders, as given in Table 7–2. Since the aim of the law is to avoid deferment of income realization, distribution of income meets the objectives of the tax law. If subpart F income is distributed, it is taxed in the usual manner. The percentages of distribution in Table 7–2 define the presumption that the U.S. corporation is not using the CFC to defer taxation. The required percentage of income to be distributed to its shareholders also depends on the relationship between the income tax rate in the country of incorporation and the income tax rate in the United States. Whenever the tax rate in the foreign country exceeds the applicable tax rate in the United States, no parts of earnings or profits are required to be distributed.

A domestic corporation may apply the relationships in Table 7–2 to one or more of its direct subsidiaries which are CFCs, or it may apply the above to one or more chains of foreign corporations, or it may apply the above to all its CFCs. Under the last method, a domestic corporation may include or exclude all corporations of less developed countries. It may, if it so desires, consider foreign branches, including those in U.S. possessions and Puerto Rico, as CFCs distributing all of their income. Should any of its subsidiaries that are considered U.S. CFCs be prevented from distributing any income as a result of currency restrictions, such income may be disregarded in this computation.

Requirement of the gross-up method

In the calculation of the U.S. tax liability, the Internal Revenue Act of 1962 made another change. It required that U.S. persons use a gross-up

TABLE 7–3

Illustration of the effects of the gross-up provision

		If foreign taxes smaller		If foreign taxes larger	
1.	Earnings before taxes	100	100	100	100
2.	Foreign taxes	30	30	60	60
3.	Dividend by foreign firm	70	70	40	40
4.	Grossed-up income (2) + (3)	—	100	—	100
5.	U.S. income tax, 50%	35	50	20	50
6.	Foreign tax credit:				
	a) Old law (3) ÷ (1) × (2)	21		24	
	b) New law (2)		30		60
7.	Net U.S. tax:				
	a) Old law (5) − (6a)	14		(−4)	
	b) New law (5) − (6b)		20		(−10)
8.	Total taxes (2) + (7)	44	50	56	50
9.	Excess U.S. tax credit, if (7) negative*			4	10

* May be used if foreign earnings are reported on an overall basis.

basis for reporting foreign earned income. The nature of the gross-up procedure is illustrated in Table 7–3, in which it is shown that the foreign taxes (line 2) are added to the net after-tax foreign income received (line 3) for reporting income for U.S. tax purposes (line 4). In Table 7–3 the old and new methods of tax computation are shown under two assumptions: (1) that foreign taxes are smaller than the U.S. income tax, and (2) that foreign taxes are larger than the U.S. income tax.

In the calculation under the old law, a U.S. person reported the net after-tax foreign earned income. This amount was subject to the U.S. tax. The foreign tax credit was the foreign taxes scaled down by the percentage of foreign income after foreign taxes to the foreign income before foreign taxes. Under the gross-up provision, the amount subject to the U.S. income tax is foreign income before foreign taxes (the gross amount). The total foreign tax can be deducted to arrive at the net U.S. tax payable. But the total tax liability is greater as a consequence of the gross-up requirement of the Revenue Act of 1962.

Treatment of capital gains as ordinary income

The Revenue Act of 1962 provides further that when stock in a U.S. CFC is sold or the corporation is liquidated, the benefits due the U.S. shareholder who is the owner of more than 10 percent of the outstanding shares are considered as dividend income (rather than a capital gain), even though the investment was held in excess of six months. Under these provisions any gain up to the proportional part of the profits made by the controlled corporation during the period of ownership of the stock is treated as dividend income. Any gain above this amount is taxed on a capital gains basis.

Example of tax treatment when shares are sold. A shareholder purchased a 20 percent interest for $5,000 and sells it two years later for $10,000. Profits after taxes of the U.S.-controlled firm during the two years were $10,000. Calculation of the tax liability when the shares are sold is:

Sale price of equity interest.	$10,000
Less cost.	5,000
Gross gain.	5,000
Shareholder's percentage of profit during period of ownership	
20% of 10,000.	2,000
Capital gain.	$ 3,000

Assuming a marginal tax rate of 40 percent, the total tax equals 40 percent of $2,000 plus 20 percent of $3,000 equals $1,400.

Also under the Revenue Act of 1962, any profit resulting from the sale or exchange of a patent, invention, model or design, copyright, secret formula, or any processes or other similar property rights is taxable on a straight tax basis if the transaction was between a U.S. corporation and a U.S. CFC.

SUMMARY

Government policies and rules generate both problems and opportunities for the manager of an international business. Regulations were classified into two broad sets: those with origins in a nation's international balance-of-payments objectives and those concerning tax regulations.

For any country to improve its balance-of-payments position it must (1) reduce the outflow of foreign exchange reserves, and/or (2) increase the inflow of foreign exchange. To reduce the outflow of foreign exchange reserves, governments first control the outflow of capital funds. Thus controls are imposed on the transfer of funds for investment abroad and on interest and dividend payments to foreigners. Foreign exchange reserves may also be conserved by restricting both the amount and kinds of imports. Such controls require appropriate policy adjustments by the multinational firm. To increase the inflow of foreign exchange, various incentives are provided by governments. These particularly aim to increase exports and may offer very attractive opportunities for multinational firms.

The international taxation of income is critical for the choice of plant location, place of incorporation, and location of management control. To avoid double taxation of income, governments negotiate tax treaties which generally provide for domestic tax credit for foreign income taxes paid. The United States taxes the income of U.S. citizens and residents irrespective of where it is earned, with few exceptions.

A multinational firm is advised to begin operations in a foreign country on a "nonestablishment basis," because income is usually taxable in the foreign country only if the seller has a "permanent establishment" there. A branch operation subjects a firm to foreign taxes based on the percentage the income of the branch is to the company's worldwide income. The uncertainty of the relationship between total income and income of the branch in any year, and hence the possibility of excessive taxation, may be avoided by the establishment of a subsidiary. Prior to the passage of the Revenue Act of 1962, the use of a subsidiary provided a tax advantage in that income from the foreign operation was not taxed by the United States until received by the parent in the form of dividends. However, the Revenue Act of 1962 provided that most income of controlled foreign corporations is taxable even if it has not been received in the form of dividends.

PROBLEM 7–1

Multinat operates in a European country by means of its own branch. Annual sales and income figures are as follows:

	Sales	EBT
Multinat.....	$100,000,000	$10,000,000
Branch......	20,000,000	2,000,000

The European government proposes that for the next three years the European branch pay taxes based on 20 percent of Multinat's worldwide profits. The branch's sales are likely to decline from their present volume, and Multinat expects a $5,000,000 capital gain from the sale of long-term assets.

A. What would be the European tax in the year of the capital gains?

B. What can Multinat do to prevent this tax increase?

PROBLEM 7–2

A U.S. investor purchased a 30 percent common equity interest in a U.S.-controlled foreign corporation for $100,000. Five years later he sold this interest for $140,000. During the five years of his ownership the firm had accumulated total after-tax profits of $50,000. His marginal tax rate is 40 percent. For this problem assume that the long-term capital gains tax rate is one half of the marginal tax rate or 20 percent.

A. What is his tax in the transaction?

B. What would the tax have been prior to the Revenue Act of 1962?

PROBLEM 7–3

The United States Manufacturing Company owns 40 percent of the outstanding common shares and 90 percent of the preferred shares of a Central American subsidiary. The common stock represents 20 percent and the preferred stock 80 percent of the equity values of the subsidiary. All other shares are owned by foreign nationals. The Central American subsidiary in turn owns a 70 percent common equity interest in a Bahamian subsidiary where the other 30 percent of the stock is owned by non-U.S. persons.

Questions:

1. Is the Central American subsidiary a U.S.-controlled foreign corporation according to the Revenue Act of 1962?
2. Is the Bahamian firm classified as a U.S.-controlled foreign corporation?
3. What is the maximum common share interest that the Central American firm can own in the Bahamian firm without making the latter a U.S.-controlled foreign firm?
4. Now assume that the United States Manufacturing Company owns only 60 percent of the preferred shares of the Central American subsidiary but that another South American joint-venture firm in which United States

Manufacturing has a 20 percent minority interest is a 30 percent owner of the Bahamian firm.

a) Is the Bahamian firm a U.S.-controlled foreign corporation?

b) What is now the maximum common share interest that the Central American subsidiary can have in the Bahamian firm without making the latter a U.S.-controlled foreign corporation?

PROBLEM 7–4

Jones, Inc., total sales are $500 million, of which $200 million are export sales. What would be the savings in income taxes if the company creates a Domestic International Sales Corporation (DISC) to handle the export sales?

The profit from total sales is $50 million per year, and the firm's marginal income tax rate is 50 percent. Its DISC, if formed, would be entitled to compute its profits on the basis of 4 percent of its sales plus 10 percent of export promotion expenditures of $5 million.

SELECTED BIBLIOGRAPHY

Bird, Richard, and Oldman, Oliver (eds). *Readings on Taxation in Developing Countries.* Baltimore, Md.: The Johns Hopkins Press, 1964.

Federal Taxes, Report Bulletin 40. *Concise Explanation of the New 1962 Tax Law.* Englewood Cliffs, N.J.: Prentice-Hall Inc., 1962.

Feinschreiber, Robert. "Disc: A New Export Tax Incentive," *Financial Executive,* Vol. 40, No. 4 (April 1972), pp. 66–70.

Gordon, Keith E. Conference Report of the National Bureau of Economic Research and the Brookings Institution. *Foreign Tax Policies and Economic Growth.* New York: Columbia University Press, 1966.

Joseph, Franz M., and Toppel, Richard V. "United States Tax Aspects of Foreign Subsidiary Operation," *Prentice-Hall Tax Ideas,* pp. 24001–24030U. Englewood Cliffs, N.J.: Prentice-Hall, Inc., 1964.

Krause, Lawrence B., and Dam, Kenneth W. Studies of Government Finance. *Federal Tax Treatment of Foreign Income.* Washington, D.C.: The Brookings Institution, 1964.

Lindholm, Richard W. "The French Value-Added Tax," *Oregon Business Review* 27, No. 2 (February 1968), pp. 1–4.

Richmond, Peggy Brewer. *Taxation of Foreign Investment Income.* Baltimore, Md.: The Johns Hopkins Press, 1963.

part two

MANAGEMENT POLICIES
AND DECISIONS

8

Institutions and instruments of international business finance

THE FINANCIAL manager seeking to contribute to the progress of his firm in international business can draw on a broad range of financing sources. These are discussed in the present chapter under five major groups: (1) international lending agencies, (2) national development banks, (3) domestic financing sources, (4) financing forms distinctive to international business, and (5) Eurodollar and Eurobond financing.

INTERNATIONAL LENDING AGENCIES

Of considerable importance for financing international business are the operations of the international financing agencies. We shall describe seven:

World Bank group:

1. International Bank for Reconstruction and Development (IBRD).
2. International Finance Corporation (IFC).
3. International Development Association (IDA).

Regional lending agencies:

1. Inter-American Development Bank (IDB).
2. Asian Development Bank (ADB).
3. European Investment Bank (EIB).
4. African Development Bank (AFDB).

Since their organization in various years following the end of World War II, international lending sources have committed an accumulated total of the equivalent in dollars of some $20 billion to financing projects and programs in which U.S. business has had an opportunity for making sales. These loans, in turn, have stimulated a substantial amount of investment from other sources and thus have increased the potential for

161

international business. Thus, the operations of these institutions have great significance for financial managers. Each will therefore be described in turn.

International Bank for Reconstruction and Development (World Bank)

The International Bank for Reconstruction and Development (IBRD) was established at the Bretton Woods Conference in 1944 as a companion institution to the International Monetary Fund (IMF). The total subscribed capital of the World Bank (as it is generally called)· is approximately $23 billion, of which about $2.5 billion has been paid in. The remainder is subject to call if required. The capital subscribed by the member governments was intended to represent the basic equity capital for the World Bank. The Bank itself has also been a borrower, having raised almost $4 billion by selling its bonds throughout the capital markets of the world. More than half of these bonds have been purchased by buyers outside the United States.

The World Bank normally finances the foreign exchange portion of the cost of projects that are designed to contribute to the productivity of the borrowing country. Its loans are made to member governments, their agencies, or to private firms within member countries whose loans are guaranteed by their governments. Loans are to be made only when other sources of private financing cannot be obtained.

Since 1948 the World Bank has emphasized development lending and an increasing proportion of its loans have been directed to the less developed areas of the world. Roughly a third of its development loans have been for electric power production and distribution. A third have been for the development of transportation in its various forms—highways, railways, air transport, waterways, and pipelines. Both of the foregoing categories of loans represent building the economic infrastructure of a nation to facilitate its further development. In the remaining third, development has been emphasized in the form of loans for water supply and for education. Loans have also been made for agriculture, particularly irrigation loans, and for industry, with emphasis on building the basic industries of a nation. In addition, the World Bank provides technical assistance to developing countries.

The World Bank has required that projects must be soundly conceived and that they must provide a basis for repayment. It further requires efficient procurement, with provision for competitive bidding on the major portion of the equipment, materials, and supplies financed by its loans. The loans are amortized over maturity periods ranging from 10 to slightly over 30 years. The terms may allow a waiting period (a period of grace) before the start of repayment of the principle, a period which is related to the estimated time required for the project to provide sufficient earnings to begin repayment. As of early 1970, the interest rate charged on loans was 7 percent per annum, dated from the time of disbursement. In addition, a commitment fee of ¾ percent per annum is charged on the undisbursed portions of loans.

Evidence of the care with which applications are analyzed by the Bank is its record of having incurred no losses on loans from its inception through the beginning of 1970. Repayment of principal to the Bank (and its participants in making loans) has aggregated over $3 billion. The excellent credit record of World Bank lending has encouraged the direct participation of private investors in its loans of more than $2 billion. In participating, commercial institutions such as banks and insurance companies generally take bonds with early maturities, receiving the same rates that the World Bank would have received.

Since the World Bank has had no losses from its loans, some critics have accused it of applying credit standards that are too high. It has been argued that the World Bank has been operating on a conservative "business-like basis" while international economic development requires more risktaking.[1] Our view is that the application of high standards has performed an important role in bringing private funds increasingly into international investments. Of course, the World Bank is not the only intergovernmental lending agency. To these others we now turn.

International Finance Corporation

The International Finance Corporation (IFC) was established in July 1956 to supplement the activities of the World Bank by making higher risk loans. As of the end of 1970, its paid-in capital, subscribed by 94 member governments, was slightly over $100 million and its reserve against losses was approximately $50 million. It is authorized to borrow amounts from the World Bank up to a limit of four times its unimpaired subscribed capital and surplus. The IFC makes nonguaranteed loans to private enterprises in developing countries. All its investments are made in association with private business. It expects its financial participation to be substantially less than 50 percent of the total cost of the project financed.

IFC's gross commitments through the end of 1970 were $477 million, of which only $280 million was held by the IFC, the remainder having been sold to private financial institutions for their own portfolios.[2] The IFC invests in both the debt securities and equities of business firms. The

---

[1] A recent article in *Barron's* has raised questions of whether the loans have made adequate contributions to world economic progress and raises further questions on future loan repayments, but no concrete evidence on the issues was provided. S. Scheibla, "Curb on Global Lenders," *Barron's*, November 12, 1971, pp. 5, 16, 18.

[2] International Financial Corporation, *Annual Report*, 1970, p. 2.

ratio of loans to shares in the portfolio of the IFC is approximately 2 to 1. The total project cost, cumulatively of the funding activities of the IFC to the end of 1970, was over $2.6 billion. Thus its activities have provided a basis for investment activity far in excess of its own portfolio. Indeed, the expansion factor is approximately 10 times the size of its own portfolio.

The IFC finances not only individual projects but also invests in development banks that in turn lend to other institutions. Examples of its recent projects include a petrochemical company in Brazil, a textile mill in Ceylon, a synthetic fiber plant in Colombia, a chemical fertilizer project in India, an iron ore mining project in Mexico, and the expansion of an automobile manufacturing operation in Yugoslavia. Illustrative of its joint participation in financing is its $8.4 million commitment to a $29.0 million polyethylene enterprise in Brazil. The financial plan for this project involved a number of sources, as indicated in the following figures:[3]

Share capital		*U.S. $ million*
National Distillers and Chemical Corp.	3.2	
Petrobras Quimica, S.A.-Petroquisa	3.2	
Unipar-Uniao de Industrias Petroquimicas, S.A.	2.7	
International Finance Corporation	2.3	11.4
Loan capital		
International Finance Corporation*	5.0	
Investbanco, Banco de Investimento do Brasil and the Banco Bozzano Simonsen de Investimento	3.9	
Dutch and Japanese suppliers' credits	3.7	
Bank of America; Manufacturers Hanover Trust Co.	2.5	
Export-Import Bank of the United States	2.5	17.6
Total		29.0

° IFC's commitment also included contingency funds of $1.1 million.

The above financial plan is illustrative of a number of projects described in the Annual Reports of the IFC. It will be noted that other private and public financing institutions are included in the financial plan presented above. In this particular project, two private U.S. institutions participated: Bamerical International Financial Corporation, a subsidiary of Bank of America, N.T. & S.A., and Manufacturers Hanover Trust Company. In addition, it will be noted that Dutch and Japanese suppliers' credits were also involved, as was the Development Bank of Brazil. This example illustrates how alert participation by financial managers can generate substantial sales for their business firms.

The International Development Association

The International Development Association (IDA) was created in 1960 to provide "soft loans" to nations with limited capacity to service conventional loans. All World Bank members are eligible to join IDA,

---

[3] Ibid., pp. 18–29.

and more than a hundred countries have done so, contributing more than $1 billion in initial subscriptions. IDA has emphasized loans to facilitate investment in social overhead projects such as power, transportation, education, and housing for the purpose of promoting economic development.

Because the servicing of general economic development loans is difficult, since they generate increases in income only after a substantial number of years, the loan terms by IDA are relatively generous. The loans are normally granted on an interest-free basis with a ¾ of 1 percent per annum service charge. The maturity period is generally 50 years. The repayment schedule starts with a 10-year grace period, which is followed by 10 years in which 1 percent of the principle is repaid annually. During the remaining 30 years, 3 percent of the principal is repaid annually.

The Inter-American Development Bank

The Inter-American Development Bank (IDB) is a western hemispheric version of the World Bank. It was founded in 1959 with the original membership composed of the United States and 20 Latin American countries. It seeks to promote economic development as well as regional economic integration. Until recently the IDB financed business from three funds separately maintained. These were: (1) ordinary capital resources, (2) a fund for special operations, and (3) the social progress trust fund. The second and third of these were combined in 1965.

From its ordinary capital resources the IDB makes loans repayable, in the currencies in which the loans are made, to private and public entities of member nations. Maturities are mostly of 10- to 20-year duration, including grace periods. The rate of interest in early 1970 was 8 percent per annum, of which 1 percent represents a commission allocated to a special reserve. Procurement is tied to those free world countries that contribute to Latin America's development through the Bank.

From the Fund for Special Operations the IDB makes loans on terms and conditions adapted to the special circumstances of specific countries. Interest rates start at about 3 percent including the service charge. Terms generally range from 10 to 30 years, including grace periods. Purchases can be made anywhere in the free world, with some emphasis on procurement from the United States, the borrower's country, and other IDB member countries. The IDB also administers funds connected with Latin American development from Canada, West Germany, Sweden, and the United Kingdom.

The Social Progress Trust Fund was organized to channel U.S. contributions to Latin America under the Alliance for Progress. After receiving its last increase in resources in 1965, this fund was combined with the Fund for Special Operations. Loans under the Social Progress Trust Fund emphasized water supply and sewage facilities, settlement and improved use of land, low-income group housing, and advanced education and training. Interest rates were as low as $1\frac{1}{4}$ percent per annum plus a service change of $\frac{3}{4}$ percent per annum payable in dollars. Terms ranged up to 30 years including a grace period.

Asian Development Bank

The United States is a participating member in the Asian Development Bank (ADB), which was founded in late 1966. The ADB was modeled after the IDB. However, one third of its subscribed capital and voting power belong to nonregional industrial nations. The ADB makes development loans using criteria similar to those of the World Bank and, like the IDB, operates through several funds making loans under liberal terms for specialized purposes.

The European Investment Bank

The European Investment Bank (EIB) was established in 1958 to help carry out the objectives of the European Economic Community (EEC)—the European Common Market. Three major types of responsibilities of the EIB stem from its assigned role of facilitating economic integration over the entire Common Market area in Western Europe. One important responsibility is to assist in financing projects that involve two or more national governments. This provides a method of coordinating the activities of the national financial agencies that may be involved. A second responsibility relates to possible adjustments required as a result of integration policies. In order to realize the potentials of economies of scale, there has been some movement toward specializing and expanding the operations of plants and firms in countries with a comparative advantage in certain lines of business. For example, major petrochemical operations might be expanded in Italy and France while basic chemicals might be centered in West Germany. A third role of the European Investment Bank is to contribute to the underdeveloped regions within the Common Market area. The aim here is to bring the various regions of the European Common Market domain into a more uniform and high level of economic maturity.

The policies of the European Investment Bank have been indicated by its annual reports. The projects which have been supported by the Bank thus far have, in the main, been development investments supporting the socioeconomic infrastructure of nations or basic industries. Illustrative projects include the construction in southern Italy of a thermoelectric power station using lignite. Another was in the Grand Duchy of Luxembourg where a hydroelectric power station feeding the interconnected European network was constructed. Still another was building in the south of France a petrochemical plant. The reports of the Bank have indicated that the initiative for creating new industries must necessarily come from relatively large enterprises.

The Bank has required that it provide only a portion of the needed funds. The borrower must provide some funds as well as obtain other funds from third parties. The European Investment Bank has sought to work through financial institutions in the individual countries. For example, in Italy the European Investment Bank made its loans through the Cassa per II Mezzo Giorno which, in turn, financed projects selected by the Bank. Also in Italy three of its operations were carried out jointly with the International Bank for Reconstruction and Development.

This kind of cooperation underscores the nature of the major function of the European Investment Bank. It is an international mechanism for mobilizing the resources of a group of nations. By pooling financial resources and staff expertise, the EIB is able to carry the risks of large-scale investment projects that would be less likely to be supported by the development banks of individual nations.

The administrative policies of the Bank may be briefly noted. Most loans have carried amortization periods of 12 to 20 years, the term being related to the durability of the project. Typically, a three- to four-year interval is established before loan repayments begin. The European Investment Bank does not require a government guarantee for each loan; but if the borrower does not provide a government guarantee, the Bank will ordinarily require appropriate collateral.

The rate of interest follows market conditions, with no attempt to associate the level of interest rate with the degree of risk of the potential borrower. The interest rate varies only with market conditions and with the monetary arrangements chosen by the borrower. Two choices are available. The first clause provides that the borrower receives currency selected by the Bank, which may be currencies of third countries, and the borrower repays in the currency he received. Under the second clause, the borrower receives the currency of whichever of the member nations he chooses, but the Bank has the right to select the currency in which repayment will be made. Most loans to date have been made under the first clause.

Related to the responsibilities of the European Investment Bank are the European Development Fund and the European Social Fund. The purpose of the European Development Fund is to establish financial aid for overseas territories which will supplement the efforts made by the Metropoles for economic and social development of those territories. With the aid of this fund, the European Economic Community will participate in the financing of social projects. These include economic investments of general interest directly connected with the implementation of programs for productive development projects. It also includes institutions for vocational training, teaching, research, and hospitals.

The European Development Fund was blueprinted in a program announced in late 1959. This initial blueprinting of European Development Fund activities stated that local savings of the less developed countries amounted to some $7.5 billion in 1957. It further said that this was barely adequate to match the increase in population. To achieve the goal of raising income per capita by 25 percent in 10 years, the report estimated that the need for outside capital would be an additional $7.5 billion. It stated that this constituted roughly just 1 percent of the total national income of the developed countries.

These initial goals may be compared with the actual total resources of the fund for the first five years—$58.25 million. Because the applications have exceeded the total funds available, the European Development Fund has given priority to infrastructure investments too costly to be met from the resources of the associated countries and territories. Considerable support has also been given to the development of agricultural production which is, of course, appropriate, given that these territories are in early stages of development. Commitments relating to infrastructure in the form of roads, railways, and ports have been the largest. These have been followed by allotments to agriculture, stock breeding, and fisheries. In addition, appropriations were made for health equipment and for projects relating to education.

The purpose of the European Social Fund is to aid in the improvement of employment possibilities and to increase the geographic and occupational mobility of labor in the community. The fund will be administered by a commission assisted by a committee presided over by a member of the commission and consisting of representatives of government, trade unions, and employers' associations. The essential purpose of the European Social Fund is to redistribute among the member governments part of the expenses of financing training centers and paying resettlement allowances to workers. As an example of its work, the European Social Fund has aided the Italian government in a program of special training for 10,000 Italian workers desirous of seeking employment in West Germany and the Netherlands.

The African Development Bank

All of the preceding regional development banks described have represented a joint partnership between developed and developing nations. The African Development Bank (AFDB), presumably in the effort to avoid undue outside influence, has excluded nonregional partners. Yet the problems and the needs faced by the African Development Bank are probably greater than those of any other region in the world. It needs a maximum amount of help from the World Bank group and the full cooperation of the developed nations.

NATIONAL DEVELOPMENT BANKS

Paralleling the functions and operations of the international and re-gional development banks discussed in the previous sections of this chapter are the national development banks of individual countries. Some of these are governmental agencies and some are private. From a financial manager's standpoint these agencies are quite important. They conduct activities to support economic growth or development within the nation as well as to support international business operations; and, of course, the two are interrelated. First, broad governmental policies affecting international business financing are summarized and examples cited of U.S. agencies in this field. Second, some foreign governmental development agencies are briefly discussed. Third, a description of private investment development organizations with international operations is set forth.

Broad governmental policies affecting international financing

Two broad forms of governmental activity are antecedent to and supportive of the operations of development banks. Of great importance are various forms of tax reductions or exemptions. Investment tax credits and accelerated depreciation encourage overall investment activity. Specific tax reductions or exemptions may be given to specific industries regarded as important to national economic needs. These include investment in individual industries or in particular regions of the country or to stimulate the development of selected types of natural resources.

In addition, government itself may undertake important forms of infrastructure investment which are essential to private projects and increase their profitability. These infrastructure projects include governmental investment in transportation, electric power, and water supply. Coming closer to the financing of private economic development is government guarantee of loans made to private companies in the individual country. One or more of a range of national or international institutions may provide the financing. The guarantees may relate to business risks, political risks, and availability of foreign exchange for servicing debt. Other direct governmental activities associated with financing include government grants to finance part of the cost of individual projects. Also, governments may subsidize the training of unskilled workers or the retraining of other workers. In addition, governments may provide reimbursement in part or in full of the expenses of moving workers geographically to new areas.

The Export-Import Bank of the United States

The Export-Import Bank of the United States, generally referred to as Eximbank, was established in 1934. Since 1953 its life has been renewed for five-year periods by the Congress of the United States. In 1968 the life of the Bank was extended to June 30, 1973, and its overall lending authority was increased from $9 billion to $13.5 billion. The fundamental purpose of the Eximbank is to provide financial assistance to encourage exports from the United States. From 1934 to 1972 Eximbank had supported a total of approximately $32 billion of credits, guarantees, and insurance to assist U.S. exports. The program of the Eximbank will be described under the following categories:

1. Direct loans.
2. Financial guarantee programs.
3. Participation financing.
4. Local-cost financing.
5. Relending credits.
6. Cooperative financing.
7. Export Expansion Facility.
8. Implications for financial managers of business firms.

Direct loans. The major program of Eximbank is represented by long-term loans made directly to borrowers outside the United States for purchases of U.S. goods and services. Disbursements under the loan agreement are made in the United States to the suppliers of the goods. The loans plus interest must be repaid in dollars by the borrowers. According to an Eximbank brochure printed in July 1971, the rate of interest charged even during the period of high interest rates in recent years has continued to be in the range of 6 percent per annum. Eximbank charges a rate of interest that represents an average of the rates paid by the U.S. Treasury on its debt obligations. Normally repayment is made in semiannual installments beginning six months after the delivery of the equipment or after completion of the project financed. A commitment fee of one half of 1 percent is charged on the undisbursed balance of an authorized loan.

The objectives of the direct lending program are to supplement private sources of financing where such sources might be unwilling or unable to assume the political and commercial risks involved, or to extend credit on terms as long as required. A related objective is to enable U.S. suppliers to provide terms on major projects competitive with those offered by government-sponsored export financing institutions of other countries. To be approved a project must be economically and technically sound. It must have promise of being financially self-supporting in order to be able to repay the Eximbank loan.

While direct loans by the Eximbank are made to foreign borrowers, they have considerable significance for the financial managers of U.S. corporations. A U.S. corporation may successfully complete a transaction in which a foreign country or foreign firm may have a project on which sales of equipment from the U.S. firm will be made. The successful application from the foreign borrower for an Eximbank loan provides the financing and hence facilitates the successful completion of the preliminary selling negotiations. The Eximbank's loan authorizations have averaged over $400 million per year during 1962–69.[4] In 1970 the loan authorizations of the Eximbank were over $600 million. Thus the programs of the Eximbank represent a substantial opportunity for financial managers by facilitating the sales programs of their companies.

Financial guarantee programs. In 1961 the Eximbank stimulated the formation of the Foreign Credit Insurance Association, an association of commercial insurance companies, to provide credit protection for exporters.[5] This FCIA program is used by firms of all sizes but is particularly helpful to small firms with limited experience in export sales. Policies issued by FCIA cover sales and can be used as collateral for bank loans.

Under a program similar to FCIA activities, Eximbank guarantees repayments to commercial banks which finance medium-term transactions for exporters. This financial guarantee program is available to U.S. financial institutions as well as to non-U.S. financial institutions. These financial guarantee programs partially substitute for direct lending by Eximbank and thus extend the impact of its programs. Under its financial guarantee loan authority, Eximbank will unconditionally guarantee repayment by a borrower of up to 100 percent of the outstanding principal plus interest of the financed portion of the transaction if the early repayments were made on schedule.

Participation financing. Participation financing represents combining Eximbank's direct lending with loans provided by private sources of funds. Combining an Eximbank direct credit at a 6 percent rate of interest with funds supplied from private sources at a higher commercial rate of interest decreases the overall effective rate of interest paid on the total financing of the transaction. Other attractive features are provided to the private lender. Eximbank will, if requested, finance through its direct lending the longer maturities of the total credit, enabling the private lender to be repaid in a shorter period of time. This also reduces the effective rate of interest to the borrower. Also, if requested by the private lender, Eximbank will, if its credit appraisal requirements are met, extend its financial guarantee to assure repayment of the private portion of the total financing.

Local-cost financing. The main purpose of Eximbank loans and guarantees is to stimulate the purchases of U.S. goods and services. Eximbank has a program to meet non-U.S. competition in providing financing for a portion of the local costs associated with major projects overseas. Local costs include expenses for engineering services, public utility connections, locally available construction materials, labor, etc. A central feature of the

---

[4] *The Economic Report of the President,* February 1971, p. 302.

[5] This program was discussed in detail in Chapter 4.

local-cost facility of Eximbank is to apply the Eximbank financial guarantee to cover loans made by non-U.S. financial institutions for the financing of local costs under specified conditions. Ordinarily Eximbank will guarantee local-cost financing up to 15 percent of the value of the goods and services exported from the U.S. in the related transaction.

Relending credits. A relending credit is a line of credit extended by the Eximbank directly to a non-U.S. financial institution. The purpose is to stimulate subloans or relending to small- and medium-sized private enterprise for financing purchases of U.S. goods and services. The rate of interest which may be charged by the relending institution on subloans is specified at 8½ percent per annum plus any taxes, devaluation insurance, or other costs typical in the country of the relending institution.

Cooperative financing. Again, in the cooperative financing program the Eximbank participates with a non-U.S. financial institution to finance the purchase of U.S. exports. Upon approval of an application for a cooperative financing facility, Eximbank will allocate a line of credit. Each transaction is then jointly financed through disbursements of funds by the cooperating institution and Eximbank. Eximbank will provide up to 50 percent of the financed portion of the loan.

Export Expansion Facility. Extension of the Eximbank by legislation in 1968 provided for the establishment of an "Export Expansion Facility." Traditionally the Eximbank was permitted to participate in transactions only where there was "reasonable assurance of repayment." This standard is now modified to encourage Eximbank participation in higher risk transactions. The new standard authorizes Eximbank to assist export transactions which offer a "sufficient likelihood of repayment to justify the Bank's support in order to actively foster the foreign trade and the long-term commercial interest of the United States."[6] During the period 1968 through March 31, 1970, the Export Expansion Facility has been used to support U.S. exports valued at $420 million.

Implications for financial managers of business firms. The large important programs of Eximbank have considerable significance for the financial manager as well as other executives of business firms. For the foreign business firm the operations of Eximbank provide a source of financing of major projects. In addition, financing is provided at rates generally below the rates in foreign countries. Export sales are stimulated. For the financial managers and executives of U.S. firms, the need to provide for financing of such external sales is eliminated. The risks of financing such sales are not borne by the private business firm. Thus the Eximbank should not be regarded as just another government agency.

---

[6] *Export-Import Bank of the United States* (4th ed.; Washington, D.C.: U.S. Government Printing Office, July 1971), pp. 3–4.

This is an agency that has considerable potential in stimulating sales and providing financing both for U.S. and foreign business firms.

The U.S. Agency for International Development

The Agency for International Development (AID) was established in 1961, implementing the Foreign Assistance Act of 1961, as an agency within the Department of State. The purpose of AID was to carry out nonmilitary U.S. foreign assistance programs. The orientation of AID is to support the international position of the United States. Emphasis is on assistance to friendly foreign governments or to support programs that will make more friends for the United States.

AID lends money to foreign governments and to other qualified foreign borrowers under Section 201 of the Foreign Assistance Act in the form of development loans, under Sections 251 and 252 in the form of Alliance for Progress loans, and under Section 401 for supporting assistance loans. The loans are repayable in dollars and are to be used to cover the U.S. procurement program of an economic development project. Loans may be made up to a 40-year maturity, including a 10-year grace period. Interest rates charged are low relative to the general level of international money rates.

AID is also responsible for the conduct of local currency loans under PL 480 agreements.[7] These loans are aimed to stimulate economic activity by providing long-term capital to private enterprise in friendly less-developed countries. The loans represent U.S.-owned foreign currency received in payment for surplus agricultural commodities. These local currency loans are available only in countries where local currencies have been allocated for this purpose under PL 480 sales agreements. A general goal of the loans is to use funds otherwise idle for the benefit of U.S. multinational firms and the local economy. These funds cannot be used to finance export sales but must be used for direct investment. Another aim is to achieve expanded markets for and the consumption of U.S. agricultural products.

The rates of interest charged are usually comparable to levels charged by local development banks. These range from 6 to 12 percent a year. The maturity of the loans ranges from 5 to 10 years with a grace period of from 1 to 3 years.

AID also has an investment guarantee program. This program covers extended risks. The specific risk guarantees are for specific new investments and projects that have been approved by the country in which they are located. The guarantees cover inconvertibility of currencies into U.S. dollars, expropriation, or losses due to war, revolution, or insurrection.

---

[7] See Chapter 9 for a discussion of PL 480.

The specific risk programs have been taken over by the Overseas Private Investment Corporation, discussed in detail in Chapter 4. The extended-risk provision authorizes insuring against a loss of any investment due to political risks, upon such terms and conditions as AID may determine. It now applies largely to Latin American pilot housing projects. This provides AID with considerable flexibility for the exercise of judgment in carrying out the aims of the Foreign Assistance Act.

The Overseas Private Investment Corporation (OPIC) was created late in 1969 to take over and expand the AID programs and to encourage private investment. It provides financial assistance to private enterprises operating in low-income countries. Its lending policies follow regular business practices. In 1974 its formal constitution will be reviewed with the possibility of transferring this agency to the private sector. The programs of the Overseas Private Investment Corporation seek to reduce the risks associated with investing in underdeveloped countries. Thus it aims to increase private investment in these countries.

Other U.S. financing agencies

Activities of governments associated with lending operations are usually conducted through specialized government or semipublic institutions generally referred to as industrial development banks. The lending operations of industrial development banks are usually at reduced rates for projects fulfilling specified social objectives. High-risk projects or business operations may be financed at interest rates close to general market levels, rates considerably lower than those ordinarily required for higher risk activities. The maturity of the credit extended by the public development banks is predominately in the 5- to 10-year range. In addition to extending credit, the development banks may also take equity positions in some projects. Development banks rarely exercise management control in these firms. The broad aim of these banks is to stimulate the establishment or expansion of industries and operations in geographic areas considered important to the growth and development of the local economy.

In the United States, Eximbank and AID are particularly important in connection with international business operations but also have considerable impact on the domestic operations of business firms. More specifically, the sector of the U.S. economy that has especially received support through these various governmental programs has been small business. Such activities have been conducted through the Small Business Administration, which makes direct loans as well as participates in loans made by private financial institutions. In addition, U.S. business is aided by the financing of highway and airport construction. In government contracting, special provisions are made favoring (1) small business and (2) depressed areas. Direct loan and loan guarantee programs are found in housing, agriculture and the maritime industry. U.S. government agencies involved are numerous.

Foreign development banks

Similar programs are found in foreign countries. This discussion will be limited to a brief identification of the industrial development banks established by foreign governments. In the United Kingdom the Industrial Reorganization Corporation (IRC) makes long-term loans of up to 10 years and takes small equity positions in business firms.

Among several developmental government units in France is the Credit Nationale (CN). CN provides long-term financing and discounts medium-term loans that have been received by business firms from commercial banks. The maturity of CN loans is primarily from 8 to 15 years and usually must be guaranteed or secured.

In West Germany the Kreditanstalt fur Wiederaufbau (KFW) is the principal industrial development bank. KFW emphasizes large-scale projects relating to public utilities and basic industries. In addition, it seeks to stimulate investment in selected areas such as the East German border, West Berlin, and the Ruhr areas.

Italy has a large number of public and semipublic agencies supplying medium- and long-term financing to business firms. The largest is the Instituto Mobiliare Italiano (IMI). IMI seeks to stimulate the establishment of new industries and to encourage the expansion or increased stability of existing industries considered important to the Italian economy. The maturity of loans is mostly in the 10- to 15-year range. Equity investments are also made. The loans are generally secured.

The main industrial development bank in the Netherlands is the Nationale Investeringsbank (NI). It is jointly owned by the government and private financial institutions. Its main aim has been to follow flexible lending policies to encourage greater balance in the amount of industrial development outside the industrial centers of Holland.

Private industrial development banks

The establishment and development of governmental development agencies has been paralleled by the creation and expansion of private-venture capital firms in the international economy. Table 8–1 provides information on a selected number of venture capital firms. For each company information is given on its ownership, capital, and the major emphasis in its operations.

Three major types of activities characterize these private investment development companies. First, they make high-risk investments. Since these investments are in new industries or in new firms in developing

TABLE 8–1

Selected venture capital firms

Name	Ownership	Capital	Specialization
Chase International Investment Co.	Chase Manhattan Bank	$5 million	Investment for new or expanding basic industry
International Basic Economy Corp. (IBEC) (1947)	Rockefeller Bros.	$18.5 million	Operates mainly in Latin America, but also in the Middle East and Southeast Asia
Lambert and Company	French interests	n.a.	Operates in Africa; interests in oil and other fields
Transoceanic-AOFC, Ltd.	IBEC and others	$15 million	Specializes in equity ownership in foreign companies, loans to new or expanding companies, and in financing capital goods exports
Atlantic Development Group for Latin America, (Adela) (1964)	Multinational	$50 million	Industrial and commercial projects to promote balanced structural development in the local economies of Latin America
Private Investment Corporation for Asia (Asian Adela) (1967)	Multinational	$40 million	Same as Adela, but for Asian countries

n.a.—not available.

economies, the risk of loss is considerable. On the other hand, these are important economic activities in new economic areas; they are generally well conceived and yield very high returns. Second, although equity investments are made, management control is usually avoided; however, managerial and technical assistance is made available, often by a subsidiary of the private venture capital firm. One aim is to provide management-technical assistance to increase the probability of success of the investment by improving managerial performance. Finally, by providing this managerial and technical assistance, the hope is to develop local management capabilities in low-income nations.

A third characteristic, of course, is the emphasis on international activities in developing countries. These private industrial development companies supply capital for private overseas operations. Their goals are not solely to obtain a high return on investment. Their aim is broader, tending toward "financial entrepreneurship." This includes assistance in the promotion and organization of overseas ventures as well as the provision of managerial and technical assistance. The operations financed relate to economic development of low-income nations. They represent a private sector contribution to the economies of developing nations.

Significance for financial managers

All of these international lending agencies offer opportunities for financing by foreign buyers either directly or indirectly. In addition, these agencies facilitate financing by the sellers of the goods. Thus, the operations of these organizations have great significance for financial managers for a number of reasons. First, the magnitude of their operations involves very large sums of money. Second, often a substantial sale by an American company will be financed either directly or indirectly through one of these international agencies. Third, the economic development stimulated by these international lending agencies may offer, with some lead time, further business opportunities for U.S. firms. This provides an opportunity for attractive returns, made possible by effective longer range planning for activities in the international sector. The financial manager has an important contribution to make in such long-range planning activities.

DOMESTIC FINANCING SOURCES

In the previous sections of this chapter, the nature of U.S. and international lending agencies was described. The very great amounts of money involved in their operations and consequently the very substantial opportunities for financial managers to support the international business operations of their firms was described. We now turn to a review and summary of financing sources from the usual private institutions and instruments connected with private financing operations. Since this material is duplicative of that covered in standard textbooks on business finance, it will be presented in summary fashion. We shall expand only on those aspects of business finance that are somewhat different in foreign countries or those forms of financing that have special importance for international business financial operations.

The major sources of financing are set forth in Table 8–2. Fifteen individual alternative sources are outlined. The basic characteristics of the financing available from each source are indicated. The alternative sources are compared and contrasted with respect to (1) the duration of the use of funds, (2) the form of financing characteristically supplied, (3) the degree of risk taken by the supplier of funds, (4) the usual stability of the availability of funds, (5) the facilities for administering mass financing, (6) the nature of the contact between the financing source and the borrower, and (7) the amount of management council provided. Elaboration of the summary characterization of each source of funds by the seven criteria listed is presented in many textbooks on business finance. Here we shall merely emphasize some general principles.

There is a wide range of sources of financing with a complex spectrum, each representing a diverse spectrum of qualities. Any one source has both

TABLE 8-2
Summary of characteristics of alternative sources of financing

Source of funds	Duration of use of funds	Form of financing supplied	Risk taken by source of funds	Availability of funds	Facilities for mass financing	Nature of contact	Amount of management counsel
1. Commercial banks	Mainly short term, some medium	Debt	Low (high quality)	Cyclical variations	Limited	Close	Moderate to considerable
2. Interbusiness suppliers	Short, medium, and long	Debt and equity	Continuing low to high	Variable	Small	Close and direct	Small to considerable
3. Life insurance companies	Medium to long term	Mostly debt	Low (high quality)	Secular growth	Limited	Limited but direct	Small to moderate
4. Finance companies	Continuing	Debt	Considerable	Cyclical	Considerable	Close	Small to considerable
5. Mutual savings banks	Long term	Debt	Secured by real estate	Stable	None	Indirect	None
6. Fire and casualty insurance companies	Long term	Debt and equity	Moderate	Variable	None	Indirect	Small
7. Investment companies	Long term	Debt and equity	Low (high quality)	Variable	None	Indirect	None
8. Pension funds	Long term	Debt and equity	Low (high quality)	Stable	None	Indirect	None
9. Savings and loan associations	Long term	Debt	Medium to low	Stable	None	Direct	None
10. Educational and religious funds	Long term	Debt and equity	Low (high quality)	Variable	None	Indirect	None

11.	Investment development corporation	Long term	Debt and equity	Moderate to high	Stable	None	Direct and close	Considerable
12.	Open market sales of debt	Short, medium, and long	Debt	Low to medium	Variable	Small	Indirect	Moderate
13.	Equity markets	Permanent	Equity	Full range	Erratic	None	Indirect	None
14.	Employees	Long term	Mostly equity	Moderate to high	Erratic	None	Direct	None
15.	Customers	Long term	Debt and equity	Moderate to high	Erratic	None	Indirect	None

advantages and disadvantages. It is important for an individual firm to seek to match its special needs to the characteristics of alternative sources of financing. Financial agencies tend to specialize in particular forms or characteristics of financing, as a consequence of their own sources of funds. Thus, in part due to the characteristics of their own sources of financing and partly as a result of the experience built up over a period of years, an individual source of funds may be advantageous with regard to some characteristics and disadvantageous in regard to others.

The nature of the alternative sources of financing is further amplified by considering these sources in conjunction with the various forms of the funds they supply, some of which are specific to individual sources of financing. Twelve alternative forms of funding and their distinctive characteristics are set forth in Table 8–3. The forms of funds differ with respect to five criteria: (1) whether or not the cost of the financing is a fixed obligation of the enterprise; (2) whether or not a fixed maturity date is involved; (3) the nature and extent of tax deductibility; (4) the possible sharing of voting control of the enterprise, directly or indirectly, and in various degrees; and (5) the extent to which choice of a particular form of funds provides potential for additional financing in the future.

The use of alternative sources and forms of financing is greatly influenced by the age and characteristics of the industry represented, the products of the firm, and other characteristics of the business firm. Thus the industries in which most new small firms predominate are mainly retail and wholesale trade. High mortality rates of firms in retail and wholesale trade reflect a tendency for too many firms to enter these industries. New small firms in trade do not have favorable profit prospect as a group; therefore, they must depend initially on the funds of owners, friends, and relatives, supplemented by credit from trade suppliers who may be striving to develop new outlets for their products.

Financing is somewhat easier for new firms and new industries with high profit opportunities, such as firms formed to expand into international business. However, risks in international business are high, commensurate with the profit potentially available. As a consequence, financing sources in the initial stages may also be limited due to the high risks. Hence, a wide variety of alternative forms and sources, supplemented by the governmental and quasi-governmental institutions described earlier, must be considered.

If a small firm or an expanding firm in international business activities grows, the owners initially will seek to finance from internal sources and an external debt. They will use straight credit and other forms of debt in an effort to avoid selling common stock to outsiders. However, at some point established by standards of debt to equity ratios for the products that are manufactured or sold in international operations, additional equity may have to be sold. At that time, since the sales and profits of the

TABLE 8–3

Characteristics of forms of funds

Forms of funds	Fixed cost	Fixed maturity date	Tax deductibility	Loss of control	Flexibility for future
		Long-term financing			
1. Common stock	Limited to dividends	No	No	Yes, if new shareholders	Widens financial base
2. Preferred stock	Limited to dividends	No	No	Some	Some restrictions
3. Debt (bonds)	Yes	Yes	Yes	Indenture provisions	Bond restrictions
4. Retained earnings	No	Avoids double taxation	No	No	No restrictions
		Intermediate financing			
5. Conditional sales contract	Interest	Yes	Yes	Some	Must meet payments
6. Leasing	Yes	Yes	Yes	Some	Must meet payments
		Short-term unsecured financing			
7. Trade credit	No	Discount date and due date	Yes	Some	Frees cash
8. Commercial banks	Interest	Yes	Yes	Some restrictions	Restricts
9. Commercial paper	Interest	Yes	Yes	No	No effect
		Short-term secured financing			
10. Accounts receivable financing	No	Yes	Yes	Some	Sales generate funds
11. Accounts receivable	No	Yes	Yes	Some	Restrict buyers
12. Inventory financing	No	Yes	Yes	Some	Inventory controls

firm are still growing, some form of option such as warrants or convertible debt will be employed in order to sell equities at an effectively higher price and lower the cost of the debt financing.

Financing costs differ not only as a consequence of the alternative sources and forms of financing employed but also on the basis of the timing and the places in the world in which the funds may be raised. The cost of debt funds characteristically declines during downturns in general business. In addition, there is distinct widening in the spread between the costs of different forms of debt during recession years. The cost of short-term debt drops much more sharply during a downturn than does long-term debt and rises more rapidly and higher during a period of tighter monetary and fiscal policies than do long-term instruments. Influences in the international markets, the characteristics of the Eurodollar and Euro-bond markets, and opportunities for financing in foreign countries were discussed in Chapter 2.

Thus, appraisal of the alternative forms, sources, timing, and the place of financing in international business finance is influenced by a large number of variables. Of primary importance are the characteristics of the individual firms involved. Important considerations are the products produced and sold, the firm's absolute size, its share of the markets in which its products are sold, the age of the firm, and its stage in the life cycle of its growth (which is influenced by the products that it sells). In addition, the life cycle of industries and the changes in general economic environmental conditions will influence the cost of financing. These represent both opportunities and challenges to the financial manager. The quality of financial management will have a major impact on whether the operations of a firm in international business will be successful.

FINANCING FORMS DISTINCTIVE TO INTERNATIONAL BUSINESS

Financing operations distinctive to international business transactions may be briefly noted. A form of commercial bank financing widely used in Europe is represented by overdrafts. An overdraft agreement permits a customer to draw checks up to some specified maximum limit. In contrast to the unfavorable connotation of overdrafts in U.S. banking until recently, the overdraft in Europe is widely used. Unlike the U.S. overdrafts, however, the European overdraft is provided for in a previous loan agreement. Thus, what is called an overdraft in Europe is really a form of a line of credit (lending arrangement) in the United States. Understood in this fashion, there is no need to elaborate its characteristics further.

Another form of financing which was until recent years much more widespread in Europe than in the United States was the use of discounting "trade bills" in both domestic and foreign transactions. One of the factors in the slow development of the discounting of trade bills and the use of acceptances in the United States was that before the passage of the Federal Reserve Act in 1913, national banks were not permitted to accept time drafts drawn on them for the benefit of their customers.[8] The Federal Reserve Act empowered national banks to accept drafts drawn on them and also gave the Federal Reserve banks the power to purchase acceptances in

---

[8] Lester V. Chandler, *Economics of Money and Banking* (5th ed.; New York: Harper & Row, 1969).

the open market, thereby helping to create a market for them. The use of discounting trade bills did not develop greatly in the United States be-cause of ability of larger firms to use wider sources of financing; they could finance their trade credit from a broad range of sources. Further-more, broad programs of accounts receivable discounting were substituted for discounting specific trade bills in individual transactions with com-mercial banks. The discounting of receivables developed as a part of the programs of mass financing by finance companies and commercial bank operations in the United States.

However, in connection with the financing of international transactions as discussed in Chapter 9 on financing imports and exports, the discount-ing of term trade bills has been a more general practice. The increased use of bankers' acceptances in the United States has been associated with the growth of the movement of goods in international trade. Bankers' ac-ceptances outstanding as of the end of June 1971 amounted to $7.6 billion. Of this total, over $3 billion were based on imports into the United States and about $1.5 billion were based on exports from the United States. Thus a total of $4.5 billion of the $7.6 billion of bankers' acceptances arose from international business transactions. The rate on bankers' acceptances in the United States generally averaged below the banks' prime rates. In foreign countries sometimes the opposite relationship may obtain.

A third variation in financing practices found in Europe as compared with the United States is the broader participation of commercial banks abroad in medium- and long-term lending activities. In Europe commer-cial banks carry on considerable activity of the kind that would be de-scribed as investment banking in the United States. However, the Banking Act of 1933 required the separation of commercial banking and the di-vestiture of investment banking operations by commercial banks in the United States. This difference thus results from a legal requirement.

A fourth and final financial practice to be noted distinctive to inter-national financing relates to arbi-loans and link financing. Both of these represent means of equalizing the supply of and demand for loanable funds in relation to sensitive interest rate levels among different countries. Under arbi-loans or international interest arbitrage financing, a borrower obtains loans in a country where the supply of funds is relatively abun-dant. These borrowings are then converted into the required local cur-rency. Simultaneously the borrower enters into a forward exchange contract to protect himself on the reconversion of the local currency into the foreign currency that will be required at the time the loan must be re-paid. The cost of an arbi-loan consists of the interest rate on the foreign loan plus the charges and differential involved on the forward exchange contract. The discount on the forward currency exchange rate may repre-sent an additional gain from the differentially lower interest rates avail-able in the foreign market. Indeed, the discount on the forward rate may be sufficient to stimulate borrowing in a higher interest rate foreign market at times. Commercial banks are typically involved in arbi-loan transactions both as lenders and as intermediaries in the foreign exchange trading.

In link financing the commercial banks take an even more direct role. A lender in a foreign country deposits funds with a bank in the borrower's country where interest rates are higher. This deposit may be earmarked for a specified borrower or it may be channeled through a money broker to borrowers of good credit standing. In the latter case, the foreign lender generally receives a portion of the broker's premium in addition to the interest rate differential. The lender, of course, would be expected to hedge his position in the foreign exchange market, since he will be repaid in the currency of the country in which the bank deposit was made. Because of the risk associated with foreign lending and with foreign exchange fluctuations, the maturity of link-financing transactions would be expected to be short term, with the possibility of renewal at maturity.

EURODOLLAR AND EUROBOND FINANCING

The nature of the Eurodollar market was described in Chapter 2. Here a number of general corporate uses for Eurodollars will be briefly described. Instead of transferring funds from the United States, American companies may borrow Eurodollars for conversion into local currencies to meet financing needs abroad. They are able to obtain funds for use abroad without a transfer of funds from the United States. Also, because of the operation of the Office of Foreign Direct Investment, some American companies borrow Eurodollars in order to repatriate the dollars to generate a credit in their capital movement position.

In addition, Eurodollars can increase the amount of available financing in the United States. During tight money periods, U.S. money-center banks have used the Eurodollar deposits of their foreign branches to increase their loanable funds in the United States. Similarly, for both foreign and U.S. corporations, international financing may be utilized when the capital markets of a particular country do not provide sufficient equity financing or are not of sufficient breadth to make local funds available. Or the international financing may be used when government controls restrict the borrowing of local currency. Thus, Eurodollar financing may be applied for both working capital purposes and for longer term investment. The proceeds of Eurodollar borrowings have been used by the foreign affiliates of U.S. firms for repayment of dollar loans from their parent companies or for the payment of dollar dividends.

A development related to the shorter term financing arrangements indicated by the Eurodollar market has been development of the Eurobond market. This refers to the development of longer term borrowing by U.S.

and other corporations in long-term U.S. dollar denominated bonds. Despite the questioning of the U.S. dollar, the dominant part of the broader international market for long-term financing and investment is in dollar denominated bonds. Other techniques were employed, but they did not develop. For example, in early 1961, the SACOR bond issue of the Portuguese Development Agency was denominated in the European unit of account. This represents a combination of European currencies whose exact composition varies with each bond contract. Such bonds reduce much of the risk of exchange rate change. However, the borrower bears the risk that his own currency may be devalued relative to the broader unit of account and the lender still runs risk that his own currency may be appreciated. The complexity of the arrangement has prevented its development to any substantial degree.

Another alternative is to offer the investor the option of receiving the repayment of the principal and interest either in U.S. dollars or a strong currency such as the German mark. The advantage to the investor is obvious, but the borrower may be hesitant to accept the increased risks that an alteration in foreign exchange rates for either currency would create.

But a surge in U.S. borrowing in the overseas capital markets came about in 1965 when monetary conditions were tightening both in the United States and in many European countries. U.S. borrowing in Europe leads to tighter credit conditions in those financial markets. Most of the early issues of U.S. firms were nonconvertible bearing an interest cost of slightly under 6 percent. In October 1965 Monsanto Chemical Company offered the first convertible debenture at an interest cost of 4.5 percent.

U.S. firms have formed subsidiaries in Luxemburg and Delaware to issue the long-term bonds. They are established for the purpose of turning over the funds raised in the foreign markets to the foreign operating subsidiaries.

These subsidiaries are established to avoid taxes. The U.S. firm must have a borrowing agency in a country where no withholding tax is applicable to the payment of interest to nonresidents. This is why the loan cannot be made by the U.S. parent firm itself. If it were, the interest paid to the nonresident investor would be subject to the 30 percent U.S. withholding tax. Six European countries, Austria, Denmark, Luxemburg, Norway, the Netherlands, and Sweden do not impose a withholding tax on interest paid by resident companies to nonresidents.

Thus a financial subsidiary in one of these six European countries may be used to raise funds overseas. But a U.S.-based corporation may also be utilized. The U.S. corporation may avoid the necessity of a withholding tax on interest paid to non-U.S. residents by proof that more than 80 percent of this gross income has been derived from foreign sources for the three taxable years preceding the payment of interest.

Most such U.S. corporations are formed in the state of Delaware because of the general advantages of incorporating in that state. Neither the Luxemburg nor Delaware subsidiaries have a clear-cut cost advantage.[9] It has been estimated that for an issue of moderate size in the $50,000,000 range, the initial and recurrent costs (notary fees, printing cost, taxes incident to creating the company, stamp duties on the issue of bonds, and the annual taxes on the company's outstanding securities) of the Luxemburg company would be roughly 0.2 percent per annum over and above the interest costs. The net cost to a Delaware subsidiary corporation is slightly less but not enough to have a major influence on the decision. Besides costs, there are other advantages in favor of the Luxemburg subsidiary. The Luxemburg company may relend and invest the proceeds of its borrowing anywhere in the world without endangering its tax-exempt status. A U.S. subsidiary must maintain at least 80 percent of its income from foreign sources. This, of course, limits its ability to invest funds even on a temporary basis in the United States.

In connection with the financing of U.S. corporations abroad, it has been proposed that a special type of holding company be formed.[10] Under Segre's proposal, the U.S. parent would turn over ownership and control of its European operation to a newly created European-based subsidiary. The parent firm would sell a portion of the equity shares of the holding company on the European market. This would enable Europeans to achieve direct ownership in American-managed enterprise in Europe to ease concern about the "invasion" of U.S. capital into Europe.

SUMMARY

A broad spectrum of financing sources is available to the manager of a firm engaged in international business. There are seven internationally sponsored agencies: three affiliated with the World Bank group and four regional lending institutions to facilitate development on four continents. Regional lending agencies include the Inter-American Development Bank, the European Investment Bank, the Asian Development Bank, and the African Development Bank.

Development banks on a national scale perform the same general functions as the international and regional development banks. They may be government or private agencies, supporting economic development within nations or internationally. Governments may encourage development projects by offering various kinds of tax reduction or exemptions. Specific tax concessions may be given to certain industries regarded as important to national economic needs. In addition, governments may undertake in-

---

[9] Carl H. Stem, "The Oversea's Dollar Bond Market and Recent U.S. Borrowing Abroad," *Staff Economic Studies No. 22* (Washington, D.C.: Board of Governors of the Federal Reserve System, 1966), p. 30.

[10] This was the proposal made by Claudio Segre, in Stem ibid., p. 31.

frastructure investment essential to the undertaking of private projects. Governments also guarantee loans made to private firms in individual countries, subsidize the training of workers, and pay moving expenses to induce workers to migrate to new areas.

The U.S. Congress established Eximbank in 1934, and has renewed its authority every five years. Its primary purpose is to provide financial aid to encourage exports from the United States. This it does by direct loans, financial guarantees, participation financing, local-cost financing, relending credits, cooperative managing, and export expansion facilities. Both foreign and U.S. business firms benefit greatly by tying in with its financing arrangements. It enables foreign firms to be U.S. customers, stimulates U.S. exports, and eliminates the risks of receiving payment.

The Agency for International Development carries out nonmilitary U.S. foreign assistance programs. It supports the international position of the United States by aiding friendly foreign governments. Its low-interest loans have maturities up to 40 years. It also has an investment guarantee program which covers extended risks, particularly of a political nature. OPIC was created in 1969 to take over and expand the AID programs to encourage private investment in underdeveloped countries.

Other U.S. industrial development banks also make a contribution in stimulating construction of projects with specified social objectives at lower than customary interest rates. Credit is usually for 5- to 10-year terms, and the banks will sometimes buy shares as well as make loans. Small business and depressed areas have been the particular beneficiary of these institutions. Foreign development banks have similar programs in other countries.

Financial managers should indeed keep abreast of the opportunities afforded by this great variety of financial institutions. In aiding the buyers, they stimulate sales and provide financing to the sellers of goods on the vast world market. The magnitude of operations and the huge sums of money involved justify careful study and long-range planning by the astute financial manager.

Only a brief review is given of the ordinary domestic financing sources, information about which is readily available. Major sources and forms of funds are summarized in tables for ready reference. The wide spectrum of choices is demonstrated, permitting the tailoring of funding to the needs of the firm. Financing forms distinctive to international operations are emphasized.

The final section of the chapter describes financing forms distinctive to international business finance. These include overdrafts, the discounting of term bills (bankers' acceptances), etc. Also, commercial banks in Europe engage in more medium-term (and longer) lending activities than commercial banks in the United States. However, term lending by commercial banks in the United States has been increasing. Arbi-loans and link financing are responses to differential interest rate levels in different countries.

More generalized mechanisms for the development of an international financial market are Eurodollars and Eurobonds. Instead of transferring funds from the United States, American companies may borrow Eurodollars for conversion into local currencies to meet financing needs abroad. They are thus able to obtain funds for use abroad without a transfer of funds from the United States. Also, because of the restrictions on the export of capital by American companies, some companies borrow Eurodollars in order to repatriate the dollars to generate a credit in their capital movement position. The proceeds of Eurodollar borrowings have also been used by the foreign affiliates of U.S. firms for the repayment of dollars loans from their parent company for the payment of dollar dividends.

The borrowing by United States and other corporations by means of long-term U.S. dollar-denominated bonds has been termed the Eurobond market. Even with the recent weakness of the U.S. dollar, a substantial volume of Eurobond financing has taken place in the form of convertible debt. Thus the buyer is protected to some degree against the potential further decline in the relative value of the U.S. dollar by the ability to participate in the rise in the equity values of the U.S. companies obtaining the financing. Even during early 1972 when the future of the U.S. dollar was uncertain and the world capital shortage had not been alleviated, large American firms were utilizing convertible debt financing from the Eurobond market at interest rates of 4.5 percent or less. This was below the prime lending rate of commercial banks in the United States for short-term loans.

PROBLEM 8–1

The United Company has a very strong product line in the United States related to the chemical industry. It is seeking to expand abroad in a developing country of South America but has had relatively little experience and has also experienced a relatively severe cash condition. Therefore it was determined that in the countries in which it is interested it would be best to enter into joint-venture operations with a local company as a joint-venture partner.

A. Indicate the kinds of planning a company seeking to expand abroad must undertake under the general circumstances described above. What should it formulate from the point of view of having access to a broad range of financing under most favorable terms?

B. On the assumption that the chemical products manufactured by the firm are considered of value in the economic development of the host country, what are the financing sources available to the joint-venture operation?

C. Compare the financing that would be available to the American company going abroad on a 100 percent financing basis as compared to the joint-venture arrangement set forth in the problem.

PROBLEM 8–2

An American company is operating with subsidiaries in the strong currency countries of Western Europe. In addition, it is also operating with subsidiaries in Latin American countries such as Brazil and Argentina.

Compare the financing strategy and policies of this American company for its operations in both Western Europe and Latin America with respect to the following:

1. Financing sources and forms.
2. Financial structure and terms of sale.

SELECTED BIBLIOGRAPHY

Baker, J. C. *International Finance Corporation.* New York, 1968.

Board of Governors of the Federal Reserve System. *Corporations Engaged in Foreign Banking and Financing Under the Federal Reserve Act—Regulation.* Washington, D.C., 1969.

Chandler, Lester V. *Economics of Money and Banking.* 5th ed. New York: Harper & Row, 1969.

The Economic Report of the President, p. 302. Washington, D.C.: Executive Office of the President, February 1971.

Ellis, C. Allen, and Wadsworth, John S., Jr. "United States Corporations and the International Capital Market Abroad," *Financial Analysts Journal,* May–June 1966, pp. 169–75.

Esslen, Rainer. "European Sources of Capital for U.S. Companies," *Financial Executive,* Vol. 39, No. 10 (October 1971), pp. 20–27.

Eurobond Borrowing Expected to Reverse Downward Trend in '71," *The Wall Street Journal,* January 6, 1971.

International Financial Corporation. *Annual Report, 1970,* pp. 2, 18–29.

Irvine, Reed J.; Maroni, Yves; and Lee, Henry F. "How to Borrow Successfully," *Columbia Journal of World Business,* Vol. 5, No. 1 (January–February 1970), pp. 42–48.

Lewis, J. Furman, and Hoskins, W. R. "The Eurodollar Markets," *Business Horizons,* Vol. 13, No. 2 (April 1970), pp. 49–60.

Main, J. "The First Real International Bankers," *Fortune,* December 1967.

Mendelson, Morris. "The Eurobond and Capital Market Integration," *The Journal of Finance,* Vol. 27, No. 1 (March 1972), pp. 110–26.

Nehrt, Lee C. *Private Development Finance Companies.* Washington, D.C.: International Finance Corporation, 1964.

Parker, George G. C. "Financing Is Still an Art and an Instrument of Growth,"

Columbia Journal of World Business, Vol. 3, No. 4 (July–August 1968), p. 43.

Richardson, D. "Investment Companies throughout the Free World," *Financial Analysts Journal,* Vol. 21, No. 1 (January–February 1965).

Scheibla, S. "Curb on Global Lenders," *Barron's,* November 12, 1971, pp. 5, 16, 18.

Smith, D. T. "Financial Variables in International Business," *Harvard Business Review,* Vol. 44, No. 1 (1966), p. 93.

Stem, Carl H. "The Oversea's Dollar Bond Market and Recent U.S. Borrowing Abroad," *Staff Economic Studies No. 22.* Washington, D.C.: Board of Governors of the Federal Reserve System, 1966.

Waterman, Merwin H. "Capital Sources for Multinational Companies," *Financial Executive,* Vol. 36, No. 5 (May 1968), pp. 25–42.

Weston, J. Fred, and Brigham, E. F. *Managerial Finance.* 4th ed. New York: Holt, Rinehart & Winston, Inc., 1972.

Zenoff, David B. "Remitting Funds from Foreign Affiliates," *Financial Executive,* Vol. 36, No. 3 (March 1968).

Zwick, Jack. "Regulation of Foreign Banks in the United States," *The National Banking Review,* Vol. 4, No. 1 (September 1966), pp. 1–19.

9

Financing worldwide commercial sales

COMMERCIAL SALES on an international basis are becoming of increasing importance to American firms. U.S. exports have increased since World War II on a year-by-year basis as total world trade has increased, even though the percentage of U.S. international trade in relation to total world trade has declined slightly. Many American firms, in efforts to broaden the markets for their products, have successfully introduced their products on an international basis. This has decreased their dependence on the level of economic activity within the United States. The recent 1969–70 recession is a good example. The export sales of many American firms increased during this period in spite of the decrease in economic activity at home.

In many instances goods can be sold at slightly higher prices on a worldwide basis than domestically. Commercial sales on a worldwide basis are particularly important to industries in which technological obsolescence in the United States is an important factor. First- or second-generation computers are still readily salable in many developing countries of the world. Even nonjet commercial aircraft are still very much in demand abroad, whereas none of these products can be sold on a profitable basis at home.

Since 1942 numerous U.S. corporations have availed themselves of the tax advantage of selling to the western hemisphere through the Western Hemisphere Trade Corporation. The maximum marginal tax rate on the profits of this corporation is 38 percent instead of 48 percent. A Domestic International Sales Corporation was authorized by the Revenue Act of 1971 in order to stimulate the export of U.S. goods and services. The advantage of the use of this latter corporation arises from the fact that income taxes can be deferred on 50 percent of its export-related profits. Both of these subsidiary forms of organization were discussed in more detail in Chapter 7.

Due to the substantial advantages of developing commercial sales on an international basis, it behooves American firms to acquire expertise to be able to conduct their international business on an efficient and effective basis. The various export procedures and financing opportunities outlined in this chapter will aid the financial executive of a multinational firm in this activity.

The terms and conditions under which exports of goods and services by U.S. exporters take place vary greatly. They go from cash with order on or before delivery in dollars at one extreme, to sales in a foreign currency with credit terms from 5 to 10 years at the other. The actual conditions and terms of any particular transaction depend on existing competition among sellers, determined by supply and demand conditions at the time of the sale.

Immediately following World War II, U.S. exporters demanded and received immediate cash payment in full in dollars. As the economies of other trading nations were rebuilt with U.S. aid and competition returned to the international trading scene, terms have gradually changed. It is not unusual now for an American exporter to sell in terms of a foreign currency on an extended time basis. This change has made it necessary for the American exporter to seek aid in financing his export transactions.

A further hindrance to sales on an international basis is the fact that many developing countries are extremely short of foreign exchange and, therefore, will not permit their citizens to import from other nations on a normal commercial basis. As a result, foreign trade may be conducted on a straight barter basis. One good is exchanged for another. This is also accomplished on a private agreement basis in which several parties are involved in the exchange of goods, or by a switch-trade arrangement made possible by the deficit position of one of the trading partners in bilateral trade agreements effected between two countries.

BASIC DOCUMENTATION IN NORMAL EXPORT-IMPORT TRANSACTIONS

Normal business transactions between persons within a country usually follow certain well-established procedures as specified by a country's commercial codes developed from past experience. International rules of business conduct have also developed as a result of historical practices observed by trading partners in the financial settlement of international transactions.

There are three basic documents instrumental in assuring the orderly conduct of business on an international basis. These are the bill of exchange, the bill of lading, and the commercial letter of credit.

Bill of exchange

A bill of exchange is an unconditional order in writing addressed by one person to another, signed by the person giving it, requiring the person to whom it is addressed to pay on demand or at a fixed or determinable future time a sum certain in money to order or to bearer. Personal checks as well as banker's checks are bills of exchange. They are drawn by a maker and instruct a bank to pay a certain sum of money to a designated person.

Sight or time drafts used in international trade are bills of exchange. They are drawn by a maker, usually the exporter, and direct the foreign importer to pay a certain definite amount of money upon receipt of the draft or at a specified future time. A sight draft is one that specifies that the funds be paid upon presentation, whereas a time draft is one that specifies that the funds be paid after a definite specified time interval.

When a foreign importer has made credit arrangements with his commercial bank whereby the bank's credit worthiness is substituted for that of the importer, the time draft becomes known as a banker's acceptance. Acceptance takes place when the time draft is presented to the importer's bank and this bank then endorses the time draft by placing on it the word "accepted," followed by the signature of an officer of the bank. Once accepted, the banker's acceptance becomes a negotiable instrument permitting the exporter to sell it in the money market to assist in financing the foreign transaction.

A "clean" bill of exchange is one to which documents of title are not attached when the bill is delivered to the person against whom the bill is drawn when he pays the amount due. A "documentary" bill of exchange, by contrast, is one to which these documents of title are attached and are delivered to the person against whom the bill is drawn at the time payment is made.

The drawer or maker is the person that issues the bill. The person against whom the bill is drawn, who eventually accepts and pays the specified amount at maturity, is known as the drawee. The payee is that person to whom the drawee will eventually pay the funds. The payee and the drawer are one and the same person if the bill of exchange has not been discounted or assigned to somebody else. However, this is usually not the case. Since the bill of exchange is a negotiable instrument, particularly after it has been accepted or guaranteed by a bank, the ownership of this bill may pass through several hands before it is finally paid.

To avoid misunderstandings, a bill of exchange must be an unconditional order or a command, not a request. It must be addressed by one person to another and must specify that a definite sum is payable upon demand or at a definite future time. A bill of exchange may be made out to order or to bearer. If it is made out to order the funds involved will be paid to the person specified. When a bill of exchange is made out to bearer the funds will be paid to the person presenting the bill of exchange for payment. For this reason bills of exchange made out to bearer must be protected the same as bearer bonds. In shipment they must be sent registered mail and insured for the full value.

Bills of lading

Bills of lading are given by transportation companies to shippers in connection with goods delivered to them for shipment. The bill of lading is a receipt that the transportation company gives to the shipper. It is at the same time a contract to ship the goods involved a certain way and to deliver them at the point of destination to a specified person or to order, as the case may be. The bill of lading also is a document of title which gives the holder of the bill of lading title to the property. It is negotiable if properly made out.

The rights of shippers as well as the liabilities of carriers and the exceptions thereto are governed by statutes. In the United States, the United States Carriage of Goods by Sea Act of 1936 governs the relationship between shippers and carriers. The majority of other trading nations have enacted similar laws, all of them based on the Brussels Convention of 1922–24, the adoption of which was participated in by representatives of most nations trading internationally.

Bills of lading are negotiable if made out to order. In contrast, a straight bill of lading is not negotiable, because it instructs that the goods be delivered to a definite specified person. In shipments to several South American countries, carriers will insist that goods be shipped on a straight bill of lading basis specifying a particular person to whom the goods are to be delivered. The reason for this insistence is due to their desire to avoid unnecessary legal actions should goods be delivered to the wrong person.

Commercial letters of credit

A commercial letter of credit is an instrument which is issued by a bank on behalf of a foreign buyer. In this letter the bank agrees to honor drafts resulting from an import transaction on behalf of its customer. To obtain such a commercial letter of credit the foreign buyer usually enters into a contractual relationship with his bank on the basis of which the letter of credit is issued. The letter is addressed to the seller and signed by the issuing bank and states the name of a person for whose benefit the letter of credit has been issued. It also indicates the approximate value and the nature of the merchandise that can be purchased with the letter of credit. Also specified are the terms of sale to be shown on the drafts to be drawn in connection with the transaction. It also specifies details of shipping charges whether on an f.o.b. or c.i.f. basis.[1] It will also specify the documents that must be attached to the drafts issued by the seller and indicates a time limit after which it becomes void. Occasionally a letter

---

[1] The abbreviation f.o.b. means "free on board," or price at factory with transportation costs additional; c.i.f. means "including cost, insurance, and freight."

of credit may also specify the percentage of the goods involved that will be covered by the letter of credit. In this instance the foreign buyer may have to meet part of the cost of the goods himself.

The *opening bank* in connection with the commercial letter of credit is the bank issuing the letter on behalf of its customer. The *notifying bank* is a correspondent bank of the opening bank located in the country of the seller. The notifying bank usually notifies the seller of the existence and the terms of the letter of credit. A *negotiating bank* is one that buys or discounts the draft of the seller that has been issued in connection with the letter of credit. The *paying bank* is the bank on which the seller's draft is drawn, which may or may not be the opening bank. A *confirming bank* is usually a bank in the country of the beneficiary that along with the opening bank assumes the obligation to honor the seller's drafts.

The commercial letter of credit greatly reduces the risk of the seller in connection with foreign export transactions. In fact, the commercial letter of credit may be used by a seller to finance the acquisition or manufacture of goods to be sold. Commercial letters of credit are issued either on an irrevocable or revocable basis. A revocable letter of credit may be revoked by the issuing bank should the credit worthiness of the foreign buyer deteriorate during the term for which the credit has been extended. An irrevocable letter of credit, on the other hand, may not be revoked by the issuing bank. It usually specifies the drawing of sight or time drafts in the currency of the seller, the buyer, or a third country and cannot be canceled by the opening bank.

The strongest commercial letter of credit is a confirmed, irrevocable letter of credit by which the payment on drafts issued in connection with the export transaction is guaranteed not only by the opening bank but also by a confirming bank, usually located in the country of the seller. A commercial letter of credit which does not involve a notifying or confirming bank is known as a circular commercial letter of credit. It is sent by the opening bank directly to the seller who may discount or sell the drafts involved to any bank that wishes to buy them. In this instance the credit worthiness of the transaction is based entirely on the credit worthiness of the foreign opening bank. It is for this reason that only the strongest foreign bank can issue circular letters of credit.

THE PAYMENT TERMS OF EXPORT TRANSACTIONS

The instruments of foreign trade discussed in the previous section make possible an infinite variety of payment terms suited to the needs of a particular transaction. At one extreme, the risks of the exporter may be completely eliminated by insisting on cash payment in dollars prior to the shipment of goods. At the other extreme, the risks may all be borne by the seller when he agrees to sell export mrchandise in terms of a foreign currency on an open account basis. In between these extremes there are all possible variations.

Cash terms

When cash payment is insisted upon by the seller, credit risk does not exist. Under these circumstances a seller may insist on cash at the time of order or he may specify that goods are to be paid for in cash prior to shipment. Another possible modification provides that a certain sum is paid at the time of order, that progress payments are to be made during the time of preparation for shipment, and that the final amount is paid prior to the release of the goods to a common carrier.

Cash-type transactions are not numerous in these days of severe international competition. Only in instances of poor credit worthiness of the foreign buyer or extreme political risks in the country of the buyer will the seller insist on such severe terms.

Credit terms

A seller can specify the credit terms under which he is willing to proceed with a foreign export transaction. However, the actual terms used are strongly influenced by the presence or absence of competition. As a result, an exporter may be forced to grant 30-, 60-, or 90-day credit even though he would prefer to be paid immediately after shipment.

Shortest credit terms are achieved when the exporter can draw a sight draft on a correspondent bank of the foreign buyer's bank. In this instance the bill of exchange will be presented to the local bank and the necessary documents will be delivered to the bank once the draft has been honored. The credit period is extended if a sight draft is drawn by the shipper and is then forwarded with the accompanying papers to the foreign importer or his commercial bank. Payment is made to the exporter at sight when the bill of exchange reaches the foreign importer or his bank.

If longer credit terms are required, the exporter can draw a time draft, instead of a sight draft, which is a bill of exchange that specifies the time period after presentation when the funds must be paid. Under this arrangement the necessary bills of lading may be forwarded to the foreign buyer so that he may obtain the merchandise prior to payment. The seller may also decide to withhold the necessary papers so that the foreign buyer does not obtain possession of the goods until they are paid for.

The risks of the bills of exchange transaction

In transactions involving an extension of credit, the risk of nonpayment or noncollection is always present. The foreign buyer may not be able to pay or he may not have made arrangements with his bank to meet his obligation. These risks are eliminated by the insistence of the exporter on a commercial letter of credit. These risks are minimized to the greatest extent by the insistence of the exporter that the foreign buyer furnish him a confirmed, irrevocable letter of credit. As discussed previously, an irrevocable letter of credit is one that has been confirmed by a bank in the exporter's country. The obligation to pay under this letter of credit has been assumed by a local bank as well as the opening bank.

The next step in the direction of increasing risks is encountered when an irrevocable but unconfirmed letter of credit is used. In this instance, payments under the commercial letter of credit are guaranteed solely by the foreign issuing bank.

A further increase of risk takes place when a letter of credit is issued on a revocable basis. In this instance there is no protection against loss should the financial standing of the foreign importer deteriorate. The bank issuing the revocable letter of credit reserves the right to terminate the letter of credit without prior notification if in its opinion the financial ability to pay of its customer deteriorates in any way.

The last move in the direction of greater risk on the part of the exporter occurs when no letter of credit is used, and the exporter sells to the foreign buyer on an open account basis.

From the above it can be seen that the commercial letter of credit transfers risk from the exporter to a foreign and/or domestic banking institution. The possession of a commercial letter of credit often makes it possible for the foreign buyer to obtain improved terms in the purchase of the goods involved. Usually payment is received by the exporter on presentation of the necessary documents as proof of shipment. If the exporter has any doubts about the credit worthiness of the foreign buyer's bank, he should insist on having the letter of credit confirmed by a local bank which will then guarantee the credit of the foreign bank.

The cost of financing a time draft

When a time draft is used in an export transaction, the exporter may carry the credit for his own account or may refinance the amounts involved through a local bank. Under the latter circumstance the letter of credit usually specifies who will pay the expenses of financing. These may be paid by the foreign importer or the U.S. exporter, a choice which is strongly influenced by existing competitive conditions at the time of the initiation of the transaction. Many commercial banks grant advances against collections to their exporter customers.

One excellent means of reducing both commercial and political risks in connection with export sales was discussed in Chapter 4. The procurement of foreign credit insurance covering the export transaction from the Foreign Credit Insurance Association or the Export-Import Bank affords this protection. There are two avenues open to the exporter to obtain this insurance which will greatly aid him in financing his foreign sales. He can obtain the necessary policies himself, and then on the basis of these policies obtain financing from his bank, or he can obtain from the insurers a guarantee that they will hold the lender harmless in the case of losses.

In the instance of large transactions over a period of years involving capital goods, it is even possible to arrange loans on behalf of a foreign credit-worthy buyer directly from the Export-Import Bank. Similarly to foreign credit insurance, which does not cover all of the financed portion of an export transaction, a loan to the foreign buyer on the part of the Export-Import Bank also does not cover all of the financed portion of the sale. In both instances the U.S. exporter is required to carry a part of this risk himself.

SOURCES OF FINANCING EXPORT-IMPORT SALES

Commercial banks

U.S. banks are prohibited from financing bills of exchange and banker's acceptances in excess of six months. However, in order to compete more effectively with foreign financial institutions, many U.S. commercial banks have formed Edge Act financing subsidiaries which are permitted to engage in export financing in excess of 180 days as a result of the 1957 and 1963 revisions of Regulation K of Section 25a of the Federal Reserve Act. An indication of the increasing use of Edge Act financing subsidiaries is that they numbered 6 in 1955 and 39 by 1965, and their use is still growing.

In countries where subsidiaries of U.S. commercial banks are not permitted or encouraged, U.S. banks will form native corporations, so-called agreement banks. The formation of these foreign-chartered banks is usually affected when a U.S. commercial bank forms a state-chartered corporation which will own the foreign bank. It will then make an agreement with the Federal Reserve System to operate the foreign bank under Provision 25a of the Reserve Act and subject to Regulation K of the Federal Reserve Board.

The use of factors in financing foreign exports

A factor organization will purchase short-term receivables as they become due. For this service the factor will charge a fee. Some factors will agree to absorb all of the risks of noncollection. However, many factors will insist that the exporter retain 20 to 30 percent of the risk for his own account. Factors will further insist on an agreement with the exporter on the extent of the receivables that they will purchase. They will usually insist on a sufficient spread of risk by insisting that they be permitted to purchase all or most of an exporter's receivables providing, of course, that the foreign customers are credit worthy.

In instances where the factor buys the receivables on a largely non-recourse basis, he will exert a strong influence on the acceptability of buyers, which may interfere with the exporter's sales effort. In the case of large dollar volume exports over a medium-term period, the factor may insist that he acquire these receivables on a case-by-case basis. Factor organizations will handle collections in terms of U.S. dollars as well as in other convertible foreign currencies. Factors usually charge a commitment fee of 1.5 to 2 percent as well as a rate of interest in excess of the prime rate.

Whether factoring companies are utilized by exporters depends upon two considerations. The first is whether the exporter can perform the credit evaluation function as efficiently as the factoring company. Since a factoring company may evaluate the same customer for a large number of companies, it may build up credit files and an expertise which enables it to evaluate credit at a lower cost than the exporter could. Second, a comparison is made between the interest charged for financing by the factor as compared with the availability of funds and the interest charged by alternative sources.

U.S. export financing companies

There exist in the United States a few private export financing companies. However, in order to reduce their risks, these companies limit their financing activity largely to covering sales to foreign exclusive distributors of U.S.-made capital goods. These buyers are usually financially strong organizations.

The risk of export financing may be further reduced by the use of Foreign Credit Insurance Association insurance policies, which permits the export financing companies to do their financing on a nonrecourse basis. Medium- or long-term credit sales payments are usually required of the buyer on a scheduled basis. Under these circumstances, the financing firm may buy these notes from the U.S. exporter and then deal with the foreign importer on a direct basis.

Export financing firms will usually insist that the foreign buyer make a 10 to 20 percent down payment and will also insist that the U.S. exporter carry part of the risk in case of noncollection. When this is the case a participation certificate is issued for the part of the risk assumed by the U.S. exporter, a certificate which he may be able to use as a collateral for other loans.

FOREIGN CURRENCY FINANCING

When a U.S. exporter makes export sales in terms of a foreign currency, there exists always the risk that the value of this foreign currency may decrease in relation to the U.S. dollar. The means of protection against foreign exchange rate risks has been discussed in Chapter 5.

Foreign currency borrowing

When a U.S. exporter wishes to assist a foreign buyer in financing his purchase, he may advance the foreign buyer dollars which the buyer then uses to pay for the goods. It is understood that there is an obligation on the part of the foreign buyer to repay the exporter in his local currency at an agreed-upon schedule. In order to eliminate foreign exchange rate risk from the transaction, the U.S. exporter, if possible, will enter the financial markets in the foreign country to obtain a loan from a local source for the amount involved in the transaction. The proceeds of this loan are then used to purchase U.S. dollars at the existing spot rate to recover the dollars advanced to the foreign buyer. When the foreign exporter meets his obligation and makes payments as required in his local currency, these funds are then used to liquidate the foreign currency loan of the U.S. exporter.

The use of a foreign currency swap

In instances where it is possible to obtain a foreign currency swap from either a commercial bank or a foreign central bank, U.S. exporters may obtain local foreign currency by means of a swap agreement. These funds are then advanced to the foreign buyer to be used by him to pay for the importation of his U.S. purchases. According to the terms of his contract he will be required to repay the exporter in his local currency at the end of the swap period, funds which are then used to liquidate the currency swap. When credits are granted to a foreign buyer by this method, the exporter must be certain that his sales price is sufficiently increased to cover costs of the swap or that the foreign buyer agrees to pay the extra costs of the swap arrangements.

PL 480 funds

PL 480 funds are blocked foreign currency owned by the U.S. government resulting from the sale of surplus agricultural commodities to foreign governments. It is not possible for a U.S. exporter to borrow PL 480 funds solely to finance exports. However, it is possible to use these funds to develop and expand foreign markets for U.S. agricultural products, as well as for purposes of business development and trade expansion. In order to take advantage of the availability of these blocked funds it is required that the U.S. exporter have some sort of an operating organization within the country where the blocked funds exist.

Link financing

The link method of financing involves borrowing funds on a short-term basis in a foreign country in which funds are plentiful and cheap. These funds are then converted into the currency of a country where the funds are needed for business purposes, and in which loans are more difficult to obtain and interest rates are higher. These loans are usually arranged through the efforts of commercial banks. Link financing widens a firm's financial horizons. It increases the supply of funds and reduces their costs.

The foreign lender makes a time deposit in a bank of the borrowing firm at the prime rate, which is lower than the cost of normal export financing. The borrower is thus *linked* through the bank deposit to a foreign private lender. The credit risk in this transaction is usually that of the local bank making the loan. The broker arranging such a transaction usually charges a 2 to 3 percent commission. He keeps 1 percent and passes the remainder on to the foreign lender who, therefore, obtains a higher rate of interest than he would receive in his own country. At the same time the firm borrowing these funds is able to get a loan at a lower rate than would otherwise be possible.

FOREIGN TRADE WITH COUNTRIES SUFFERING AN EXTREME SHORTAGE OF FOREIGN EXCHANGE RESERVES

Barter

Barter represents an exchange of goods between two countries without the involvement of currencies. Surplus goods are offered for barter instead of being sold at a lower price than on the normal market. Usually barter deals are arranged between countries on a bilateral basis. An exporter of one country sends certain goods to an importer of another country and in return takes goods in trade that he sells in his own country.

As with all trade transactions there must be an advantage for both parties involved. The exporter to the foreign-exchange-short country must obtain a relatively larger quantity of goods in exchange for his goods than would be the case in transactions involving currencies. In turn, the importer in the foreign-currency-short country must be able to obtain goods as a result of this barter transaction that he would not otherwise be able to obtain, and, if possible, he must receive for his goods a normal or higher value. By far the largest volume of barter deals in the world today are made between governments. However, in countries where barter is the custom, it is not difficult for individual firms to receive official approval for barter transactions.

Compensating agreements among three parties usually involve the export of commodities which are surplus in the countries involved. An exporter of one country will ship goods to a foreign-currency-short country in exchange by barter for goods which are then sent either to a third country or to the first exporter's own country as the occasion requires. To complete this transaction the original exporter then settles accounts on either a barter or currency basis with the firm that received his goods. As in a straight two-country barter deal, there must be an advantage to all parties concerned to make such a transaction desirable.

Switch exchange financing

A number of developing countries that have a shortage of foreign exchange have entered into bilateral clearing agreements to make foreign trade possible between them. The agreements usually set forth an anticipated volume of trade between the two countries and the amount of each country's currency that is deposited into a bilateral clearing account. Exports to each other are then paid out of this clearing account.

Unfortunately, however, too often one of the countries will not live up to its end of the bargain by failing to export sufficient goods to its trading partner. When this happens a shortage in clearing funds will develop for the deficit country. One of the countries becomes a creditor country and the other a debtor country due to the fact that the latter country's volume of exports is running below the agreed-upon volume. When this occurs, bilateral trade agreements have a tendency to break down. A breakdown is harmful to both countries but is usually of particular disadvantage to the debtor country.

There is a limit to the deficit that is permitted under the bilateral agreement. It is usually specified that amounts in excess of allowable variations must be paid the creditor country in gold or convertible currency. This requirement, however, often makes possible exports from a third country to the creditor country. Both partners to the clearing agreement usually realize that it is to their best interests to remove the imbalance. This is achieved by procuring desired goods from third countries for export to the creditor country via the debtor country. In effect the debtor country procures goods from others for export to the creditor country in order to bring the bilateral trading agreement back into the required balance. This means that the debtor country will spend gold or convertible currencies in the procurement of goods sent to the creditor country. However, this is often more advantageous than exporting debtor-country goods to the trading partner.

It is at this point that a switch-trade broker enters the picture. He determines the goods that are wanted and is instrumental in procuring them from third countries. The goods are paid for by the debtor country in a currency required by the third-country exporter.

The goods are then shipped to the creditor country, often at inflated or above-cost prices, a practice normally ignored by the creditor country due to its need for the goods involved, since it could not purchase these for its own account due to its extreme shortage of convertible foreign exchange. The procedure is equivalent to settling a clear account deficit on a discount basis. However, the expenditure of convertible currency on the part of the debtor country is required unless the goods can be procured from a third country that is willing to accept the debtor country's currency in payment for the goods.

A number of variations are possible from the above-outlined procedure. Excess clearing funds which represent a claim against the debtor country are sometimes used to pay for needed imports into the creditor country. An exporter willing to export the desired goods to the creditor country will engage a switch broker to arrange for someone to buy the clearing funds for convertible currency at a discount. This is made possible by charging a higher than normal price for the exports to the creditor country. The purchaser of the clearing funds against the debtor country then has the option of selling these funds to an importer from the debtor country or of making a deal on a discount basis to sell these funds to the central bank of the debtor country to be used in clearing its deficit position in the bilateral trading agreement with its trading partner.

Bilateral trading agreements exist between many developing countries and east-bloc countries who find it advantageous to increase exports to each other on this basis. Information on existing bilateral trade agreements is readily available from financial sources. However, negotiations required to take advantage of deficits in these agreements are quite often sensitive, since they require the approval of at least both of the governments of the firms that are partners to the bilateral trading agreement. At times the consent of the exporter's own government is also required, since the goods are sometimes shipped directly from the third country to the creditor country instead via the debtor country. This saves time as well as unnecessary expense.

A firm desiring to take advantage of bilateral clearing agreement deficits should employ a knowledgeable switch-trade broker to develop these export opportunities and to carry out the required negotiations. This avoids involving the firm in possible problems should the complicated negotiations fail to reach a successful conclusion.

SUMMARY

This chapter outlined various export procedures and financing options, familiarity with which will enhance a U.S. firm's ability to export its products on an efficient and effective basis. We first described three basic documents used in normal export-import transactions. These are the bill of exchange, the bill of lading, and the commercial letter of credit.

Bills of exchange, frequently used in international trade, are sight or time drafts. A sight draft requires that the funds be paid upon presentation, whereas a time draft specifies that the payments be made at a fixed or determinable future time. A bill of exchange is called "clean" or "documentary" depending upon whether or not documents of title are attached to it.

The bill of lading is a receipt that the transportation company gives to the shipper. It is at the same time a contract specifying how, where, and to whom the goods are to be shipped. It is also a document of title and is negotiable if made out to order. The rights of shippers, as well as the liabilities of carriers, are governed by statutes established in major trading nations based on the Brussels Convention of 1922–24.

A commercial letter of credit is a letter addressed to the seller and signed by the issuing bank which agrees to honor drafts resulting from an import transaction by a foreign buyer. The letter specifies various terms and details of the transaction. The commercial letter of credit reduces the risk of the seller so much that it is often used by him to finance the acquisition or manufacture of the goods to be sold. These letters are issued either on an irrevocable or a revocable basis.

These instruments of foreign trade make possible a variety of payment terms appropriate for a particular transaction. The risks of the exporter may be completely eliminated, of course, by his insisting on cash payment in strong currencies prior to the shipment of goods. If the transactions involve an extension of credit, the risk of nonpayment is always present. These risks are to various degrees avoidable by requiring the foreign buyer to furnish a commercial letter of credit. The risks are minimized with a confirmed, irrevocable letter of credit. With an irrevocable, but unconfirmed letter of credit, the risks are a little higher. They are further increased if the letter is issued on a revocable basis. The greatest risk is encountered when transactions are made on an open account basis.

The use of foreign credit insurance reduces both commercial and political risks connected with foreign transactions. The exporter can obtain the necessary policies himself and on the basis of these policies obtain financing with his bank; or, he can obtain a guarantee that will hold the lender harmless in case of losses. Export transactions on credit involve various costs such as financing expenses and premiums for insurance. The letter of credit usually specifies who will pay these expenses, a choice strongly influenced by existing competition.

We next discussed various financing options. U.S. financial institutions involved in export-import business include commercial banks, their Edge Act subsidiaries, "agreement banks," factor organizations, and export financing companies. Commercial banks are prohibited from financing bills of exchange in excess of six months. The Edge Act subsidiaries formed by U.S. commercial banks can engage in export financing in excess of 180 days. Native agreement banks are established by U.S. commercial banks in countries where subsidiaries of these banks are not permitted nor encouraged.

Factor organizations purchase short-term receivables from exporters and then collect these receivables as they become due. For this service, factors usually charge a fee of 1.5 to 2 percent, as well as a rate of interest in excess of the prime rate. The costs of credit evaluation of a foreign customer by the seller and the interest rate on financing from other sources are the major considerations in deciding whether a factor should be used. There are only a few private export financing companies in the United States. In order to reduce their risks, these companies usually limit their financing to sales by large foreign distributors dealing exclusively in U.S.-made capital goods.

We next described some financing opportunities using foreign currencies. Sometimes advancing dollars to a foreign buyer facilitates U.S. exports; repayment is made in the foreign currency at an agreed rate. Or, a U.S. exporter may borrow a foreign currency directly from a foreign bank or from a foreign private lender through link financing arrangements. Sometimes a foreign currency swap may be advantageous. For some limited purposes, especially to develop foreign markets for U.S. agricultural products, the use of PL 480 funds is possible. In trading with countries suffering from a shortage of foreign exchange reserves, transactions take the form of barter, private compensating agreements, or switch exchange financing.

An increasing number of American firms have found it advantageous to increase the scope of their markets by selling their products on an international as well as national basis. The added complexities of exporting are not insurmountable but make it desirable to establish an export department staffed by knowledgeable people to conduct the firm's export business with the greatest possible efficiency and lowest cost.

PROBLEM 9-1

A U.S. exporter sells $100,000 of machinery with a down payment of $10,000 on a six-month open account basis. His cost of financing the amount of the sale is 10 percent without FCIA insurance. This cost drops to 8 percent with an FCIA policy, the premium of which would be one half of 1 percent of the insured portion. His customer can arrange for a confirmed irrevocable letter of credit at a cost of $1,000; the banker's acceptance resulting from this transaction can be discounted at 6 percent.

A. What is the cost to the exporter of each of these variations?

B. Which should he choose?

PROBLEM 9-2

A U.S. exporter enjoys an annual sales volume of approximately $10 million. His sales are typically on a six-month open account basis with a down payment of 10 percent. He is analyzing the formulation of a policy in regard to insuring his foreign sales with the Foreign Credit Insurance Association. The FCIA requires that an exporter must cover all of his foreign sales in order to avoid the possibility of protecting only the sales to poor credit risks.

The company estimates that on the $10 million volume of sales it could probably obtain confirmed irrevocable letters of credit on at least 60 percent but not on the remaining 40 percent. By means of the letters of credit, exports can be financed by means of banker's acceptances discounted at 6 percent. Sales protected by FCIA insurance can be financed at 7 percent. Sales made on an open account basis without protection or credit guarantee require a cost of 10 percent. The FCIA insurance premium is estimated to cost $1 per $100 of the insured portion of each sale. Due to the 10 percent down payment and the requirement that the insured carry 10 percent of the financed portion at his own risk, the FCIA will insure only 81 percent of the export sales. Since the sales to importers that cannot furnish letters of credit are made to more financially risky firms, it is estimated that a reserve for noncollection of receivables of 10 percent is advisable.

What is your recommendation as to the policies that the firm should adopt?

PROBLEM 9-3

A U.S. exporter sells to a South American importer machinery worth 2 million pesos on a one-year open account basis. His opportunity cost of funds is 8 percent. The expected rate of devaluation of the peso during the year is 10 percent and the spot rate is presently 10 pesos per U.S. dollar. The exporter has the following choices:

1) Purchase a one year forward contract at a cost of 15 percent per year.
2) Borrow the required pesos from a bank in the country of his customer at an annual cost of 20 percent. Convert the pesos into U.S. dollars at the present spot rate.
3) Obtain a swap from a commercial bank in the country of his customer. The proposed swap discount is 20 percent and the interest on the pesos is 15 percent per year. Convert the pesos thus obtained into U.S. dollars at the spot rate.

In both alternatives (2) and (3) the peso loans would be repaid from the funds obtained when the customer pays his bill at the end of one year. Determine which of the alternatives is lowest in cost and risk.

SELECTED BIBLIOGRAPHY

Bankers Trust Company. *Washington Agencies That Help Finance Foreign Trade.* 4th ed. New York: Bankers Trust Co., 1964.

Fayerweather, John. *International Marketing.* Englewood Cliffs, N.J.: Prentice-Hall, Inc., 1965.

Fischer, Edward P. "Financing Foreign Operations," *Financial Executive,* Vol. 32, No. 10 (October 1964), pp. 12–16.

Greene, James H. *Organizing for Exporting.* New York: National Industrial Conference Board, 1968.

Nehrt, Lee C. *Financing Capital Equipment Exports.* Scranton, Pa.: International Textbook Co., 1966.

10

The foreign investment decision

FOREIGN INVESTMENTS may be short term or long term. Short-term investments are represented by a firm's funds that are temporarily not needed in operations and invested in higher yield instruments abroad. Long-term foreign investments may be portfolio investments or direct investments. Portfolio investments do not represent a control position in holdings of foreign bonds and foreign stocks. Direct investments are represented by funds placed in controlled entities operating abroad. This chapter is focused on direct investments in plant and equipment in controlled entities operating in foreign countries.

SOME GENERAL PRINCIPLES

A general framework for viewing the reasons for direct foreign investment may be set forth succinctly. Some countries have a comparative overabundance of capital and a relative shortage of labor. Evidence of a relative abundance of capital would be a general low and declining return from investments. Evidence of a comparative labor shortage would be the rapid rising of wage rates in a country compared with wage rates in other nations. A country in such a situation will need either to import labor to offset the labor shortages or to export capital. One form of exporting capital is represented by the increase in foreign direct investment, the subject of this chapter.

The situation of the recipient of this investment, the host country, is the reverse. Countries that represent attractive places for foreign investment are those characterized by relative capital shortages and a relative abundance of labor, plus local raw materials that may be utilized in the production process. A country in such a situation must either export its labor and raw materials or import capital.[1]

---

[1] Note that this represents an operation of the price system in terms of providing for resource movements to bring about a greater equality in returns, both to capital and labor in the worldwide market.

It should be emphasized that these differences need only be situations of comparative or relative advantage. These differences are likely to be most pronounced between developed and less developed nations. But even among developed nations or among less developed nations, all that is required is that in particular industries there be a comparative advantage either in terms of physical equipment and/or management know-how. The case is similar with regard to raw materials or labor.

The only requirement is that the comparative situation be such that related to the values of other products and the total product pattern of the individual nations, a comparative advantage exists in some industries for one country and in other industries for other countries. This is likely to occur since it simply reflects the most general principle of all trade—comparative advantage and specialization.

These general statements on factors leading to international and foreign direct investment are clearly illustrated in the recent experience of Japan.[2] It has been stated that Japan has traditionally viewed the rest of Asia and the rest of the world in the "classic role of an economic colony."[3] She purchased raw materials, used them in manufacturing, and sold the finished goods abroad. In Southeast Asia Japan had been buying $3 billion worth of goods per year and selling $5 billion per year. This could not go on indefinitely because the unfavorable trade balance of Southeast Asia could be covered only by the export of Japanese capital, that is, various forms of investment by Japan in these countries. This could be in the form of loans by Japan or by direct investment.

More generally, it would be expected that Japan's total direct investment would increase because of its previous relatively low level. By contrast, the United States has been making gross direct investments of $6–$7 billion per year, cumulating to a total of direct private long-term investments of American companies as of the end of 1969 of almost $71 billion. Japan's total investment outflow totaled only $3 billion during all of the quarter century following the end of World War II to 1970.

Particularly, the considerable imbalance in Japan's trade with Southeast Asia created pressures for investment in that area by Japan. In addition to pressures from the southeast Asian countries there were specific economic stimuli from Japan. Wages in Japan had been increasing 15 to 20 percent per year in a number of industries, reflecting a chronic labor shortage. Productivity increases had not been sufficient to offset these increases in wage rates in recent years. Also, it was stated, "Japan's air and water have become so fouled with pollutants that many businessmen and civil leaders feel further oil refineries, chemical plants and metal

---

[2] This illustration is summarized from an analysis by Mr. W. D. Hartley, "After Years of Selling, Japan Begins Investing in Neighboring Lands," *Wall Street Journal,* May 5, 1971, pp. 11, 17.

[3] Ibid., p. 1.

smelters, must be placed outside Japan."[4] This shift on the part of Japanese business received endorsement by the Japanese government. Japan's Minister of Finance, Takeo Fukuda, had indicated that advanced countries must export capital and simple technology to developing countries and then produce new technologies at home, industrialize these, and move on to even higher industrial levels.[5]

This change in policy on the part of the Japanese government has been matched by a strong interest in the nations of Southeast Asia to encourage industrialization, but particularly to replace imports with homemade goods. The Director of Industrial Development of Malaysia, Yeo Beng Poh, was quoted as stating, "Now we have reached a stage of wanting export-oriented industries to use our natural resources and our low-cost labor. So any country that comes in [to build a factory] must be export-minded."[6]

The foregoing provides a summary of the kinds of broad overall patterns that stimulate direct foreign investment. The host country's government is interested and indeed may provide various forms of tax and other incentives. It is clear that the industrialized country, as in the case of Japan, also has strong incentives for investment abroad. These are not only economic incentives but incentives related to the quality of life as well.

SUMMARY OF WORLD PATTERNS OF INVESTMENT

With these general principles as background, we may see their implications as reflected in world patterns of investment with the data organized from the standpoint of the United States. Table 10–1 sets forth a summary of the U.S. international investment position. The overall net position of the United States is positive as a net creditor to the rest of the world by $69 billion. In fact, this position has been improving by $2 billion per year.[7] However, despite this favorable overall balance, there are some less favorable relations from a liquidity standpoint. Table 10–1 shows that most of the U.S. assets abroad are held in the form of nonliquid claims ($150 billion of the total $167 billion U.S. assets abroad). But almost one half of the U.S. obligations are liquid claims by foreigners on the United States ($47 billion of a total of $98 billion foreign claims).

---

[4] Ibid.

[5] Ibid., p. 17.

[6] Ibid.

[7] The U.S. investment position has been improving despite a continuing balance-of-payments deficit due in part to increases in both direct (investment in plant and equipment) and portfolio (investment in foreign bonds and stocks) foreign investments. For example, a purchase of foreign bonds by Americans or investment in foreign subsidiaries of $2 billion would result in an adverse flow in our balance of payments by $2 billion but would improve the U.S. investment position by $2 billion.

TABLE 10-1

International investment position of the United States, year-end 1970 (preliminary) (in billions of dollars)

	Total*	Western Europe	Japan	Western hemisphere Canada	Western hemisphere Other	Other foreign countries	International org.§
I. U.S. assets abroad:							
Total	167	41	7	37	29	32	20
A. Nonliquid	150	40	6	36	28	32	7
1. Private	118	32	6	36	22	16	5
a) Long-term	105	30	2	35	18	14	5
(1) Direct	78	24	1	23	15	11	4
(2) Other†	27	5	1	12	3	3	—
b) Short-term	13	2	4	1	4	2	†
2. U.S. government	32	8	1	1	6	16	1
B. Liquid	17	2	†	1	†	†	14
II. U.S. liabilities to foreigners:							
Total	98	60	6	13	9	6	3
A. Nonliquid	50	36	1	7	4	2	2
1. Private	49	35	1	6	3	1	2
a) Long-term	45	32	1	6	3	1	2
(1) Direct	13	10	†	3	3	†	†
(2) Other†	32	22	1	3	†	1	2
b) Short-term	4	3	†	†	†	†	†
2. U.S. government	2	2	†	†	†	†	†
B. Liquid	47	24	5	6	5	4	1
III. *Net international investment position of the United States*	69	(19)	1	24	20	26	17

* Minor discrepancies in totals and subtotals due to rounding.
† Less than $0.5 billion.
‡ Foreign bonds, foreign corporate stocks, claims, or liabilities of U.S. bank, and others.
§ Includes U.S. gold stock.
Source: David T. Devlin, "The International Investment Position of the United States," *Survey of Current Business*, October 1971, p. 21.

FIGURE 10–1

Annual additions to direct investments by industry and major area

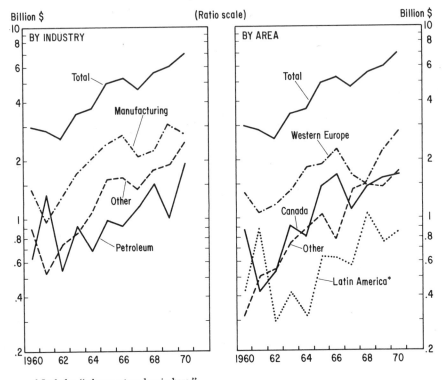

° Includes "other western hemisphere."
Source: R. David Belli and Julius N. Freidlin, "U.S. Direct Investments Abroad, 1970," *Survey of Current Business*, October 1971, p. 26; data from U.S. Department of Commerce, Office of Business Economics.

Furthermore, the United States is a net debtor to the developed countries of Western Europe by $19 billion.

Figure 10–1 demonstrates that U.S. annual additions to foreign direct investments have grown since 1960 with only moderate and temporary reversals. This has been the situation for all major categories of industry. A general increase has also occurred in all major areas.

Figure 10–1 presents data on rates of return on U.S. direct investments abroad. The rates of return are much higher in less developed countries than in the developed countries. However, the risks in the less developed countries are also greater. Manufacturing rates of return are compared in this U.S. Department of Commerce study for developed countries and for foreign direct investment and U.S. domestic investment (excluding petroleum). The chart is misleading for the latter in that the returns being compared are returns for total assets for the foreign investments and returns on net worth for U.S. domestic investments. Return on net

FIGURE 10-2

Rate of return° on U.S. direct investments abroad and domestic manufacturing excluding petroleum

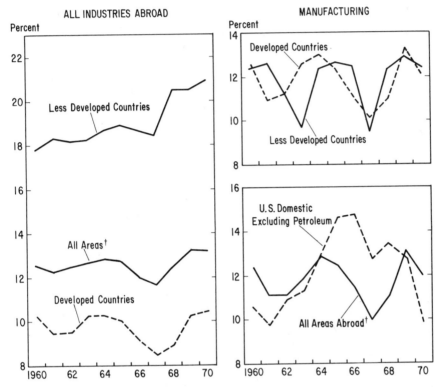

° Return on direct investments represents earnings plus interests (on intercompany accounts) applied to book value at beginning of year. Return on domestic manufacturing represents net income applied to net worth at beginning of year (as computed by First National City Bank of New York).

† Data in the direct investments category "international unlocated" is included in the figures for all areas but excluded from the figures for developed and less developed countries.

Source: R. David Belli and Julius N. Freidlin, "U.S. Direct Investments Abroad in 1970," *Survey of Current Business*, October 1971, p. 31; data from U.S. Department of Commerce, Office of Business Economics.

worth is generally about 3 to 5 percentage points higher than return on total assets, reflecting benefits by accounting measures of trading on the equity (the use of debt leverage). After adjustment to achieve comparability, the returns from foreign investments would have been 3 to 4 percentage points higher than the returns on domestic investments in the early 1960s, and averaged about the same for the second half of the decade of the sixties, rising above domestic returns during the U.S. recession of 1969–70.

Finally, in this broad overall survey, it is useful to review the technical measurement of investment earnings in connection with foreign investments for understanding better the additional factors that are included in the analysis of individual direct foreign investment projects discussed later in this chapter. Eleven different measures of direct investment earnings are explained in Table 10–2. Net earnings of the foreign corporations

TABLE 10–2

Direct investment earnings measurement, 1970—Derivation and relationship based on 1970 preliminary data (millions of dollars)

1. Net earnings of foreign corporations.................. 6,256   reported
2. Net earnings of foreign branches.................... 2,477   reported
3. Earnings... 8,733 = 1 + 2

4. Gross dividends (on common stock)................. 3,371 = 5 + 6
5. Foreign withholding tax (on common stock dividends).. 390   reported
6. Dividends (on common stock)...................... 2,981 = 4 − 5
   (reported)

7. Preferred dividends.............................. 15   reported
8. Interest... 553   reported
9. Interest, dividends, and branch earnings............. 6,026 = 2 + 6 + 7 + 8

10. Reinvested earnings............................. 2,885 = 1 − 4
    or 3 − 2 − 4
11. Adjusted earnings.............................. 8,911 = 9 + 10
    or 3 + 7 + 8 − 5

Technical note: The various direct investment earnings items are defined below and their derivation and relationship to each other are detailed.

Item and definition

1. Net earnings of foreign corporations: The U.S. parents' equity in the earnings of their foreign subsidiaries after provision for foreign income taxes, preferred dividends, and interest payments.

2. Net earnings of foreign branches: The earnings of foreign branches of U.S. companies after foreign income taxes, but before depletion charges and U.S. taxes. Included with net earnings of branches are the U.S. share in the net earnings of foreign partnerships, sole proprietorships, and other types of foreign organizations. All branch earnings are assumed to be repatriated to the United States and thus are balance of payments flow items. To the extent that branch earnings are left abroad they are implicitly entered as offsetting capital outflows.

3. Earnings: Net earnings of foreign corporations plus net earnings of foreign branches.

4. Gross dividends on common stock: Dividends paid out by foreign corporations before deduction of withholding taxes paid to foreign governments.

5. Foreign withholding tax: A tax withheld on the payment of dividends as distinguished from income taxes, which are imposed on the earnings of a business. Taxes are also withheld by the payor on payments of interest and preferred dividends but both interest and preferred dividends are reported to the Balance of Payments Division on a net basis and, therefore, our data on withholding taxes relate only to those on common stock dividends.

6. Dividends: Dividends on common or voting stock only, net of foreign withholding taxes; dividends are included in income as balance of payments flow items.

7. Preferred dividends: Dividends received on preference or nonvoting shares after deduction of any foreign withholding taxes. Preferred dividends are included in income as balance of payments flow items. Preferred dividends are treated like interest in these accounts even though on the foreign company's books they are not charged as an expense.

8. Interest: The net interest received on intercompany accounts or on long-term debt of foreign affiliates held by the parent or other nonbank U.S. investors, after deduction of any foreign withholding taxes. Interest is not included in earnings since it is deducted as an expense item by the foreign firm, but, it is included in income as a balance of payments flow item.

9. Interest, dividends, and branch earnings: The sum of dividends, preferred dividends, and interest received by or credited to the account of the U.S. owner—all net after foreign withholding taxes—plus branch earnings after foreign taxes: all before U.S. taxes.

10. Reinvested earnings: Net earnings of foreign corporations less gross dividends on common stock.

11. Adjusted earnings: The benefits of ownership accruing to a U.S. foreign direct investor after all foreign taxes, including withholding taxes, have been paid; this is comprised of (1) funds returned to the United States as income in the form of dividends, preferred dividends, branch profits, and interest, plus (2) funds left abroad to increase the investor's equity in the foreign enterprise as a reinvestment of earnings.

Source: *Survey of Current Business,* October 1971, pp. 37, 38.

refers to U.S. parent companies' equity in the earnings of their foreign subsidiaries after provision for (1) foreign income taxes, (2) preferred dividends, and (3) interest payments of the foreign subsidiary. These last three numbered items must be treated as "outflows" in any analysis of the funds available from the foreign investment on a project analysis basis.

Many foreign countries impose a withholding tax on the payment of dividends comparable to U.S. income tax withholding on wage and salary earnings. Thus the gross dividends paid out by the foreign subsidiary to the U.S. parent have been decreased by the foreign withholding tax on dividends at the source (this is in addition to the tax already paid on the earnings of the foreign subsidiary). The final term, "11. Adjusted earnings," represents the total of all fund flows received by the U.S. parent plus funds left abroad as a reinvestment of earnings in the foreign subsidiary.

STIMULI TO DIRECT FOREIGN INVESTMENT

Valid principles are broadly and generally applicable. Thus the basic concepts of capital budgeting and cost of capital are applicable in an international setting. But the success of business decisions and their social effects are greatly influenced by implementation considerations. While the basic principles of capital budgeting and cost of capital in international investments are the same as for domestic investments, the subject requires discussion for a number of reasons. A wider range of stimuli are involved. Important differences are involved in the application of the principles. New variables must be considered, and hence the decision model must be enlarged.

The basic economic principles of capital budgeting decisions apply: accept those investments which increase the present value of the owners' wealth. But, the considerations in constructing the analysis to reflect the relevant criteria are broadened. The decision rules for accepting or rejecting investment will be the same. But the soundness of the decisions will be greatly affected by the kinds and quality of information used in applying the criteria for evaluating investment decisions. These generalizations will now be made more concrete.

The basic principle is that investment flows to areas in which rates of return are high in relation to risks. Within this broad principle many important specific influences may be operating. Illustrative of the special characteristics of international business finance is the fact that the major portion of U.S. direct investments during the last decade were made in the developed countries of Western Europe. The stimuli represented opportunities and threats. The establishment of the European Economic Community (the Common Market) created a large market comparable in economic size to the United States. The establishment of the European

Economic Community achieved by political and economic agreement what had been accomplished in the United States by the completion of the transcontinental railroad systems which made the United States the first broad common market from a geographic, political, and economic standpoint. The creation of a comparable large market in Western Europe afforded opportunities to American firms for the utilization of their years of experience in mass-production operations and in mass-merchandising operations. Thus attractive rates of return were offered by these new opportunities in the European Common Market.

A further stimulus was the threat of heightened tariff barriers against the outside world. A time-phased schedule for the European Common Market provided for successive reductions in tariff barriers within its broad area, with a successive raising of tariff barriers against the outside world. Thus, for the United States to participate profitably in this broadened market required U.S. manufacturing operations within the Common Market countries.

Tariffs and other barriers to export sales into the Common Market area may have been responsible for heightening other incentives and considerations. Product sales in foreign countries may require different forms and styles. An example would be the automobile industry. The lower average income levels, the narrower roads, and the higher costs of fuel make small cars predominate in the European markets. The same is true of many household appliances such as refrigerators and stoves. Since different products were required, this required separate manufacturing facilities anyhow. The use of some local machinery and local personnel might provide for more efficient operations than manufacturing different types of products in domestic countries for foreign markets.

Thus, when compared with the export of products, some new factors may lead to establishing manufacturing operations abroad. Tariff barriers as well as the requirement of different types of products have been described. In addition, for some products, it is cheaper to ship raw materials and parts to manufacture or to assemble abroad. Transportation costs are lower for those types of products with raw materials or parts that can be prepared for shipment in relatively compact form, whereas the final product is relatively bulky. The extreme example in this regard, of course, would be houses. It is also true for automobiles and other consumer durable goods to a considerable degree. Thus, in some cases, it may be necessary to establish manufacturing operations abroad as the only means by which sales of products in foreign markets could be achieved. To establish operations abroad might thereby continue to utilize some portion of materials and parts manufactured in the United States. The alternative might be losing out completely in the foreign markets.

Another business incentive for starting an establishment abroad is that it represents a form of geographic diversification. For example, if a shift in demand patterns has taken place so that more rapid growth in demand is likely to take place abroad, this form of geographic diversification enables the firm to participate in the more rapidly growing market segments.

The further use of top corporate staff personnel is another business incentive. This represents a form of spreading some of the firm's overhead expenses. The same basic general competence in the general management functions of planning, organizing, staffing, directing, and controlling can be applied abroad. In addition, the domestic manufacture of certain parts or components may provide for utilization of unused physical capacity. Thus many firms have commented that the establishment of foreign manufacturing operations has stimulated domestic manufacturing activity and export sales from domestic plants.

In addition to these general economic and business incentives for investing abroad, incentives may be provided by host governments. This is particularly true in developing countries which are seeking to broaden the range of industrial operations carried on in their own countries. Their motives for this may include a combination of considerations. A primary motive may be to conserve the nation's foreign exchange reserves.

Local manufacturing operations, even if owned by outsiders, may conserve foreign exchange reserves in a number of important ways. Even if all the materials and parts were shipped in from abroad, their value as parts would be smaller than the price of the final product. In addition, manufacturing in the less developed country may provide for economic utilization of local materials and parts. In addition, local labor will be trained and develop experience in manufacturing a broader range of products. This may lead to the future establishment of domestically or locally owned operations, employing some of the labor force skills developed by foreign operations.

This progress may be stimulated and hastened by the requirement of the local government that the operations be established on a joint-venture basis with local, national investors as well as with the outside foreign investors. Under these circumstances, the establishment of foreign operations may represent sharing some of the special management know-how of the U.S. firm.

A wide range of considerations, then, may make direct investment abroad economically sound. All of these stimuli may contribute to a favorable return-risk pattern from this enhanced form of geographic diversifications. However, because there are important differences between multinational and national capital budgeting decisions, the range of new variables to be considered should be understood clearly. We, therefore, next consider this aspect of the foreign investment decision.

NEW VARIABLES WHICH MUST BE CONSIDERED

A broadened range of variables must be considered in the foreign investment decision as compared to the domestic investment decision. These include:

1. Environmental complexity and diversity.
2. New cultural-institutional factors.
3. Legal-political constraints.
4. More diverse labor laws.
5. Differences in tax laws.
6. Differential rates of inflation.
7. New and increased risks.
    a) Change in exchange rates and devaluation.
    b) Exchange controls.
    c) Restrictions on the flow of funds.
    d) Expropriation risks.
    These were discussed in Chapters 1 through 3.

Thus, the variables to be considered in a foreign investment decision are substantially broadened in range. Both the kind of variables and their rate of change involved in foreign investment decisions are greatly expanded. This affects the application of capital budgeting or investment decision models to foreign investment decisions. This aspect of the subject is next considered.

PROJECT EVALUATION IN FOREIGN INVESTMENT DECISIONS

The basic principles are the same in project evaluation for foreign investment decisions as in domestic investment decisions. Hence, the same general pattern of analysis applies.[8] This involves comparing cash inflows and outflows on the project, applying a relevant cost of capital to determine the net present value of the project. With no capital rationing, for independent investments, all projects with net present value are accepted. For mutually exclusive investments, the project with the highest net present value is selected. With capital rationing, mathematical programming techniques must be used to achieve a formally correct decision.

For project analysis of foreign investment decisions at least three aspects are distinctive: (1) The range of variables to be considered in the analysis is expanded. (2) The estimates of both inflows and outflows may be subject to wider margins of error. (3) The analysis of risks and returns is likely to be more complex.

---

[8] Cf. H. Bierman and S. Smidt, *The Capital Budgeting Decision* (2d ed.; Macmillan Co. 1966), chap. 13.

These concepts will be developed by use of an illustrative case example for the Celan Company. The Celan Company is contemplating the establishment of a specialty instrument manufacturing plant in Latin America. It has developed the following information: Sales are estimated to be LC 20 million per year for the first two years and LC 50 million per year for the third to the fifth year. The terms of sale are such that it is estimated that at the end of each year 20 percent of sales will be in receivables. For simplicity it will be assumed that all the receivables in the previous period are collected during the current period. During the fifth year, the raw materials purchased during the period are reduced because there is no requirement for inventory to be held at the end of the fifth year in contemplation of operations for the sixth year. It is assumed that the raw materials purchased during this period are entirely on a credit basis. Further all the accounts payable in the preceding period must be paid off during the current period.

The investment required will include LC 20 million in new fixed assets and LC 10 million in used equipment. These investments plus outlays for cash on hand and inventories will be required before the start of the first year. Cash on hand equal to 10 percent of the estimated first-year sale will be required. Inventories on hand equal to 50 percent of next year's raw material usage will also be necessary. However, the cash outflow for the purchase of inventories will be reduced because accounts payable will represent 50 percent of raw material purchases. At the end of the project (end of the fifth year) all the receivables are collected and all payables are paid off. Finally, all of the taxes incurred during a given period must be paid at the end of that period.

It is estimated that raw materials cost will constitute 40 percent of sales. Labor costs will be 10 percent of sales. Selling and administrative costs will be 10 percent of sales. The costs of hedging against foreign exchange losses and insuring against other losses from foreign operations will be LC 1 million per year for the first two years and LC 2 million per year for the third through the fifth year.

The parent company will charge the subsidiary project a supervisory fee of LC 1 million per annum. Taxes imposed by the local (foreign) government will be 30 percent of before-tax profits each year.

For determining the profit and loss for the project, use straight-line depreciation over a 10-year period for both the new fixed assets and the used equipment. It is assumed further for analysis of the project over a five-year time horizon that both the new fixed assets and used equipment can be sold at their book depreciated value as of the end of the fifth year.

The project will return in dividends to the U.S. parent one half of its after-tax net income each year. These dividends will be subject to a 10 percent foreign withholding tax, which is deductible from the applicable U.S. income taxes. The U.S. income tax will be calculated by the method outlined in Chapter 7. A U.S. corporate income tax rate of 50 percent will also be applied directly to the supervisory fee income which will not be subject to any foreign country withholding tax. The exchange rate throughout this problem will be LC 10 equals $1.

The following are required:

1. A five-year capital budgeting analysis from the standpoint of the project (Table 10–3).
2. A five-year cash flow analysis (cash budget) from the standpoint of the project (Table 10–4).
3. A five-year pro forma balance sheet from the standpoint of the foreign project (Table 10–5).
4. A five-year pro forma income statement from the standpoint of the project (Table 10–6).
5. The computation of the tax obligations of the U.S. parent over the five-year period (Table 10–7).
6. The parent company cash flows and cumulative net present values from the project calculated at a present value factor of 15 percent (Table 10–8).

Analysis of the Celan Instrument project proposal

The information provided in this illustration is formulated so that the solution to the problem provides a review of the basic procedures of financial forecasting. While all of the individual steps will not be explained in detail, the results reflect the systematic relations required for financial planning.

In Table 10–3 the Celan Instrument project proposal is analyzed from a capital budgeting standpoint over the five-year time horizon. The cash inflows represent sales less the increase in receivables that takes place in a given year, the net result in cash collections each year.

The cash outflows begin in period 0 before the start of operations in the first year. The project is charged for the value of the new fixed assets that are purchased as well as the used equipment. Sometimes in the establishment of a foreign subsidiary it may be advantageous for the parent company to transfer used equipment from its domestic operations. The used equipment may provide an adequate rate of production for the foreign operations. This may enable the parent to substitute new and modern equipment for its domestic operations, realizing higher salvage values than otherwise possible for the older equipment. The depreciated value of the used equipment in the parent company's accounting records is not the relevant cost we are charging the project. The relevant cost we are charging the project is the opportunity cost of acquiring such equipment in the foreign country. In this example that cost is estimated to be LC

TABLE 10-3

CELAN INSTRUMENT PROJECT PROPOSAL
Subsidiary five-year capital budgeting project analysis (in thousands of LC)

	0	1	2	3	4	5
Cash inflows:						
Sales..............		20,000	20,000	50,000	50,000	50,000
Less: Increase in receivables........		4,000	.....	6,000	......	......
Cash collections........		16,000	20,000	44,000	50,000	50,000
Cash outflows:						
Cash investment......	2,000	......	......	......	......	(2,000)
New fixed assets......	20,000	......	......	......	......	(10,000)
Used equipment.......	10,000	......	......	.....	......	(5,000)
Inventories*.........	2,000	2,000	3,000	3,000	......	......
Raw material*.......	......	4,000	8,000	14,000	20,000	10,000
Labor costs..........	......	2,000	2,000	5,000	5,000	5,000
Selling and administrative costs..........	......	2,000	2,000	5,000	5,000	5,000
Costs of hedging and insuring.............	......	1,000	1,000	2,000	2,000	2,000
Supervisory fee.......	......	1,000	1,000	1,000	1,000	1,000
Local taxes (from Table 10-7).............	......	900	900	4,200	4,200	4,200
Total Outflows....	34,000	12,900	17,900	34,200	37,200	10,200
Net cash inflows (to Table 10-8)........	(34,000)	3,100	2,100	5,800	11,800	39,800
Cumulative cash inflows.............	(34,000)	(30,900)	(28,800)	(23,000)	(11,200)	28,600

° These figures are based on the assumptions that outlays for inventories are required to increase the level of ending inventory compared with the preceding period, and that current raw material usage is from current purchases—essentially a last-in, first-out approach.

10 million. Hence, the appropriate cash outlay that would have been required by the project for the used equipment is LC 10 million. This is shown as an outflow from the standpoint of the project itself.

The cash investment represents a flow of funds that will have to be assigned to the project. The inventory investment before operations are begun is calculated as follows: Inventories are required to be 50 percent of next year's raw material usage. Next year's raw material usage is LC 2 million. Therefore, beginning inventory would be LC 4 million. However, the purchase of LC 4 million of inventory gives rise to accounts payable of LC 2 million. Hence, the net investment that would be allocated to the project would total LC 34 million. This would represent a negative cash flow in period 0 in the cash flow statement. The inventory figures for the following years are calculated on the basis of similar reasoning.

Continuing with the following items in the cash budgeting analysis, labor costs are 10 percent of sales as indicated. The same is true of selling and administrative costs. The costs of hedging and insuring are next considered. The costs of hedging against foreign exchange losses may represent the use of the forward exchange markets or the use of currency swaps as described in Chapter 5. These costs are likely to be a percentage of sales. In addition, costs of insuring against the loss of investment and the accumulated profits from investments will also be required. These costs are likely to be a function of the balance sheet net worth values. To simplify matters for convenience of exposition, we have assumed that the costs of hedging and insuring will be LC 1 million for the first two years and LC 2 million for the final three years when the level of sales have increased.

The supervisory fee may represent a combination of elements. Foreign investments represent the application of the parent company management know-how to the new project. This represents the utilization of important capabilities built up over a period of years. This know-how is used to guide the operations of the foreign subsidiary. It is assumed that a flat fee of LC 1 million per year is charged to the subsidiary for the services so rendered. This is based on a fee equal to 2 percent of the volume of sales attained from the third year on.

The final line, local taxes, is taken from Table 10–6 which is the five-year pro forma income statement. The tax rate is 30 percent of profit before taxes from the subsidiary operations. The outflows are totaled. The differences between cash collections and the total outflows are the net cash inflows for each year. The net cash inflows from a capital budgeting standpoint are a negative LC 34 million during period 0 and generally increasingly positive thereafter. However, on a cumulative basis, net cash inflows do not become positive until the fifth year, when they are LC 16.6 million.

This capital budgeting analysis is critical for determining whether the project will be profitable, that is, whether it will have a positive net present value. However, for making this final determination with reference to the parent company cash flows from the project, some additional financial statements are required.

The next financial statement is the pro forma cash budget set forth in Table 10–4 which summarizes the cash flows in connection with the project and thus provides an overview of the total investment proposal. The total equity capital contribution by the parent is LC 34 million. Since the total cash outflows before the beginning of operations are LC 32 million, the cash balance at the beginning of the first period of operation is LC 2 million. The remainder of the inflows and outflows reflect the relationships set forth in the statement of the illustrative case study and can be verified by reference to the relationships set forth. Following the standard procedures for the development of a cash budget, the cash balance at

TABLE 10–4

CELAN INSTRUMENT PROJECT PROPOSAL
Five-year pro forma cash budget (in thousands of LC)

	0	1	2	3	4	5	6
Cash inflows:							
Contributed capital.....	34,000						
Cash sales.............	......	16,000	16,000	40,000	40,000	40,000	......
Receivables collections..	......	0	4,000	4,000	10,000	10,000	10,000
Cash received..........	34,000	16,000	20,000	44,000	50,000	50,000	10,000
Cash outflows:							
New fixed assets.......	20,000	......	......	......	......	(10,000)	......
Used equipment........	10,000	......	......	......	......	(5,000)	......
Inventories............	2,000	2,000	5,000	5,000	5,000	......	......
Raw material..........	......	2,000	2,000	5,000	5,000	......	......
Accounts payable......	......	2,000	4,000	7,000	10,000	10,000	10,000
Labor costs...........	......	2,000	2,000	5,000	5,000	5,000	......
Selling and administrative costs............	......	2,000	2,000	5,000	5,000	5,000	......
Costs of hedging and insuring................	......	1,000	1,000	2,000	2,000	2,000	......
Supervisory fee........	......	1,000	1,000	1,000	1,000	1,000	......
Dividends.............	......	1,050	1,050	4,900	4,900	4,900	......
Local taxes (from Table 10–6)..............	......	900	900	4,200	4,200	4,200	
Total Cash Outflows*.......	32,000	13,950	18,950	39,100	42,100	17,100	10,000
Cash inflows..........	34,000	16,000	20,000	44,000	50,000	50,000	10,000
Net change in cash.....	2,000	2,050	1,050	4,900	7,900	32,900	......
Cash at beginning......	0	2,000	4,050	5,100	10,000	17,900	......
Net change...........	2,000	2,050	1,050	4,900	7,900	32,900	......
Cash balance at end of period..............	2,000	4,050	5,100	10,000	17,900	50,800	......

° Note that a cash outflow is a negative cash inflow.

the end of each time period can be developed. It will be noted that the final line of Table 10–4, the cash balance at the end of each period, must and does reconcile with the first line of Table 10–5, the five-year pro forma balance sheet. We therefore turn to that financial statement.

In period 0 the total assets are LC 36 million. This reconciles to the capital budgeting analyzed in the two preceding tables in which the cash outflows for period 0 were LC 34 million. The difference is represented by the financing provided by the accounts payable of LC 2 million during period 0. In the balance sheet, receivables for each year are 20 percent of sales. Inventories are one half of the following year's raw material usage. Net fixed assets decline by LC 3 million each year representing the amount of depreciation for each year.

Accounts payable grow in relationship to the purchases made as ex-

TABLE 10–5

CELAN INSTRUMENT PROJECT PROPOSAL
Five-year pro forma balance sheet (in thousands of LC)

	0	1	2	3	4	5
Cash.....................	2,000	4,050	5,100	10,000	17,900	50,800
Receivables................	......	4,000	4,000	10,000	10,000	10,000
Inventories...............	4,000	4,000	10,000	10,000	10,000	......
Current Assets..........	6,000	12,050	19,100	30,000	37,900	60,800
Gross fixed assets............	30,000	30,000	30,000	30,000	30,000	......
Less: Reserve for depreciation...............	......	3,000	6,000	9,000	12,000	......
Net fixed assets............	30,000	27,000	24,000	21,000	18,000	......
Total Assets..........	36,000	39,050	43,100	51,000	55,900	60,800
Accounts payable............	2,000	4,000	7,000	10,000	10,000	10,000
Common stock..............	34,000	34,000	34,000	34,000	34,000	34,000
Retained earnings...........	......	1,050	2,100	7,000	11,900	16,800
Total Liabilities and New Worth.........	36,000	39,050	43,100	51,000	55,900	60,800

plained in connection with inventory and raw material outflows. The initial common stock investment is LC 34 million. Retained earnings grow by the amount of one half of profit after taxes which is also equal to the amount of dividends paid out. The difference between total liabilities plus net worth and all of the other asset items except cash is made up by the cash amount. Cash begins at a minimum of 10 percent of the following year's sales and satisfies this minimum for each of the subsequent years. It will be noted that the cash account grows to almost LC 26 million by the end of the fifth year. The implications of this will be discussed after the net present value of the project is analyzed.

In Table 10–6 the pro forma income statement is set forth. It differs from the cash flow statement of Table 10–4 in a number of respects. Income is based upon sales recorded rather than on actual receipt of cash. Expenses are on an accrual basis rather than on actual cash outflows. The income statement records noncash outlays such as depreciation not included in the cash flow statement.

In Table 10–7 the computation of tax obligations of the parent is made in accordance with the procedures set forth in Chapter 7. In line 1 is the dividend received by the parent from the subsidiary. Line 2 shows 50 percent of the foreign taxes paid by the subsidiary since its dividend payout ratio is 50 percent. In line 3 the dividend withholding tax paid by the subsidiary is set forth.

As described in Chapter 7, the gross-up income from the standpoint of the U.S. parent is the sum of the first three lines. U.S. income tax is shown in line 5, on the basis of a 50 percent tax rate, and is 0.5 of line 4.

TABLE 10–6

CELAN INSTRUMENT PROJECT PROPOSAL
Five-year pro forma income statement (in thousands of LC)

	1	2	3	4	5
Sales..............................	20,000	20,000	50,000	50,000	50,000
Less:					
Raw material.....................	8,000	8,000	20,000	20,000	20,000
Labor...........................	2,000	2,000	5,000	5,000	5,000
Depreciation on equipment..........	3,000	3,000	3,000	3,000	3,000
Selling and administrative costs......	2,000	2,000	5,000	5,000	5,000
Supervisory fees..................	1,000	1,000	1,000	1,000	1,000
Costs of hedging and insuring........	1,000	1,000	2,000	2,000	2,000
Total Costs..................	17,000	17,000	36,000	36,000	36,000
Profit before taxes..................	3,000	3,000	14,000	14,000	14,000
Taxes............................	900	900	4,200	4,200	4,200
Earnings after taxes................	2,100	2,100	4,800	9,800	9,800
Dividends........................	1,050	1,050	4,900	4,900	4,900
Less: Dividend withholding tax (10%)..	105	105	490	490	490
Dividends to the U.S. parent..........	945	945	4,410	4,410	4,410

The foreign tax credit is the sum of line 2, the foreign income tax paid by the subsidiary, and line 3, the dividend withholding tax paid by the subsidiary. The net U.S. tax due, therefore, is the tax obligation of line 5 less the foreign tax credit. The net after U.S. tax income, line 8, is obtained by subtracting the U.S. taxes paid from the dividend received from the subsidiary. The net U.S. tax due will be required in Table 10–8 in which the capital budgeting analysis of the project was made from the standpoint of the parent.

Since this is an international project it is plausible to make an analysis

TABLE 10–7

CELAN INSTRUMENT PROJECT PROPOSAL
Computation of tax obligations of U.S. parent
(in thousands of dollars)

	1	2	3	4	5	5t
1. Dividends received..............	94.5	94.5	441	441	441	1,512
2. Foreign income tax paid by subsidiary,......................	45	45	210	210	210	720
3. Dividend withholding tax paid by subsidiary.....................	10.5	10.5	49	49	49	118
4. Gross-up income (1 + 2 + 3).....	150	150	700	700	700	2,400
5. U.S. income tax (50% of 4).......	75	75	350	350	350	1,200
6. Foreign tax credit (2 + 3).......	55.5	55.5	259	259	259	888
7. Net U.S. tax due (5 − 6).........	19.5	19.5	91	91	91	312
8. Net after U.S. tax income (1 − 7)..	75	75	350	350	350	1,200

based on the possibility that the project will be terminated at the end of the planning horizon. The value of this analysis is to require that some judgments be formulated about what might be received from the project on liquidation.

Accordingly when we calculate the tax obligations of the U.S. parent, we will assume that all of the accumulated retained earnings of the subsidiary will be paid out to the parent at the termination of the fifth year. We then calculate the net U.S. tax due, following the principles we have already set forth. This accounts for the column 5_t in Table 10–7.

TABLE 10–8

CELAN INSTRUMENT PROJECT PROPOSAL
Parent company capital budgeting analysis of the project
(in thousands of dollars)

	0	1	2	3	4	5	5_t
Cash inflows from project:							
Net cash flows from project.	(3,400)	310	210	580	1,180	3,980	
Supervisory fee.	. . . . .	100	100	100	100	100	
Total Inflows.	(3,400)	410	310	680	1,280	4,080	
Cash outflows:							
U.S. income tax.		19.5	19.5	91	91	91	312
U.S. tax on supervisory fee income.		50.0	50.0	50	50	50	. . .
Dividend withholding tax paid by sub.		10.5	10.5	49	49	49	168
Total Outflows.		80	80	190	190	190	480
Net inflows.	(3,400)	330	230	490	1.090	3,890	(480)
Present value factor at 15%. . .	1,000	0.870	0.756	0.658	0.572	0.497	0.497
Net present values.	(3,400)	287	174	322	623	1,933	2.39
Cumulative net present values from project.	(3,400)	(3,113)	(2,939)	(2,617)	(1,994)	(61)	(300)

The parent company cash flow analysis is set forth in Table 10–8. We begin with the cash inflows from the project translated to dollars. Therefore, the figures in the final line of Table 10–3, the five-year capital budgeting analysis, are divided by 10 and carried in the first line of the parent company cash flows from the project. The parent company charges the subsidiary project a supervisory fee of LC 1 million or $100,000 which will represent an increment to the domestic net income of the parent company. It will therefore be subject to the company's U.S. tax rate of 50 percent in the capital budgeting analysis of the project from the standpoint of the parent. These figures are summed up in the following line.

Cash outflows from the standpoint of the parent are next analyzed. First, we present the U.S. income tax which represents line 7 of Table

10–7. The 50 percent on the supervisory fee income is next set forth. Since the dividend withholding tax paid by the subsidiary is all applicable to the parent, this is next deducted as a cash outflow. The three cash outflows are then totaled. The net cash inflows from the standpoint of the parent are shown next.

The applicable cost of capital to the project, 15 percent, is used as a present value factor. This is multiplied times the net inflows to obtain net present values as indicated. These are then cumulated in the final line. The cumulated net present values from the project are negative in every year including the fifth year.

Just as we had to consider the effects of terminating the project in connection with the computation of tax obligations of the U.S. parent, similarly we must consider, in the capital budgeting analysis of the project from the parent company standpoint, the additional U.S. tax obligations at the termination of the fifth year. As a result the negative net present value of $61,000 is increased to $300,000—the additional tax obligations stemming from the remittance to the parent of the terminal or liquidating cash. This further aggravates the indicated unprofitability of the project, but additional analysis might alter the outlook.

A review and analysis of the project might then be made. Perhaps the sales forecasts are too low. Perhaps some of the cost estimates are too high. A probability analysis of alternative forecasts of cash inflows and cash outflows might be made to determine the expected return from the project and some measures of variation from the project's expected returns.

We emphasize that the appropriate cost of capital to assign to the project is the project cost of capital and not the company's overall cost of capital. Some writers have suggested using the company's overall cost of capital. However, we believe this to be an error. The company's overall cost of capital represents in some sense the weighted average of the cost of capital of all of its individual projects and divisions. Both analysis and logic would suggest the application of the cost of capital specific to the division or project rather than the company's overall cost of capital.

It is of interest to note that on the basis of the five-year pro forma income statement, this project has a profit both before and after taxes in each year. Indeed, the cumulative nondiscounted cash flows for the project on Table 10–3 are positive in the fifth year. Thus the project would meet a five-year payback requirement. Nevertheless, the project is unattractive.

Although the project is profitable according to the pro forma income statement, it does not earn the firm's cost of capital of 15 percent. Thus, it is important to analyze the project from a discounted cash flow standpoint rather than from the standpoint of a pro forma income statement.

Another aspect of interest from the balance sheet is that the cash accumulates to an LC 25.8 million level by the fifth year. This is also consistent with the cash budget in Table 10–4 where positive cash flows are shown for each of the individual years after period 0. The analysis of the cash flow demonstrates that the project throws off cash after the initial outlay of LC 34 million in period 0. Given this favorable cash throw-off of the project, it might have been desirable for the parent to have provided one half of the initial capital required, for example, and to have borrowed the other half locally with a three- to five-year payout on the amounts borrowed locally. If the local (foreign) country were subject to depreciation of its currency relative to the U.S. dollar, this would have been a desirable financial policy from the standpoint of monetary balance.

Of course, the parent company would not have permitted the large indicated amounts of cash to accumulate in idle balances. The financial statements represent a part of the planning stage for analysis of the project. The accumulations of cash in excess of the cash balance requirements of the project would be employed either by the parent or subsidiary. The capital budgeting analysis assumes that the excess funds are utilized at the firm's opportunity cost.

At a number of points in the foregoing analysis it has been recognized that the figures used represent the best estimates. These figures are, of course, subject to variation. Investments in foreign countries are subject to considerable risk or variation. Some of the risk aspects of the project will now be considered more explicitly.

Risk considerations in project analysis

Risk considerations are especially important in foreign investment decisions. Hence, the models for the treatment of investments under uncertainty take on special importance. Because of the wider range and severity of possible risks in the foreign environment that can be only partially hedged or insured against, the range of possible outcomes may be much greater for the foreign investment than for a domestic commitment.

The appropriate procedure is to set forth the cumulative net present values that would occur under alternative possible future states and outcomes for the investment project. A comparison of expected returns and the dispersion of expected returns as measured by the variance and standard deviation of alternative outcomes must be taken into consideration. Thus on a return-risk consideration, some difficult choices may be involved. Domestic investments are likely to offer lower expected returns and lower standard deviations; foreign investments may offer higher expected returns and higher standard deviations of returns. Management's need for models of investment opportunities under uncertainty is increased for foreign investment decisions. A detailed discussion of investments under uncertainty can be found in Appendix C.

Another aspect of investment decisions under uncertainty becomes of increased importance in an analysis of foreign investment decisions. The variance or standard deviation of returns contains elements of both diversifiable and nondiversifiable risk. While the standard deviation of returns from foreign investments may be large, a portion of this risk may be diversified away if the firm makes a portfolio of foreign investments or combines domestic and foreign investments in its portfolio.

The economic characteristics of foreign markets are likely to be more different from investments in the United States than other U.S. domestic investments because of the diversity of economic characteristics of individual countries. Levy and Sarnat found that the correlation coefficient among returns for nine countries was negative or below 0.25 in 27 out of 45 possible observations in the correlation matrix.[9] Thus although the risks of foreign investments may be greater than for domestic investments, their negative covariance with domestic investments *may improve* the overall risk-return relations for the total "portfolio" of the firm which includes foreign investments in its activities.

SUMMARY

Direct foreign investment is a form of exporting capital from relatively capital-abundant countries to relatively labor-abundant countries. In the first section of this chapter we discussed the basic economic principles underlying the international movement of capital and the kinds of broad overall patterns of direct foreign investment. In the second section, we then summarized world patterns of investment with data organized from the standpoint of the United States.

With this general background, the factors that stimulate the individual firm's foreign investment were analyzed in the third section. The major factors are (1) high rates of return relative to risks, (2) tariffs and other barriers to export sales, (3) the requirements for different types of products in the foreign market, (4) savings in transportation expenses, (5) increased growth potential of the firm through geographic diversification, (6) further utilization of top corporate staff personnel, (7) employment of local talent, and (8) the favorable policies of host governments. Consideration of these factors adds a range of new variables to the list of variables in the domestic investment decision.

Finally, we illustrated the basic principles and techniques of project evaluation in foreign investment decisions. While the same basic principles as for domestic investment decisions apply to the analysis of foreign investment decisions, there are three salient differences: (1) The range of variables to be considered in the analysis is expanded. (2) The estimates

---

[9] H. Levy and M. Sarnat, "International Diversification of Investment Portfolios," *American Economic Review*, Vol. 60 (September 1970), p. 672.

of both outflows and inflows may be subject to wider margins of error. (3) The analysis of risks and returns is likely to be more complex.

New cost elements include costs of hedging against foreign exchange losses, costs of insuring against higher commercial credit risks, costs of insurance and guarantees against expropriation, additional taxes in the foreign country, and supervisory fees charged by the parent company. The transfer abroad of used equipment from the parent company and the potential substitution of sales from the new subsidiary for export sales made by other components of the multinational company constitute additional elements in the investment analysis.

Risk considerations are particularly important in foreign investment decisions since the range of possible outcomes is much wider. A comparison of prospective returns with risks is required. Foreign investments are likely to offer higher prospective returns with higher risks as well. Because the results of foreign operations are not likely to vary directly with the results of domestic operations, foreign investments offer attractive opportunities for diversification. The negative covariance of foreign investment with the results of domestic operations may strengthen the growth prospects of the firm and improve its overall risk-return position.

PROBLEM 10–1

A number of investment-type activities are described in the following list of transactions.

Indicate their effects on: (1) the U.S. balance of payments and on (2) the U.S. investment position.

1. American individuals purchase $5 million worth of bonds issued by a foreign company operating in France from (*a*) checks drawn on U.S. banks and (*b*) from deposits in foreign banks.

2. A U.S. parent company loans $20 million to a subsidiary in Mexico from bonds sold in the United States.

3. A U.S. parent loans $10 million to a foreign subsidiary by drawing a check on its U.S. bank. The subsidiary uses the $10 million to purchase equipment manufactured in Mexico.

4. An American parent company borrows $50 million in the Eurodollar market for nine months and uses these funds to establish a subsidiary in Brazil. It plans to raise the money on a more permanent basis later.

5. An American company transfers a patent to a joint venture with a foreign company in a foreign country. The American company receives a 49 percent interest in this joint venture in return for the patent. The joint venture is capitalized at 5 million Swiss francs.

6. A wholly owned British subsidiary of an American company had earnings of one million pounds during the previous year but paid no dividends to the American parent. The American parent is a large corporation whose securities are listed on the New York Stock Exchange and are widely held. The foreign subsidiary is engaged in manufacturing operations and sells the products produced wholly within the United Kingdom.

7. A U.S. parent invests $10 million from funds raised in the United States to establish a wholly owned subsidiary in France. In the following five years, the direct export sales of the U.S. parent are taken over completely by the foreign subsidiary from goods manufactured abroad. The export sales of the American parent over this period would have totaled $5 million. The total sales of the foreign subsidiary during this period aggregated $40 million representing $15 million worth of goods produced by the U.S. parent in the United States and sold to the foreign subsidiary in France. None of the goods produced by the foreign subsidiary are sold in the United States.

PROBLEM 10–2

The Carbon Company is contemplating the establishment of a manufacturing plant in a Latin American nation. It has developed the following information: Sales are estimated to be 20,000 pesos the first year, 30,000 pesos the second year, and 60,000 pesos per year through the fifth year. An investment of 24,000 pesos in new fixed assets and of 6,000 pesos in used equipment will be made at the beginning of the first year. Raw materials costs will be 30 percent of sales. Labor costs will be 20 percent of sales. Selling and administrative costs will be 10 percent of sales. Assume for simplicity that there are no accounts payable, all sales being for cash. The parent company will charge the project a supervisory fee of 1,000 pesos per annum to cover its actual dollar costs. There will be no local taxes for the first two years because the Latin American government is seeking to attract investments of the type involved by tax forgiveness. Local taxes in the third, fourth, and fifth years will be 30 percent of the before-tax profits.

For determining the profit and loss of the project, assume straight-line depreciation over a 10-year period for both the new fixed assets and the used equipment. Assume further for a cash flow analysis that both the new fixed assets and used equipment can be sold at their depreciated value as of the end of the fifth year. Cash on hand at the beginning of each period will be 10 percent of the sales of the next period. This investment in working capital will be returned at the end of the investment period.

The project will return in dividends to the U.S. parent one half of its after-tax net income each year. These dividends will be subject to a 10 percent withholding tax in the country of operation. The U.S. income tax will be calculated under the gross-up basis as outlined in Chapter 7. Assume a U.S. corporate income tax rate of 50 percent. The host country government has entered into a tax treaty with the U.S. government which provides that the 10 percent dividend withholding tax may be offset against U.S. income taxes. The foreign country does not tax the sale of used equipment at book value. All funds will be returned home at the end of the five-year period. The exchange rate is LC 10 to $1; no devaluation is expected.

A. Make a five-year cash flow analysis for each year in terms of the local currency.

B. Calculate the profit or loss after taxes for each year in the local currency.

C. Set out the parent company cash flow for each year expressed in dollars at an exchange rate of LC 10 per $1.

D. Calculate the U.S. income tax that will be paid by the parent on the dividends received from the Latin American project.

E. Calculate the cash inflows and cash outflows from the project on a capital budgeting basis.

F. Calculate the net present value of the cash flows from the standpoint of the parent company on a capital budgeting basis using a 15 percent cost of capital.

SELECTED BIBLIOGRAPHY

Aharoni, Yair. *The Foreign Investment Decision Process.* Cambridge, Mass.: Harvard Business School, 1966.

Behrman, Jack N. "Planning for and against Foreign Investment Controls," *Worldwide P & I Planning,* July–August 1968, p. 64.

Belli, R. David, and Freidlin, Julius N. "U.S. Direct Investments Abroad in 1970," *Survey of Current Business,* October 1971, pp. 26–38.

Devlin, David T. "The International Investment Position of the United States: Developments in 1970," *Survey of Current Business,* October 1971, pp. 19–25.

De Vries, Henry P. "Legal Climate for Investment," *Columbia Journal of World Business,* Vol. 4, No. 6. (November–December 1969), pp. 81–82.

Farmer, Richard N., and Richman, Barry M. *Comparative Management and Economic Progress,* pp. 74–237. Homewood, Ill.: Richard D. Irwin, Inc. 1965.

Kwack, Sung Y. "Effects of Interest Rates on Foreign Investment Income," *The Quarterly Review of Economics and Business,* Vol. 12, No. 1 (Spring 1972).

Penrose, E. T. "Foreign Investments and the Growth of the Firm," *The Economic Journal,* June 1956.

Proceedings of 1963 Institute the Southwestern Legal Foundation. *Private Investments Abroad and Foreign Trade.* New York: Matheco Bender & Co., 1963.

Singer, Stuart R. "Financial Planning Within the Foreign Direct Investment Regulations," *Financial Executive,* Vol. 38, No. 6 (June 1970), pp. 62–67.

Stonehill, A., and Nathanson, L. "Capital Budgeting and the Multinational Corporation," *California Management Review*, Summer 1968, pp. 39–54.

Treuherz, Rolf M. "Re-evaluating ROI for Foreign Operations," *Financial Executive*, Vol. 36, No. 5 (May 1968), pp. 64–71.

Williams, Simon. "Negotiating Investment in Emerging Countries," *Harvard Business Review*, January–February 1965, pp. 89–99.

11

Working capital management in the international enterprise

INTERNATIONAL cash management involves the minimizing of exposure of foreign-located funds to foreign exchange rate risk and the avoidance of prohibitions on the movement of funds from one country to another. Basically all funds denominated in any foreign currency, particularly that of developing countries, are subject to a potential decrease in value in terms of the home currency. To avoid foreign exchange rate risk and prohibitions against the international movement of funds requires that the financial manager continually assess political and economic trends in the countries of operation in order to anticipate changes that would have a detrimental effect.

COMPARISON OF DOMESTIC AND INTERNATIONAL CASH MANAGEMENT TECHNIQUES

The general principles that apply to the management of cash on an international basis are very similar to those that are used successfully by many American firms on a domestic basis. Multinational firms try to speed up the collection of cash by having bank accounts, identified by number, in the banking system of each country, as well as a "giro" account in the country's postal banking system. In many countries bills are paid by the customer requesting his bank or postal administration to deduct from his account and transfer to a specified account the amount owed.

However, many types of cash management techniques, such as lockbox systems to speed up the collection of funds, are available only in the United States. Arrangements are made with commercial banks whereby customers send payments directly to these lockboxes and the commercial banks credit the company's accounts with the funds received several times a day. Telegraphic transfer is used whenever available in connection with international operations to speed up the flow of funds. International banks with branches and correspondent banks in many foreign countries are employed to shorten the transfer time of funds between countries and reduce the foreign exchange rate risk during the transfer time.

Concentration banking, involving the movement of company funds to one or more cash centers for accumulation, temporary investment, and eventual reassignment is practiced by multinational firms whenever possible. However, the obstacles that prevent the effective execution of these policies on an international basis are many. The elimination or minimizing of the effect of these obstacles, which requires the attention of the financial executive of the multinational firm on a continuing basis, will be discussed in this chapter.

On a domestic basis funds are all denominated in the same currency. The same rules apply to the movement, accumulation, and reinvestment of all these funds. Commercial practices are uniform and are understood by everyone in the organization. Domestic currencies may lose purchasing power with an increase in price levels, but receivables and payables will always have a constant numerical value.

By contrast, as soon as international boundaries are crossed, these same conditions no longer apply. American firms doing business on an international basis 15 to 20 years ago solved the foreign currency problem by insisting on immediate payment in dollars. Credit granted, if any, was denominated in the home currency. However, due to the rapid rise of competition on an international basis, these policies no longer apply. The multinational firm of today must be ready and willing to do business in terms of the currencies used in the countries of its customers as well as the countries in which it has made investments or has established operations. Attempts by the International Monetary Fund to maintain a fixed relationship between all currencies of international trading nations have not been successful. Whenever the value of one currency changes in relation to others, the value of receivables or liabilities in terms of that currency changes in terms of the home currency of the multinational firm. It is these changes that cause the losses due to foreign exchange rate risk, a topic which has been discussed in detail in Chapter 5.

The problem of float, funds immobilized during the fund transfer process, differs between domestic and international transactions. Float from a domestic point of view involves only the temporary loss of income of these funds. In international operations, however, the problem of float is twofold. It involves the loss of income on the funds tied up during the longer transfer process and their exposure to foreign exchange rate risk during the transfer period. This requires an evaluation of the potential loss due to foreign exchange rate risk in addition to the loss of income while the funds are tied up as float.

Operations on a domestic basis are carried on according to the desires, policies, and aims of one government. By contrast, the political and economic goals among several nations are not likely to be the same. It is these conflicts between the policies and goals of the various national governments that create problems for the multinational firm as it attempts to conduct business on an effective and efficient commercial basis across national boundaries.

The governments of all nations have a never-ending requirement for funds, both domestic and international, to be used in achieving their national goals. For this reason the multinational firm operating within the political boundaries of a foreign country either by means of a subsidiary, branch, or joint venture is required to do its part in providing the domestic funds for its host government by the payment of taxes and assessments of various kinds. The firm is also required to do its part in assisting its host government to acquire and to husband foreign exchange reserves by obeying an endless stream of directives—all aimed at maximizing the foreign exchange reserves of the host country.

Concentration banking readily practiced domestically is not always possible on an international basis. At the present time even the majority of the developed nations in Europe will not permit the movement of funds across international boundaries for purposes of concentration, even though they will still permit the free flow of funds resulting from commercial transactions. This is due to the fact that any outflow of funds from a particular country will cause a decrease in foreign exchange reserves; thus the transfers of funds to other nations are very closely watched as well as regulated. In general, the ease or difficulty with which funds can be moved out of a particular country is directly related to the international balance-of-payments position of the country involved. It is these differences between national governments and the fact that various national currencies are not rigidly related to each other that prevent the multinational firm from executing a policy of effective cash management.

Business decisions made and operations executed by a multinational firm doing business in many countries on a sales, investment, and operational basis will cause a continuing flow of funds in both directions between the parent and its subsidiaries and branches, as well as between the subsidiaries and branches themselves. The inflow of funds from the parent or any of its branches or subsidiaries to any sister corporation may include initial or additional investment funds, loans, and the payments for goods and services obtained from that particular subsidiary. The outflow of funds from the same organization to its parent, branches of its parent, and sister corporations may include dividends, interest on loans, the repayment of loans, royalty payments, licensing fees, technical service fees, management fees, export commissions, and payments for goods and services received.

An ideal arrangement would be to adjust these fund flows within the multinational organization in such a way that as nearly as possible the flows to and from any particular subsidiary cancel each other. This goal is not impossible of attainment, particularly in multinational organizations where the various component parts carry on an active trade not only with the parent but also with each other. If the inflow from sister organizations is very strong, it may be possible to reach an equilibrium between the in and out flows for a particular subsidiary. In order to evaluate this problem it is of interest to take a look at the component parts of the funds flow.

THE COMPONENTS OF THE FUNDS FLOW

The flow of funds from subsidiary to parent

The principal components of the flow of funds from subsidiary to parent are dividends, interest on loans, principal reduction payments, royalty payments, license fees, technical service fees, management fees, export commissions, and payments for merchandise obtained from the parent.

The flow of dividends from subsidiary to parent is strongly influenced by the overall dividend policies of the multinational organization. In large multinational organizations the average of the dividend payout ratios of the subsidiaries is similar to that for the parent. This does not mean that the payout ratio is exactly the same for all of the subsidiaries. Usually the payout ratio for newly formed subsidiaries and subsidiaries engaged in very profitable operations is lower. On the other hand, subsidiaries of long standing and those that are engaged in operations that are not as profitable as others may have a higher than average dividend payout ratio.

The magnitude of the flow of dividends is not entirely within the control of the parent organization for all subsidiaries. In many countries, particularly those where chronic foreign exchange shortages prevail, there may exist severe limitations on the amount of dividend payments. Some countries may not permit the payment of dividends in a foreign currency. Other countries strongly limit the amount of dividends paid to foreign owners to a percentage of equity or earnings. Many governments impose a dividend withholding tax of up to 15 percent at the time dividends are remitted to foreign owners. This is a form of taxation on the foreign owners. Since not all countries grant tax credits on dividends received from subsidiaries, this may represent a form of double taxation.

In other countries penalties are levied by the taxing authorities on companies that pay out either too high or too low a ratio of earnings in the form of dividends. For this reason the payout ratio in any particular subsidiary may be strongly influenced by national laws as well as the fund needs of the subsidiary and the desires of the national joint-venture partners. It is often these national joint-venture partners that most strongly object to large dividend payments to the foreign (U.S.) parent. These citizens of the country of operation have a high regard for cash and often cannot understand why the liquidity of their particular organization should be endangered by the withdrawal of dividend payments.

Interest on loans. Most countries usually permit the payment of interest, whether of a short- or long-term duration, even if the lender is the parent or a sister organization. It is only under extreme conditions of foreign exchange reserve shortage that countries will not permit the payment of interest. Interest payments are fully taxable to the recipient in most countries. However, they are also fully deductable from income on the part of the organization making these payments. Another advantage to interest payments lies in the fact that they serve as evidence that an indebtedness exists between the subsidiary and the parent.

Return of loan principal. Return of loan principal is quite often restricted in amount, particularly by developing countries. In most of these countries the repayment of principal cannot exceed 10 percent of the original loan in any one year. During periods of extreme foreign exchange reserve shortage, the return of loan principal may not be possible until the severe shortage condition passes. Since the return of principal is not taxable to the recipient, it may actually be desirable for a firm to make these payments first before increasing materially the dividend payout ratio, if low dividends are not penalized by the taxing authority in a particular country.

Royalty payments and licensing fees. Royalties and licensing fees in general are recognized as valid obligations to foreign firms or individuals. In a number of countries, however, royalty payments are limited to a particular percentage of annual sales. The magnitude of patent or license fees for technical production processes also must be in a reasonable percentage relationship to the subsidiary's volume of business.

Technical service and management fees. Technical service and management fees must be assessed to a subsidiary on a fair and defensible basis. The distribution of these fees among parts of a multinational firm must bear resemblance to services actually rendered. If this is not the case, either the government of the country in which the subsidiary is located or the parent country's taxing authority will investigate the problem and levy additional taxes, often in the form of penalties. In the case of joint ventures with nationals of the country of operation, the levying of royalty payments, license fees, technical service fees, and management fees often makes it possible for the minority owner to receive a majority of funds. In fact, the patent, royalty, and licensing agreements makes possible the effective control of a subsidiary by a group that is not the majority owner.

Payment for goods. The payment for goods offers probably the greatest possibility of adjusting the flow of funds. Transfer pricing, if not practiced to excess, can make it possible to shift profits from the subsidiary to the parent by pricing goods sent by the parent to the subsidiary slightly higher than to other buyers. As a result the operating or manufacturing expenses of the subsidiary are increased, thus lowering profits and local taxes.

The flow of funds from parent to subsidiary

The largest flow of funds from the parent to the subsidiary usually consists of initial as well as added investment funds. These may be for the purpose of equity investment or for loans that will be repaid at a later time. The purchase of goods from a subsidiary at perhaps slightly decreased prices from what would normally be required offers another opportunity to remove earnings from a subsidiary and the transfer of these to the parent. As mentioned previously, this transfer pricing must be done with care, since the taxing authorities of most countries watch this very carefully. Under conditions of extreme foreign exchange reserve shortage, the transfer of funds resulting from merchandise trade may be the only way to obtain funds from a subsidiary. This at times is made possible because under such extreme conditions, most national governments offer inducements to firms that are able to increase their exports. If, then, as part of this export drive the parent purchases goods from the subsidiary and pays for these funds in a convertible currency, this may make it possible for the subsidiary, as a result of its government's export promotion drive, to keep a portion of these funds to spend at its own discretion. The remainder of the convertible currency funds, of course, must be turned over to the country's national bank for conversion into local currency.

The flow of funds between subsidiaries

Subsidiaries of a multinational firm may loan funds to each other. This results in interest as well as principal reduction payments passing from the debtor to the lender. The subsidiaries may also sell or purchase parts and supplies as well as finished goods from each other. If this movement of goods and materials and finished equipment is large in scale, it will permit reasonable freedom to regulate the flow of funds from and to any particular subsidiary. It is not impossible, under conditions of extreme foreign exchange reserve shortage, that two subsidiaries may be able to trade with each other on a strictly barter basis with the approval of their governments.

POLICIES AFFECTING THE SHORT-TERM FLOW OF FUNDS

From an economic point of view the worldwide funds of a multinational firm should migrate toward the points of highest profitability and safety. They should also move toward those locations from which they can again be readily reassigned to other places of the world. Idle funds should migrate toward cash centers for accumulation and temporary investment prior to reassignment elsewhere. If the proper country is chosen for such a cash center, the funds will be relatively safe from foreign exchange rate risk, will not be subject to undue taxation, and can be readily assigned to any country of the world in which the multinational firm wishes to operate. This concentration of idle cash will improve control over it, will likely improve its income prior to reassignment, and most importantly will permit the immediate undertaking of new investment opportunities once decisions to proceed have been made. Germany, Hong Kong, Liechtenstein, and Switzerland presently offer the best accommodations. The following considerations should serve to achieve the above specifications.

These cash centers should be located in countries whose governments are politically stable, whose currency has a relatively constant value and is readily convertible into other currencies, and a country that has no prohibitions against fund transfers either into or out of the country. The government of a country in which such a cash center is located should also have a friendly attitude toward foreign-owned subsidiaries and should permit 100 percent foreign-owned subsidiaries. It should tax income only at the source and have no taxes on capital.

At the location of the cash center should exist an international financial market which should include an effective foreign exchange market, with an active forward market involving the currencies of the majority of trading nations. An active money market should exist in which funds can be invested gainfully on a short-term basis with minimum risk prior to reassignment. It is also desirable that the country of location of such a cash center have a foreign investment guarantee program which can be used for protective purposes when funds are sent for investment from the cash center to other countries.

The financial planning pertaining to the transfer of funds on an international basis must be done on a worldwide basis. This planning should obviously be done at the head office of the parent organization. The pattern and timing of the flow of funds must be determined by the parent organization because local managers are often strongly influenced by their own business problems and by the attitudes of national partners in the case of joint ventures.

The need for the transfer of funds away from a foreign subsidiary should be governed by the worldwide needs of the parent as well as of all its subsidiaries. The opportunity cost of the funds to be removed from a foreign subsidiary must be considered. A comparison between this cost and the borrowing cost of funds in other parts of the world may dictate leaving particular funds with a subsidiary, if they are earning a higher rate of profit than would result from transferring them. Conversely, if the opportunity costs of funds for a particular subsidiary are low, funds should be moved from this organization toward others where investment would prove more profitable. These considerations make it necessary that financial planning be done on a worldwide basis.

The international transfer of funds should be effected on the most direct basis consistent with safety from foreign exchange rate risk. The planning of fund transfers involves a comparison between loss of income on the float and probability of a loss due to a devaluation in one country or the other on the funds during the transfer period. The transfer period between two countries is shortest if the funds transferred are denominated in the currency of one of the two countries. When the funds are denominated in a third-country currency, the transfer period is lengthened, since the clearing process always takes place in the country of the currency used.

Example of transfer risk of short-term funds

A Hong Kong subsidiary for a U.S. multinational firm wishes to transfer funds to a Belgian exporter. The shortest transfer period will be achieved by the Hong Kong firm buying Belgian francs in Hong Kong and transferring them to Belgium. These funds will be cleared by reducing the Belgian account of a Hong Kong bank. If the funds are transferred in Hong Kong dollars, they are exchanged into Belgian francs after arrival and are cleared by increase of a Hong Kong dollar account of a Belgian bank. This transfer may take two or three days.

If, on the other hand, the Hong Kong subsidiary wishes to reduce foreign exchange rate risk by making the transfer in U.S. dollars, this transfer would be cleared via the United States. The purchase of the U.S. dollars would decrease the U.S. account of a Hong Kong commercial bank, and the sale of the U.S. dollars in Belgium and conversion to Belgian francs would cause an increase in the balance of a Belgian bank's U.S. dollar account in the United States. The final clearing process would take place in the United States by the transfer of a credit from the Hong Kong bank's account to that of a Belgian bank. The time interval for this transaction may be six days. The larger loss of the income on the float of the Hong Kong firm must be considered a cost of the protection against exchange rate risk.

At the present time it would be advisable to make the transfer in terms of the Belgian franc, since the probability of a decrease in its foreign exchange value is less than that for U.S. and Hong Kong dollars and at the same time the transfer time is shorter, reducing the loss on the float. The services of an international commercial bank with branches and correspondents in major countries will greatly help to reduce transfer time and foreign exchange rate risk during the transfer period.

Policies on payments by subsidiaries

International cash flow policies practiced by American multinational firms are strongly influenced by the relationship between a company's foreign and domestic income. If the firm's international income is small in relation to that from domestic operations, it is generally found that international cash flow policies are less stringent and that there is a tendency to reinvest foreign-earned funds in the countries of operation rather than withdrawing them for parent or other subsidiary use. However, when the international income represents a large share of total income of the multinational firm, cash flow policies must be much more definite and transfers should be carried out according to an overall plan.

Policies on the dividend payout ratios for the various entities in a multinational organization as well as on the allocation of overhead expenses, management fees, and loan and financing policies must be made on a worldwide basis. When these are uniform and applied equally to all subsidiaries and branches, the governments of host countries are more likely to accept them than would otherwise be the case. Overhead costs must be allocated on a basis of service rendered in order to make these allocations defensible before the taxing authorities of the foreign countries of operation.

Licensing fees under home-country patents, royalties resulting from the use of company trademarks, and charges for technical services or manufacturing processes should be uniform for general acceptance on a worldwide basis. Patents and licensing agreements on technical processes are an effective means of virtual control in the case of joint ventures that are less than 50 percent owned. These licensing fees as well as transfer pricing practiced on a moderate basis are effective means of transferring income from one subsidiary to another or to the parent. Excessive use of transfer pricing to influence the flow of worldwide funds is usually not possible over an extended period of time because of the close attention paid to these practices by the governments of host countries and foreign joint-venture partners as well as the taxing authorities of the home country.

In order to minimize exposure to foreign exchange rate risk, equity investments in foreign subsidiaries should be held to a minimum. If a foreign subsidiary requires additional funds, they usually should be provided on a loan basis denominated in U.S. currency because permission to pay interest and make loan repayments is usually more readily obtainable from the foreign country than is payment of dividends on shares. In addition, any funds advanced on either an equity or loan basis should be registered with the foreign country's banking authorities so that in the case of equity funds, dividend payments may be later permitted, and in the case of loan funds, the payment of interest as well as the return of the capital may also be expedited.

As a subsidiary's volume of business grows in a foreign country, this will usually cause an increase in monetary assets such as operating cash and accounts receivable. The loss of the purchasing power of these monetary assets may be minimized by obtaining offsetting loans providing that these can be obtained at reasonable rates of interest in relation to the expected rate of devaluation. Furthermore, if a subsidiary's product market is proprietary, that is, it has distinctive products and other suppliers are few, a subsidiary should limit the granting of trade credit to an absolute minimum or charge a rate of interest in line with expected devaluation. At the same time, if the subsidiary should be so fortunate as to obtain its supplies in a competitive market where supplies as well as suppliers are large in number, the subsidiary should make fullest use possible of trade credit obtainable on a free basis. If, on the other hand, the opposite should be true, where demand is strong in the factor market and the supply is abundant in the product market, then the foreign subsidiary usually has no choice except to pay a high rate of interest on the credit obtained and at the same time grant trade credit to its customers on a free basis.

Minimizing erosion of short-term funds

Multinational firms must minimize tax liability from an overall point of view. This requires a detailed knowledge of the tax codes in the various countries of operation, because many nations charge transfer taxes on fund transfers such as payment of dividends or interest. These charges are made in part to discourage the outflow of funds and also to exact a tax from the recipient of the funds. Multinational firms usually take for granted that the home country will eventually tax all foreign earned income, with credit, of course, for taxes paid to other governments.

If excess funds exist in the hands of a subsidiary which cannot be transferred out of the country, steps must be taken to protect the purchasing power of these funds as the local currency continues to decrease in value. When idle funds or dividends declared cannot be moved due to national government restrictions, it is best to invest these funds in real assets, preferably real assets of a short-term nature such as inventory, which will again turn to cash in a reasonably short time. This investment in inventory can be repeated until the conditions improve so that transfers out of the country are again possible. These unpaid dividends should also be recognized on the books of the subsidiary as a liability to the parent.

Occasionally it is possible to make excess funds available to another foreign-owned organization in the same country. To offset the loan made in a foreign country the parents of the two organizations can effect a loan in the opposite direction that will have the same termination date. In this way the parent of the cash-surplus subsidiary has the opportunity, at least on a temporary basis, to make use of these funds in the home country. A later cancellation of liability between the two foreign organizations, as well as between the two parents, is not legal in most foreign countries since this would be considered an illegal transfer of funds out of the country.

When operating in a country subject to chronic increases in price levels, it is advisable that the foreign subsidiary operate with as little cash on hand as is possible. If permitted, such subsidiaries should liquidate foreign debt denominated in convertible currencies. It should endeavor to keep trade receivables as low as possible, or charge a rate of interest in line with the change in price levels. If it does need funds on a short-term basis, it should obtain these, if possible, from local commercial banks. However, under conditions of a fairly rapid increase in price levels, loans from commercial banks are usually not obtainable. It then becomes necessary to go into the private money market and obtain short-term loans on a discounted 90- to 120-day basis, a practice which customarily proves to be very expensive.

It will be worthwhile to practice all the normal procedures of speeding up the collection and movement of cash and to borrow on an overdraft basis whenever necessary. If loans on a normal basis are not available, it may be advisable to seek out another firm which may have a temporary excess of cash that it wishes to employ until needed. Whenever additional foreign funds are brought into the country, it is very important that these be registered with the country's national bank so that it may be possible to pay interest and eventually return them when desired. It is advisable to obtain forward contracts wherever available to protect the convertible currency value of funds between accumulation and transfer. Since working capital shifts are usually of short duration, it is not likely that a currency swap can be employed to protect local cash balances from purchasing power deterioration.

THE USE OF MULTINATIONAL BANKS

Multinational commercial banks, particularly those that have branches or affiliates in a large number of countries, may be very helpful to a multinational firm. Several of the larger American multinational commercial banks have foreign departments whose sole purpose is to aid American multinational firms in their problems of international cash management. An international bank can speed the flow of funds of a multinational firm and thereby decrease the exposure of these funds to foreign exchange rate risk. It can make suggestions as to the routing of these transfers as well as the national currency to be used. Whereas in the United States the average time between the initiation and completion of a financial transaction is two to three days, the time interval between these dates in connection with foreign transactions may be as long as two or three weeks. These long delays tie up large funds unnecessarily and should be avoided. In this instance, the multinational commercial banks can be of great help. Transfer of funds from one country to another, providing government restrictions do not interfere, is possible on a same-day basis as long as the multinational bank has a branch or an affiliate in the two countries involved.

In the case of a multinational firm with large international intercompany transactions, an international bank can be of the greatest service. After a new year's operations forecast has been completed by the multinational firm, the international bank on a consulting basis can help the firm to establish cash flow systems in which the bank may or may not be involved operationally. Their study would involve all of the firm's receivables and payables as well as investments both on a domestic and an international basis.

In addition, the multinational commercial bank can be of considerable aid to the financial executive of the multinational firm by providing him with knowledge about the banking laws and procedures in any of the countries of his firm's operations. Only an international commercial bank's foreign department can have complete and detailed information about the banking systems in 50 or more countries. To achieve this same level of competence within the multinational firm would prove extremely expensive, if not impossible. Also, since banks usually have the latest information on government restrictions and prohibitions of fund transfers or changes in these rules, a multinational commercial bank can be of great aid to the financial vice president of a multinational firm and alert him when added restrictions against the transfer of funds are being considered in a particular country or when the removal of existing restrictions is near.

An alert multinational commercial bank can actually make additional cash available to the corporation for business purposes as a result of the reduction in the amount of float that is tied up unnecessarily due to slow transfer habits based on past antiquated practices. These freed funds when invested profitably will increase the income of the multinational firm. The assistance of such a bank will definitely improve a multinational firm's cash planning.

To the multinational firm the proper planning for, and the execution of, the correct movements of funds on a worldwide basis is of utmost importance. The movement of funds to points of greatest profitability and safety will be very important in assuring the success of the firm's efforts. A financial vice president well versed in the details of international finance can play an important part in assisting the management of his firm in making the proper decisions.

SUMMARY

International cash management techniques are basically similar to those employed domestically, but additional problems are involved. Some techniques used in the United States, such as telegraphic transfers and lockbox systems, may not be available in other countries. In this country, arriving funds can be credited several times a day. Similar use should be made of concentration banking, whereby funds are accumulated in cash centers ready for immediate transfer. Concentration banking is, however, difficult to practice when foreign governments forbid the outflow of funds.

In domestic financial operations all transactions are subject to the same rules of movement, accumulation, and reinvestment. But, across national boundaries the rules vary. The international firm must be willing to do business in other currencies with no fixed relationship between them. Funds are immobilized by the float during transfer, sometimes for long periods of time. This means loss of interest during the transfer process and exposure to exchange rate risk as well. Many governments are involved, each watching out for its own national interest.

Policies adopted for the short-term flow of funds ideally should result in worldwide funds migrating toward the points of highest profit and safety. But international financial managers must take many factors into consideration in deciding policy, contending with impediments to the economic ideal all the way. Transfer of funds within a multinational firm must be governed by the worldwide needs of the parent as well as of all its subsidiaries and so must be managed by the head office. It must likewise be influenced by the relationship between a company's foreign and domestic income. Funds should be accumulated in centers from which they may be reassigned readily to new opportunities for profit.

Erosion of short-term funds by taxation as well as by exchange rate risk should be avoided. Detailed knowledge of the tax codes of various countries is required. Multinational commercial banks, particularly those with branches or affiliates in many countries, can speed the flow of funds and decrease exposure to foreign exchange rate risk. They can suggest routing of transfers and the national currency which is best to use. They can transfer funds on a same-day basis and provide consulting service on most aspects of international financing.

PROBLEM 11–1

The Hong Kong subsidiary of a U.S. multinational firm desires to pay U.S. $100,000 to a Belgian supplier. The transfer time of funds in terms of Hong Kong dollars or Belgian francs is six days, whereas the transfer time in U.S. dollars is two weeks. What is the cost of avoiding foreign exchange rate risk by making the transfer in U.S. dollars on the basis that the firm's opportunity cost is 12 percent?

PROBLEM 11-2

The subsidiaries and branches of Multinat each month collect the equivalent of U.S. $600,000 in European and North African countries. These funds are transferred to a cash center in Switzerland as received. The average transfer time is 12 days.

An international bank has approached Multinat and has offered its services to handle these fund transfers. It has guaranteed that the average transfer time will not exceed two days. Multinat's opportunity cost of funds is 14 percent. What is the maximum that Multinat should pay for this service?

PROBLEM 11-3

Why would an American company manufacturing in the United States but having a substantial amount of export sales to Japan and Western European countries make use of the local U.S. branches or agencies of large foreign banks?

SELECTED BIBLIOGRAPHY

Stonehill, Arthur, and Stitzel, Thomas. "Financial Structure and Multinational Corporation," *California Management Review,* Fall 1969, pp. 39–54.

Verroen, John. "How ITT Manages Its Foreign Exchange," *Management Services,* January–February 1965, pp. 27–33.

12

The multinational firm

TECHNICALLY the multinational company may be defined as a firm which owns and manages business operations in two or more countries.[1] The multinational corporation has direct investments in foreign countries which involve the ownership and management of physical assets as well as the managers and workers required to make those physical assets productive. This is in contrast to owning portfolio investments in securities. Almost every large enterprise has some impacts from international elements on its operations. It may import some materials or export some products. It may have agents or offices abroad, and it may even license foreign firms to manufacture some of its products. However, a firm takes on the important characteristics of a multinational enterprise only when it must carry out the responsibility of financing, producing, and marketing products within foreign nations.

An analysis of the multinational corporation is useful for integrating many aspects of the topics discussed in previous chapters of this book. The subject will be discussed under four broad topics:

1. Stages in development to multinational status.
2. Some illustrative case studies of the development of multinational firms.
3. Multinational firms and the U.S. economy.
4. Tailoring strategy to country's stage of development.

STAGES IN DEVELOPMENT TO MULTINATIONAL STATUS

While the formal definition of a multinational firm has elements of arbitrariness, the characteristics of multinational operations may be best conveyed by analyzing the stages in development from a domestic firm to

---

[1] See Neil H. Jacoby, "The Multinational Corporation," *The Center Magazine,* Vol. 3 (May 1970), p. 38.

a truly international operation. Usual steps in the process are set forth in Table 12–1.

It has been estimated that something over 100,000 U.S. business enterprises have reached stage 4—engaging in direct exports using its own personnel. Fewer have reached stages 5 and 6 of establishing branch sales offices abroad or engaging in licensing operations. The next fundamental stages are those in which manufacturing facilities are established abroad through joint venture, branch manufacturing operations, mergers, acquisitions, or subsidiaries developed by internal expansion. These stages have been reached by about 45,000 American firms. However, probably not more than 200 of the largest business firms engaged in international opera-

TABLE 12–1

Stages in the development from a domestic firm to a multinational firm

1. Development of a strong product for domestic sales.
2. Import of raw materials or parts.
3. Exports through brokers.
4. Direct export sales.
5. Foreign branch sales office.
6. Licensing.
7. Licensing with partial ownership.
8. Joint ventures.
9. Wholly owned manufacturing branch plants or subsidiaries.
10. Multinational management organization.
11. Multinational ownership of equity securities.

tions have reached truly multinational status and orientation as indicated by steps 10 and 11.[2] The nature of each of these stages will be briefly described from the standpoint of decision making and international business operations.

Development of a strong product for domestic sales

A fundamental precondition necessary to lay a foundation for international operations requires a firm to develop a reliable product with a good reputation. This provides a basis for realizing a favorable market potential of sales in the firm's own country. Use of international operations cannot provide a sound substitute for managing domestic operations effectively. If domestic operations are poorly managed, the problems cannot be solved by going international. International operations should not be viewed as an escape hatch for failing to face up to the challenges of domestic operations. Indeed, if domestic operations are not being conducted efficiently, the prospects of successful operations in international business

[2] Ibid.

are small. The likelihood is high that the firm will make even greater mistakes in international operations than in domestic because the problems are more complex and the dynamism of market changes and wider forms of competition are even greater.

Imports of raw materials or parts

A firm may develop some exposure to international operations by importing a portion of the raw materials or parts used in its domestic production. This contact with international operations may represent various degrees of participation. It may simply represent purchases from an import agent or through a distributor who may be utilizing both domestic and foreign sources.

Exports through brokers

A firm begins to meet the requirements of understanding international business more completely when it begins to export its products. Here a decision must be made about the regions in which sales will be made and whether the firm's own personnel will be employed or export brokers will be used.

The use of an export broker or agent is favored under some circumstances. An important consideration is whether the firm has in its employ sales personnel with experience or aptitude for international sales. If the firm has only personnel with little or no experience in export sales, and particularly if the products sold are consumer goods which require a broad foreign marketing organization or contact with intermediary marketing institutions abroad, the use of an export broker or agent is favored. This procedure may be employed initially as a method of acquainting the firm and its personnel with the international export business.

Direct export sales

Beginning an export operation with a company's own personnel is favored when two conditions are met: (1) the cost is lower than, and quality of the firm's product is superior to, that of foreign competitors', and (2) the products are industrial goods that require relatively few customers and, therefore, a small marketing organization will suffice.

When a firm seeks to develop its own direct foreign sales operations, it can receive much help from U.S. government agencies. Both the Department of State and the Department of Commerce have a wide range of facilities to help a firm obtain experience in international sales. The State Department has consular representatives who are a source of considerable information about individual countries. These agencies conduct trade fairs and other forms of expositions in order to provide opportunities for displaying the products of individual firms abroad.

In addition, the Department of Commerce has a considerable staff of experienced personnel and substantial data to provide a basis for sound planning of foreign operations. In a number of areas of the country, local department of commerce offices conduct seminars in which individual businessmen describe their experiences in developing sales in international markets for the benefit of potential newcomers. Seminars are also held in which the problems of individual firms seeking to expand operations in the international market are discussed. In these the experience of both department of commerce officers and the combined experience of the managers of private firms can be drawn upon.

Much information can be obtained for determining whether and to what extent export potential exists for a product. A basic approach to estimating a product's export potential starts with an analysis of the product's total volume of exports from the United States. Such data are obtainable in the Foreign Trade Series of the U.S. Department of Commerce. The Commerce Department FT410 and FT420 series provide data on U.S. exports by commodity groups and subgroups by country of destination. If countries are already importing the product in quantity, clearly the conditions necessary for the use of the commodity in that country already have been met. If the product a firm wants to introduce is new, then it should be related to products already used abroad. Although a country may not import the particular product nor consume it but buys a product with similar characteristics, there is a possibility of commercial feasibility of selling the new product in that country.

The basic factors determining the export potential to a foreign market include: its population, income level, literacy, climate, resources, and economic production patterns; its social, cultural, and religious character; the transportation facilities and costs; the foreign exchange situation; and the nature and role of its government. These factors have been discussed in some detail in previous chapters.

Foreign branch sales office

Shortly after some initial sales have been made, if the conditions favoring direct export are favorable, the firm may seek to establish a branch sales office abroad. This has a number of advantages: It enables the firm to establish more direct contacts and enables its personnel to obtain more detailed familiarity with the foreign market. Inevitably, modifications will be required for a product to fit the foreign market needs exactly. The establishment of a branch sales office enables the firm to have a base for researching the foreign market more effectively. Also, technical sales personnel may be placed in the foreign branch office and thus be able to provide some service for the product if it is a durable good. In addition, the firm can begin to accumulate information more directly on the reactions of foreign users of the product. This may be a basis for providing more prompt communication and service and, in addition, for making plans to modify the initial characteristics of the product to more nearly meet the needs of foreign customers.

Licensing

Intermediate to the step of actually establishing foreign manufacturing operations is licensing a local or foreign firm to manufacture the firm's

TABLE 12–2

Appraisal of licensing

Advantages:

1. Local licensee takes care of—
   a) Forecasting domestic needs.
   b) Timing of bringing in new facilities.
   c) Competing with existing industries over—
      (1) High quality material.
      (2) Skilled labor.
   d) Political considerations.
2. Avoids the fear of nationalization.
3. Achieves better public relations.
   a) Employs local skills and labor.
   b) Immediate expansion of employment in the country.
   c) Husbands potential earnings of foreign exchange.
4. Help available from the licensor:
   a) Technical.
   b) Financial.
   c) Marketing.
5. Minimizes the financing of international operations in this area.
6. Provides continuous income.
7. Enables the licensor to protect foreign sales and his local manufacturing as well as his subsidiaries, foreign and domestic.
8. Minimum involvement in foreign problems for companies not established to cope with problems overseas.
9. Overcomes overseas import and export restrictions, including prohibitive duties.
10. Provides good profit margins.

Disadvantages

1. Proposed licensee may become a serious competitor in the future in one or more areas.
2. Local conditions could be detrimental as to—
   a) Patent and trademark regulation.
   b) Taxes.
   c) Royalty and fee regulations and tax on these.
3. Probable double taxation where treaties with the United States do not exist.
4. Antitrust and monopoly laws may hinder some aspects of license operation (e.g., exclusive licenses beyond one country become increasingly sensitive to antitrust enforcement).
5. Sometimes, to insure exportability of money, the license contract must be approved by the local authorities.
6. In know-how agreements, the retention of confidential information is difficult.

product abroad. Licensing has a number of advantages and disadvantages. These are set forth in Table 12–2. In summary, a number of conditions favor the use of licensing. One determining factor may be that the foreign country, such as Japan, for example, may be very restrictive with regard to the conditions under which a foreign manufacturing operation may be established. If the foreign government absolutely prohibits the establishment of operations on any other basis, obviously there is no choice for the firm.

On the other hand, where the firm does have a choice, it may go the licensing route for two primary reasons. First, the problems of foreign operations may be highly complex in individual countries. Even though an absolute prohibition against foreign operations may not exist, there may be highly restrictive regulations. In such circumstances, there may be an advantage to licensing in order to have the wide range of problems of foreign conditions taken over by the licensee.

The second factor that may favor licensing is that this is likely to contribute to a high return on investment by the licensing firm. The reason is that very little investment is required on the part of the firm licensing, but the royalty returns may be relatively substantial. On the other hand, licensing may represent a very short-term point of view. At some future date the foreign licensee may, after the expiration of the licensing contract, determine to set up its own independent operations. Or, individual personnel from the foreign licensee may set up a new independent firm before the expiration of the license period. This new competition may mean that a very considerable investment has actually been made by the licensing firm in the form of the loss of future profit potentials that may be foreclosed by virtue of the experience and know-how conveyed to local personnel in the licensing agreement.

Licensing with partial ownership

Another intermediate arrangement is to establish a foreign licensee but take a partial ownership position in the operation. Licensing a foreign-owned company with minority ownership interest on the part of the licensing firm may represent a long-term method of participating in the future profits from the licensing operation. This, then, brings us to the next step of considering the establishment of manufacturing operations abroad, either through a joint venture or a wholly owned foreign subsidiary.

Joint ventures

Sometimes there are also some advantages of providing for local participation through joint ventures. These are set forth in Table 12–3. Joint ventures are sometimes the only alternative open for a firm. Government

TABLE 12–3

Reasons for use of joint ventures

Reasons for foreign company participation with a U.S. firm:

Business considerations:

1. To obtain franchise, license, or other special concessions held by the foreign partner.
2. To obtain local partners whose influence or knowledge of local conditions is required.
3. To take advantage of manufacturing facilities or distribution organization of an existing company.
4. To obtain local capital to finance the venture.
5. To receive participation in exchange for licensing process or formation of joint venture representing a pooling of know-how from two or more participants.
6. To share risk with local investors because of special economic or political considerations.
7. To permit small U.S. concerns to expand abroad with minimum capital outlay.

Legal and tax considerations:

8. To take advantage of tax or duty exemptions held by an existing company.
9. To comply with foreign legal stipulations requiring local participation or reserving certain kinds of business for nationals.
10. To avoid higher tax rates sometimes applied to companies which are wholly foreign owned.
11. To utilize tax credits which may be available to an existing company.

Political considerations:

12. To obtain official and popular goodwill where local pride or nationalism is an important factor.

Pitfalls and disadvantages to U.S. firms of foreign capital participation:

1. The danger of deadlock where foreign and local control are evenly divided and closely held.
2. The risk of being "frozen out" if local interests hold majority control.
3. If the U.S. company has majority control, the risk of legal action or obstructionism from dissatisfied minority shareholders.
4. Conflict of interest between local shareholder seeking high return and the usual American objective of plowback and expansion.

restrictions in either relative or absolute terms may be such that it becomes of overriding importance to joint venture the foreign operation. In addition, if legal business or political considerations are complex and troublesome, the use of a joint-venture operation may be the only practical way to deal with them.

Wholly owned manufacturing branch plants or subsidiaries

The advantages and disadvantages of establishing wholly owned subsidiaries are summarized in Table 12–4. Wholly owned foreign manufacturing operations have been historically favored for a number of reasons: (1) There are no local partners to deal with, and this facilitates ease of administration and quality control. (2) There is maximum security for protecting business methods and know-how. (3) There is maximum fi-

TABLE 12–4

Appraisal of use of wholly owned foreign subsidiaries

Advantages of establishing wholly owned subsidiaries abroad:
1. Earnings are not subject to U.S. tax until remitted to the U.S. company as dividends.
2. Effective rate of tax on profits (dividends to the parent company) may be less than the rate under a branch form of operation.
3. Subsidiary company abroad—
   a) Has same status as local company.
   b) Offers possibility for a variety of functions.
   c) Is particularly suited when several exporters combine in export trading or when exporter associates with an overseas concern in marketing certain goods.

Disadvantages of establishing wholly owned subsidiaries abroad:
1. Dividends from foreign subsidiary operation are not included in 85 percent dividends-received deduction.
2. Must obtain ruling from Internal Revenue Service that exchange of branch assets for stock of subsidiary (in case of switch of the form of foreign operation) is not for tax avoidance.
3. If a country imposes a dividend-withholding tax in addition to the taxes it imposes on profits (commercial and industrial) earned within the country, the total effective tax rate on distributed profits of a subsidiary may be greater than that for branch operation.
4. Subsidiary may be subject to the double taxation in the absence of treaty agreement between the two countries as to double taxation, provided that the subsidiary is managed and directed by the parent.
5. Subject to local laws and regulations:
   a) Labor legislation.
   b) Employment of nationals.
   c) Payroll rules for nationals.
   d) Business or company laws, e.g., licenses.
6. Possible government discrimination or nationalization.

Wholly owned operations are historically favored for these reasons:
1. Ease of administration and quality control.
2. Maximum security for proprietary business methods and know-how.
3. Maximum financial flexibility with respect to dividend policy, reinvestment of earnings, intercompany transactions, etc.
4. No necessity to share profits with outsiders.
5. U.S. tax advantage if parent company owns 95 percent or more of subsidiary—in certain loss situations, such as expropriation.
6. Absence of any problem of relationship with local owners.

nancial flexibility with respect to dividend policy, reinvestment of earnings, intercompany transactions, etc. (4) There may be important tax advantages (see Chapter 7).

The wholly owned approach is most suitable for relatively small-scale operations where the primary objective is the performance of specialized services or the manufacture and distribution of products very similar to the parent firm's domestic products. Also, the wholly owned approach is favored when the establishment of a new manufacturing enterprise is involved in which U.S. know-how or capital investment is of overriding importance to its success and the manufacturing activity is of considerable value to the host country. Another condition under which wholly owned branches or subsidiaries are favored obtains in developing countries where local capital and managerial know-how have not yet been developed. However, the clear trend is for local participation to an increasing degree in both ownership and managerial activity, reflecting strong nationalistic feelings. To respond to such an emphasis by the host nation, therefore, would represent a gesture of enlightened self-interest on the part of the parent firm.

In a study of the financing of direct investment operations in the United Kingdom in 1965, Professor Jacoby records that 77 percent of the net assets of American firms were held by wholly owned subsidiaries.[3] Fourteen percent were held by subsidiaries more than 50 percent American-owned, and only 9 percent were held by firms financed mainly by British citizens. However, these patterns may be less characteristic for other countries. The percentage of U.S. ownership would be lower particularly for Japan and Mexico, which permit foreign manufacturing operations with foreigners only as minority investors in joint ventures.[4]

Multinational management organization

Two basic organizational forms for multinational firms have been distinguished by Professor Jacoby in his thorough-going analysis of the multinational corporation.[5] In a *world corporation format*, the basic business functions of research and development, manufacturing, marketing, and finance are merged for domestic and foreign operations. In the *international division format*, all foreign operations are separated from their domestic counterparts in an "international division." Both forms have been used successfully.

In both types of multinational organizations and operations, the corporate headquarters normally makes the final decision on strategic policy decisions such as the determination of product lines and capital budgets. The chief executives of its foreign affiliates are given broad authority to operate within the general policy guidelines in their respective countries. The main pattern of planning and control parallels that of domestic operations. Periodic budgets initiated by the foreign affiliate set forth goals and targets for operations. There is also a periodic review and evaluation of progress. The review is performed jointly by corporate headquarters and the affiliate managers.

---

[3] Ibid., quoting a study by John H. Dunning, *American Investment and British Manufacturing Industry* (London: Allen & Unwin, 1958), pp. 58–60.

[4] Ibid.

[5] Ibid., p. 42.

Multinational ownership of equity securities

It is becoming increasingly recognized that firms operating in a large number of host countries should encourage widespread international participation in their ownership. The importance of this policy and the reasons for it have been stated in his McKinsey Foundation Lectures by Frederic G. Donner, then chairman of the board of General Motors Corporation.[6]

In my view, one of our greatest challenges in the years ahead is to find ways to accomplish the objective of world-wide participation in the ownership of multinational business. . . . What we in General Motors would like to be able to do is to extend the opportunity for stock ownership participation to people overseas on the same basis as it is made available to people in the United States. . . . Our desire to broaden our base of ownership is consistent with General Motor's world-wide business approach, as well as being aimed directly at our larger objective to help raise the level of economic opportunity wherever we operate in the world.

Mr. Donner also described the methods by which share ownership has been encouraged: (1) Annual reports are printed in four foreign languages for overseas distribution. (2) Summaries of annual reports were placed in 30 newspapers and periodicals in Western Europe. (3) The stock is listed in four major stock exchanges overseas and traded in many other overseas markets. (4) Secondary offerings of stock were made abroad issued in the form of Bearer Depositary Receipts Units with a "unit" representing one twentieth of a full share of common stock to reduce the unit price for small investors. As a result, at least 6.5 million shares were held for overseas investors in more than 80 different countries.[7]

It is probable that this important trend toward worldwide ownership of multinational companies will increase. This is a salutory development toward achieving multinational goodwill, along with multinational management or rapport and employees.

The characteristic steps by which a firm may reach multinational status have been described. We have outlined the stages in the evolution of a firm's progression in international operations to attain a multinational point of view and organization. The format has not been uniform for all firms in all circumstances. To indicate something of the range of approaches and developments, the following section provides a summary of two case studies.

---

[6] Frederic G. Donner, *The World-Wide Industrial Enterprise—Its Challenge and Promise* (New York: McGraw-Hill Book Co., 1967), pp. 98–106.

[7] Ibid., pp. 103–5.

SOME ILLUSTRATIVE CASE STUDIES OF THE
DEVELOPMENT OF MULTINATIONAL FIRMS

CPC International Inc.[8]

CPC International Inc. is the successor to the Corn Products' Refining (Co.) established in New Jersey on February 6, 1906. It had been in operation for a number of years domestically before its incorporation in 1906. The firm has long been a leader in the corn-refining industry. In grinding and refining corn, five major products are derived—starch, syrup, sugar, oil, and farm animal feed. Many of the refined products are sold in package and/or bottled forms such as cornstarch, Karo syrup, Mazola oil, and Linit. The firm also makes Bosco, a chocolate flavored milk modifier, Nucoa margarine, and Knorr soups. Best Foods Division is the domestic marketing organization for the company's table and household products. A self-rising cake flour is merchandised under the trademark of Presto. It also carries the shoe-dressing line of Shinola.

The firm began its foreign operations by establishing sales offices in Europe as far back as 1906. It did not establish manufacturing affiliates in Europe until after World War I. One of its wholly owned subsidiaries, Deutsche Maizena Werke, bought a 28 percent interest in C. H. Knorr, a German maker of packaged soups in 1922. The investment in Knorr was continuously increased until by the mid-1950s Deutsche Maizena had a 75 percent interest in Knorr. In 1957 it completed its take-over of C. H. Knorr. In 1958 a merger between the Corn Products Company, to which its name had been changed, and Best Foods took place. The name CPC International was adopted April 23, 1969.

In 1962 its foreign affiliates began producing and distributing Gerber Baby Foods in Western Europe and the United Kingdom under a license agreement with Gerber Products Company. In 1969 the company formed an operating group in Greece to manufacture, sell, and distribute yogurt, cheese, wine, olives, and oil. Aerobol, S.A. in Mexico City is a subsidiary which produces and packages hair spray, deodorants, other toiletry items, and specialty products. The company now has 75 foreign affiliate plants operated in 38 countries. Its foreign sales in 1969 were $609 million. Its U.S. sales reached the same amount in 1969. However, its foreign sales have been rising while its U.S. sales have been declining recently. During the previous 10 years CPC's international sales approximately doubled while its U.S. sales grew by only one third. During the same 10 years its profits from abroad almost doubled to reach over $27 million in 1970. During the same 10-year period, its U.S. earnings rose from $22 million to $28 million.

---

[8] This summary is based on a presentation in *Business Week*, December 19, 1970, pp. 64–69.

CPC's total affiliates number 150 of which one half are foreign based. It has almost 44,000 employees, two thirds are based overseas. CPC's worldwide activities are organized into six operating groups. Three of the groups cover the United States, dealing with consumer products, industrial products, and corporate research and development. The three groups operating overseas are CPC Europe, CPC Latin America, and CPC Far East. The corporate organization philosophy is to consider the six groups as individual "companies." There is an aim to seek a continuous flow of knowledge among the six groups in order to "maximize the sales and profits of the entire organization and not just their own units." One company emphasis is to approach a problem facing the firm by drawing on the previous experience of other segments or groups. The presidents of the six operating companies meet with the chairman of the board and the president of CPC and their assistants at least four times a year for as long as a week at a time. The purpose of these meetings is to emphasize the overall corporate point of view.

The Carborundum Company

This company was originally incorporated in Pennsylvania on September 28, 1891. Its original business was the manufacture of fabricated abrasive products and abrading machinery and systems. After making a number of domestic affiliations in recent years, Carborundum has emphasized acquisitions abroad to add to its product lines, which now range from tableware to industrial equipment and ceramic armor.

In its multinational operation Carborundum is pursuing a two-pronged strategy. First, it is seeking acquisitions abroad where it feels there are better opportunities than in the United States. Second, it emphasizes multiple sourcing, which means supplying customers from plants around the world in order to permit Carborundum to take advantage of lower production costs and changing business conditions in different countries. In 1966 the company took over a 200-year-old British firm, W. T. Copeland & Sons, which makes Spode china. In 1963 it added subsidiaries in France; in 1965 it acquired an abrasive machinery manufacturer in England; in 1969 it acquired the remaining 75 percent of Spencer & Halstead, Ltd., England.

The officials of the company have stated that they will engage in any type of operations overseas "that will enable our presence to be profitably established." They indicated no objection to operating as a minority interest. Carborundum treats a plant as a turnkey operation, providing equipment and know-how. In return Carborundum receives about 20 percent of equity. In addition, it seeks to obtain a contract to supply materials. It also obtains royalty payments for the continuing right to Carborundum's know-how.

Carborundum feels that it achieves added marketing strength by its flexibility in supplying customers from plants in different countries around the world. "Anytime we set up a subsidiary, associated company, or licensee, he automatically becomes our distributor in that area for all the products we make any place in the world, and he is free to choose any source he wants to."[9] Competition within the organization is encouraged. It has been stated that the company would not object if its Mexican affiliate put a distributor on the southern border of the United States.

This is an example of a multinational business with a worldwide point of view and a flexible approach as to how it will operate in any particular foreign country.

MULTINATIONAL FIRMS AND THE U.S. ECONOMY

The economic consequences of multinational corporations are currently in dispute. Important challenges have been raised by a bill introduced into Congress in September 1971 by Senator Vance Hartke of Indiana and Congressman James A. Burke of Massachusetts. The Burke-Hartke Bill contains a large number of sections, but its provisions can be summarized into two major parts. One is to discourage foreign direct investment or to prohibit it altogether if a net loss in American jobs is involved. The other part provides for new forms of trade protectionism. It has been urged and supported by some labor groups.

If unfavorable trends in the U.S. balance-of-payments position and problems in individual industries continue, the President of the United States would be empowered by a provision of the Burke-Hartke Bill to prohibit the transfer of capital to make foreign direct investments if a net decrease in jobs will result. The proposals are based on the alleged decline in individual industries' ability to compete successfully with foreign firms in the production of certain goods, either in the international marketplace or in the United States. Certain industries, such as consumer electronics, nonrubber footwear, shoes and slippers, textile products, and steel have been particularly affected. Overall it is asserted that "between 1966 and 1969 U.S. foreign trade produced the equivalent of a *net loss* of half a million American jobs."[10] Other estimates place the loss of American jobs because of the establishment of manufacturing operations abroad from 300,000 to 600,000.

The basic fallacy in the Burke-Hartke Bill's position with regard to "loss of jobs" is looking at only immediate and direct results. If goods are now imported which formerly were produced in the United States, this is

---

[9] Ibid., p. 72.

[10] "IUD Save Our Jobs Rally," *Summary Fact Sheet of Foreign Trade and Investment Act of 1972, S-2592, HR-10914,* October 4, 1971, pp. 3–4.

treated as a loss of U.S. jobs. If an American company is producing an item in a foreign country and produces similar items in the United States, it is presumed that this represents a loss of U.S. jobs. There are a number of errors involved in this position. The fundamental error is the failure to recognize that if these manufacturing operations were not being conducted abroad, a substantial portion of the sales resulting from these operations would be completely lost to American companies. For example, characteristics must be altered for the Western European market of such products as automobiles, all types of household durable goods, and a wide range of other consumer goods. In addition, service, distribution, and warehousing facilities are necessary for an effective sales effort. Without this kind of manufacturing and distribution backup, those foreign sales would not be made. The foregoing example has been for developed countries.

For the less developed countries local materials and labor content percentages are frequently established. These require that manufacturing be done in the foreign country. Thus, the realistic alternative to producing abroad might well be that U.S. firms' sales would not be made at all. The future holds great opportunities for U.S. contributions to the development of other economies as well as our own. We need to take the long view in recognizing that with the continued evolution of the world economies, there are increasing opportunities for benefiting from a worldwide division of labor to increase jobs and standards of living for ourselves as well as the people of other countries of the world.[11]

Our analysis is supported by additional factual evidence. Surveys by government agencies have established that at least one fourth of all nonagricultural U.S. exports represent sales to the foreign subsidiaries of American companies.[12] By enabling the U.S. companies to compete suc-

---

[11] For an early analysis of the implications of foreign direct investment, see J. Fred Weston, "A Framework for Product-Market Planning," in Norman N. Barish and Michel Verhulst (eds.), *Management Sciences in the Emerging Countries—New Tools for Economic Development*, selected papers from a TIMS Conference in Brussels, August 1961 (New York: Pergamon Press, 1965). See also J. Fred Weston and Peter D. Duncan, *Economic Development Patterns* (Stanford Research Institute, 1963).

[12] "The activities of U.S. enterprises abroad directly induce considerable U.S. exports of capital goods, component parts, and associated products for sale through distribution channels established by foreign subsidiaries. The most recent publicly available data indicate that in 1965, foreign affiliates of the 330 U.S. corporations surveyed purchased $5.1 billion from the United States, representing almost 25% of total nonagricultural exports in that year. Moreover, by raising levels of living and contributing to economic development abroad, foreign investment stimulates further U.S. exports." Commission on International Trade and Investment Policy, *United States International Economic Policy in an Interdependent World*, Report to the President submitted by the Commission on International Trade and Investment Policy (Washington, D.C., July 1971), p. 173.

cessfully abroad in making sales, the American companies are able to exploit the comparative advantage they have in producing certain parts and components in the United States and thereby provide an outlet for those production activities via their foreign manufacturing and sales operations. In addition, government surveys demonstrate that of the sales resulting from the manufacturing operations of American subsidiaries manufacturing and selling abroad, only 8 percent are made in the United States.[13]

Thus, the net gain in American jobs from foreign manufacturing operations abroad is clearly positive rather than negative. It was on the basis of an analysis such as the foregoing that Professor Stobaugh of Harvard University has estimated that the net positive gain to American jobs resulting from U.S. manufacturing operations abroad is approximately 600,000.[14]

U.S. direct investments abroad have also been criticized for their adverse balance-of-payments effects. It has been said that if $3 to $4 billion flow abroad in the form of direct investments, this must be adverse to the U.S. balance of payments. But the facts are contrary to this simplistic view. As direct investment outflows have risen to over $4 billion per year, the reverse flows have also risen. As U.S. direct investments have accumulated over a period of time to a book value of some $80 billion, they generate a flow of investment income, including fees and royalties, that reached $7.9 billion in 1970. Thus the favorable positive contribution of direct investments to the U.S. balance-of-payments position during the years 1968–70 averaged $3.6 billion per year (see Table 12–5).

Another aspect of the unrealistic preconceptions of the proponents of the bill is that it ignores the fundamental mobility of capital. If opportunities for profitable operations exist abroad, capital will respond to these

---

[13] "Many foreign markets for our products are growing rapidly but, at the same time, are growing more competitive. Both the size of the markets and their competitiveness have made it attractive or necessary to invest abroad in order to tap them. . . . Most sales of U.S. foreign manufacturing affiliates are in the local market abroad—78% in 1968. When we add another 14% of sales that go to third markets overseas, we find that only about 8% of sales are back to the United States. This last figure has grown in recent years—though it appears on closer examination that a dominant portion of increasing exports to the U.S. by American affiliates abroad results from the U.S.–Canada Auto Agreement." Peter G. Peterson, "Background Material," *The United States in the Changing World Economy* (Washington, D.C.: U.S. Government Printing Office, December 1971), Vol. II, p. 46.

[14] "In total, we estimate that the jobs of at least 250,000 workers, most of which are production workers, would be lost if there were no U.S. foreign direct investment. These 250,000 jobs, combined with the 250,000 jobs estimated by Raymond Vernon to exist in the main offices of U.S. multinational enterprises because of foreign direct investment, plus an additional allowance for supporting workers that Professor Vernon has not included in his estimates, gives a total of perhaps 600,000 jobs." Robert B. Stobaugh and Associates, *U.S. Multinational Enterprises and the U.S. Economy: A Research Study of the Major Industries That Account for 90 Per Cent of U.S. Foreign Direct Investment in Manufacturing* (Boston, Mass.: Harvard Business School–U.S. Department of Commerce, Bureau of International Commerce, January 1972), p. 31.

TABLE 12–5

Comparison of investment income with direct investments and trade balance (billions of dollars)

	Average 1960–64	Average 1965–67	1968	1969	1970
Investment income, including fees and royalties........................	3.8	5.5	6.5	7.3	7.9
Direct investment outflows..........	−1.8	−3.5	−3.2	−3.3	−4.4
Balance on direct investment account.....................	2.0	2.1	3.3	4.0	3.5

opportunities. The reasons for investing abroad are complex and numerous. The most freqently mentioned are:[15]

a) To jump tariff and import barriers and regulations, including local-content regulations or a requirement that *local* exports be made in order to receive an import license;

b) To reduce or eleminate high transportation costs;

c) To obtain or use local raw materials;

d) To obtain incentives offered by host governments;

e) To maintain existing market positions;

f) To participate in the rapid expansion of a market abroad;

g) To control quality in the manufacture of specialized products;

h) To follow customers abroad;

i) To follow a competitor abroad;

j) To obtain foreign technical, design, and marketing skills;

k) To bid on foreign infrastructure projects.

If U.S. firms are prevented from participating in this form of international economic activity, other firms will respond to the opportunities. Firms that are already operating in those places in which opportunities exist will expand their operations, or new firms from other countries will enter into these markets to participate in the opportunities available. This would result in curtailing the present level of American exports to subsidiaries and income returning from U.S. investment abroad.

TAILORING STRATEGY TO COUNTRY'S STAGE OF DEVELOPMENT

Economic historians have suggested that the nations of the world may be grouped on the basis of their stage of development. A vast body of em-

---

[15] National Foreign Trade Council, "The Impact of U.S. Foreign Direct Investment on U.S. Employment and Trade—An Assessment of Critical Claims and Legislative Proposals," November 1971, p. 11.

pirical data provides a profile of the economic characteristics of a large number of countries at varying levels of development. This descriptive information reveals similarities and differences between countries in the process of economic change. These systematic patterns provide a useful basis for grouping so that countries may be analyzed as parts of classes rather than their economic development being viewed as unique for every individual nation. Five stages, with characteristics of the countries at each stage, are set forth in Table 12–6. In turn, business planning for international operations can be time-phased in relation to the stage of development of each nation.

The economic development patterns that exist in various countries at different stages provide a basis for the development of strategies for business firms in both developed and developing countries. The processes and timing of economic change are sufficiently systematic to afford a base for planning by the individual business firm. This planning should be related to a time phasing of business policies and strategies for participating in

TABLE 12–6

Stages of economic development

1. *Traditional society*
   - a) Low per capita income.
   - b) Stagnant or declining per capita income.
   - c) Population mainly in agriculture.
   - d) Little international trade except agricultural and mineral products.
   - e) Special social customs and political factors must be considered.

2. *Transitional society*
   - a) Increased contact with outside world.
   - b) Need to solve periodic social and economic breakdowns.
   - c) Simple equipment and strategic fertilizers increase productivity of agriculture.
   - d) Some agricultural surplus permits some foreign exchange.
   - e) Outside grants and some loans help build roads, schools, power, and transport.
   - f) Political and social stresses; periodic upheavals.

3. *Takeoff society*
   - a) Emergence of strong individual growth sectors in some parts of manufacturing.
   - b) Production more generally diversified.
   - c) Per capita income begins to rise more rapidly.
   - d) Self-sustaining growth can profitably employ foreign loans.

4. *Technologically mature society*
   - a) No gaps in ability to engage in all forms of economic activity.
   - b) New leading sectors determined by comparative resource advantages.
   - c) Emergence of national surplus over basic needs.

5. *Developed society*
   - a) Surplus national income used for consumer affluence, welfare state, etc.
   - b) Must depend on emergence of new industries to sustain growth thrusts.
   - c) Sound national economic policies necessary for full-employment growth.
   - d) Favorable foreign trade balance depends on strong research by advanced industries.

Source: W. W. Rostow, *The Stages of Economic Growth: A Non-Communist Manifesto* (New York: Cambridge University Press, 1961).

the economic processes of countries at different stages. Interaction between firms in developed countries and developing countries can produce benefits both for the individual firms in whatever stage of development, by providing a basis for effective operations and long-range planning, and contribute to the success of economic development plans and processes of their respective countries.

Business strategies in developed nations

The key implication of the patterns of growth that accompany a country's economic rise is that a framework is provided which helps in identifying areas of opportunity. Managers of an individual firm are usually not able to study the entire world for opportunities—at least in the detail required for investment decisions. Therefore, the determination of what appear to be areas of major opportunity can aid a company in allocating its limited resources and establishing a priority for analysis of business opportunities, even though these generalizations about the patterns of growth provide only a rough approximation of the anticipated trends.

Pinpointing opportunities. The first use of industrial growth patterns is that businessmen who are concerned in their future planning with the products with which they are familiar should be able to narrow their interests to countries where opportunities for these products are particularly favorable. For instance, importers of mineral products or timber would probably look first at countries in the traditional stage, as would the seller of mineral extraction machinery and timber milling equipment. Manufacturers of consumer durables would look to countries in the transitional stage for expanding sales, and to countries moving toward takeoff for investment in the production of consumer durables. The exporter of transportation equipment or the civil works contractor looking for overseas business would probably be interested in the transitional countries. The financier looking for good investments overseas would be most interested in the takeoff and maturing countries.

There are relatively few industry sectors in which there are strong growth opportunities in the traditional stage of development. The spectrum of opportunity widens as the country moves through the transitional and takeoff stages and continues to do so through the stage of technological maturity. Some industries begin to have lower growth rates at this period; however, this condition is accentuated in the developed economy stage. At this point, each of the sectors is large in absolute volume, but some are growing very slowly. As a country reaches the technological maturity stage, opportunities must be analyzed more discriminatingly to insure participation in growth fields.

Generally speaking, a vigorous investment program would be undertaken immediately preceding and during the early growth of the particular sector. For example, the transportation and utilities sectors are expected to begin growing as a country moves into the transitional stage. Thus, a firm supplying equipment or materials in these areas should look to countries in the early stages of progress beyond the traditional stage.

The risk of investment at the traditional and transitional stages are great. Slow and uncertain economic progress may be associated with social and political instability and turmoil. However, sometimes a small commitment will provide a necessary foundation of knowledge and understanding as the nation develops. A firm must analyze how it may best establish its interests in the early stages of development. The business firm must also determine the amount of participation required for the continued growth rate expected to carry through the next stage.

The changing patterns of industrial growth emphasize the limitations of using a straight-line extrapolation of trends. The fact that new industries emerge in different stages means that new sources of supply and demand are also emerging. Thus, as countries move through the various phases of economic development, there will be alterations in the world supply and demand picture for every product industry.

The key factor in a country's growth from the transitional to technological maturity appears to be substitution of domestic production facilities for imports from the development of comparative advantage in some goods. Consequently, import trends are a good indicator of investment opportunities, since it is in these areas that much of the country's growth will take place at a given stage. This is especially true in investment-type products (machinery, equipment, etc.), since most of the growth is internally generated as the country shifts from handicraft to factory production.

Substitution of local production for importation will generally be relevant for the smaller and less developed countries. As a country approaches technological maturity or a developed economy, there is less relative reliance on imports. Its size and income generally create markets large enough to support a production facility. A firm selling consumer goods will need to rely more on joint ventures rather than on imports, which are likely to be restricted.

Determining technique of entry. A variety of business techniques is available to the firm wishing to operate in international markets: (1) importing or exporting, using a firm's own offices or agents or representatives; (2) direct investment in the form of a wholly owned operation or joint venture with another firm; or (3) licensing of production when direct investment is not appropriate. (Seven options were named in Table 12–1.) Just which approach is most suitable will depend on the type of product involved, as well as the requirements of the particular firm and the stage of economic development of the country involved.

In *traditional* and *transitional* economies, the U.S. businessman would be wise to keep his fixed capital investment at as low a level as possible, unless he is able to acquire concessions that give him the prospect of operating over a long enough period to recover his investment. In such countries, a firm should generally think in terms of using its own or established agents for importing and exporting. Investment in production to replace imports is not likely to offer favorable prospects, except where markets are very large. Investment to produce exports frequently offers a range of favorable prospects. Negotiations should be conducted at the government level, preferably supplemented by U.S., other national, or international authorities, in order to fit best into the economic development plans of the country. Insofar as possible, nationals of the country concerned should be associated with the undertaking.

The most likely investments for export opportunities from developing countries are in agriculture and mineral resources. Investments with export potential are especially attractive to the governments of traditional and transitional countries because of the need for foreign exchange to provide the purchasing power for the imports required for the country's development efforts.

Licensing agreements are generally not a good alternative in these early stages. Such agreements are usually used for the more complex production processes for which there are frequently only very limited markets in traditional or transitional countries. Furthermore, the education and experience level of technical personnel is too low. Some consumer product areas, however, have large enough markets to warrant installation of production facilities and licensing of consumer products that require only limited investment and technical capabilities—Coca Cola is an example that may be appropriate here. Nevertheless, the wide use of licensing at this stage may preempt later efforts to invest directly in joint ventures as the markets grow in size.

Finding operation to fit stage of development. The *transitional* stage may be a good period in which to begin laying the foundation for future investment opportunities in particular countries by becoming acquainted with the marketing problems and obtaining an understanding of the mechanics of working with the local governments. This is particularly true for firms interested in transportation, utilities, consumer durables and materials, industries that generally begin to grow rapidly at this stage. While the complex equipment required for these industries is not likely to be produced locally, the various materials and supplies would be locally produced. Consequently, firms should analyze local conditions and develop the plan of action that appears most appropriate for the anticipated growth in the next stage of development. Generally it is most practical to do this reconnoitering on a low-cost basis over a period of several years rather than by heavy initial commitments.

In *takeoff* countries, there will usually be more opportunities for investment. In this stage the long-term future lies in association with nationals who are committed to support the growth of the economy. Businessmen should be alert for two types of investment opportunities: (1) Production to substitute for imports should be undertaken as soon as possible, because import restrictions are always imminent. (2) Production to expand exports has promise because export earnings are of vital importance to the growth of an economy during takeoff, and they will be encouraged. In both cases, investment should be joint ventures with nationals to insure access to the concessions that are a feature of development at this stage.

As countries move into *technological maturity* and the *developed* stage, in almost all industries the relative dependence on international trade decreases but the absolute amount of trade increases. With the achievement of economic maturity most markets are large enough to support domestic producers, which leaves a much smaller proportion of the total market to foreign exporters trying to supply the market from abroad. While wholly owned operations may be the most appropriate investment when the foreign firms supply only a small part of the total market, some sort of joint venture with nationals may be more appropriate if foreign firms supply a large segment of the market.

Licensing may be the quickest way to tap markets in countries in the advanced stages, but it would probably bring only short-run profits, since the licensee could soon become a competitor and eventually squeeze out the licensor. Consequently, it might be better to invest directly and continue participating in the profits for a longer period of time. At this point, U.S. firms might find it particularly advantageous to obtain licenses to the advanced know-how of other countries.

Particularly for countries in the developed stage, the full complex of techniques may be effectively used at the same time. Licensing arrangements should be regarded as a less satisfactory alternative than joint ventures with nationals and should be used only if the opportunity for investment has been missed.

Initial market development or testing can generally best proceed on an export basis and by working closely with local distributing firms. Local distributors are especially important since it is difficult to use other forms of promotion. Usually not much public information is available abroad on the detailed trends of narrow market segments. This is especially true in the traditional and transitional countries. Import records are readily accessible, but data about most demand trends are best obtained from established commercial organizations (for example, The United African Company in Nigeria).

Units of consumption—in both the industrial and consumer fields—are smaller and necessitate more breaking of bulk in the newly developing countries than in developed areas. Local tastes and requirements often are also quite different and frequently demand product alterations if the market is to be tapped. However, this tends to be less of a problem as an economy becomes more developed, although it is still a continuing and important one.

The differences in trade and investment opportunities among countries in different stages of economic development are indicated by Table 12–7. For each stage of economic development, individual countries are illustrated. The types of products that can be bought and sold are also set forth. From analysis of the patterns of commercial opportunities by this stage of a country's economic development, guidance is provided to

TABLE 12–7

Appropriate business strategies for various stages of economic development

Stage and country	What we can sell	What we can buy
I. Bolivia	Fertilizers	Foods
Jordan	Simple agricultural tools	Minerals
II. India	Same as I plus some industrial materials for simple fabrication	Same as I plus fabricated materials
III. Brazil	Parts for assembly	Same as II plus consumer
Chile	Industrial machinery for simple processing	durables and nondurables
IV. Japan	Machine tools	Same as III plus some mass
Ireland	Industrial machinery	produced electrical products
V. West Germany	Complex; see C in	Specialty items such as chemicals, paints, photographic
United Kingdom	Table 12–8	icals, paints, photographic equipment ·

business firms on the development of a time-phased plan for expanding multinational operations, as set forth in Table 12–8.

Firms must recognize that in their efforts for rapid development, countries in stages II through IV are likely to impose limitations on import or manufacture of consumer durables. These use up people's savings and take resources from the producers' industries.

The framework also provides perspective on political developments. Stage I is tradition-dominated with tribal political groups. As a country moves to a national state, fierce rivalries develop between a large number of tribal leaders. Considerable government controls are found in stages II through IV. This necessitates liaison with government officials for permits, etc., in countries in these stages. Stages II and III represent great dangers to political stability. Because of lack of democratic experience, diverse interest groups and inequality of wealth and income, the military emerges as the group which can exercise balance of power.

The strategies discussed in Table 12–8 have been presented from the point of view of firms in the most highly developed countries. For a more

TABLE 12–8

Uses of the stages of development concept in international business planning

A. Provides a framework for international market planning.
    1. Export what you have successfully produced at home.
    2. Do not be too quick to license. You are developing future competitors. Joint venture with a local concern is likely to be better.
    3. Portfolio investments can be made to develop contacts for trading technical know-how for mutual license agreements.
    4. The converse of A1 is to import products successfully developed abroad. This is a method of obtaining new products without costly research and development and high product failure rate.
B. It is not as important to predict the precise timing of a country's movement from stage to stage as is forward planning and the time phasing of product sales in each country.
C. Export sales to fully developed countries become more complex. Consider sales to the Common Market countries:
    1. Those commodities which will not be affected by tariff differentials (because no tariffs exist) are corn, coal, raw cotton, crude rubber, scrap iron, steel.
    2. Those goods not affected because European producers are inefficient are: oil seeds, animals fats, vegetable oils.
    3. Those goods whose prospects are uncertain because of potential competition from their associated territories—tobacco, copper.
    4. Aircraft exports are likely to be determined more by technological than by price factors.
    5. Those goods which will be highly affected are manufactured products, chiefly machinery and others, for example, petroleum products, chemicals, pigments, paints.

balanced perspective on the types of business operations that will be encouraged by the host country, the viewpoint of firms in the developing economies should also be understood. This is discussed in the following section.

Opportunities for native firms in the developing economies

Much of the literature on implications of national economic develop-ment to business firms is from the view of firms in the developed countries. The analysis is usually from the standpoint of how business firms in de-veloped countries can most appropriately time their entry into the de-veloping countries and the different cultural patterns in the world. Equally important is an analysis of the opportunities for local business enterprise in the developing countries.

Among the techniques which may be employed by U.S. business firms to evolve international business strategies for local firms in underdevel-oped countries are the following: Licensing can effectively be employed by the small domestic business. It has a relative advantage in using licens-ing arrangements. The local business managers can and ought to know im-portant aspects of local conditions which contribute to success both in manufacturing and in marketing. This know-how is very difficult for a foreign firm to obtain, particularly knowledge of local market require-ments. At a minimum the local business operation can make a substantial contribution to effective operations in the local market. In addition, local entrepreneurs can be a source of new ideas for manufacturing.

Since the local firm has a relative advantage in marketing operations, it can use this advantage as a trade-off for obtaining a manufacturing-licensing arrangement from the foreign firm of a relatively more de-veloped country.

Where licensing arrangements cannot be worked out, again the local firm is in a strong position to insist on the joint-venture arrangement. It can provide strategic inputs on local manufacturing and marketing re-quirements. In addition, it can provide some local capital. Importantly, intimate knowledge of cultural factors can enable local people to make a substantial and valuable input. Both of these devices can make significant contributions to the developmental process of the foreign country and the domestic company.

With regard to the development of domestic industry in a foreign land, one useful approach begins at a local planning level. This approach argues that the prime ingredient for local participation in the development pro-cess is the availability of raw materials. Whatever the overall scheme of the development process a nation may be employing, a substantial contribution may be achieved by following these basic criteria: Give priority to (1) operations related to the availability of raw materials, and (2) a relatively simple manufacturing process which requires few link-ages either in inputs or for market outlets. The training process that will be achieved by employing local workers in such activities will contribute to the development of an experienced (if not skilled) labor supply.

Such small-scale projects involve relatively small capital requirements. In many cases, therefore, the financing may be achieved from local sources. Such sources of financing may contribute to the development of a middle class in the community. However, one should remember that projects involving relatively greater financing may require broader gov-ernment support.

SUMMARY

A multinational firm owns and manages business operations in more than one country by making direct investments in foreign countries. Multinational status is usually achieved by degrees, usually starting with the marketing abroad of a successful domestic product. Detailed case studies of CPC International Inc. and The Carborundum Company, and their evolution into multinational status, were then described.

The effects of U.S.-based multinational firms on the U.S. economy were next explored. Claimed unfavorable effects have been brought into the limelight by the Burke-Hartke Bill introduced into the U.S. Congress in September 1971. This would curtail or prohibit direct foreign investment when a net loss in American jobs is threatened. It would also provide for severe protective tariff measures—the most far-reaching in U.S. history.

The basic fallacy in the Burke-Hartke Bill's position is that it takes into account only immediate and direct results. If an American company is now producing goods abroad formerly manufactured in the United States, it is presumed that this represents a loss of U.S. jobs. However, if these products were not now being made abroad, a large part of their sales would be lost to American companies anyway, for several reasons. This applies both to developed countries and to less developed countries. The U.S. economy will benefit most from additional opportunities for world-wide division of labor, which will increase jobs and standards of living for ourselves and for the people of other countries. The net gain in jobs from American manufacturing activities abroad is clearly positive rather than negative.

U.S. direct investments abroad have also been criticized as having adverse effects on our balance of payments. As the direct investment outflows have risen over the years, the reverse flows have also increased. Capital must be free to migrate to the area of greatest opportunity; and if U.S. firms are prevented from participating in these opportunities, the void will be filled by companies of other countries which can then produce at lower costs than we can.

In developing strategies for international business activities, the U.S. multinational firm must recognize the stage of development of various countries in planning its moves. Five broad stages of economic development have been recognized: traditional, transitional, takeoff, technologically mature, and developed. The processes and timing of economic change are sufficiently systematic to afford a basis for planning of appropriate strategy by multinational firms to take advantage of economic opportunities. Planning of business operations should be time-phased to participate most effectively in the economic processes of countries in various states of development. This will be advantageous to the host country in its hopes for economic development as well as to the U.S. businessman.

In developed countries, such a framework permits a U.S. manager to pinpoint his research into desirable business opportunities by country and by industry. Firms needing to import mineral products or timber would likely look first at countries in the traditional stage, as would exporters of mineral extraction machinery or lumber milling equipment. The civil works contractor should probably look to transitional countries. However, since new industries emerge in different stages, there will be continuing changes in the world supply and demand for every product.

There are also opportunities for native firms in developing economies. U.S. companies can help these firms as well as themselves by licensing, joint ventures, and other arrangements. Local businessmen know local conditions and can have informed opinions on the cultural climate and acceptability of new products. They may be useful in obtaining raw materials; they also have a head start on marketing techniques and may be of help in obtaining local financing.

PROBLEM 12-1

The Cryogenic Company has been manufacturing and selling a patented product in the United States. It is a specialized industrial product with the total market in the United States of about $50 million per year. Five firms produce the product in the United States, each protected by patents which make the individual product of each firm somewhat different from that of the other four firms, but the functions performed by the product are similar. The product is a self-contained unit that can be shipped as a finished product in inexpensive crates. On arrival it is uncrated and operates as an independent unit with gasoline equivalent to that used in automobiles.

Each firm has roughly an equal share of the U.S. market. The size of the market in Europe is now equal to that of the United States, but the potential for this product in Europe is expected to grow at a much faster rate so that within five years the size of the market in Western Europe will be triple that in the United States because of differences in demand.

The product manufactured by the U.S. firms is superior to that produced by Western European companies. Each U.S. firm now operates on a one-shift basis. Transportation costs to ship the product to Western Europe are low relative to the value of the product.

Outline a time-phased program for one of the U.S. companies to enter and develop the Western European market.

PROBLEM 12-2

The Catton Company has been producing a successful line of small tractors in the United States. It has been selling the tractors in Western Europe through a European branch sales office. A few problems have been developing. The European buyers have been requesting special configurations of the tractors of the kind not required by U.S. buyers. Requests by Catton's export department to the manufacturing department to produce a wide variety of special-purpose tractors have met with objections. Their U.S. labor force is accustomed to relatively long production runs. Assembly operations take place on two long assembly lines which efficiently produce a relatively uniform product.

Another difficulty has arisen in that distributors in Western Europe complain that repair parts are often not available. Furthermore, it would at times be more economical to return defective equipment to the factory for inspection and replacement of critical parts and renovating the tractor completely. Furthermore distributors have complained that frequently they encounter repair and maintenance problems requiring factory assistance.

What should the Catton Company do to deal with these problems that have developed?

PROBLEM 12-3

The Weadon Engineering Company has developed superior equipment for tin plating steel sheets used in making tin cans. Over a period of years it has developed machinery superior to that produced by any other firm in the United States or in Western Europe. It has fully patented the critical elements of its engineering, production, and product concepts. It has been making some sales abroad but suffers from the handicap that foreign steel manufacturing firms have been accustomed to dealing with local suppliers and have been dependent upon the local manufacturers for servicing their equipment. Machinery to perform the functions described is large and complex, and the service and maintenance activities require a high degree of technical competence. It was generally sold on a turnkey operation. When it was installed the user could simply turn a key and it began operating. Nevertheless, maintenance was required involving technical competence. In addition, the foreign steel companies were accustomed to buying from local manufacturers of tin plating equipment. Therefore the Weadon Company encountered marketing problems in spite of a superior product.

A French company manufacturing tin plating equipment approached the Weadon Engineering Company with a proposal to obtain a license. They proposed to pay a royalty for the privilege of using the patents and being provided with personnel to give them the engineering and manufacturing knowhow. The proposal of the French company was presented to the board of directors of the Weadon Engineering Company. There was considerable support for the patent proposal because it would provide a very substantial dollar return to Weadon Engineering Company and, as one member of the board pointed out, this would represent virtually an infinite return on the company's investment, because there was virtually no additional investment required to achieve a considerable increase in income.

However, another member of the board pointed out that if the French company were licensed, it would before too long learn the know-how of the Weadon Company. He stressed that the present superior product of Weadon was developed over a period of years based on the company's experience. Hence, after a time the French company would be in a position to patent its own developments and become relatively independent of the Weadon Company. He proposed as a counteroffer that Weadon enter into a joint venture with the French company in which Weadon would own 70 percent and the French company 30 percent of the foreign operation.

You have been called in as an outside consultant to evaluate the proposal for a patent license versus the counterproposal for a joint venture operation. Present the advantages and disadvantages of each approach and conclude by giving your recommendation to the board of directors.

SELECTED BIBLIOGRAPHY

Behrman, Jack N. *Direct Manufacturing Investment, Exports and the Balance of Payments.* New York: National Foreign Trade Council, 1968.

Commission on International Trade and Investment Policy. *United States International Economic Policy in an Interdependent World.* Report to the President submitted by the Commission on International Trade and Investment Policy. Washington, D.C., July 1971.

————. *United States International Economic Policy in an Interdependent World.* Papers submitted and published in conjunction with the Commission's Report to the President. Compendium of Papers: Vols. I and II. Washington, D.C.: U.S. Government Printing Office, July 1971.

Donner, Frederic G. *The World-Wide Industrial Enterprise—Its Challenge and Promise.* New York: McGraw-Hill Book Co., 1967.

Edwards, C. "The World of Antitrust." *Columbia Journal of World Business,* July–August 1969.

Friedmann, W. C., and Kalmanoff, George. *Joint International Business Ventures.* New York: Columbia University Press, 1961.

Gennard, John. *Multinational Corporations and British Labour: A Review of Attitudes and Responses.* British-North American Research Association, January 1972.

Gray, H. Peter, and Makinen, Gail E. "Balance of Payments Contributions of Multinational Corporations," *Journal of Business,* July 1967, pp. 339–43.

Greene, James, and Duerr, Michael G. *Intercompany Transactions in the Multinational Firm.* Managing International Business, No. 6. New York: The Conference Board, 1970.

International Chamber of Commerce, Inc., U.S. Council. *U.S. Direct Investments and the Balance of Payments,* "Report of the Committee on Foreign Investment."

Litvak, I. A., and Maule, C. J. "Guidelines for the Multinational Corporation," *Columbia Journal of World Business,* July–August 1968, p. 35.

Lovell, Enid Baird. *Appraising Foreign Licensing Performance.* Business Policy Study No. 128. A Research Report from The Conference Board. New York, 1969.

National Foreign Trade Council. "The Impact of U.S. Foreign Direct Investment on U.S. Employment and Trade—An Assessment of Critical Claims and Legislative Proposals," November 1971.

National Planning Association. *U.S. Foreign Economic Policy for the 1970's: A New Approach to New Realities.* A Policy Report by an NPA Advisory Committee. Planning Pamphlet No. 130. Washington, D.C., November 1971.

Peterson, Peter G. "A Foreign Economic Perspective," *The United States in the Changing World Economy,* Vol. I. Washington, D.C.: U.S. Government Printing Office, February 1971.

————. "Background Material," *The United States in the Changing World Economy,* Vol. II. Washington, D.C.: U.S. Government Printing Office, December 1971.

276   *International managerial finance*

Polk, Judd. *U.S. Production Abroad and the Balance of Payment,* chap. 6, "Exports and Production Abroad." A Survey of Corporation Investment Experience, 1966.

Rolfe, Sidney E. *The Multinational Corporation.* Foreign Policy Association No. 199, February 1970.

Stobaugh, Robert B., and Associates. *U.S. Multinational Enterprises and the U.S. Economy: A Research Study of the Major Industries that Account for 90 Per Cent of U.S. Foreign Direct Investment in Manufacturing.* Boston, Mass.: Harvard Business School–U.S. Department of Commerce, Bureau of International Commerce, January 1972.

U.S. Department of Commerce, Bureau of International Commerce. *Policy Aspects of Foreign Investment by U.S. Multinational Corporations,* Part I. Office of International Investment, January 1972.

———. *Trends in Direct Investments Abroad by U.S. Multinational Corporations 1960 to 1970,* Part II. Office of International Investment, February 1972.

Vernon, Raymond. "International Investment and International Trade in the Product Cycle," *Quarterly Journal of Economics,* May 1966, pp. 190–207.

Vogel, Joseph O. "The Real Culprit in International Monetary Crises," *Business Horizons,* Vol. 15 (April 1972), pp. 41–46.

Weston, J. Fred. "A Framework for Product-Market Planning," in *Management Sciences in the Emerging Countries—New Tools for Economic Development* (eds, Norman N. Barish and Michel Verhuls), selected papers from a TIMS Conference in Brussels, August 1961. New York: Pergamon Press, 1965.

Weston, J. Fred, and Duncan, Peter D. *Economic Development Patterns.* Stanford Research Institute, 1963.

13 .

International financial trends and their business implications

On August 15, 1971 the President of the United States, Richard M. Nixon, announced some fundamental changes in the economic policy of the United States with regard to both international and domestic matters. In the midst of a severe foreign exchange crisis, the U.S. dollar lost what had formerly remained of its convertibility. A transition between two eras thus occurred in 1971.

The year 1933, when the United States changed the price of gold from $20.67 per ounce to $35 per ounce, marked the close of the post–World War I prosperity era. It came between 1931 and 1933, to be followed by a new period of international economic tension culminating in World War II. The year 1971 marked the close of an era that had begun at the termination of World War II, when certain hopes and goals for the international economy had been developed. A new period of relationships in international economic affairs began in August 1971. To provide perspective on these developments and offer a basis for understanding what their implications may be for business managers, it will be useful to review briefly the developments after World War II.

AN ERA OF NEW INTERNATIONAL COOPERATION

The basic objective of the International Monetary Fund (IMF) was to achieve the advantages of the gold standard without its disadvantages. The advantage of the gold standard was the relative stability in exchange rates that it was supposed to achieve. The IMF was formed in 1946 by 39 member nations as a result of the Bretton Woods Conference. Today almost all of the "free world" nations with the exception of Switzerland are members of the Fund. Each member country is required to subscribe to the capital of the Fund in accordance with a quota which is determined on the basis of the new member's monetary reserves, volume of foreign

277

trade, and national income. Quotas can be reexamined and changed upon request of a member country or an increase in the volume of world trade. Each member is required to pay in gold 25 percent of its quota or 10 percent of its net official holdings in gold and U.S. dollars, whichever is less. The remainder of the quota is paid in the member's currency.

The International Monetary Fund has three major functions that were aimed to avoid the problems and difficulties that had developed in international financial relations before World War II. These three main functions are: (1) providing short-term credit facilities, (2) consulting among nations to achieve mutually consistent policies, and (3) attaining upward and downward changes in the value of individual country currencies.

Short-term credit facilities

In the long run a nation must pay for its imports or equivalent by means of exports or equivalent, or by long-term borrowing. In the interim, however, a country may need short-term credit to meet temporary imbalances. By the extension of international short-term credit it was hoped that a temporary imbalance would not be aggravated into a massive disequilibrium. One of the principal purposes of the IMF is to assist member nations in meeting temporary needs for foreign exchange funds. Any member may on an automatic basis purchase from the Fund foreign currency with its own currency in an amount equal to or less than its gold tranche, the amount of gold the member paid into the IMF as part of its quota. Any purchases of foreign currencies that are made in excess of the gold tranche require the Fund's approval. The largest purchase of foreign currencies permitted is 200 percent of a member's quota. After the individual nation's balance-of-payments situation has improved, it is able to buy back with its improved foreign exchange reserves the local currencies that have been deposited with the Fund. Thus the IMF provided a mechanism for adjusting short-term disequilibriums. This function is similar to providing a commercial banking service on an international scale for the nations of the world in the same way that a commercial bank meets the seasonal or temporary financing needs of individual business firms within a given country.

Coordination of economic policies among nations

The Fund, like an individual bank, monitors individual countries to be certain that they are not piling up too much indebtedness. Also, analyses are made to determine that the economic policies of an individual country are not leading to cumulative imbalances. Indeed, the Fund seeks to arrange for consultations with individual nations and among groups of nations in order to provide for coordinated policies. It might counsel a nation that is developing balance-of-payment surpluses to lower its import barriers and reduce its export subsidies. It might counsel such a nation to lend abroad to a greater extent. A country with severe domestic inflation and continuing balance-of-payments deficits might be counseled to moderate its rate of monetary expansion or to cut back on government expenditure programs. The Fund seeks to achieve through objective studies and consultations an era of new international economic cooperation.

Orderly adjustment of exchange rates

Recognizing, however, that fundamental changes in productivity or changes in costs of production between countries might progressively take place over time, the IMF makes provision for orderly changes in exchange rate relationships. A member of the IMF is permitted to depreciate or appreciate its currency by 10 percent as its international situation might require. Prior to such an action, the IMF sought to prevent destabilizing activity of speculators. The IMF would provide to a nation contemplating devaluation, substantial loans from the IMF and coordinated direct loans by other individual countries. But, despite the institution of the International Monetary Fund, the world faced increasing international financial imbalances and disequilibriums, particularly after the mid-1960s, culminating in a major international financial crisis associated with the events leading up to August 15, 1971.

CAUSES OF THE DOLLAR PROBLEM

A number of factors contributed to the deterioration in the position of the U.S. dollar, causing a major disequilibrium and leading to a departure from convertibility. Each of these factors will now be discussed.

Exchange values of 1946 were unrealistic

At the close of World War II the economies of Western Europe and Japan appeared to have been prostrated by devastation. Their need for the import of materials to rebuild their economies augured substantial balance-of-payments problems for these countries. There was widespread talk of a dollar shortage. The exchange rates established were based on the expectation of the overwhelming strength of the U.S. economy. However, some major developments altered the relative position of the U.S. economy as compared with those of the other major nations, making the 1946 exchange rates increasingly unrealistic as time went on.

The grant and loan program of the United States

The United States launched a major program of foreign aid to many other countries of the world following 1945. The United States helped finance and was a substantial contributor to the United Nations Relief and Rehabilitation Administration (UNRRA) to help meet immediate postwar emergency needs. The Marshall Plan was directed primarily to European recovery. Between July 1, 1945 and the end of 1970, the foreign aid expenditures of the U.S. government totaled over $120 billion. Of this amount $55 billion represented economic and technical aid grants. An additional $25 billion represented net loans to foreign governments. The U.S. net military grants during this period totaled $40 billion. The foreign aid program of the United States increasingly shifted toward grants to the North Atlantic Treaty Organization (NATO) nations and other military alliances.

One of the strong motives for the program was to combat the spread of communism. Thus, aid was directed to nations that appeared to be threatened by communism, such as Greece, South Korea, and even Yugoslavia, to help those countries maintain their independence from influence by the USSR. Similarly, large aid programs were provided to the neutral nations of Latin America, Asia, and Africa. In addition to seeking to limit the spread of communism, another motive was the realization that in an increasingly interdependent world, the health of the American economy would depend upon reasonable stability in the international economy.

Since the Soviet Union was also engaged in a foreign aid program there was an added element of competition for goodwill and influence, particularly among the neutral nations. An effort was made to increase economic progress in certain countries by the U.S. technical aid program. Since the idea for the program was set forth as the fourth point in the 1949 Inaugural Address of President Truman, it became known as the "Point Four" program. It involved a government plan for exporting some of the technological know-how of the U.S. economy.

U.S. foreign aid programs had mixed effects on American business firms. On the one hand, a number of the spending programs involved tied outlays in the sense that the monies had to be spent for U.S.-produced goods. This provided an artificial stimulus to some industries and firms in the United States. Even where the aid programs were not tied, the increased spending power in the foreign countries made available to them by these aid programs augmented their ability to import U.S. goods of all kinds. On the other hand, programs such as the "Point Four" program, which reduced the size of the technological gap that had existed in favor of the United States and aided in rebuilding of a number of foreign industries increased competition for U.S. industries.

Of particularly substantial impact was the rebuilding of a number of European and Japanese industries with the latest modern equipment and technology. The productivity of a number of foreign industries increased by leaps and bounds to offer increasing competition to U.S. industries. The problem was aggravated in particular industries, such as steels and chemicals. These industries were modernized, often with direct government aid, because they represented prestige industries for developed and developing nations alike. As a result, world overcapacity resulted in such industries, causing particular problems to U.S. industry, which had to compete with foreign industries that we had subsidized in varying degrees. Postwar U.S. labor problems that resulted in strikes and threats of strikes facilitated the entry of foreign products, particularly steel, into the United States. The balance-of-payments position of individual industries such as the steel industry deteriorated. This had an unfavorable effect on the overall balance-of-payments position as well.

Development of the European Economic Community

In 1957, under provisions of the Treaty of Rome, six nations formed a European Common Market. These were France, West Germany, Italy, Belgium, the Netherlands, and Luxembourg. The agreement for the European Economic Community provided that by 1973 tariffs and import quotas on nonfarm products produced within the European Common Market area were to be eliminated. There would be a free movement of labor and capital within the Common Market. A common tariff against goods from countries outside the Common Market would be established.

The advantages of the Common Market idea caused seven other European nations to form a European Free Trade Association (EFTA). The "Outer Seven" free trade areas consisted of the United Kingdom, Switzerland, Sweden, Austria, Denmark, Norway, and Portugal. EFTA represented a somewhat looser federation than the EEC, but generally had the same aims. However, the EEC represented a much larger and stronger Common Market area than EFTA. For some years several EFTA countries made gestures toward joining the EEC.

On January 22, 1972 the six founding members of the Common Market signed treaties in Brussels with the United Kingdom, Ireland, Denmark, and Norway providing for the enlargement of the EEC. After the treaties have been ratified by the four countries concerned, they will enter the Common Market on January 1, 1973. The EEC will then include a population of over 250 million, gross national products that total over $560 billion, and foreign trade in excess of $200 billion.

The formation of the Common Markets in Western Europe had two very substantial influences on U.S. business firms. First, the creation of the Common Market areas provided opportunities for U.S. firms to utilize their considerable historical experience in managing mass-production and mass-distribution entities in the new Common Market areas of Western Europe. This was done by acquisitions and mergers as well as by the establishment of new entities by U.S. firms in the Common Market areas. The stimulus of these opportunities was reinforced by a serious threat. The threat aspect was represented by the prospect of the common tariffs moving up to successively higher levels against foreign imports. Thus, it appeared to American business firms that if sales to Common Market countries were to be continued, it would be increasingly necessary to have manufacturing and marketing facilities within those areas. This threat was the second factor causing an increase in the magnitude of direct investment by American firms in European countries.

Military expenditures in Western Europe and the Far East

At the end of World War II the United States maintained troops in Western Europe and in various parts of Asia to keep a defensive posture in the outer perimeters from which a threat to the United States might be initiated. A broad complex of diplomatic and military considerations was involved in these expenditures. It is inappropriate in this presentation to attempt an evaluation of the soundness of the considerations which lead to the military and nonmilitary foreign expenditure programs of the U.S. government. Nor will an evaluation be made of the highly controversial wars that developed in Korea in the early fifties and subsequently in Southeast Asia on an escalated basis beginning in 1966. But, the economic consequences of these programs are beyond dispute. They are reflected in the trends in the U.S. balance-of-payments position.

TRENDS IN THE U.S. BALANCE-OF-PAYMENTS POSITION

The U.S. balance-of-payments position deteriorated in successive stages. The data are shown in Table 13–1, in which six time periods are shown. In the immediate post-World War II years the United States was running a very substantial positive balance on goods and all services. Unilateral transfers, the export of capital through government loans and private direct investment partially offset this favorable balance on goods and services. But foreign countries also exported gold into the United States, which shows up as a debit or negative entry in the balance-of-payments account. The official reserve transactions balances were held down to relatively moderate amounts because the large balance on goods and services was substantially offset by unilateral transfers and long-term capital outflows from the United States.

In the decade of the 1950s the balance on merchandise and other services was cut to about half the level that had been achieved during the

1946–49 period. Unilateral transfers and long-term capital outflows continued at their levels of the immediate postwar period. As a consequence, the official reserve transactions balance was actually unfavorable to the United States and a small export of gold took place. The total of U.S. official assets declined by about $3 billion during the 10-year period, 1950 through 1959 inclusive.

During the years 1960 to 1964, the current accounts balance continued moderate. Unilateral transfers were large, and long-term capital outflows

TABLE 13–1

Shifts in the U.S. balance-of-payments position, 1946–71 (amounts in $billions)

	1946–49	1950–59	1960–64	1965–69	1970	1971†
Merchandise and other services	+7	+3	+3	−2	− 3	− 6
Investment income	+1	+2	+3	+6	+ 6	+ 8
1. Balance on goods and services	+8	+5	+6	+4	+ 3	+ 2
Unilateral transfers	−4	−4	−3	−3	− 3	− 4
2. Balance on current account	+4	+1	+3	+1	*	− 2
Long-term capital	−3	−3	−4	−3	− 3	− 8
3. Balance on current account and long-term capital	+1	−2	−1	−2	− 3	−10
Nonliquid claims on U.S.	+2	+1	−2	−1	− 1	−13
4. Net liquidity balance	+3	−1	−3	−3	− 4	−23
Liquid claims on U.S.	−1	−1	+1	+3	− 6	− 8
5. Official reserve transactions balance	+2	−2	−2	0	−10	−31
Liabilities to foreign official agencies	*	*	+1	*	+ 7	+28
Gold	−2	+1	+1	*	+ 1	*
Other U.S. official reserve assets	*	+1	*	*	+ 2	+ 3

* Less than $0.5 billion.
† First three quarters on an annualized basis.
Source: Summarized from *Economic Report of the President, January 1972* (Washington, D.C.: U.S. Government Printing Office), pp. 150, 296–97.

actually increased somewhat. There was a small official reserve transactions negative balance which was covered by a continued small export of gold from the United States and some building up of liabilities to foreign official agencies.

During 1965–69 the United States began to experience a negative balance on merchandise and other services. This resulted from an increase in foreign travel and an increase in transportation outlays incurred. However, investment income as a result of prior long-term capital outflows reached the very substantial level of $6 billion per year. Thus the balance on goods and services was a favorable $4 billion. Unilateral transfers and long-term capital outflows continued large. There was some buildup of liquid claims on the United States. The net result was that the official reserve transaction balance was zero. However, a number of unfavorable trends were underway.

In 1970 the deficit on merchandise and other services continued to increase. This was aggravated by the cumulative increase in military expenditures associated with the escalation of the war in Southeast Asia after 1965. In 1970 serious doubts about the ability of the United States to remedy its balance-of-payments problems began to spread. Unilateral transfers and long-term capital outlays continued at a combined $6 billion level. Private liquid claims on the United States began to be liquidated as the flight from the dollar was underway. The official reserve transactions balance reached some $10 billion which was covered primarily by the increase in U.S. liabilities to foreign official agencies.

In 1971 the trends which had begun in 1970 were aggravated. Although investment income rose to $8 billion, the deficit on the merchandise and other services account reached $6 billion. All types of short-term claims on the United States were liquidated in large amounts. The official reserve transactions balance for the first three quarters of 1971 on an annual basis reached the astounding level of over $30 billion. This had to be covered primarily by an increase in U.S. liabilities to foreign official agencies.

INTERNATIONAL FINANCIAL DEVELOPMENTS AFTER 1967

Overview

The international currency crisis which finally resulted in the suspension of convertibility into gold of U.S. dollars on August 15, 1971 was preceded by a number of significant currency developments beginning in 1967. These will be briefly summarized for perspective; then some individual events will be described more fully.

November, 1967. The pound sterling was devalued on November 18, 1967 by 14.3 percent from $2.80 to $2.40 to the pound. A similar devaluation was made by 13 other countries generally closely related to the United Kingdom in international trade relations. These included Ireland, New Zealand, Spain, and Denmark.

March, 1968. After a three-billion-dollar loss of gold to private and corporate buyers within the space of weeks, support by the United States and six other countries of the gold price was suspended. A two-tier gold price system was established. On March 18, 1968 the gold cover requirement of 25 percent on U.S. Federal Reserve notes was eliminated by an Act of the U.S. Congress.

August, 1969. The French franc was devalued by 11.1 percent from $0.20255 to $0.180044. Shortly thereafter, on September 29, 1969 the West German mark was permitted to float upward. The parity rate of the mark on October 24, 1969 was raised from $0.250 to $0.273224, a level 9.3 percent higher.

June, 1970. With a continued large inflow of U.S. dollars into Canada, Canadian authorities permitted the Canadian dollar to float beginning June 1, 1970. The Canadian dollar rose from $0.925 to just under $1 in the early part of 1970 and at approximately $1 by the end of 1971.

May, 1971. The Swiss franc was revalued upward from $0.228685 to $0.244852. On the same, May 9, 1972, date the West German mark was again permitted to float as was the Dutch guilder.

August, 1971. On August 15, 1971 the convertibility of U.S. dollars

TABLE 13-2

Changes in exchange rates of major currencies against the dollar, January 1, 1971 to December 31, 1971

Currency	Percentage increase*
Japanese yen	16.88
Swiss franc	13.88
West German mark	13.58
Netherlands guilder	11.57
Belgian franc	11.57
French franc	8.57
United Kingdom pound	8.57
Swedish krona	7.49
Italian lira	7.48
Canadian dollar	†

  ° "Central value" of currency relative to January 1 dollar parity rate.
  † Canada has announced that it will continue to allow the Canadian dollar to float. The value of the Canadian dollar on December 31, 1971 (99.79 U.S. cents) was 7.9 percent greater than the pre-May 1970 par value (92.5 U.S. cents).
      Source: *Economic Report of the President, January 1972* (Washington, D.C.: U.S. Government Printing Office), p. 152.

into gold was suspended and a 10 percent import surcharge was introduced. Many of the strong currencies of Europe were permitted to float, and after a slight delay the Japanese yen was permitted to float also.

December, 1971. On December 18, 1971 agreement was reached for a realignment of major currencies. The devaluation of the dollar in terms of gold by a rise in the official price from $35 to $38 per fine ounce would be proposed to the U.S. Congress as soon as agreement on trade matters could be reached with EEC, Canada, and Japan. This represented a 7.89 percent devaluation, equivalent to an 8.57 percent increase in the U.S. monetary gold price. The other strong currencies of Western Europe and Japan were realigned as set forth in Table 13–2. Following the currency realignment agreement, the U.S. import surcharge was eliminated on December 20, 1971.

Effects of inflation in the United States

Although there had been relative price stability in the United States between 1958 and 1965, with the acceleration of the war in Southeast Asia, a period of rampant inflation began in the United States. Of course, inflation has been taking place in other countries of the world as well and probably to a greater degree overall than in the United States. But the inflation in the United States hit particularly unfavorably the prices of U.S. export goods.

TABLE 13-3

Changes in U.S. relative price position, 1961-71

	United States	Competitors*	Ratio of U.S. to competitors†
	1964 = 100‡		
Unit value of exports of manufactured goods:			
1961..........................	99.5	99.6	99.9
1962..........................	99.5	98.3	101.2
1963..........................	99.3	98.5	100.8
1964..........................	100.0	100.0	100.0
1965..........................	103.3	101.0	102.3
1966..........................	106.2	102.7	103.4
1967..........................	109.4	104.0	105.2
1968..........................	111.9	103.9	107.7
1969..........................	116.8	107.7	108.4
1970..........................	122.8	114.9	106.9
1971, 1st half§..............	126.7	117.7	107.6

* Weighted average for Belgium, Canada, France, Germany, Italy, Japan, Netherlands, Sweden, and United Kingdom.
† Ratio multiplied by 100.
‡ Adjusted for changes in exchange rates.
§ Preliminary.
Source: *Economic Report of the President, January 1972* (Washington, D.C.: U.S. Government Printing Office), p. 143.

Table 13-3 shows that the unit prices of exports of manufactured goods of the United States continuously rose compared to the unit value of exports of manufactured goods of nine nations competitive with the United States in international trade. Table 13-3 shows that by the first half of 1971 the ratio of U.S. export prices of nine competitive nations of the United States was almost 8 percent higher than those prices had been in 1961. Thus the relative prices of U.S. export goods had risen compared to the prices of the products of competitor countries.

Thus the United States began to exhibit the characteristics that we had outlined in Chapter 3 of a country that was facing foreign exchange difficulties. Domestic inflation was limiting the ability of the United States to compete on merchandise and service exports. Continued large U.S. government capital outflows could be supported only by a favorable balance on goods and services which no longer could be achieved. In 1968, a run on U.S. gold began.

The two-tier gold system

During March 1968 meetings were held among 10 of the leading commercial nations of the world to develop policies to defend the U.S. gold position in the face of the continuing balance-of-payments difficulties of the United States. Agreement was reached to suspend all gold payments from official central banks to the free market and to establish a two-tier system. All the gold in the official reserves as of March 1968 was to be frozen. In the official tier, gold payments were to be made only among governments and always at official IMF parities.

Outside the IMF group gold is completely demonetized. A free market tier is established in which the price of gold is freely set by supply and demand, as with other commodities. In the free market in gold, its price has fluctuated from about $36 an ounce to $60 per ounce since the establishment of the two-tier gold system. In 1970, agreement was reached that newly mined gold from South Africa could be sold in the free market and the IMF agreed to buy the residual new-mined gold at the official $35 an ounce. In turn South Africa agreed not to manipulate the free price of gold but received the equivalent of a floor under the free market in return.

The establishment of the two-tier gold market was aimed at least in part to protect the gold reserves of the United States. But this stop-gap measure did not succeed in eliminating the continued pressures on the U.S. dollar. During 1970 a major portion of the dollar outflow moved to West Germany. West Germany's large trade surplus and its restrictive credit policy which maintained high interest rates in the country indicated continued strength in the West German mark. In February 1971 West Germany's authorities sought to push down the forward value of the mark by selling marks for forward delivery against the dollar. But the demand for marks was so great and the surplus of dollars was so massive that it was not feasible to continue these efforts.

The United States suspends convertibility

During the second quarter of 1971 the U.S. balance of payments on merchandise and services continued to deteriorate. Confidence in the ability to maintain the dollar's exchange value fell further. Substantial reductions in U.S. reserve assets continued. By mid-August 1971 the U.S. Treasury had used up over $3 billion in reserve assets, of which about 40 percent took place in early August. This decline in U.S. reserve assets took place despite substantial drawings of foreign currencies under swap lines of credit with other central banks by the U.S. Federal Reserve System. The Federal Reserve used these drawings of foreign currencies to buy dollars that the Central Banks might otherwise have presented at the U.S. Treasury for conversion into gold or other reserve assets.

As the pressures mounted, the United States suspended convertibility of the dollar on August 15, 1971. Essentially, the value of the dollar in terms of other major currencies began to float. In addition, the President announced a 10 percent surcharge on goods imported into the United States and ordered a 10 percent cut in foreign aid. The surtax applied only to goods on which duties had been reduced under reciprocal trade agreements and was limited to the statutory ceiling on import duties. For example, on automobiles the tax was 6.5 percent. All goods subject to mandatory import quotas were exempt from the additional tax, so that the surcharge affected only about one half of U.S. imports.

The Smithsonian Agreement

After August 15, 1971 a period of floating rates and negotiations on setting new exchange rates got underway. An agreement referred to as the Smithsonian Agreement (because the meeting took place at the Smithsonian Institution) was reached on December 18. A set of exchange rates was negotiated aimed to correct the relative overvaluation of the U.S. dollar. The United States agreed to devalue the dollar in terms of gold to $38 per ounce. The changes in the exchange rates of major currencies in relationship to the dollar during the year 1971 are summarized in Table 13-2. In relationship to the dollar the exchange value of other currencies moved up ranging from over 7 percent for the Italian lira to almost 17 percent for the Japanese yen.

In addition, the Smithsonian Agreement also provided that the band of permissible exchange value fluctuations would be broadened. The original IMF articles of agreement required that each member maintained the exchange value of its currency against gold or the U.S. dollar within a range no wider than 1 percent on each side of its official parity value. The Smithsonian Agreement provided that this band be widened to 2.25 percent on each side of official parity, thus providing for a total range of 4.5 percent.

At the time of adoption of the Smithsonian Agreement on December 18, 1971, it was hoped that the uncertainties that had existed would be resolved. Unfortunately, however, such has not proved to be the case. By the middle of January 1972 a strong upward trend in a number of currency values had started. In a number of instances the currencies were selling at their plus intervention points. This meant that the governments involved would have to intervene in their foreign exchange markets if the prices of their currencies in terms of U.S. dollars were to be kept within the permitted limits.

U.S. policy in 1972

In a speech on March 15, 1972 the U.S. Secretary of the Treasury, John B. Connally, reemphasized U.S. opposition to early efforts to restore convertibility of the U.S. dollar either into gold or other forms of convertible currency. He also stated that the United States did not contemplate another devaluation of the dollar, and that the United States expected the surplus countries in Europe as well as Japan to defend the net rate structure by accumulating more dollars. It has been estimated that by the end of January 1972 the foreign exchange reserves of Central Banks of the IMF member countries and Switzerland had risen to almost $80 billion, 90 percent of which is estimated to consist of U.S. dollars.

As an indication of their concern over the general uncertainty, members of the European Economic Union drew up an agreement that became effective April 24, 1972. Under this agreement the countries involved agreed that they would keep the value of each other's currency within plus or minus 1⅛ percent of the central rates. They also agreed that in order to maintain the agreements made in Washington December 18, 1971 none would buy unwanted U.S. dollars.

If all six of the early members of the European Economic Union, and England, Denmark, Ireland, and Norway, each of which officially agreed to become members of the European Economic Union by the Treaty of Adhesion signed in Brussels, January 22, 1972 adhere to the pledges made, there will be two markets for the U.S. dollar within the European Economic Union. There will be a commercial market in which the dollar is traded at fixed rates and a financial market in which the rate is permitted to fluctuate freely depending on supply and demand conditions. However, to make this possible will require the application of strict foreign exchange controls and an absolute refusal on the part of the governments to buy any more unwanted U.S. dollars. This would also require that all European Economic Union countries act in unison, which means that the floating of the U.S. dollar would have to be on a "clean" rather than "dirty" floating basis, that is, no government intervention. Under this agreement, imbalances among the members of the union would be settled in gold or other foreign currencies. It also provides that imports from the United States are to be paid for in commercial dollars.

It is unlikely that this agreement will work out successfully, for two reasons. One, it will be nearly impossible, due to the trading volume involved, to separate successfully the markets in commercial dollars and so-called financial dollars. Any leakage or breakdown in the separation of those two markets will mean that individuals or firms will be able to purchase U.S. exports on a financial dollar basis, thus making these exports highly competitive with European Economic Union goods and services. Two, another obstacle to the effective operation of the plan results from the fact that not all members of the European Economic Union are equally strong from an economic as well as foreign exchange reserve point of view. This means that if Italy, France, and the United Kingdom run short of gold or foreign exchange reserves to support their own currencies in relation to those of other members of the EEU, other members will be required to purchase Italian, French, and British currencies in order to keep the relative rates of these currencies within the agreed-upon limits. It appears to us highly unlikely that the strong countries of the European Economic Union will follow such required policies for an extended period of time. This, to us, is an indication that from a long-range point of view other actions are required that will lead to further changes in the world's international monetary system.

PROPOSALS FOR REFORM OF THE INTERNATIONAL FINANCIAL SYSTEM

The continued negotiations and continued uncertainty as to the future of the dollar in relation to other currencies emphasize the need for more fundamental and long-run solutions to the international imbalances and uncertainties in international finance. This chapter will, therefore, be concluded with an analysis of longer run proposed solutions to international financial problems. We emphasize that these discussions are not academic. They are of critical importance for business decisions. We are seeking to provide a brief and compact framework that provides the business manager with a vehicle for understanding and putting in perspective the financial developments that affect his firm. Otherwise, the businessman operates in his own private world of increasing bewilderment and uncertainty. As a consequence of lack of understanding of these international developments, the businessman may withdraw from the international business, or miss valuable opportunities because it appears too complicated and he feels unwilling to expose himself to its great uncertainties. However, as we pointed out in the first chapter and elsewhere, no firm in a world of major international financial changes is free from the impact of the events that have been taking place. Chapter 1 provided examples of how firms that thought they were domestic firms were greatly influenced by international developments.

Therefore, we feel that without getting into the technical economic apparatus for understanding all aspects of these developments, it is essential to understand them at a broad conceptual level. This is necessary so that from a business planning standpoint these large issues can be translated into practical terms. If any one large nation pursues an inflationary policy or embarks on a program that requires large foreign exchange outflows, such as the U.S. war activity in Southeast Asia, there will be international repercussions. In turn, these international developments will affect firms engaged in both international operations and, presumably, purely domestic pursuits. Therefore, the president of even a solely domestic firm simply has to shift his horizon to the increasingly important international economic developments of the type covered in this book. This is essential if he is to protect the long-run future of his individual firm. Thus, we have felt it important to summarize these major developments in compact fashion. Without this kind of overall framework and understanding, very great costs and losses to individual firms may result.

Would restoration of the gold standard be a solution?

The first proposal that has been made to achieve international financial stability is a return to the gold standard. Let us analyze the implications of the return to gold.

Attachment to gold as the standard. There are two broad reasons for the strong attachment to gold as an international monetary standard. First is the apparent very great interest of speculators in investing in gold. Some people then reason that if speculators see gold as a continued strong store of value, there must be some fundamental virtue attached to it. One of the reasons gold was used as an object of speculation is that a downside risk protection was provided by the United States, which offered to buy and sell it at $35 an ounce. Speculators were certain of a floor under the price of gold. It is very rare that a speculator can find an opportunity that provides such protection. Even under the new two-tier gold system, the IMF assures the Union of South Africa of purchasing its gold at $35 an ounce. Hence, something of a floor still remains. Of course, with the assurance that the United States is going to increase the price of gold by some degree, this further encourages speculators. In addition, rumors are rampant that the United States might even increase the price of gold in massive proportions. But it would be interesting to see how its price would behave if there were truly a free market in gold.

Second, the nostalgia for a return to the gold standard is not based on reality and has many elements of fiction in it. Somehow the feeling has grown up that when most nations were on the gold standard this was an era of stability and economic well-being. Virtually the opposite is the truth. The gold standard era was generally one of great international instability. Domestic economies under the gold standard suffered from deflation as well as inflation. In fact, it was because of the impossibility of the international economy functioning well under a strict gold standard that nations departed from an absolute gold standard. They modified the effects and discipline of the gold standard in various ways through fractional reserve banking systems in which gold support of the domestic currency varied. Indeed, a number of countries found it more advantageous to hold strong currencies that were based on gold in differing degrees rather than gold itself. Thus a number of countries during the gold standard era were actually on a gold exchange standard.

New proposals for the gold standard. In recent years proposals have been made for large increases in the price of gold. The French economist, Jacques Rueff, has proposed an increase in the price of gold to $70 or $100 an ounce. The price of gold would be raised and then nations would return to a rigid gold standard. Gold would then function as a strict economic discipline for all the governments in the world. If a given nation tended to inflate, it would lose gold and be forced into deflation. After a nation suffered deflation for a period, the wringing out of its prices and costs would improve its international trade position, bring about a return of gold, and ameliorate the deflation.

The inherent lack of logic in the position of Professor Rueff is suggested by the position of Professor Roy Harrod, a British economist. Harrod has also supported doubling or tripling the price of gold at this time *and again later,* whenever required to give nations the ability to pursue expansionary policies. But, if periodically the price of gold is to be changed, then gold is not, in fact, serving as a discipline on the economic policies of governments and individual nations.

Reasons for unacceptability of gold standard. The reality of modern economies is that nations simply will not accept a stagnating economy, mass unemployment, and deflation in deference to the rules of an automatic gold standard. The fundamental problem is one of the proper balance in individual government economic policies and in relationship to the policies of other nations of the world. Since the gold standard never did provide the proper international coordination, it has lost its acceptability as the primary basis upon which international economic relations are to be conducted. This being the fact, the main effect of doubling or tripling the price of gold would simply be to divert resources to mining gold rather than producing other commodities—and to reward speculators. While there is no sound basis for a massive increase in the price of gold, we recognize that for traditional reasons gold will continue to be one of the important official reserve assets. Hence, gold will play some role in the international monetary standards of the future, but will no longer have a central or dominant position.

Once we have departed from a strict gold standard, a basic and fundamental issue arises. Should the international financial community attempt to operate with fixed exchange rates or with flexible exchange rates? The recent international financial crises have sharpened the argument between the two opposed points of view. We will next analyze these two positions.

Fixed versus flexible exchange rates

A fixed exchange rate system has long been the mechanism under which international financial relations have been conducted. Its main advantage is that it encourages international trade by enabling transactions to be conducted at definite prices based on fixed exchange rates. An argument against fixed exchange rates is that large capital flows are required to achieve equality in the balance of payments of individual countries at fixed and inflexible prices. In addition, speculative activity may act as a further destabilizing force in a world with fixed prices represented by pegged exchange rates.[1]

Arguments for flexible rates. The argument for flexible exchange rates is that exchange rates are nothing more than price ratios between two currencies and that the principle of free market prices should be permitted to operate. Exchange rates, like other prices, should reflect actual supply and demand conditions and changes therein. Flexible prices, it is argued, would prevent imbalances and disequilibria from developing. Furthermore, it is claimed that flexible exchange rates would have avoided the kind of cumulative speculative investment flows that have developed since the late 1960s. Finally, there would be less need for international capital flows, and a smaller need for international liquidity reserves, because there would be less need for capital flows to make adjustments for differences in balance-of-payments positions. It would be expected that the frequency of exchange rate fluctuations would be greater. Exchange rate fluctuations, as the adjustment mechanism, will be carrying the greater burden of adjustment relative to capital flows. As a consequence, the uncertainties of conducting international business, particularly those involving durable goods and longer term contracts, will be increased. Proponents of flexible exchange rates argue, however, that the uncertainties of price changes in business transactions can be reduced through hedging operations in the forward market. The argument that such hedging operations might be unduly expensive and an unnecessary burden on international commerce is said to be unfounded. Freely flexible exchange rates would result in the development of more active forward markets with specialists of increased experience and resources who would perform the forward exchange market functions with increasing efficiency. This would reduce the costs of using the forward exchange markets for hedging and other operations over time. It is argued that the estimates of expenses that are said to be associated with forward exchange market

---

[1] The gold standard was a symbol of discipline. If nations were willing to be disciplined by the recognition that gold flows would be the corrective capital flows, and that these gold flows would have major impacts on domestic policies, the gold standard would work. A gold standard really represents an extreme form of fixed exchange rates, and all of the weaknesses of a fixed exchange rate system are magnified in a fixed gold standard system.

operations and hedging are based upon experiences under fixed exchange rates. Under flexible exchange rates, institutions and specialist services would develop so that the functions would be performed at relatively minimal costs.

Arguments for fixed rates. In reply it is argued that nothing in this world is free. There is a basic trade-off between the two approaches to the international exchanges. With fixed exchange rates, larger capital flows are required and these may be, in fact, destabilizing. With fluctuating exchange rates, smaller capital flows are required but the frequency and magnitudes of fluctuations in exchange rates may be greater. Speculative trends may also develop in relation to exchange rate fluctuations which might be amplifying and destabilizing. Economical hedging operations will be feasible and international trade facilitated only if under freely flexible exchange rates; the exchange rates do not move persistently in one direction. But this in turn implies that individual nations are not pursuing policies causing chronic inflation or chronic deflation in relation to other nations of the world. This implies, therefore, that individual nations must exercise self-discipline and that there is effective coordination of economic policies between the major nations of the world. But, if individual nations exercise intelligent self-discipline and if there is effective coordination between the nations of the world, then a system of fixed exchange rates would also work very well.

Compromise proposals. It is precisely because the arguments between the two schools of thought are somewhat even that the Smithsonian Agreement of December 18, 1971 represented something of a compromise position between the fixed exchange rate school and the freely flexible exchange rate school. One of the provisions provided for "widening the band." Widening the band of permissible exchange rate fluctuation from 1 percent on either side of the official rates to $2\frac{1}{4}$ percent on either side introduces a degree of exchange rate flexibility. Thus the total band permitted is now 4.5 percent.

Another proposal has been to introduce a crawling or sliding peg. This would provide that within any one year the exchange rate parity of a nation's currency would be permitted to move by some specified amount, for example, 1 or 2 percent per year. The crawling or sliding peg would be combined with the concept of a widened band to introduce two elements of flexibility in exchange rates. An important advantage of combining these two elements is that speculative tendencies would be blunted by dampening the pace of movement in any given direction. Speculative tendencies would be dampened because continuous moderate changes reduce potential speculative gains in relation to the cost of borrowed funds or the opportunity costs of funds tied up in speculative positions. Given that these continuous moderate changes in par values are bleeding off the pressures of adjustments, this reduces the required amounts of capital flows and thus reduces the potential speculative gains from this direction as well.

Special drawing rights

Another major development in international institutions was the provision in the creation of special drawing rights (SDRs) by the International Monetary Fund. Agreement was reached in 1970 for the IMF to issue a total of $9.5 billion SDRs over the three years 1970–72.[2] Empowering the IMF to create special drawing rights was another important step for the international economy. The SDRs have been referred to as paper gold representing the creation of an international currency. It provides for a leadership role for an international agency, the IMF, to try to achieve multilateral agreements among the nations of the world for determining an optimal rate of growth in international reserves. Thus the rate of growth in international reserves would not be determined by the degrees of inflation in an individual country such as the United States, whose deficits expanded the Eurodollar system from the mid-1960s. Nor would the amount of international reserves be influenced by the interaction between pressures for increasing the price of gold and the resulting gold mining activity or gold hoarding or dishoarding. The SDRs provide an opportunity for introducing some rational economic analysis into the determination of the required level of international reserves.

But no individual set of institutions can bring about the required stability in international financial relations. The fundamental requirement is that there has to be an accord for an understanding in the world international financial economic community. Each nation must recognize that it cannot pursue independent policies inconsistent with the long-range balance situation in the world as a whole. If any single nation or group of nations pursues policies inconsistent with those of the rest of the world, there is no institution nor international exchange policy that would solve this problem. There is no international financial arrangement that can be pursued effectively that does not depend upon some kind of amity, understanding, and coordination among nations from both the political and economic standpoints.

Individual nations must exercise a degree of self-discipline and follow policies that are responsible in relation to the position they hold in the international economy. Also a necessity is a spirit of general international cooperation which makes it feasible to have fruitful periodic negotiations.

---

[2] An increase in international liquidity was achieved on October 30, 1970 as a result of the fifth general increase in quotas to the IMF.

In addition, a permanent mechanism such as the IMF must be accorded sufficient authority to insure a reasonable degree of coordination of economic policies among all the nations of the world.

SUMMARY

This chapter has traced the development of the events leading up to the depreciation of the U.S. dollar and its departure from convertibility. Some of these pressures were a consequence of special historical circumstances. In part, they were due to the unrealistic level of exchange values established in 1946, which were based on temporary conditions which then changed substantially as the postwar restructuring of the European and Japanese economies took place. An additional complication resulted from a broad set of diplomatic and military situations which led to large unilateral governmental loan and grant programs by the United States. The development of the European Economic Community stimulated private direct investment by U.S. persons in Western Europe at a greater pace than otherwise would have occurred without this large trading area. Finally, the escalation of hostilities in Southeast Asia resulted in strong inflationary pressures in the United States and substantial foreign exchange losses with outlays associated with these hostilities.

All of these events and pressures resulted in a series of developments observed in a number of leading indicators of U.S. economic conditions. Increasingly large federal deficits were incurred. The money supply in the United States grew intermittently, but at a relatively high rate in relationship to the growth of real products. Domestic goods grew at an even faster pace and larger in amount than the increases in the prices of export goods of countries that are competitors of the United States.

These influences increasingly showed up in the U.S. balance-of-payments position. The surplus which the United States had long achieved on the merchandise account continually dwindled until in 1971 it actually became negative. Unilateral transfers, the export of capital for U.S. government grant and loan programs, and private direct investment further aggravated the deficit on current accounts. In 1971, the short-term claims against the United States held by nongovernmental interests were increasingly liquidated. The official reserve transaction balance grew to enormous dimensions and had to be covered by substantial increases in liabilities to foreign official agencies. The pressures became overwhelming, culminating on August 15, 1971 when President Nixon announced the suspension of convertibility of the U.S. dollar.

Subsequently, a realignment of exchange rates took place. Depreciation and the devaluation of the U.S. dollar took place at the same time as appreciation and upward revaluation of the strong Western European and Japanese currencies took place.

The fundamental requirements for international financial stability have not yet been established. Two strong positions have developed. Some protagonists have argued that it has now been effectively proven that fixed exchange rates do not work. If true, it establishes even more strongly that the traditional gold standard works even less effectively. Some arguments have been made for full flexible exchange rates. One reason given is that the size of capital flows would be much smaller and less likely to aggravate instability.

A fear expressed in connection with flexible exchange rates is that the uncertainties of pricing of international transactions would contract the level of international trade. In response, it is urged that increased specialization in international currency exchange in foreign exchange markets would greatly reduce the cost of hedging operations as they become more frequent and more widespread.

Agreement has not been reached as to which of the two types of exchange rates, fixed or flexible, would function most effectively in international finance. The Smithsonian Agreement of December 18, 1971 represented something of a compromise. It provided that the band of permissible exchange rate fluctuations would be broadened. In addition, it has been suggested that a crawling or sliding peg be introduced. This would provide that within one year the exchange rate parity of a nation's currency would be permitted to move only by some specified amount, for example, 1 or 2 percent per year. The combination of a widened band and a sliding peg would, it is hoped, blunt speculative tendencies by dampening the pace of movement of exchange rates in any given direction. In addition, increased power has been provided to the International Monetary Fund by giving it limited authority to create new special drawing rights representing a form of paper gold.

Of particular significance to businessmen, however, is that the fundamental problems of international finance have not yet been solved. Uncertainties and risks will continue. This emphasizes the need for the continuing understanding by businessmen of the fundamental forces in operation. Furthermore, business executives must follow closely the critical economics that provide indicators of changes in exchange rates and international economic and financial conditions. There are both tremendous opportunities and pitfalls rapidly changing in international business operations. The opportunities are so great that this area of business activity cannot be ignored. Many of the pitfalls are avoidable with understanding.

The fundamental pressures on the United States in terms of diplomatic and military commitments have by no means been resolved. Further, there is no international institution or financial agreements that do not depend upon some kind of self-discipline of individual nations and coordination among nations from both political and economic standpoints. Thus, change and uncertainties will continue in the international economy. These will require the continual study and analysis by executives of business firms—indeed, by responsible citizens—of all nations.

PROBLEM 13-1

You are given selected transactions for seven different countries.

A. From the data given compute the five concepts of balance in the balance of payments.

B. Characterize the situation of each country as suggested by your analysis of each of the five concepts of the balance of payments.

Item	I	II	III	IV	V	VI	VI
Merchandise and all other services......	+700	+300	+300	−200	−500	+400	−1(
Investment income....................	+100	+200	+300	+600	+700	+800	+8(
1. Balance on goods and services	—	—	—	—	—	—	—
Unilateral transfers...................	−400	−400	−300	−300	−400	−400	−1(
2. Balance on current account	—	—	—	—	—	—	—
Long-term capital....................	−300	−300	−400	−300	−500	−300	−4(
3. Balance on current account and long-term capital	—	—	—	—	—	—	—
Nonliquid short-term claims...........	+200	+100	−200	−100	−200	−200	−1(
4. Net liquidity balance	—	—	—	—	—	—	—
Liquid claims.......................	−100	−100	+100	+300	−300	−300	−1(
5. Official reserve transactions balance	—	—	—	—	—	—	—
Liabilities to foreign official agencies......	—	—	+100	—	+900	—	—
Gold...............................	−200	+100	+100	—	—	—	—
Other official reserve assets.............	—	+100	—	—	+300	—	—

(Country header spans columns I–VI)

PROBLEM 13-2

Discuss the implications for executives of multinational corporations of some of the possible ways in which the approximately $70 billion of U.S. dollars held by the Central Banks of Western Europe and Japan might affect the operations of U.S. multinational corporations.

In your answer first discuss the pros and cons of the likelihood of each particular alternative taking place and then discuss the implications of the actions that you think are the most likely for the operations of U.S. multinational corporations.

Alternative A: The sum of $70 billion, held by foreign Central Banks, might be used to make direct investments in industries in the United States. This would be the reverse of what has been taking place since the end of World

War II when the United States made large direct investments in Western European industries.

Alternative B: The Western European Central Banks could nationalize some or all of the companies controlled by Americans in Western Europe and pay for the nationalization by returning the dollars they hold at the present time. This has been referred to as the De Gaulle plan since it was proposed by the late President De Gaulle of France some four years ago.

Alternative C: Another possibility is a trend noted in the April 8, 1971, issue of *The Wall Street Journal* that the government of Japan, for example, is investing in long-term U.S. government securities.

Alternative D: These dollars might be used to increase the purchases of goods and services in the United States, thus increasing our balance of merchandise trade.

Alternative E: It has been proposed that since most of the military expenditures of the United States abroad are for the defense of Western Europe and Japan, their accumulated dollar balances might be used to finance U.S. military expenditures abroad rather than having the United States continue to finance them.

Alternative F: The European Central Banks might step up their level of portfolio investments in U.S. securities, both stocks and bonds.

SELECTED BIBLIOGRAPHY

Aliber, Robert Z. *The Future of the Dollar as an International Currency.* New York: Frederick A. Praeger, Inc. 1966.

Borch, F. J. International Trade: What Is the Problem? an address, Detroit, Michigan, Economic Club, October 12, 1971.

"The Deadlock over the Dollar," *Business Week*, September 25, 1971, pp. 82–107.

Friedman, M., and Rosa, R. V. *The Balance of Payments: Free versus Fixed Exchange Rates.* Washington, D.C.: American Enterprise Institute for Public Policy Research, 1967.

Grove, David L. "Defending the Dollar or Passing the Buck," *Financial Executive,* Vol. 36, No. 7 (July 1968), pp. 15–26.

Horie, Shigeo. *The International Monetary Fund.* New York: St. Martin's Press, Inc., 1964.

Horsefield, J. Keith. *The International Monetary Fund: 1945–1965,* Vol. I. Washington, D.C.: The International Monetary Fund, 1969.

———. (ed.), *The International Monetary Fund: 1945–1965,* Vol. II and III. Washington, D.C.: The International Monetary Fund, 1969.

Jacobson, M. Allen. "Why Not Flexible Exchange Rates?" *Columbia Journal of World Business,* Vol. 4, No. 6 (November–December 1969), pp. 88–89.

Johnson, Harry G. *An Overall View of International Economic Questions Facing Britain, the United States, and Canada during the 1970's.* British-North American Committee, June 1970.

Krause, Lawrence B. *Sequel to Bretton Woods.* A Staff Paper. Washington, D.C.: The Brookings Institution, 1971.

Lanyl, Anthony. *The Case for Floating Exchange Rates Reconsidered.* Princeton, N.J.: Princeton University, International Finance Section, 1969.

Officer, Lawrence H., and Willett, Thomas D. (eds.). *The International Monetary System.* Modern Economic Issues. Englewood Cliffs, N.J.: Prentice-Hall, Inc., 1969.

Triffin, Robert. *Our International Monetary System: Yesterday, Today, and Tomorrow.* New York: Random House, Inc., 1968.

14

An integrated view of international managerial finance

IT IS of value to review the materials presented in the previous chapters to synthesize the effects of various factors on the foreign business entity. We may thereby derive useful policies which will aid in the successful operation of the foreign business venture.

From a theoretical point of view no great differences exist between domestic and international finance. The various models of investment evaluation are the same whether they are applied to domestic or to international investment problems. The problems of valuation of a business firm are similar, as are financing mix decisions. The foregoing statements do not imply that the problems of international finance are identical to the problems of domestic finance.

INFLUENCE OF INTERNATIONAL ENVIRONMENTAL FACTORS

We start with environmental factors—demographic, social, political, and financial. In domestic finance many of the environmental factors that influence the outcome of financial decisions are reasonably well known and understood, since all of these are influenced and guided by the political and economic objectives of one government. By contrast, when international financial problems are considered, their outcome is influenced by many environmental factors whose complexities increase, the larger the number of countries that are involved in the firm's operations. It is a task of major proportions to understand the motivation and functioning of a large number of foreign governments. By comparison it is less difficult to achieve an understanding of one's own government—its goals and desires over an extended period of time. On a domestic basis the rules of the game are better understood, so that business policies can be shaped to coincide with the aims of one's own government. But the same is not true when operating on an international basis.

301

Demographic environmental factors strongly influence the success or failure of a foreign business enterprise. The problems of vertical as well as horizontal mobility of the population and the social structure of the national society must be considered. In many foreign countries the existing social structure prevents the upward movement of workers in the ranks of management as they acquire additional skills. The resistance or aversion to individuals moving from one stratum to a higher one is strongest where the separations between classes in the population are severe. For this reason the multinational firm must exercise caution and care when initially hiring its work force. A firm must recognize that in some foreign countries it cannot always follow the U.S. custom of advancing people directly as a result of increased competence.

A multinational firm must also be aware of the social legislation existing in a country of intended operations, since the cost attached to this legislation often strongly affects the profitability of the planned enterprise. Social security taxes equal to 30 percent of payroll are not unusual in many foreign countries. In addition, many countries require the payment of an annual bonus, usually at Christmas time, that has no relation to profitability of the venture. Required annual vacations in many countries are also longer than customary in the United States. In the majority of foreign countries a native employee, after his initial probationary period, has to be paid a severance payment of 1 month per year of service for the first 10 years and 2 months per year of service for all years thereafter.

In the United States the laws, rules, and regulations that the government issues are generally obeyed and adhered to by business. This is not so in many foreign countries. In some, national businesses will deliberately ignore existing laws, making every effort to avoid their effect. However, a foreign-owned firm would not dare follow these same practices, because a foreign-owned firm is judged differently from those owned by nationals of the country. The employment of competent local attorneys and accountants will usually avoid possible mistakes in the observance of laws, rules, and regulations that apply to the operations of the foreign-owned business entity. With the help of these local experts it is quite often possible to obtain a better understanding of the foreign government's attitude towards business and particularly that which is foreign owned.

INTERNATIONAL TRANSACTIONS AND THE BALANCE OF PAYMENTS

The nature of exchange rates and the characteristics of foreign exchange markets were presented as background for use in later analysis. The nature of primary transactions in international trade and finance was analyzed as a basis for understanding how they are reflected in the balance-of-payments accounts. The use of the balance-of-payments statement as a tool of analysis, planning, and forecasting by financial managers was set forth. We have presented the basic framework for understanding the key terminology and mechanisms needed for developing managerial policies in international business finance.

The export of goods by the United States represents a plus or a credit in the U.S. balance of payments. If the foreigner pays by increasing the deposits of U.S. banks in foreign countries, this represents an increase in U.S. claims on foreigners. It represents an extension of credit by the United States and may be regarded as the import of an IOU obligation of foreigners. It is, therefore, a debit. If, on the other hand, the export of goods is offset by a decrease in the liabilities of the U.S. banks to foreigners, this decrease represents a reduction in credit extended by the United States. It represents an import of an IOU obligation of the United States and therefore also represents a debit.

Similarly, if the United States imports goods, this represents a minus or a debit. If payment is made by decreasing U.S. deposits in foreign banks, this represents a reexport or cancellation of an IOU by the United States. Or, alternatively, the imports could be made by increasing the liability of U.S. banks. This represents an increase in credit obligations incurred—thus it represents an export of an IOU or an import of capital and represents a credit to the U.S. balance-of-payments account.

What is the meaning of the balance of payments? In one sense, the balance of payments is always in balance—the debits always equal the credits. But in another sense the balance of payments is an analytical tool for studying the trends in a nation's economic and financial positions. Six concepts of balance of payments are currently employed by the United States Department of Commerce. These are: (1) balance on goods and services, (2) balance on goods, services, and remittances, (3) balance on current account, (4) balance on current account and long-term capital, (5) net liquidity balance, and (6) official reserve transactions balance. Analysis of the relation between these measures of "balance of payments" yields information on the pattern of trade and capital flows taking place. Such study will provide a barometer, or a basis, for forecasting changes in a nation's foreign exchange position, the exchange rates, its policies with regard to convertibility of its currency, freedom to import and export goods, as well as the freedom of currency to move in and out of its national boundaries.

THE RISKS OF INTERNATIONAL BUSINESS FINANCE

The principal risks of international managerial finance discussed were commercial risk, political risk, and foreign exchange rate risk. The risks of foreign investment differ both in degree and kind from the risks of domestic investment. Differential rates of inflation have a major impact on the profitability of operations. Changes in foreign exchange rates and devaluation may also have a number of effects.

Exchange controls also have an impact. The ability to transfer funds from one country to another may be constrained. Exchange controls may involve a number of different kinds of exchange rates. These greatly complicate the problems of determining the real cost of raw materials and parts that are imported, as well as the effective prices that are realized from sales by a foreign manufacturing operation. Finally, the commitment of investment funds abroad makes a firm a hostage to the political and legal environment of the host country. Such investments become vulnerable to many forms of indirect and direct expropriation.

Two sets of measures for dealing with these risks may be used. First are insurance and guarantee programs for commercial and political risks. Second are three financial techniques to minimize foreign exchange rate risk: (1) forward contracts, (2) currency swaps, and (3) monetary balance.

INSURANCE AND GUARANTEE PROGRAMS IN INTERNATIONAL FINANCE

Foreign credit insurance and guarantees

Insurance policies are available from the Foreign Credit Insurance Association (FCIA) for short-term credit sales of less than 6 months covering the sale of consumer goods and for medium-term transactions of from 181 days to normally 5 years, involving transactions in capital or producer's goods. Terms up to 7 years are available in order to meet foreign competition.

The cost of this insurance protection varies with the country of destination, the length of the credit period, and the credit worthiness of the foreign buyer or his credit institution (which may or may not guarantee that obligations incurred will be met at the end of the credit period). A two-month confirmed irrevocable letter of credit transaction will carry a very much lower premium than an open account transaction for a one-year term. In the same way among medium-term export sales a transaction guaranteed by a foreign bank for its customer over a one-year period will call for a very much lower premium than an open account transaction without credit guarantee for a period of five to seven years.

Insurance policies may be obtained on a comprehensive basis covering both commercial and political risk, or they may be had on a political-risk-only basis, as desired by the exporter. There are times when it is more advantageous to cover an export transaction with comprehensive coverage rather than political-risk-only coverage. Political-risk-only coverage costs about 70 percent as much as comprehensive coverage, but the latter includes protection against the inability of the foreign buyer to purchase the currency needed to discharge his obligation.

The principal advantage of obtaining commercial- and political-risk insurance is that it makes possible the financing of foreign export transactions at lower costs. This is a particular advantage to the small multinational firm or exporter who may need the FCIA insurance in order to be able to finance foreign exports with normal commercial banking sources. When these transactions cannot be financed with a commercial bank, the financing usually proves to be much more expensive. It is for this reason that quite often the difference in costs of various forms of financing will determine the advantage and/or desirability of obtaining commercial as well as political-risk coverage.

A number of new insurance programs have been made available since 1967 by the Foreign Credit Insurance Association in conjunction with the Export-Import Bank. Among these are a castrophe policy which is designed for high-volume, low-profit exporters and as such usually covers only the political risks involved. Under this policy premiums are relatively low due to the fact that the U.S. exporter assumes a larger share of the risk than is the case with normal policies. In other words, it is a policy designed to protect the excess of risk rather than all of the risk. A comprehensive master policy has also been made available which is worldwide in scope. Under this policy, a U.S. exporter is able to obtain certain specified buyer limits for all of his customers, an arrangement under which he can make credit decisions up to these limits without resorting to the FCIA or Export-Import Bank for an evaluation. After the transactions have taken place, at regular intervals his credit transactions are evaluated. However, he does have the opportunity to proceed with his business transactions without unnecessary delays.

A small business exporter policy was also initiated during the last several years in order to encourage many American firms to engage in foreign exports that had previously not done so. Under this policy a minimum amount of paper work is required. The rates are reasonable, and protection nearly automatic. However, these policies are limited to small firms whose volume of exports is less than $200,000 per year and who have not been in the export business for more than two years.

The Export-Import Bank of the United States as a U.S. government-owned corporation makes available all of the political-risk insurance contained in the comprehensive policies and reinsures the commercial risk coverage in large policies. However, in addition to this cooperation with the Foreign Credit Insurance Association, the Export-Import Bank by itself will cover export transactions of a medium-term nature where the Export-Import Bank will issue comprehensive and political-risk-only policies which will enable the exporter to finance his transactions with normal credit sources. In connection with this activity the Export-Import Bank will often make direct guarantees to the exporter's lender.

The new OPIC program

The Overseas Private Investment Corporation (OPIC) was organized January 19, 1971, when it assumed responsibility over the major portion of investment guarantees formerly offered by AID. The purpose of this corporation is to mobilize and facilitate the participation of U.S. private capital and skills in the economic and social progress of less developed friendly countries and areas, thereby complementing the development assistance objectives of the United States.

In order to carry out its investment incentive programs, OPIC is authorized to do the following:

1. Investment insurance:
   a) Issue investment insurance in the instance of approved projects to protect against:
      (1) Inability to convert into U.S. dollars credits or proceeds from earnings or profits from approved projects, or funds for the repayment or return of invested amounts, or the sale or disposition in whole or in part of the funds invested.
      (2) The loss of the investment in approved projects in whole or in part if due to expropriation or confiscation on the part of the foreign government.
      (3) Any loss due to war, revolution, or insurrection.
   b) Join other governments in the issuance of investment insurance in the case of projects financed by investors of various nationalities, providing that OPIC's coverage of risks is not greater than the participation of eligible U.S. investors.
2. Investment guarantees: Issue investment guarantees against loss to eligible investors in the case of loans and other investments due to risks and on such terms as determined by OPIC.
3. Direct investments: Make loans in U.S. dollars, or such foreign currencies as the Secretary of the Treasury may determine to be in excess, to firms privately or privately and publicly owned. OPIC is not permitted to purchase stock of any kind except convertible debt securities which are not permitted to be converted during the period of OPIC's ownership. No loans may be made to finance development or extraction of mineral resources.
4. Investment encouragement: Initiate, support, and participate in investigations seeking out private investment opportunities outside of the area of natural resource development.

5. Special activities: Administer and manage special projects designed to develop human resources, capital savings, and intermediate financial and investment institutions.

As a result of the above, OPIC is presently offering the following:

1. Incentives to investors, including insurance against loss due to specific political risks of currency inconvertibility; expropriation; and war, revolution, or insurrection.
2. Financial assistance through (1) guarantees against loss from commercial as well as political risk; (2) direct loans in dollars or foreign currencies; and (3) preinvestment information, counseling, and cost sharing.

OPIC-assisted investment must be financially sound new investments or expansions of existing projects in lower income countries. They should be competitive, approved by the local government, and must contribute to the social and economic progress of the country.

During the time when the Agency for International Development was issuing specific risk investment guarantees, these guarantees did not cover profits resulting from the investment. However, this feature was added by OPIC at the time it took over the foreign investment guarantees from AID. The Agency for International Development has continued to insure Latin American housing projects on an extended-risk basis. This means that these projects are insured against the risks of nonconvertibility, confiscation, and war, and that the policies are such that they protect profits up to 100 percent of the cost of the investment. The cost for this type of policy is approximately 2 percent per year.

MANAGEMENT OF FOREIGN EXCHANGE RATE RISKS

Exchange rate risk protection can be achieved by three methods: (1) forward contracts, (2) foreign currency swaps, and (3) monetary balance.

Forward contracts

Contracts to purchase or sell a foreign currency on a forward basis in terms of the U.S. dollar can be obtained for all developed countries and a number of the more stable developing countries. Forward contracts fix a definite dollar value for foreign currency payments or receipts that are scheduled to take place at the end of the forward contract period. Forward contracts are usually available on a 30-, 60-, 90-, or 180-day basis. Under special conditions it is sometimes possible to negotiate forward contracts for a longer term of up to two years.

The cost of this protection is the premium or discount that is required over the spot rate—the exchange ratio in effect when the forward contract is purchased. The premium or discount required varies from 0 to 2 or 3 percent per annum for reasonably stable currencies. For currencies undergoing devaluation in excess of 4 to 5 percent per year, discounts required may be as high as 15 to 20 percent per year. When risk of future devaluation exceeds 20 percent per year, forward contracts are usually no longer available.

Since members of the financial communities in the two countries are usually well informed as to the future expectancy of the forward exchange value of their respective currencies, the premiums or discounts quoted are very closely related to the probable occurrence of changes in the exchange rates. Therefore, the forward market is chiefly used as protection against *unexpected* changes in the foreign exchange value of a currency.

The foreign currency swap

When investments are made in a foreign country in terms of its local currency and under conditions of substantial currency devaluation, the foreign currency swap provides an effective hedge. The currency swap can prevent the erosion of the dollar value of the invested funds during the swap period. It also presents an advantageous alternative to the borrowing of local currency funds on the part of a foreign subsidiary, since interest rates in countries of unstable currencies are usually very high. Whether it is profitable or not to use swaps depends upon the probable degree of exchange rate deterioration of the local currency compared with the effective costs of obtaining a swap arrangement.

Monetary balance

As a general rule, branches and foreign subsidiaries of U.S. firms operating in foreign areas are monetary creditors. Among their assets are cash in the foreign currencies and accounts receivable from foreign customers. Indebtedness, if any, is usually owed the parent company in terms of the foreign currency. Therefore, the achievement of monetary balance requires the borrowing of foreign currency and the spending of these funds for business purposes. The cost of obtaining monetary balance is the interest that must be paid on the borrowed funds.

The benefits of monetary balance result from the fact that if there is any downward change in the value of the foreign currency in relation to the U.S. dollar, losses incurred due to the possession of monetary assets are balanced by profits resulting from the possession of an equal amount of monetary liabilities. U.S. firms are well advised to have their branches and subsidiaries operate on a monetary debtor basis in countries with an inflationary bias. Conversely, prior to the recent shift in exchange rates, it would have been desirable for U.S. firms to have their subsidiaries in Western Europe on a net monetary creditor basis.

ACCOUNTING TREATMENT OF FOREIGN OPERATIONS

The same concepts of monetary balance just discussed are the key to accounting policies for foreign operations. Of particular significance at the present time is that "international companies with investments and affiliates abroad must translate their foreign financial results into dollars in their annual consolidated reports to shareholders."[1] It appears that the

TABLE 14–1

Direction of the exchange adjustment account as a function of the position of the foreign subsidiary

	Net monetary position of foreign subsidiary	
	Net monetary debtor	*Net monetary creditor*
Devaluation of parent country currency relative to the currency of the foreign country in which the subsidiary is located.................	Downward	Upward
Revaluation upward of parent country currency relative to the currency of the foreign country in which the subsidiary is located..........	Upward	Downward

Accounting Principles Board will follow the "so-called monetary rule that provides for restatement of all balance sheet items that have a specific dollar value."[2]

The Accounting Principles Board is further recommending that after calculating a "loss" or "exchange adjustment" due to inflation and new exchange rates, the full amount will not be charged in the year in which reported. The total of these "exchange adjustments" will be deferred over the life of the debt involved.

The application of the net monetary rule which is being proposed provides for the following: Real assets, inventories, and fixed assets are translated at the exchange rate at the date of acquisition. Monetary assets and liabilities are translated at the current exchange rate. There will be an exchange adjustment in the net worth of the subsidiary upward or downward as shown in the pattern of relationships shown in Table 14–1.

---

[1] Charles N. Stabler, "Accounting Panel, in Reversal, Now Favors Deferring Losses in Dollar Cheapening," *The Wall Street Journal,* December 15, 1971, p. 2.

[2] Ibid.

When the value of the currency of the country of the parent company increases in relation to the value of the currency of the foreign country in which the subsidiary is located, the revaluation adjustment in the net worth of the foreign subsidiary will be upward if the subsidiary is in a net monetary debtor position and downward if the subsidiary is in a net monetary creditor position. When the value of the currency of the parent country is decreased in relation to the value of the currency of the foreign country in which the foreign subsidiary is located, the net worth revaluation adjustment for the subsidiary is downward if the subsidiary is in a net monetary debtor position and upward when the subsidiary is in a net monetary creditor position.

Accounting practice is not uniform with regard to the treatment of inflation in individual countries. Conceptually, current operations should be charged with the current costs of the use of both fixed assets and inventories. With respect to inventories, this is accomplished by using the last-in, first-out (Lifo) method. This charges current operations with the most recent cost of inventories and results in balance sheet values of inventories at historical costs. With regard to fixed assets, a number of countries make provision for writing up their values based on a government index. The higher value is used as a basis for reducing taxable income by increasing the depreciation deduction. This avoids applying taxation to overstated profits.

A rise in the value of a nation's currency is not necessarily an unmitigated gain or benefit for each individual company. The situation of the Volkswagen Company in 1970 is a good illustration. The statement of Mr. Lotz, the outgoing chairman of Volkswagen in this connection, is of interest. He states, "thus Volkswagen says the 9.3 percent upward revaluation of the mark against other currencies in late 1969 cost the company $65.6 million in 1970"—a major reason, along with rising production costs, for a profit decline that year. Similarly, Mr. Lotz has said that "in the present currency float, every percentage point the mark rises against its mark-dollar parity would cost the company $19 million a year."[3]

GOVERNMENT POLICIES AND RULES AFFECTING INTERNATIONAL BUSINESS

We discussed the government rules and regulations applicable to international business. These rules affect (1) the flow of funds in connection with business transactions, (2) the import and export of needed materials, and finally (3) the taxation of the income of the subsidiaries or branches of multinational firms.

Since August 15, 1971, there is hardly a country that still permits the

---

[3] Lorana O. Sullivan, "The Battered Beetle," *The Wall Street Journal,* September 23, 1971, p. 1.

free and unhindered inflow and outflow of funds, be it for short-term or long-term investments. In the majority of the developed countries of Europe, domestically owned funds are still not permitted to flow freely from one country to another. Only foreign-owned funds have this privilege. If the problems of the balance of payments of certain nations of the world do not materially improve, it is likely that the free flow of funds across international boundaries will be further restricted.

Governments, including that of the United States, will continue their efforts to increase exports in order to improve their foreign balance-of-payments position. The majority of developing nations control the outflow of foreign exchange and regulate the demand for foreign exchange by control over imports. In many developing countries, foreign exchange can only be obtained through commercial banks, which require the permission of the central bank. Under conditions of severe foreign exchange shortage, the multinational firm is in an excellent position to propose to the national government in the country in which one of its branches or subsidiaries is operating that the U.S. firm may be able to supply a much-needed import without any burden on the other country's foreign exchange position by the foreign country working out a barter arrangement with the U.S. subsidiary. It is also possible at times to obtain permission to import certain spare parts that are needed in an operation by furnishing these parts to the branch or subsidiary on a no-charge basis.

A multinational firm must keep fully abreast of any change in rules and regulations as they are issued by various national governments as these governments strive to increase the volume of their exports. A case in point is the creation by the United States of the Domestic International Sales Corporation (DISC), which was included in the Revenue Bill of 1971. The principal purpose of DISC is to facilitate export of U.S. goods and services by making this more attractive to American firms from a tax point of view.

Taxation of international business

On an almost uniform basis, all countries tax income that has been derived from sources within their borders. The profits resulting from the operation of productive assets within a country are always taxed by the government of that country.

The negative impact of double taxation on international business was early recognized by the United States. In order to remove the inequity, the U.S. government entered into tax treaties with the governments of many trading nations of the world which spell out the rights of their citizens and the taxes that apply as they conduct business ventures in or with each other's countries. Tax treaties and conventions usually define the terms of residence, nationality, domicile, and control.

The Revenue Act of 1962 has greatly affected the foreign operations of

American businesses. The provisions of the Revenue Act of 1962 may be generally divided into two groups: (1) those affecting business operations in foreign countries and (2) those affecting foreign portfolio investments or the foreign income of individuals.

Definition of control of a foreign corporation

A U.S.-controlled foreign corporation (CFC) is any foreign corporation in which more than 50 percent of the total combined voting power is owned or deemed to be owned by U.S. shareholders, each owning 10 percent or more of the voting stock of such foreign corporation. Thus the Revenue Act of 1962 classifies American shareholders in foreign corporations into two groups, those holding less than a 10 percent interest and those holding 10 percent or more of the outstanding shares of the foreign corporation.

The control of a first-tier foreign corporation is judged on the basis of percentage of ownership of its common shares, whereas the ownership of subsidiaries and sub-subsidiaries of this foreign corporation are judged on the basis of value of ownership.

Income subject to taxation prior to remission of dividends

If it has been determined, upon the basis of the considerations described above, that a U.S. person (this includes corporations since corporations are treated as "persons" in law) controls a foreign corporation, certain forms of income of the foreign corporation are subject to taxation to the U.S. person prior to the actual receipt of income from the CFC.

To avoid tax deferment, the Revenue Act of 1962 identified certain forms of income regarded as characteristically involved in such foreign-based company devices for deferment of income realization. These types of income were discussed in a section of the Internal Revenue Code at paragraphs identified as "subpart F," so have been referred to as "subpart F income." Subpart F income has also been called "foreign-based company income." If a foreign corporation's subpart F income is less than 30 percent of its total income, it is not taxed as such. If the subpart F income is equal to or greater than 70 percent, all of the firm's income is considered subpart F income. Percentages in between are taxed on the actual percent of subpart F income to the total.

The "foreign-based company income" which is subject to U.S. taxation before remission in the forms of dividends consists of three main categories: (1) foreign personal holding company income, (2) foreign-based company sales income, and (3) foreign-based company service income. Each of these forms of income in the case of a U.S.-controlled foreign corporation is defined in the tax code.

Certain items received from unrelated persons are not treated as sub-part F income. These are rents and royalties derived in the active conduct of the business. Examples are rents received by a corporation in the real estate renting business; dividends, interest, and gains received by those in the banking and finance business; and dividends, interests, and gains received by an insurance company from investments of its reserves.

Treatment of capital gains as ordinary income

The Reveue Act of 1962 provides further that when stock in a U.S.-controlled foreign corporation is sold, or the corporation is liquidated, the benefits due the U.S. shareholder who is the owner of more than 10 per-cent of the outstanding shares are considered as dividend income (rather than a capital gain) even though the investment was held in excess of six months. Under these provisions, any gain up to the proportional part of the profits made by the controlled corporation during the period of ownership of the stock is treated as dividend income. Any gain above this amount is taxed on a capital gains basis.

Requirement of use of the gross-up method

In the calculation of U.S. tax liability, the Internal Revenue Act of 1962 made another change. It required that U.S. persons use a gross-up basis for reporting foreign earned income, in which the foreign taxes are added to the net after-tax foreign income received for reporting income for U.S. tax purposes.

The United States taxes the income of U.S. citizens and corporations irrespective of where their income is earned or received, with few excep-tions. This applies even to U.S. noncitizen residents who have foreign source incomes, even though they may have no income from within the United States. An exception, however, is made in the case of nonresident U.S. citizens in regard to earned foreign income. Under these provisions, a U.S. citizen earning his livelihood and being at the same time resident in a foreign country for a period in excess of 510 "full" days within 18 months is not taxed on the earned income obtained in his country of residence. The internal revenue rules limit this exclusion to $20,000 per year during the first three years and $25,000 per year thereafter. How-ever, such a U.S. citizen residing in a foreign area must still report and pay taxes on all "nonearned" income such as royalties, dividends, and interest.

Some further exceptions are made in the case of income resulting from investments in U.S. possessions and Puerto Rico. If a U.S. corporation derives more than 80 percent of its gross income from sources within a possession for a three-year period, and if for such period 50 percent or more of the gross income is derived from the active conduct of a trade or business within a possession of the United States, then such income is not subject to U.S. taxes until it is received within the United States in the form of dividends.

Another exception to normal tax methods of taxation is offered by the *Western Hemisphere Trade Corporation.* This business entity was created by the Revenue Act of 1942, which provides that the maximum marginal tax rate is 38 percent instead of the usual 48 percent. This decrease in taxation results from a special credit against net income. A Western Hemisphere Trade Corporation is defined as being a domestic corporation that conducts all of its business in the western hemisphere and obtains 95 percent of its gross income from sources outside of the United States and 90 percent or more of its gross income from the active conduct of a trade or business venture. This type of organization was created as a result of an effort on the part of the U.S. government to encourage trade with Latin America after World War II.

Domestic International Sales Corporations

The Revenue Act of 1971 permitted the establishment of Domestic International Sales Corporations (DISC). The purpose of these U.S.-incorporated firms is the encouragement and expansion of U.S. exports by the deferral of one half of the income taxes on the income of a DISC related to export activity. The DISC does not pay any income taxes; its shareholders pay its income tax for it, but only on one half of the qualified export-related income.

A corporation can qualify as a DISC if certain precise conditions are met. Limitations are imposed on the profits that a DISC may make to avoid shifting profits arbitrarily by the parent to the DISC by the method of transfer pricing employed. The most advantageous of the alternative definitions of profits listed below may be chosen:

1. Profits may be equal to 4.5 percent of qualified export sales plus 10 percent of the DISC's export promotional expenditures.
2. DISC profits may be 50 percent of the profits of both the DISC and the parent that are export related plus 10 percent of the export promotional expenses.
3. DISC may claim all of the profits related to all marginally produced export goods. That is, the DISC may claim credit for all increases in export volume over previous levels. Administrative rules are expected to be issued to clarify this alternative but have not been issued as yet.
4. DISCs may claim all of the profits on export sales of goods that have been transferred to it on an arm's length basis.

If a DISC pays a dividend from tax-deferred earnings, this is fully taxable without the usual dividend credit applying in the instance of corporate shareholders.

INSTITUTIONS AND INSTRUMENTS OF
INTERNATIONAL BUSINESS FINANCE

The financial manager seeking to contribute to the progress of his firm in international business can draw on a broad range of financing sources: (1) international lending agencies, (2) national development banks, (3) domestic financing sources, (4) financing forms distinctive to international business finance, and (5) Eurodollar and Eurobond financing.

Of considerable importance for financing international business are the operations of the international financing agencies. We described seven.

World Bank group:
1. International Bank for Reconstruction and Development (IBRD).
2. International Finance Corporation (IFC).
3. International Development Association (IDA).

Regional lending agencies:
1. Inter-American Development Bank (IDB).
2. Asian Development Bank (ADB).
3. European Investment Bank (EIB).
4. African Development Bank (AFDB).

Since their organization at various years following the end of World War II, international lending sources have committed an accumulated total of the equivalent of some $20 billion to finance projects and programs which have enhanced the opportunity for U.S. business to make foreign sales. These loans, in turn, have stimulated a substantial amount of investment by other sources, public and private, and thus have further increased international business potentials.

All of these international lending agencies offer opportunities for financing by foreign buyers, either directly or indirectly. In addition, they facilitate financing by the sellers of the goods. Thus, the operations of these international financing agencies have great significance for financial managers for a number of reasons. First, the magnitude of their operations involves very substantial sums of money. Second, often a sizable sale by an American company will be financed either directly or indirectly through the operation of one of these agencies. Third, the economic development stimulated by these international lending agencies may stimulate, with some lead time, further business activity offering opportunities for U.S. firms. This provides a chance for attractive returns made possible by effective longer range planning for entering the international field. The financial manager has an important contribution to make in such long-range planning activities.

Decisions by international firms on alternative forms, sources, timing, and the place of financing are influenced by a large number of variables. Of primary importance are the characteristics of the individual firms themselves. Important considerations are the products produced and sold, the firm's absolute size, its share of the markets in which its products are sold, the age of the firm, and the stage in the life cycle of its growth as influenced by the product that it sells. In addition, the life cycles of industries and changes in general economic environmental conditions will influence the cost of financing. These represent both opportunities and challenges to the financial manager.

Some financing operations are distinctive to international business finance. A form of commercial bank financing widely used in Europe is represented by overdrafts. An overdraft agreement permits a customer to draw checks up to some specified maximum limit. The practice is similar to a line of credit arrangement in the United States.

Another form of financing which was until recent years much more widespread in Europe than in the United States was the discounting of "trade bills" in both domestic and foreign transactions. The increased use of banker's acceptances in the United States has been associated with the growth of the movement of goods in international trade.

A third variation from U.S. financing practices is the broader participation of commercial banks in medium- and long-term lending activities found in Europe. In Europe commercial banks carry on considerable activity of the kind that would be described as investment banking in the United States. However, the Banking Act of 1933 required the divestiture of investing banking operations by commercial banks in the United States. This difference, then, results from a legal requirement.

A fourth financial practice distinctive to international financing relates to arbi-loans and link financing, both of which represent forms of equalizing the supply of and demand for loanable funds in relation to sensitive interest rate levels among different countries. Under arbi-loans or international interest arbitrage financing, a borrower obtains loans in a country where the supply of funds is relatively abundant. These borrowings are then converted into the required local currency. Simultaneously the borrower enters into a forward exchange contract to protect himself on the reconversion of the local currency into the foreign currency that will be required at the time the loan must be repaid. Commercial banks are typically involved in the arbi-loan transactions both as lenders and as intermediaries in the foreign exchange trading.

In link financing the commercial banks take an even more direct role. A lender in a foreign country deposits funds with a bank in the borrower's country where interest rates are higher. This deposit may be earmarked for a specified borrower, or it may be channeled through a money broker to borrowers of good credit standing. In the latter case, the foreign lender generally receives a portion of the broker's premium in addition to the interest rate differential. The lender, of course, would be expected to hedge his position in the foreign exchange markets, since he will be repaid in the currency of the country in which the bank deposit was made. Because of the risk associated with foreign lending and with foreign exchange fluctuations, the maturity of link-financing transactions would be expected to be short term, with the possibility of renewal at maturity.

U.S. industry must finance its foreign operations from credit sources mainly outside the United States. The major sources of the financing of foreign operations have been new debt issues, loans from internal and domestic banks, and trade credits, in addition to internal funds. The variations and combinations of these are virtually infinite.

Some American companies use local sources of financing in the individual countries where their financing needs exist. In functioning in local financial markets, a company must conform to the regulations established by each individual government, which controls the financial practices within its own national market. Generally, most countries impose restrictions on the amount of local currency financing that can be obtained by U.S. industry. This is generally a function of the percentage of local ownership involved in the operations. With the weakening of the U.S. dollar abroad in recent years, there is an increasing tendency for many large, multinational companies to tap the capital markets in Germany, Switzerland, and the Netherlands. All of these have been able to provide medium-term sources of capital at coupon rates below those of the Eurobond market.

The Eurocurrency market offers a number of advantages to the affiliate of the U.S. company seeking financing abroad. The Eurocurrency market encompasses any currency which is available in the international marketplace to finance U.S. industries. The choice may be among dollars, pounds, French francs, Swiss francs, Deutsche marks, or Dutch guilders. The analysis must take into consideration the exchange rate risks as well as interest costs. Available in European currency is a variety of types of financing. The method of financing that has been a major source of financing by individual business firms has been bank credit lines under a medium-term commitment, with interest rates tied to the cost of deposits to Eurocurrency market banks. An operating and profit margin is added to the cost of time deposits paid by these Eurocurrency market banks. Historically, the revolving Eurodollar or Eurocurrency credit line has ranged from one to five years. Medium-term credits, of course, are most appropriate to finance temporary working capital. They are not appropriate for financing long-term investments.

These revolving credits have generally been arranged on a syndicated basis through London-based banking houses or the London branches of the large U.S. banks. Credit obtained in the Eurocurrency market is arranged through European banking houses. The objective is not only to raise funds but also to develop relationships with banking houses in a number of countries to provide various forms of assistance to the firm's operations in those local countries.

Commercial paper, as a vehicle for providing Eurocurrency finance to U.S. industry, has been growing. This represents a recent major breakthrough which has enabled U.S. industry to tap capital in the hands of private foreign investors. This enables the private investors to purchase short-dated debt notes of the U.S. borrower. The Eurocurrency commercial paper market has grown to the point where some 15 issuing companies have been utilizing it. All of them have at least an A Bond rating in the United States. Their commercial paper has been successfully placed at rates of interest which are consistently below the interest cost associated with borrowing under the Eurodollar revolving bank credit line.

Subsidiaries which engage in international financing to raise funds abroad are widely used. The major reason U.S. companies adopt this financing vehicle is that interest payments made to foreign lending institutions from U.S.-based companies are subject to a 30 percent U.S. withholding tax. This tax can be eliminated or reduced, however, depending upon reciprocal tax treaties between the U.S. and the country of the lending bank. This problem can be completely overcome, however, by establishing an international financing subsidiary. The best known of these are domiciled in Delaware and the Netherlands Antilles.

The Eurobond market is a very important segment of the Eurocurrency market. It is available in a range of currencies both on a straight debt basis and through the use of convertible securities. The Eurobonds are usually denominated in dollars, have a fixed maturity between 12 to 15 years, with annual sinking fund requirements commencing after two to four years. In recent years increasing use has been made of convertible securities. This has enabled large U.S. companies to borrow at rates of interest of $4\frac{1}{2}$ percent or lower.

FINANCIAL INSTRUMENTS AND POLICIES IN CONNECTION WITH EXPORT TRANSACTIONS

The commercial letter of credit reduces the risk of the seller in connection with foreign export transactions. In fact, the commercial letter of credit may be used by a seller to finance the acquisition or manufacture of goods to be sold. Commercial letters of credit are issued either on an irrevocable or revocable basis. A revocable letter of credit may be revoked by the issuing bank should the credit worthiness of the foreign buyer deteriorate during the term for which the credit has been extended. An irrevocable letter of credit, on the other hand, may not be revoked by an issuing bank. It usually specifies the drawing of sight or time drafts in the currency of the seller, the buyer, or a third country, and cannot be canceled by the opening bank. The strongest commercial letter of credit is a confirmed, irrevocable letter of credit where the payment of drafts issued in connection with the export transaction is guaranteed, not only by the opening bank but also by a confirming bank, usually located in the country of the seller. A commercial letter of credit which does not involve a notifying or confirming bank is known as a circular commercial letter of credit. It is sent by the opening bank directly to the seller, who may discount or sell the drafts involved to any bank that wishes to buy them. In this instance, the credit worthiness of the transaction is based entirely on the credit worthiness of the foreign opening bank.

The instruments of foreign trade make possible an infinite variety of payment terms suited to the needs of a particular transaction. At one extreme, the risks of the exporter may be completely eliminated by insisting on cash payment in dollars prior to the shipment of goods. At the other extreme, the risks may all be borne by the seller when he agrees to sell export merchandise in terms of a foreign currency and on an open account basis. In between these extremes there are all possible variations.

U.S. banks are prohibited from financing bills of exchange and banker's acceptances with maturity in excess of six months. However, in order to compete more effectively with foreign financial institutions, many U.S. commercial banks formed Edge Act financing subsidiaries which are permitted to engage in export financing in excess of 180 days.

PL 480 funds are blocked foreign currency owned by the U.S. government resulting from the sale of surplus agricultural commodities to foreign governments. U.S. exporters may use these funds to develop and expand foreign markets for U.S. agricultural products, as well as for purposes of business development and trade expansion. In order to take advantage of the availability of these blocked funds, the U.S. exporter is required to have some sort of an operating organization within the country where these blocked funds exist.

PROJECT EVALUATION IN FOREIGN
INVESTMENT DECISIONS

The basic principles are the same in project evaluation for foreign investment decisions as in domestic investment decisions. Hence, the same general pattern of analysis applies. This involves comparing cash inflows and outflows of the project and applying a relevant cost of capital to determine its net present value. With no capital rationing, for independent investments, all projects with net present value are accepted. For mutually exclusive investments, the project with the highest net present value is selected. With capital rationing, mathematical programming techniques must be used to achieve a formally correct decision.

Project analysis

For project analysis of foreign investment decisions, at least three aspects are distinctive: (1) the range of variables to be considered in the analysis is expanded; (2) the estimates of both inflows and outflows may be subject to wider margins of error; and (3) the analysis of risks and returns is likely to be more complex. The broad outlines of the patterns for project analysis of foreign direct investments parallel those for domestic investments. Some distinctive elements reflect the characteristics of foreign investments. Some elements of cost are introduced in the cash outflow section which are characteristic of foreign investments. Costs of hedging against foreign exchange losses may represent use of the forward exchange markets or the use of swaps. In addition, costs of insuring against expropriation may be required. Additional taxes in the foreign country may also be involved. These include local fees and taxes on income and withholding taxes on dividends. An additional cost to the subsidiary may be supervisory fees charged by the parent company. However, such fees may also be involved in parent-subsidiary relations in domestic investments as well.

Sometimes in the establishment of a foreign subsidiary it may be advantageous for the parent company to transfer used equipment from its domestic operations. The used equipment may provide an adequate volume of operations for its foreign demand. This may enable the parent to substitute new and modern equipment for its domestic operations, realizing higher salvage values than otherwise possible for the older equipment. The used equipment may have a depreciated value in the accounting records of $200,000. However, the opportunity costs of acquiring such equipment in Mexico is (for illustration) $500,000. Hence the appropriate charge to the project is $500,000.

The asset acquisition requirements will then be reflected in the summary inflow and outflow analysis. Additional items involved in foreign investments may also be noted. The firm may have been exporting instruments from its U.S. or other manufacturing operations. Some of the sales of the new subsidiary may substitute for these export sales. Hence an item is introduced to reflect this offset—the after-tax decline in cash flows resulting from the decline in export sales resulting from the substitution of sales by the new foreign subsidiary.

In addition, foreign investments represent the application of management know-how to the new project. This represents the utilization of important capabilities built up over a period of years, representing an important organizational investment. A portion of this know-how is inevitably shared with the nationals who will be employed in operating the foreign plant. A portion of this investment know-how is likely to be "used up" in various ways in the foreign operation. Hence, it is appropriate to charge the investment with a portion of this valuable accumulated investment in know-how. The pattern of the analysis then follows the standard form for capital budgeting decision models.

Risk considerations in project analysis

Risk considerations are especially important in foreign investment decisions. Hence, the models for the treatment of investment under uncertainty take on special importance. Because of the wider range and severity of possible risks in the foreign environment, that can only be partially hedged or insured against, the range of possible outcomes may be much greater for the foreign investment.

The appropriate procedure is to set forth the cumulative NPVs that would occur under alternative possible future states and outcomes for the investment project. A firm must consider expected returns, and the dispersion of expected returns as measured by the variance and standard deviation of alternative outcomes. Thus, on a return-risk basis some different choice combinations may be involved. Domestic investments are likely to offer lower expected returns and lower standard deviations; foreign investments offer higher expected returns and higher standard deviations of possible returns.

WORKING CAPITAL MANAGEMENT IN INTERNATIONAL ENTERPRISE

For multinational business enterprise short-term finance functions take on increased significance. The multinational firm operates in a wide diversity of environment and obtains financing from a wide diversity of sources. While some degree of autonomy may be granted to international subsidiaries, at some point the financing activities must be coordinated at central headquarters of the multinational enterprise. Tax considerations, investment decisions, and cash-flow management must be centralized. Management information systems take on increased importance. To control cash throughout its operations, the multinational firm requires frequent reports from subsidiaries to headquarters. Some firms have established "mobilization points" as centers for transferring funds on a semi-decentralized basis.

Multinational corporate treasurers must achieve efficient worldwide corporate cash management. Large multinational banks have expanded their operations to provide services to multinational corporations to this end. They help to achieve maximum speed in moving funds. They cooperate with corporate management in establishing daily control over the firm's international cash flow.

Thus, increasingly, the arena for business finance is the global market. At the start of each day, the corporate treasurer determines whether he will be borrowing or lending in the international financial market. He will be making investment decisions in domestic product markets or in foreign countries. The financial manager of the multinational corporate enterprise must consider the form and extent of protection against risks of devaluation on sales of his product to companies abroad. He must be concerned with the long-run political and commercial risks in his foreign sales and investments.

If he has surplus cash, he must compare the returns from investing in his domestic money market with utilizing the international financial market. Similarily, if short-term financing needs arise, he must make comparisons between financing sources abroad as compared with domestic sources. He must consider the advantages and disadvantages of the more impersonal international financial markets, with the development of long-term financing relations with international commercial banks or financial groups in London, Paris, Zurich, and Bonn.

THE MULTINATIONAL FIRM

The multinational corporation technically may be defined as a firm which owns and manages business operations in two or more countries. It has direct investments in foreign countries which involve the ownership and management of physical assets as well as the managerial and worker personnel to make these physical assets productive. This is different from portfolio investments in securities. Almost every large enterprise has experienced some effects of international forces on its operations. It may import materials and export some products. It may have agents or representative offices abroad; it may even license foreign firms to manufacture some of its products. However, a firm takes on the important characteristics of a multinational enterprise only when it must carry out the responsibility of financing, producing, and marketing products within foreign nations.

The characteristics of multinational operations were analyzed by tracing the stages in the development from a domestic firm to truly international operation:

Stages in the development from a domestic firm to a multinational firm:
1. Development of a strong product for domestic sales.
2. Import of some products.
3. Use of export brokers.
4. Direct export sales.

5. Branch sales office abroad.
6. Licensing.
7. Licensing with joint venture.
8. Joint venture.
9. Wholly owned manufacturing subsidiary.
10. Multinational management organization.
11. Multinational ownership of equity securities.

In both types of multinational organizations the corporate headquarters normally makes the final decision on strategic policy decisions such as the determination of product lines and capital budgets. The chief executives of its foreign affiliates are given broad authority to operate within the general policy guidelines within their respective countries. The main pattern of planning and control parallels that of domestic operations. Periodic budgets initiated by the foreign affiliate set forth goals and targets for operations. There is also a periodic review and evaluation of progress. The review is performed jointly by corporate headquarters and the affiliate managers.

Economic historians have suggested that the nations of the world may be grouped on the basis of their stage of development. In turn, business planning for international operations can be time-phased in relation to the stage of development of a particular nation. The economic development patterns that exist in different countries at different stages provide a basis for the development of business strategies appropriate for business firms in both developed and developing countries. Interaction between firms in developed countries and developing countries can produce benefits both for the individual firms, by providing a basis of effective operations and long-range planning, and contribute to the reinforcement of economic development plans and processes of their respective countries.

It is probable that the important trend toward worldwide ownership of multinational companies will increase. This is a salutory development toward achieving multinational bonds along with a mutuality of interest that can lead to better international relations.

INTERNATIONAL FINANCIAL TRENDS

Until after the mid-1960s the United States had a large surplus of goods and services which was offset by government and private capital flows. In the late 1960s, the U.S. surplus of goods and services began to shrink sharply for several reasons. The steady worsening in the U.S. overall balance-of-payments position had to be offset by increased holdings by foreign official agencies and by using up U.S. official reserve assets. A most important issue from a managerial standpoint is its possible future additional devaluation.

The overall investment position of the United States is positive as a net creditor to the rest of the world. In fact, this position has been improving by $2 to $3 billion per year. However, despite this favorable overall balance, there are some less favorable relations from a liquidity standpoint. Most of the U.S. assets abroad are held in the form of nonliquid claims, but almost one half of the U.S. obligations are liquid claims by foreigners on the United States.

The causes of the U.S. balance-of-payments deficit when running a very substantial surplus on goods and services exports were the following: (1) large direct investments made abroad, (2) portfolio investments made by Americans abroad, (3) direct U.S. government loans and grants for economic development to the less developed countries, and (4) military grants and expenditures abroad. The latter were increased substantially both directly and indirectly with the expansion of hostilities in Southeast Asia beginning in 1965.

After President Nixon's actions on August 15, 1971, meetings of the International Monetary Fund and of smaller groups of nations took place. The purpose of the meetings was for major developed nations of the world to seek agreement on what actions to take with respect to their currencies and general trade policies. Tentative agreements have been reached for the revaluation upward of the major currencies that had become undervalued in relationship to the U.S. dollar. To bring this action about, the United States raised the price of gold in relationship to the U.S. dollar by approximately 10 percent.

From the foregoing discussion of international managerial finance it can be seen that basically international managerial finance and managerial finance on a domestic basis are not significantly different in principle. However, the details of execution vary considerably. This is due to the fact that in multinational operations one deals with the goals, desires, laws, rules, and regulations of many governments whose aspirations vary over a wide range. For this reason, a multinational firm operating in many countries can never make international business decisions on a routine basis. Uniform business and financial policies on a worldwide basis are just not possible due to the differences between the aspirations and goals of the many governments involved.

The greater risks and dispersion of returns from foreign business ventures can be mitigated to some degree by the accumulation of know-how on a worldwide basis. That this is possible is demonstrated by the increasing number of multinational firms that have established a record of successful worldwide operations.

PROBLEM 14–1

Select a company that has been engaged in international business operations. Write a report on its experiences using the outline below. Cover all items for which you can obtain information. The purpose of this case study is to test the principles that have been set forth in this book. Comment on information that you encounter that appears to agree with concepts set forth or that appears to be in contradiction.

The following is an outline of a suggested study project on a multinational firm. Its aim is to trace the development of the international activities of the individual firm over an extended period of time. Emphasis should be placed on the types of problems and opportunities that presented themselves in connection with international operations and how they were met by the firm.

Case Study of a Firm in International Financial Operations

I. General history of the firm
    A. Founding date
    B. Products—early; later
    C. Location in U.S.
    D. Corporate headquarters
II. Entry into international operations
    A. Dates and volume of foreign sales
    B. Use of licensing to foreign companies
    C. Licenses from foreign countries
    D. Years when foreign sales branches were established
    E. Date of establishment of foreign manufacturing branches
III. Mergers and acquisitions
    A. Dates and nature of foreign acquisitions
    B. Manufacturing operations conducted by joint venture
        1. Percent ownership by U.S. company if majority ownership
        2. Any minority ownership joint ventures
IV. Relative proportions of domestic versus foreign sales volume and profits
    A. Percent of parts imported from foreign subsidiaries
    B. Percent of total sales by foreign subsidiaries
    C. Percent of sales abroad from U.S. manufacturing plants
    D. Profits from domestic operations versus profits from foreign operations
    E. Growth rates of foreign sales during last 5 or 10 years compared with domestic sales
    F. Growth rates of profits from foreign operations versus profits from domestic operations during last 5 or 10 years
V. Multinational organization
    A. Number of foreign sales offices and manufacturing plants
    B. Form of organization
        1. Foreign division to handle international operations
        2. Complete integration of foreign operations
VI. Financing
    A. Practices in financing foreign sales—letters of credit, banker's acceptances, etc.
    B. Place of incorporation of foreign subsidiaries
    C. Sources of financing foreign operations

    D.   Financial structure of foreign subsidiaries

    E.   Describe and provide prospectuses on foreign financing

    F.   Use of Eurodollar market by the firm

Information sources:

1. *Moody's Investment Manuals*
2. Annual reports of the firm
3. Prospectuses in connection with financing of the firm
4. Published histories of the firm
5. Special stories and write-ups in:

   a)   *Business Week*

   b)   *Fortune*

   c)   *Dun's*

   d)   *Finance*

   e)   *International Management*

   f)   *Barron's*

   g)   *The Wall Street Journal*
6. Direct correspondence with the executives of the company after compiling summary information to send along when you ask for additional detailed and specific information
7. Include citations of all sources used
8. Include direct quotations to illustrate some of the points made

PROBLEM 14–2

You are on the board of directors of a multinational company. Your company has for a period of years had investments in the Union of South Africa. A number of members of your board of directors have urged that such an investment makes your company very unpopular with an increasing number of religious and protest groups in the United States and have proposed that the company liquidate its investment in South Africa.

Present the pros and cons of continuing or liquidating your investment in the Union of South Africa.

SELECTED BIBLIOGRAPHY

Bower, Marvin. "Personal Service Firms Venture Abroad," *Columbia Journal of World Business,* Vol. 3, No. 2 (March–April 1968), pp. 49–58.

Hauge, Gabriel. "The Financial Dimension of International Operations," *Financial Executive,* Vol. 38, No. 2 (February 1969), pp. 47–54.

Kolde, E. J. "Business Enterprise in Global Context," *California Management Review,* Vol. 8, No. 4 (Summer 1966), pp. 31–48.

Rose, S. "Rewarding Strategies of Multinationalism," *Fortune,* Vol. 78, No. 4 (September 15, 1968), pp. 100–105.

Yoshino, M. Y. "Toward a Concept of Managerial Control of a World Enterprise," *Michigan Business Review,* Vol. 18, No. 2 (March 1966), pp. 25–31.

glossary

Glossary

Absolute advantage.   A country can produce a particular product at lower cost than other countries can.

Annual turnover.   Total sales divided by total assets, inventories, or other individual asset items. Turnover represents a measure of the degree of utilization of a company's investments.

Arbi-loans.   Loans obtained outside the country of the borrower in response to the relative abundance of funds in the foreign country and the relatively lower rates of interest. The expression "arbi" refers to the arbitrage nature of this borrowing activity.

Barter.   The direct exchange of commodities for commodities or services, without the use of money.

Bilateral trade agreement.   An agreement or treaty of trade between two nations under which various privileges are granted only to each other, and are not extended to other nations.

Bill of exchange (or draft).   An unconditional written order calling on the person to whom it is addressed to pay on demand or at a future date, a sum of money to the order of a specified person or bearer. Examples are the ordinary commercial bank check and the draft used in import transactions.

Bill of lading.   A receipt given by a carrier to a shipper for goods received, stating that the goods have been accepted for shipment and detailing the terms and provisions under which they will be transported. The original copy of a bill of lading carries with it title to the goods shipped. When the original copy is attached to the bill of exchange used to effect payment for the shipment, it entitles the holder to receive the goods.

Branch organization.   A division of a business located at a different place from the principal operation, possibly even in a foreign country. In contrast to a subsidiary, which is a separate legal entity, it is a part of the corporate legal entity .

cif (cost, insurance, and freight).   A term indicating that the quoted price includes the cost of the goods, the freight charges to a named destination, and the insurance charges on the shipment of the goods. The seller is responsible for the transportation and insurance of the shipment. The buyer is only responsible for local delivery of the goods and for paying any import duty.

Commercial letter of credit. A letter addressed by an importer's bank to the exporter guaranteeing payment for goods received according to specified terms.

Commercial risk. Risk of nonpayment due to the inability of the buyer to meet his obligations, or when due to the inability of the buyer to convert the currency of his own country into the currency of the seller's country.

Commitment fee. A payment made by a borrower to a lender for the assurance that a specified total amount of funds will be made available to the borrower for a specified time interval, whether actually used or not.

Comparative advantage. When the ratios of the costs of producing internationally traded goods differ between individual countries, the low-cost country is said to have a comparative advantage.

Concentration banking. The movement of funds from scattered locations to a central location to increase prompt availability of the funds by reducing time lag, to increase safety from exchange rate losses, for greater ease of reassignment, and to achieve the highest returns from their use.

Confirming bank. A correspondent bank of the importer's bank that notifies the exporter of the existence of the commercial letter of credit. By this act, the confirming bank joins the issuing bank in guaranteeing eventual payment.

Correspondent bank. A formal relationship between two or more banks providing for reciprocal services on an agreed-upon basis. A domestic correspondent bank for a foreign bank accepts the bills of exchange of that foreign bank according to a standing agreement between the two banks.

Currency swap. A currency swap provides for the exchange of one currency into another at an agreed ratio, the swap rate, with the exchange being reversed at exactly same ratio at the end of the swap contract period.

Depreciation of a currency. The reduction in the value of a currency by changing its relationship to gold or another currency which is a standard of value. "Depreciation" and "devaluation" are generally used interchangeably.

Direct investments. Investments in foreign corporations or other enterprises in a form that provides for active participation by the investors in the management or control of the foreign firms.

Discounting of a trade bill. The sale of a time draft to a lending institution by the holder before maturity at a discount representing a charge by the financial institution for the loan of the funds by making them available before their due date.

Drawee. The person or institution who is ordered to make payment on a draft, bill, or check.

Drawer. The person who draws or orders in a check, draft, or bill that the money held by a second party be paid over to a third party by the drawee.

Earned income. Income derived from personal efforts or labor or through active participation in a business venture and received in the form of salaries, wages, or proprietors' withdrawals. This is distinguished from unearned income which represents a return on invested capital such as dividends, rents, etc.

Economies of scale. The reduction in cost achieved through more intensive utilization of productive assets as a result of a larger volume of production.

Eurobond. A long-term promissory note (bond) denominated in a currency other than that of the country of the borrower.

Eurodollar. A deposit in a foreign bank denominated in dollars.

European Economic Community (EEC). An agreement of originally six (now ten) European countries to establish initially a customs union, and to seek eventually a common economic policy and later perhaps political unity.

Exchange rate risk. Losses that may occur as a result of a change in the value of one currency in relation to another.

First-in, first-out inventory costing (Fifo). The profit and loss statement is charged with the cost of inventory on the assumption that the first goods received are the first used.

Fiscal policy. The plans affecting the relationship between the stream of expenditures and receipts of a governmental unit.

f.o.b. (free on board). The seller assumes all responsibilities and costs up to some specified point or stage of delivery named, including transportation, packing, insurance, etc.

Foreign-based company income. Income to a U.S.-controlled foreign corporation. It may be in the form of income from investments, from sales, or from various forms of services for, to, or on behalf of related persons.

Foreign exchange reserves. Gold, SDRs, and other assets readily convertible into foreign currencies.

Foreign personal holding company income. The income from investments of U.S.-controlled foreign corporations.

Forward contract. A contract to exchange currencies at a specified exchange rate at a future date, usually 30, 60, or 90 days.

Forward rate. The rate of exchange specified in the forward contract.

Gold tranche position. The amount of gold paid in to the International Monetary Fund by a nation as part of its contributed capital.

Gross-up method of taxation. Provides for the addition of foreign taxes paid plus dividends received by a U.S. person for purposes of determining his U.S. tax liability.

Horizontal mobility. Refers to the ability of an individual to move without restriction from one geographic location to another.

Infrastructure. Refers to the basic transportation, sanitation, water, highway, communication facilities, electric power, etc., which represent the necessary prerequisites for the production of other goods and services in the economy.

Interest Equalization Tax. Refers to a tax levied by the United States on foreign issuers of debt obligations sold to U.S. persons.

International Development Association (IDA). One of the members of the World Bank group organized to make high risk, flexible loans to less developed countries.

International Finance Corporation (IFC). A member of the World Bank group making loans of somewhat higher risks than those made by the World Bank itself. Some of its financing includes taking an equity position with the intention of selling out as soon as feasible.

Joint venture. An arrangement whereby two or more independent entities pool their resources in a business project.

Leading indicators. Economic time series which perform as barometers in predicting the direction of the subsequent movement of other economic series.

Lifo inventory costing. A method of costing in which the goods last purchased are first charged to profit and loss. The goods remaining in inventory, therefore, are valued at historical costs.

Link financing. Sometimes used to refer to arbi-loans defined previously. Some writers refer to the situation when more than two countries are involved in a chain of arbi financing.

Long-term capital gain. Profits realized from the sale or exchange of a capital asset held for six months or longer.

Maker of a bill of exchange. The party who executes and signs a negotiable instrument; hence, the maker is the same as the drawer.

Monetary balance. A relationship between a firm's monetary assets and monetary liabilities that is appropriate to prospective changes in the value of a domestic currency or to the relationship between the values of two currencies.

Monetary policy. Refers to government actions with respect to the rate at which the monetary base, the money stock, or availability of funds is expanded or contracted, or the cost is raised or lowered.

Multinational firm. A firm which conducts manufacturing and other related commercial activities across national boundaries.

Negotiating bank (commercial letter of credit). This is the bank that buys or discounts the draft of a seller that has been issued in connection with a letter of credit.

Net monetary position. This refers to whether the monetary assets exceed monetary liabilities or whether the monetary liabilities exceed the monetary assets.

Nondiversifiable risk. The variance of returns on an investment that remains after broad diversification has been achieved. This remaining variation is the covariance of returns on an investment from a broader index referred to as market returns.

Notifying bank. The same as the confirming bank.

Opening bank (*in a commercial letter of credit transaction*). The originating bank.

Portfolio investment. Investments in which the holder takes no active role in the companies whose securities he holds.

Price level indicator. A measure of price level changes. This may be the GNP price deflator, the consumer price index, the wholesale price index, the prices of imported goods, or the prices of exported goods.

Private compensating agreements. A triangular exchange on a barter basis of goods which are surplus in the countries involved.

Revaluation of a currency. The change in value upward of one currency in terms of other currencies.

Revaluation reserve account. This is an earmarked net worth account in which are recorded changes in the net worth of a firm resulting from translation from one currency to another. If a change resulted from a drop in home currency value of a foreign-denominated debt this is amortized, usually over the life of the debt obligation.

Sight draft. A bill of exchange payable immediately upon presentation or on demand. An ordinary bank check is a sight draft.

Source income. Income which is generated at the place of operations of productive assets.

Special drawing rights. Credits (paper gold) distributed by the International Monetary Fund to its members on a quota basis in an effort to expand international liquidity—represents an increase in funds available to settle international transactions.

Spot rate or spot quotation. Refers to exchange rates between currencies existing at the present or current period of time.

Subpart F income. The income of a U.S. foreign-controlled corporation subject to special tax provisions under the Revenue Act of 1962.

Swap discount. The reduction from official exchange rates made by the foreign country or a commercial bank in a foreign country when executing a swap contract for a foreign party.

Switch trading. The elimination of imbalances in bilateral clearing accounts of trade between two nations by exporting to the creditor country goods it needs on behalf of the debtor country. These goods are shipped from third countries directly or via the debtor country and are paid for by the debtor country with convertible currencies or barter.

Takeoff economies. Economies that have reached the point where a sufficient number of interacting industries have been established so that further economic development takes place from the country's own internal momentum.

Tax-haven country. A nation which permits the formation of foreign subsidiaries and which does not levy taxes on foreign source income or local capital funds.

Tax incentives. Tax reductions or outright subsidies to induce foreign investors to make investments in certain countries or specific industries in specific geographic locations in the countries offering the tax incentives.

Time draft.   A bill of exchange payable at a specified future date.

Trade deficit.   Refers to an excess of merchandise imports over merchandise exports.

Traditional economy.   A traditional economy is predominantly agricultural; the growth of income does not exceed the growth of population so income per capita is stagnant or declining.

Transitional economy.   An economy which has developed a sufficient surplus to provide the basis for capital investment and hence movement out of the stagnation of a constant or declining per capita income.

Unearned income.   Income derived from investments rather than an individual's personal efforts. Examples of unearned income are dividends from investments, rentals on property, interest on indebtedness owned, etc.

U.S.-controlled foreign corporation.   A foreign corporation owned by five or fewer U.S. persons, each of whom owns 10 percent or more of the outstanding common stock.

Venture capital.   An equity investment in a small or new enterprise regarded as subject to high risk.

Vertical mobility.   The ability of a person to move from one social class to another in a society, or progress within a company from one level to a higher one.

World Bank (IBRD).   An international institution resulting from the meetings at Bretton Woods in 1944. It provides for pooling the resources of member nations to make international investments possible particularly to developing countries, and especially to aid in the creation of an infrastructure.

appendixes

APPENDIX A

Answers to selected end-of-chapter problems

BELOW are given the final answers to selected end-of-chapter problems. The answers are given for those problems that are most likely to have a single solution. Problems or parts of problems requiring extended verbal discussion are not included. It must be kept in mind that the answers to some problems may differ depending on the assumptions that are made. However, we thought that it would be of value to provide these answers as an indication to the problem solver to see if he is "on the right track."

2–1. Part **A:**
  1. Too high.   2. Too low.   3. Too high.   4. Too low.
  5. In New York City traders would sell LCs and buy dollars.
  6. In the foreign country, traders would buy LCs and sell dollars.
  Part **B:**
  Americans would buy LCs with dollars, next sell LCs for francs, and finally convert francs into dollars.

2–2. Line $11 = (\$500)$; line $13 = (\$800)$; line $15 = (\$1,000,800)$; line $26 = (\$3,000,800)$; line $33 = (\$2,991,800)$; and line $42 = (\$11,000,000)$.

4–1. **A.** Yes.   **B.** Yes, however the profit would not be as high as in **A.**

4–2. Insure via OPIC; it permits the insurance of profits as well as the original investment.

4–3. Yes, it would remove commercial and political risks.

5–1. **A.** 1. $200,000.
      2. $188,700.
      3. $223,600.

5–2. **A.** 1. $190,000.
      2. $200,000.
      3. $181,000.

5–4. **A.** 1. 26.4 percent.   2. 10 percent.
      B. 1. (2.9 percent).   2. 5.7 percent.
      C. 1. 26.4 percent.   2. 0 percent.

337

5–5. Borrow locally because $r_F - r_{US} = 0.22 < 0.25 =$ the rate of currency devaluation.

7–1. **A.** Tax equals $3 million.

B. Form a subsidiary to own the foreign branch.

7–2. **A.** $11,000.

B. $8,000.

7–3. 1. No.   2. Yes.   3. 62.5 percent.   4a. No.   4b. 54. percent.

7–4. $2,125,000.

9–1. **A.** 1. $4,500.   2. $4,095.   3. $3,700.

10–2. **B.** 1. LC 4,000.   2. LC 8,000.   3., 4., and 5. LC 14,000.

C. Total net U.S. income tax = $1,160.

D. Net present value = $2,903.

11–1. $26.64 or 0.00027 percent.

11–2. $27,936 or 0.388 percent.

APPENDIX B

The interest factor in international financial decisions

AT A NUMBER of places in the text, international financial decisions required a comparison between receiving payment immediately, or periodically over a number of months or years, or at the end of a period of years. Therefore, it is essential for making sound decisions to take into consideration the influence of interest costs over periods of time. For this reason an understanding of compound interest relationships is required.

Fortunately it is not a difficult subject despite some of its apparent complications. High school algebra is the only mathematics needed in order to understand compound interest relationships. Furthermore, all of the situations involving compound interest can be handled by utilizing only a small number of basic formulas.

Annual compound interest rates

Suppose that your firm is negotiating an export sale. Two alternatives are being explored as to how the customer will pay for his purchase. One is to receive the payment immediately. The other is to be paid a somewhat higher amount at the end of a period. For example, suppose that you are offered $1,000 today or $1,200 at the end of the fifth year. Which should you take? The use of compound interest concepts helps to determine which choice is most advantageous.

Another critical item of information is the rate of return (or interest rate) that could be earned by the company if it had the money immediately. For purposes of illustration we will assume that if a company received the money immediately it could earn a 6 percent return (or 6 percent interest rate) on those funds. We could then state the problem as follows: Let

$$P = \text{principal, or beginning amount} \quad = \$1,000$$
$$r = \text{interest rate} \quad = 6\% = .06$$
$$n = \text{number of years} \quad = 5$$
$$S_n = \text{the value at the end of the year } n$$

TABLE B-1

Compound sum of $1

$$S_n = P(1 + r)^n$$

Year	1%	2%	3%	4%	5%	6%	7%	8%	9%	10%	11%	12%	13%	14%	15%	16%
1	1.010	1.020	1.030	1.040	1.050	1.060	1.070	1.080	1.090	1.100	1.110	1.120	1.130	1.140	1.150	1.160
2	1.020	1.040	1.061	1.082	1.102	1.124	1.145	1.166	1.188	1.210	1.232	1.254	1.277	1.300	1.322	1.346
3	1.030	1.061	1.093	1.125	1.158	1.191	1.225	1.260	1.295	1.331	1.368	1.405	1.443	1.482	1.521	1.561
4	1.041	1.082	1.126	1.170	1.216	1.262	1.311	1.360	1.412	1.464	1.518	1.574	1.631	1.689	1.749	1.811
5	1.051	1.104	1.159	1.217	1.276	1.338	1.403	1.469	1.539	1.611	1.685	1.762	1.842	1.925	2.011	2.100
6	1.062	1.126	1.194	1.265	1.340	1.419	1.501	1.587	1.677	1.772	1.870	1.974	2.082	2.195	2.313	2.436
7	1.072	1.149	1.230	1.316	1.407	1.504	1.606	1.714	1.828	1.949	2.076	2.211	2.353	2.502	2.660	2.826
8	1.083	1.172	1.267	1.369	1.477	1.594	1.718	1.851	1.993	2.144	2.305	2.476	2.658	2.853	3.059	3.278
9	1.094	1.195	1.305	1.423	1.551	1.689	1.838	1.999	2.172	2.358	2.558	2.773	3.004	3.252	3.518	3.803
10	1.105	1.219	1.344	1.480	1.629	1.791	1.967	2.159	2.367	2.594	2.839	3.106	3.395	3.707	4.046	4.411
11	1.116	1.243	1.384	1.539	1.710	1.898	2.105	2.332	2.580	2.853	3.152	3.479	3.836	4.226	4.652	5.117
12	1.127	1.268	1.426	1.601	1.796	2.012	2.252	2.518	2.813	3.138	3.499	3.896	4.335	4.818	5.350	5.936
13	1.138	1.294	1.469	1.665	1.886	2.133	2.410	2.720	3.066	3.452	3.883	4.363	4.898	5.492	6.153	6.886
14	1.149	1.319	1.513	1.732	1.980	2.261	2.579	2.937	3.342	3.797	4.310	4.887	5.535	6.261	7.076	7.988
15	1.161	1.346	1.558	1.801	2.079	2.397	2.759	3.172	3.642	4.177	4.785	5.474	6.254	7.138	8.137	9.266
16	1.173	1.373	1.605	1.873	2.183	2.540	2.952	3.426	3.970	4.595	5.311	6.130	7.067	8.137	9.358	10.748
17	1.184	1.400	1.653	1.948	2.292	2.693	3.159	3.700	4.328	5.054	5.895	6.866	7.986	9.276	10.761	12.468
18	1.196	1.428	1.702	2.026	2.407	2.854	3.380	3.996	4.717	5.560	6.544	7.690	9.024	10.575	12.375	14.463
19	1.208	1.457	1.754	2.107	2.527	3.026	3.617	4.316	5.142	6.116	7.263	8.613	10.197	12.056	14.232	16.777
20	1.220	1.486	1.806	2.191	2.653	3.207	3.870	4.661	5.604	6.728	8.062	9.646	11.523	13.743	16.367	19.461

Source: Adapted from Jerome Bracken and Charles J. Christenson, *Tables for Use in Analyzing Business Decisions* (Homewood, Ill.: Richard D. Irwin, Inc., 1965).

The formula that applies is the compound interest formula. In general terms it may be stated as follows:

$$S_n = P(1 + r)^n \qquad (1)$$

Actually, the details of the formula do not have to be known because a compound interest table will be used (see Table B–1). We now have all the information needed to compute the value at the end of the fifth year.

$$S_5 = \$1,000(1.06)^5$$

We then look in the compound interest table to find that at 6 percent a dollar over a 5-year period grows to $1.338. Since the amount we have is $1,000, it is multiplied times the interest factor:

$$S_5 = \$1,000(1.338) = \$1,338$$

Therefore, if the firm can earn 6 percent with the money, it is more worthwhile for it to receive the $1,000 today rather than $1,200 at the end of the fifth year.

Future amounts and their present values

A similar type of problem occurs when a company is offered an amount to be received in the future. It is desirable to compare that amount with the value of whatever amount could be received today. This requires the computation of the present value of the amount to be received in the future. The determination of present values involves the same formula except that it is solved for P, representing present value, instead of for S_n which, in this situation, is known. By simple algebra the required formula would be:

$$P = S_n/(1 + r)^n \qquad (1.1)$$

Using our previous example, we determined S_n to be $1,338. Since the appropriate interest rate is 6 percent and the number of years is five, this is what is required to determine P. This can be done by using our previous information and making a division. We would be dividing $1,338 by 1.338 to obtain the result $1,000. But, for most combinations of numbers there is a simpler method. We can use a present value interest table (Table B–2), which is the reciprocal of a compound interest table. In this case the formula is:

$$P = S_n(1 + r)^{-n} \qquad (2)$$

We can now insert the illustrative numbers:

$$P = \$1,338(0.747)$$
$$P = \$1,000$$

TABLE B-2
Present value of $1

$$P = S_n(1 + r)^{-n}$$

Years Hence	1%	2%	4%	6%	8%	10%	12%	14%	15%	16%	18%	20%	22%	24%	25%	26%	28%	30%	35%	40%	45%	50%
1	0.990	0.980	0.962	0.943	0.926	0.909	0.893	0.877	0.870	0.862	0.847	0.833	0.820	0.806	0.800	0.794	0.781	0.769	0.741	0.714	0.690	0.667
2	0.980	0.961	0.925	0.890	0.857	0.826	0.797	0.769	0.756	0.743	0.718	0.694	0.672	0.650	0.640	0.630	0.610	0.592	0.549	0.510	0.476	0.444
3	0.971	0.942	0.889	0.840	0.794	0.751	0.712	0.675	0.658	0.641	0.609	0.579	0.551	0.524	0.512	0.500	0.477	0.455	0.406	0.364	0.328	0.296
4	0.961	0.924	0.855	0.792	0.735	0.683	0.636	0.592	0.572	0.552	0.516	0.482	0.451	0.423	0.410	0.397	0.373	0.350	0.301	0.260	0.226	0.198
5	0.951	0.906	0.822	0.747	0.681	0.621	0.567	0.519	0.497	0.476	0.437	0.402	0.370	0.341	0.328	0.315	0.291	0.269	0.223	0.186	0.156	0.132
6	0.942	0.888	0.790	0.705	0.630	0.564	0.507	0.456	0.432	0.410	0.370	0.335	0.303	0.275	0.262	0.250	0.227	0.207	0.165	0.133	0.108	0.088
7	0.933	0.871	0.760	0.665	0.583	0.513	0.452	0.400	0.376	0.354	0.314	0.279	0.249	0.222	0.210	0.198	0.178	0.159	0.122	0.095	0.074	0.059
8	0.923	0.853	0.731	0.627	0.540	0.467	0.404	0.351	0.327	0.305	0.266	0.233	0.204	0.179	0.168	0.157	0.139	0.123	0.091	0.068	0.051	0.039
9	0.914	0.837	0.703	0.592	0.500	0.424	0.361	0.308	0.284	0.263	0.225	0.194	0.167	0.144	0.134	0.125	0.108	0.094	0.067	0.048	0.035	0.026
10	0.905	0.820	0.676	0.558	0.463	0.386	0.322	0.270	0.247	0.227	0.191	0.162	0.137	0.116	0.107	0.099	0.085	0.073	0.050	0.035	0.024	0.017
11	0.896	0.804	0.650	0.527	0.429	0.350	0.287	0.237	0.215	0.195	0.162	0.135	0.112	0.094	0.086	0.079	0.066	0.056	0.037	0.025	0.017	0.012
12	0.887	0.788	0.625	0.497	0.397	0.319	0.257	0.208	0.187	0.168	0.137	0.112	0.092	0.076	0.069	0.062	0.052	0.043	0.027	0.018	0.012	0.008
13	0.879	0.773	0.601	0.469	0.368	0.290	0.229	0.182	0.163	0.145	0.116	0.093	0.075	0.061	0.055	0.050	0.040	0.033	0.020	0.013	0.008	0.005
14	0.870	0.758	0.577	0.442	0.340	0.263	0.205	0.160	0.141	0.125	0.099	0.078	0.062	0.049	0.044	0.039	0.032	0.025	0.015	0.009	0.006	0.003
15	0.861	0.743	0.555	0.417	0.315	0.239	0.183	0.140	0.123	0.108	0.084	0.065	0.051	0.040	0.035	0.031	0.025	0.020	0.011	0.006	0.004	0.002
16	0.853	0.728	0.534	0.394	0.292	0.218	0.163	0.123	0.107	0.093	0.071	0.054	0.042	0.032	0.028	0.025	0.019	0.015	0.008	0.005	0.003	0.002
17	0.844	0.714	0.513	0.371	0.270	0.198	0.146	0.108	0.093	0.080	0.060	0.045	0.034	0.026	0.023	0.020	0.015	0.012	0.006	0.003	0.002	0.001
18	0.836	0.700	0.494	0.350	0.250	0.180	0.130	0.095	0.081	0.069	0.051	0.038	0.028	0.021	0.018	0.016	0.012	0.009	0.005	0.002	0.001	0.001
19	0.828	0.686	0.475	0.331	0.232	0.164	0.116	0.083	0.070	0.060	0.043	0.031	0.023	0.017	0.014	0.012	0.009	0.007	0.003	0.002	0.001	
20	0.820	0.673	0.456	0.312	0.215	0.149	0.104	0.073	0.061	0.051	0.037	0.026	0.019	0.014	0.012	0.010	0.007	0.005	0.002	0.001		
21	0.811	0.660	0.439	0.294	0.199	0.135	0.093	0.064	0.053	0.044	0.031	0.022	0.015	0.011	0.009	0.008	0.006	0.004	0.002	0.001		
22	0.803	0.647	0.422	0.278	0.184	0.123	0.083	0.056	0.046	0.038	0.026	0.018	0.013	0.009	0.007	0.006	0.004	0.003	0.001	0.001		
23	0.795	0.634	0.406	0.262	0.170	0.112	0.074	0.049	0.040	0.033	0.022	0.015	0.010	0.007	0.006	0.005	0.003	0.002	0.001			
24	0.788	0.622	0.390	0.247	0.158	0.102	0.066	0.043	0.035	0.028	0.019	0.013	0.008	0.006	0.005	0.004	0.003	0.002	0.001			
25	0.780	0.610	0.375	0.233	0.146	0.092	0.059	0.038	0.030	0.024	0.016	0.010	0.007	0.005	0.004	0.003	0.002	0.001	0.001			
26	0.772	0.598	0.361	0.220	0.135	0.084	0.053	0.033	0.026	0.021	0.014	0.009	0.006	0.004	0.003	0.002	0.002	0.001				
27	0.764	0.586	0.347	0.207	0.125	0.076	0.047	0.029	0.023	0.018	0.011	0.007	0.005	0.003	0.002	0.002	0.001	0.001				
28	0.757	0.574	0.333	0.196	0.116	0.069	0.042	0.026	0.020	0.016	0.010	0.006	0.004	0.002	0.002	0.002	0.001	0.001				
29	0.749	0.563	0.321	0.185	0.107	0.063	0.037	0.022	0.017	0.014	0.008	0.005	0.003	0.002	0.002	0.001	0.001	0.001				
30	0.742	0.552	0.308	0.174	0.099	0.057	0.033	0.020	0.015	0.012	0.007	0.004	0.003	0.002	0.001	0.001	0.001	0.001				
40	0.672	0.453	0.208	0.097	0.046	0.022	0.011	0.005	0.004	0.003	0.001	0.001										
50	0.608	0.372	0.141	0.054	0.021	0.009	0.003	0.001	0.001	0.001												

Source: Adapted from Jerome Bracken and Charles J. Christenson, *Tables for Use in Analyzing Business Decisions* (Homewood, Ill.: Richard D. Irwin, Inc., 1965).

Therefore, we see that the results of compound interest and present value computations are just two different ways of looking at the same relationship.

Income flows and their values

Income flows are a series of periodic payments made over a span of time. This is probably the most frequently encountered type of compound interest situation encountered by a business firm. For example, a firm may sell some goods that will be paid for in installments. A basic question is, what is the present value of those installment payments? Or, the firm makes a foreign investment from which it expects to receive a series of cash returns over a period of years. At an appropriate discount rate what would the series of future income receipts be worth today? The firm needs this information in order to determine whether it is worthwhile to make the investment.

Some specific examples will further illustrate these ideas. The firm makes an investment in a foreign enterprise. It is promised the payment of $1,000 a year for 10 years with an interest rate of 10 percent. What is the present value of such a series of payments?

The basic formula involved is the present value of an annuity.

$$A_{\overline{n}|r} = a\left[\frac{1 - (1 + r)^{-n}}{r}\right] \tag{3}$$

Where:

$$A = \text{present value of an annuity}$$
$$a = \text{amount of the annuity}$$
$$r = \text{interest factor}$$
$$n = \text{number of years}$$

The expression in brackets is somewhat cumbersome. It represents the present value of an annuity factor of $1 at an interest rate, r, for n periods. This interest factor may be found directly in Table B–3 for the designated interest rate and number of years. In some calculations of actual international financial cases and decisions, a number of kinds of compound interest relations may be involved. For convenience, therefore, we shall use instead of the cumbersome expression set out above, the symbol $P_{n,r}$ where:

$P_{n,r}$ = present value of an annuity factor for n years at r percent.[1]

Equation (3) above can, therefore, be rewritten as:

$$A_{\overline{n}|r} = aP_{n,r} \tag{3.1}$$

---

[1] Except for the use of this "shorthand" expression and another in connection with the sum of an annuity formula, the reader will find that we have adopted the symbols most generally employed.

TABLE B–3
Present value of $1 received annually

$$A_{\overline{n}|r} = \$1\left[\frac{1 - (1+r)^{-n}}{r}\right] = \$1 P_{n,r}$$

Years (n)	1%	2%	4%	6%	8%	10%	12%	14%	15%	16%	18%	20%	22%	24%	25%	26%	28%	30%	35%	40%	45%	50%
1	0.990	0.980	0.962	0.943	0.926	0.909	0.893	0.877	0.870	0.862	0.847	0.833	0.820	0.806	0.800	0.794	0.781	0.769	0.741	0.714	0.690	0.667
2	1.970	1.942	1.886	1.833	1.783	1.736	1.690	1.647	1.626	1.605	1.566	1.528	1.492	1.457	1.440	1.424	1.392	1.361	1.289	1.224	1.165	1.111
3	2.941	2.884	2.775	2.673	2.577	2.487	2.402	2.322	2.283	2.246	2.174	2.106	2.042	1.981	1.952	1.923	1.868	1.816	1.696	1.589	1.493	1.407
4	3.902	3.808	3.630	3.465	3.312	3.170	3.037	2.914	2.855	2.798	2.690	2.589	2.494	2.404	2.362	2.320	2.241	2.166	1.997	1.849	1.720	1.605
5	4.853	4.713	4.452	4.212	3.993	3.791	3.605	3.433	3.352	3.274	3.127	2.991	2.864	2.745	2.689	2.635	2.532	2.436	2.220	2.035	1.876	1.737
6	5.795	5.601	5.242	4.917	4.623	4.355	4.111	3.889	3.784	3.685	3.498	3.326	3.167	3.020	2.951	2.885	2.759	2.643	2.385	2.168	1.983	1.824
7	6.728	6.472	6.002	5.582	5.206	4.868	4.564	4.288	4.160	4.039	3.812	3.605	3.416	3.242	3.161	3.083	2.937	2.802	2.508	2.263	2.057	1.883
8	7.652	7.325	6.733	6.210	5.747	5.335	4.968	4.639	4.487	4.344	4.078	3.837	3.619	3.421	3.329	3.241	3.076	2.925	2.598	2.331	2.108	1.922
9	8.566	8.162	7.435	6.802	6.247	5.759	5.328	4.946	4.772	4.607	4.303	4.031	3.786	3.566	3.463	3.366	3.184	3.019	2.665	2.379	2.144	1.948
10	9.471	8.983	8.111	7.360	6.710	6.145	5.650	5.216	5.019	4.833	4.494	4.192	3.923	3.682	3.571	3.465	3.269	3.092	2.715	2.414	2.168	1.965
11	10.368	9.787	8.760	7.887	7.139	6.495	5.937	5.453	5.234	5.029	4.656	4.327	4.035	3.776	3.656	3.544	3.335	3.147	2.757	2.438	2.185	1.977
12	11.255	10.575	9.385	8.384	7.536	6.814	6.194	5.660	5.421	5.197	4.793	4.439	4.127	3.851	3.725	3.606	3.387	3.190	2.779	2.456	2.196	1.985
13	12.134	11.343	9.986	8.853	7.904	7.103	6.424	5.842	5.583	5.342	4.910	4.533	4.203	3.912	3.780	3.656	3.427	3.223	2.799	2.468	2.204	1.990
14	13.004	12.106	10.563	9.295	8.244	7.367	6.628	6.002	5.724	5.468	5.008	4.611	4.265	3.962	3.824	3.695	3.459	3.249	2.814	2.477	2.210	1.993
15	13.865	12.849	11.118	9.712	8.559	7.606	6.811	6.142	5.847	5.575	5.092	4.675	4.315	4.001	3.859	3.726	3.483	3.268	2.825	2.484	2.214	1.995
16	14.718	13.578	11.652	10.106	8.851	7.824	6.974	6.265	5.954	5.669	5.162	4.730	4.357	4.033	3.887	3.751	3.503	3.283	2.834	2.489	2.216	1.997
17	15.562	14.292	12.166	10.477	9.122	8.022	7.120	6.373	6.047	5.749	5.222	4.775	4.391	4.059	3.910	3.771	3.518	3.295	2.840	2.492	2.218	1.998
18	16.398	14.992	12.659	10.828	9.372	8.201	7.250	6.467	6.128	5.818	5.273	4.812	4.419	4.080	3.928	3.786	3.529	3.304	2.844	2.494	2.219	1.999
19	17.226	15.678	13.134	11.158	9.604	8.365	7.366	6.550	6.198	5.877	5.316	4.844	4.442	4.097	3.942	3.799	3.539	3.311	2.848	2.496	2.220	1.999
20	18.046	16.351	13.590	11.470	9.818	8.514	7.469	6.623	6.259	5.929	5.353	4.870	4.460	4.110	3.954	3.808	3.546	3.316	2.850	2.497	2.221	1.999
21	18.857	17.011	14.029	11.764	10.017	8.649	7.562	6.687	6.312	5.973	5.384	4.891	4.476	4.121	3.963	3.816	3.551	3.320	2.852	2.498	2.221	2.000
22	19.660	17.658	14.451	12.042	10.201	8.772	7.645	6.743	6.359	6.011	5.410	4.909	4.488	4.130	3.970	3.822	3.556	3.323	2.853	2.498	2.222	2.000
23	20.456	18.292	14.857	12.303	10.371	8.883	7.718	6.792	6.399	6.044	5.432	4.925	4.499	4.137	3.976	3.827	3.559	3.325	2.854	2.499	2.222	2.000
24	21.243	18.914	15.247	12.550	10.529	8.985	7.784	6.835	6.434	6.073	5.451	4.937	4.507	4.143	3.981	3.831	3.562	3.327	2.855	2.499	2.222	2.000
25	22.023	19.523	15.622	12.783	10.675	9.077	7.843	6.873	6.464	6.097	5.467	4.948	4.514	4.147	3.985	3.834	3.564	3.329	2.856	2.499	2.222	2.000
26	22.795	20.121	15.983	13.003	10.810	9.161	7.896	6.906	6.491	6.118	5.480	4.956	4.520	4.151	3.988	3.837	3.566	3.330	2.856	2.500	2.222	2.000
27	23.560	20.707	16.330	13.211	10.935	9.237	7.943	6.935	6.514	6.136	5.492	4.964	4.524	4.154	3.990	3.839	3.567	3.331	2.856	2.500	2.222	2.000
28	24.316	21.281	16.663	13.406	11.051	9.307	7.984	6.961	6.534	6.152	5.502	4.970	4.528	4.157	3.992	3.840	3.568	3.331	2.857	2.500	2.222	2.000
29	25.066	21.844	16.984	13.591	11.158	9.370	8.022	6.983	6.551	6.166	5.510	4.975	4.531	4.159	3.994	3.841	3.569	3.332	2.857	2.500	2.222	2.000
30	25.808	22.396	17.292	13.765	11.258	9.427	8.055	7.003	6.566	6.177	5.517	4.979	4.534	4.160	3.995	3.842	3.569	3.332	2.857	2.500	2.222	2.000
40	32.835	27.355	19.793	15.046	11.925	9.779	8.244	7.105	6.642	6.234	5.548	4.997	4.544	4.166	3.999	3.846	3.571	3.333	2.857	2.500	2.222	2.000
50	39.196	31.424	21.482	15.762	12.234	9.915	8.304	7.133	6.661	6.246	5.554	4.999	4.545	4.167	4.000	3.846	3.571	3.333	2.857	2.500	2.222	2.000

Source: Adapted from Jerome Bracken and Charles J. Christenson, *Tables for Use in Analyzing Business Decisions* (Homewood, Ill.: Richard D. Irwin, Inc., 1965).

Substituting actual numbers and using the present value of an annuity interest table (Table B–3) we would have the following for 10 years at 10 percent:

$$\$6,145 = \$1,000(6.145)$$

In other words, a series of payments of $1,000 received for 10 years, and applying an interest factor of 10 percent, would be worth $6,145 today. Hence, if the amount of investment we were required to make were $8,000, for example, or any amount greater than $6,145, we would be receiving a return of less than 10 percent on our investment. Conversely, if the investment required to receive annual payments of $1,000 for 10 years at 10 percent were $5,000 or any amount less than $6,145, we would be earning a return greater than 10 percent.

A number of other questions can be answered using these same relationships. Suppose the decision facing the firm requires determining the rate of return on an investment. For example, suppose we would have $6,145 to invest and that an investment opportunity promises an annual return of $1,000 for 10 years. What is the indicated rate of return on our investment? Exactly the same relationship is involved, but we are now solving for the interest rate. We can, therefore, rewrite our equation as follows:

$$P_{10,10\%} = A_{\overline{10}|10\%}/a$$

We can now substitute the appropriate figures.

$$P_{10,10\%} = \$6,145/\$1,000 = 6.145$$

In Table B–3 showing present value of periodic payments received annually we look across the year 10 row until we find the interest rate that corresponds to the interest factor 6.145. This is, of course, 10 percent.

We have illustrated the idea with simple numbers. Now let us consider another situation. Suppose that we are going to receive a return of $2,000 per year for 5 years from an investment of $8,200. What is the return on our investment? This is generally referred to as the internal rate of return on the investment, or it is also sometimes referred to as the DCF or discounted cash flow approach to valuing an investment.

We follow the same procedure as before.

$$P_{5,r} = \$8,424/\$2,000$$
$$= 4.212$$

We look again for the present value of an annuity in Table B–3 along the row for the year 5 to find the interest factor 4.212. We then look at the interest rate at the top of the column to find that it is 6 percent. Thus, the return on that investment is 6 percent. If our required rate of return were 8 percent we would not find this investment attractive. On the other hand, if the required return on our investment were only 5 percent we would consider the investment attractive.

These relationships can be used in still another way. Taking the facts of the preceding illustration we may ask the question, what is an investment worth today that yields $2,000 per year for 5 years, using an appropriate discount factor (or cost of capital) of 6 percent? What is the present value of a series of future income flows? For example, if a firm were to make a sale of goods on an open account with a down payment of $1,000 plus yearly payments of $2,000 for 5 years, what would the present value of all of the payments be at a 6 percent interest rate? From our previous calculations we know that the series of payments of $2,000 for 5 years at a 6 percent interest rate are worth $8,424 today. When we add the $1,000 down payment to this figure we would have a total of $9,424.

Compound sum of an annuity

Instead of needing to know the present value of a series of future payments, we may need to know the future value or future sum to which a series of payments will accumulate. The reason may be to determine whether we have enough funds to repay an obligation in the future. The sum of an annuity can be determined from the following basic relationship:

$$S_{\overline{n}|r} = a\left[\frac{(1+r)^n - 1}{r}\right] = aC_{n,r} \qquad (4)$$

Where:

$S_{\overline{n}|r}$ = the future sum to which an annuity will accumulate in n years at rate r

a = the annuity

$C_{n,r}$ = repeated event or annuity compound interest factor for n years at rate r

Suppose the firm were to receive annual payments of $1,000 a year for 5 years and is charging an interest rate of 8 percent. What will be the amount that the firm will have at the end of 5 years? We can solve this problem by consulting Table B–4. Utilizing our equation we would have:

$$S_{\overline{n}|r} = \$1,000(5.867)$$
$$S_{\overline{n}|r} = \$5,867$$

The 5 payments of $1,000 each would accumulate to $5,867 by the end of the fifth year. Thus, if we had obligated the firm to repay a $5,000 obligation in 5 years it would be able to do so. On the other hand, if the obligation amounted to $7,000 there might be a problem of insufficient funds.

Sometimes the question is asked in a different way. Suppose we need to

TABLE B-4

Sum of an annuity for $1 for *n* years

$$S_{\overline{n}|r} = \$1\left[\frac{(1+r)^n - 1}{r}\right] = \$1C_{n,r}$$

Year	1%	2%	3%	4%	5%	6%	7%	8%	9%	10%	11%	12%	13%	14%	15%	16%
1	1.000	1.000	1.000	1.000	1.000	1.000	1.000	1.000	1.000	1.000	1.000	1.000	1.000	1.000	1.000	1.000
2	2.010	2.020	2.030	2.040	2.050	2.060	2.070	2.080	2.090	2.100	2.110	2.120	2.130	2.140	2.150	2.160
3	3.030	3.060	3.091	3.122	3.152	3.184	3.215	3.246	3.278	3.310	3.342	3.374	3.407	3.440	3.473	3.506
4	4.060	4.122	4.184	4.246	4.310	4.375	4.440	4.506	4.573	4.641	4.710	4.779	4.850	4.921	4.993	5.066
5	5.101	5.204	5.309	5.416	5.526	5.637	5.751	5.867	5.985	6.105	6.228	6.353	6.480	6.610	6.742	6.877
6	6.152	6.308	6.468	6.633	6.802	6.975	7.153	7.336	7.523	7.716	7.913	8.115	8.323	8.536	8.754	8.977
7	7.214	7.434	7.662	7.898	8.142	8.394	8.654	8.923	9.200	9.487	9.783	10.089	10.405	10.730	11.067	11.414
8	8.286	8.583	8.892	9.214	9.549	9.897	10.260	10.637	11.028	11.436	11.859	12.300	12.757	13.233	13.727	14.240
9	9.369	9.755	10.159	10.583	11.027	11.491	11.978	12.488	13.021	13.579	14.164	14.776	15.416	16.085	16.786	17.518
10	10.462	10.950	11.464	12.006	12.578	13.181	13.816	14.487	15.193	15.937	16.722	17.549	18.420	19.337	20.304	21.321
11	11.567	12.169	12.808	13.486	14.207	14.972	15.784	16.645	17.560	18.531	19.561	20.655	21.814	23.044	24.349	25.733
12	12.683	13.412	14.192	15.026	15.917	16.870	17.888	18.977	20.141	21.384	22.713	24.133	25.650	27.271	29.002	30.850
13	13.809	14.680	15.618	16.627	17.713	18.882	20.141	21.495	22.953	24.523	26.212	28.029	29.985	32.089	34.352	36.786
14	14.947	15.974	17.086	18.292	19.599	21.051	22.550	24.215	26.019	27.975	30.095	32.393	34.883	37.581	40.505	43.672
15	16.097	17.293	18.599	20.024	21.579	23.276	25.129	27.152	29.361	31.772	34.405	37.280	40.417	43.842	47.580	51.659

Source: Adapted from Jerome Bracken and Charles J. Christenson, *Tables for Use in Analyzing Business Decisions* (Homewood, Ill.: Richard D. Irwin, Inc., 1965).

have a specified amount of money, such as $5,867, by the end of five years. How much would we have to set aside each year at an interest rate of 8 percent in order to have that amount? We would solve the equation above for a, the annuity. We would have:

$$a = S_{\bar{n}|r}/C_{n,r}$$

Since we know that we need to have $5,867, we look in the interest table for the sum of an annuity, Table B–4, to see what the interest factor is at 8 percent for 5 years. This is 5.867. Therefore, we would need to set aside $1,000 each year.[2]

Now that the basic idea has been set forth let us take a more complex example. Suppose the amount of money that the firm must have at the end of 10 years is $29,000. The applicable interest rate is 8 percent. We wish to know how much we would have to set aside each year in order to accumulate the required amount. The general expression is

$$a = S_{\overline{10}|8\%}/C_{10,8\%}$$

Inserting the numbers given in thé illustration we would have:

$$a = \$29,000/14.487 = \$2,002$$

It would be necessary to set aside slightly over $2,000 each year in order to have the required amount.

Annual receipts from an annuity

Suppose that the firm has made an investment of $30,725 and will be repaid in annual installments at an interest rate of 10 percent. What is the annual amount the firm will receive for each of the 10 years? The general equation for this problem is

$$a = A_{\bar{n}|r}/P_{n,r}$$

Inserting the amounts given for the problem we have:

$$a = \$30,725/6.145$$
$$= \$5,000$$

The result is exactly $5,000. If the question is somewhat altered we still are able to solve it. Suppose the question is, what amount would we have to have to receive $5,000 for 10 years at a 10 percent interest rate? In this instance we would solve the general expression for the present value as shown:

$$A_{\bar{n}|r} = a\,P_{n,r}$$

---

[2] It will be observed that in this presentation we are assuming that the payments are made at the end of each year. This is called a regular annuity or a deferred annuity. If the payment is made at the beginning of the year it is referred to as an annuity due.

In this problem the annual annuity of $5,000 is given and the interest factor is determined by the knowledge that the interest rate is 10 percent and the annuity will continue over a 10-year period. Thus, when we insert the numbers we would have the following result:

$$A_{\overline{10}|\,10\%} = \$5,000(6.145)$$
$$= \$30,725$$

Overview

The formulas that we have used are the following:

$$S_n = P(1 + r)^n \tag{1}$$
$$P = S_n(1 + r)^{-n} \tag{2}$$
$$A_{\overline{n}|r} = a\left[\frac{1 - (1 + r)^{-n}}{r}\right] = a\,P_{n,r} \tag{3}$$
$$S_{\overline{n}|r} = a\left[\frac{(1 + r)^n - 1}{r}\right] = a\,C_{n,r} \tag{4}$$

Of course, the first two equations give us the relationship for both the compound future sum and for the present value of a sum that will be received in the future. For annuities there are different expressions for the interest factor in calculating the present value as compared with the future sum. But, only three basic equation relationships are involved.

These three basic equations enable us to solve at least twelve types of problems. We have three equations and we can solve each one of them for each of the four terms in the equation (present value, future sum or annuity, interest rate, number of years). Thus, with a relatively small number of relationships and with the help of the compound interest tables a large variety of problems involving the time value of money can be handled. Before closing we will consider three variations on the basic themes we have set forth.

Compounding periods within one year

In the illustrations set forth thus far the examples have been for returns that were received once a year or annually. If the interest rates are calculated for periods of time within one year a simple relationship can be followed, utilizing the principles already set forth. For compounding within one year, we simply divide the interest rate by the number of compoundings within a year and multiply the annual periods by the same factor. For example, in our first equation for compound interest we had the following:

$$S_n = P(1 + r)^n$$

This was for annual compounding. For semiannual compounding we would follow the rule just set forth. The equation would become:

$$S_n = P\left(1 + \frac{r}{m}\right)^{nm}$$

Where:

m = the number of compoundings during a year.

We may apply this to the first numerical illustration employed. The question originally was to how much would $1,000 at a 6 percent interest rate accumulate over a 5-year period. The answer was $1,338. Now, we apply semiannual compounding. The equation would appear as follows:

$$S_{5/2} = \$1,000\left(1 + \frac{.06}{2}\right)^{5(2)}$$

Thus, the new expression is equivalent to compounding the $1,000 at 3 percent for 10 periods. Looking in the compound interest table (Table B–1) for 10 years the interest factor would be 1.344. Our equation would, therefore, read:

$$S_{5/2} = \$1,000(1 + .03)^{10}$$
$$= \$1,344$$

It will be noted that with semiannual compounding the future sum amounts to $1,344 as compared with the $1,338 we had before. Frequent compounding provides compound interest paid on compound interest, so the amount is higher. Thus, we would expect that daily compounding, as some financial institutions advertise, or continuous compounding, as is employed under some assumptions, would give somewhat larger amounts than annual or semiannual compounding. But, the basic ideas are unchanged.

The same logic is equally applicable to all of the categories of relationships we have described. For example, in the first illustration on the present value of an annuity the problem was stated as the payment of $1,000 a year for 10 years with an interest rate of 10 percent, compounded annually. If the compounding is semiannual we would employ an interest rate of 5 percent and apply the compounding to a period of 20 years. With compounding semiannually we also have to divide the annual payment by the number of times the compounding takes place within the year. Utilizing, then, our previous example we would have the following expression:

$$
\begin{aligned}
A_{\overline{nm}|r/m} &= \$500(P_{nm,r/m}) \\
&= \$500[P_{10(2),10\%/2}] \\
&= \$500(P_{20,5\%}) \\
&= \$500(12.462) \\
&= \$6,231
\end{aligned}
$$

It will be noted that with annual compounding the present value of the annuities was $6,145. With semiannual compounding the present value is

TABLE B-5

Present value of $1/12 received monthly in year n

Year (n)	1%	2%	4%	6%	8%	10%	12%	14%	15%	16%	18%	20%	22%	24%	25%	26%	28%	30%	35%	40%	45%	50%
1	0.995	0.989	0.979	0.969	0.959	0.950	0.941	0.932	0.928	0.924	0.915	0.907	0.899	0.892	0.888	0.884	0.877	0.870	0.853	0.837	0.822	0.808
2	0.985	0.970	0.941	0.914	0.888	0.864	0.840	0.818	0.807	0.796	0.776	0.756	0.737	0.719	0.710	0.702	0.685	0.669	0.632	0.598	0.567	0.539
3	0.975	0.951	0.905	0.862	0.823	0.785	0.750	0.717	0.702	0.686	0.657	0.630	0.604	0.580	0.568	0.557	0.535	0.515	0.468	0.427	0.391	0.359
4	0.965	0.932	0.870	0.814	0.762	0.714	0.670	0.629	0.610	0.592	0.557	0.525	0.495	0.468	0.455	0.442	0.418	0.396	0.347	0.305	0.270	0.239
5	0.956	0.914	0.837	0.768	0.705	0.649	0.598	0.552	0.531	0.510	0.472	0.438	0.406	0.377	0.364	0.351	0.327	0.305	0.257	0.218	0.186	0.160
6	0.946	0.896	0.805	0.724	0.653	0.590	0.534	0.484	0.461	0.440	0.400	0.365	0.333	0.304	0.291	0.278	0.255	0.234	0.190	0.156	0.128	0.106
7	0.937	0.879	0.774	0.683	0.605	0.536	0.477	0.425	0.401	0.379	0.339	0.304	0.273	0.245	0.233	0.221	0.199	0.180	0.141	0.111	0.088	0.071
8	0.928	0.861	0.744	0.644	0.560	0.488	0.426	0.373	0.349	0.327	0.287	0.253	0.224	0.198	0.186	0.175	0.156	0.139	0.104	0.079	0.061	0.047
9	0.919	0.844	0.715	0.608	0.518	0.443	0.380	0.327	0.303	0.282	0.244	0.211	0.183	0.160	0.149	0.139	0.122	0.107	0.077	0.057	0.042	0.032
10	0.909	0.828	0.688	0.574	0.480	0.403	0.339	0.287	0.264	0.243	0.206	0.176	0.150	0.129	0.119	0.110	0.095	0.082	0.057	0.041	0.029	0.021
11	0.900	0.812	0.661	0.541	0.444	0.366	0.303	0.251	0.229	0.209	0.175	0.147	0.123	0.104	0.095	0.088	0.074	0.063	0.042	0.029	0.020	0.014
12	0.892	0.796	0.636	0.510	0.411	0.323	0.271	0.221	0.199	0.180	0.148	0.122	0.101	0.084	0.076	0.070	0.058	0.049	0.031	0.021	0.014	0.009
13	0.883	0.780	0.612	0.482	0.381	0.303	0.242	0.193	0.173	0.156	0.126	0.102	0.083	0.067	0.061	0.055	0.045	0.037	0.023	0.015	0.010	0.006
14	0.874	0.765	0.588	0.454	0.353	0.275	0.216	0.170	0.151	0.134	0.106	0.085	0.068	0.054	0.049	0.044	0.035	0.029	0.017	0.011	0.007	0.004
15	0.865	0.750	0.565	0.429	0.327	0.250	0.193	0.149	0.131	0.116	0.090	0.071	0.056	0.044	0.039	0.035	0.028	0.022	0.013	0.008	0.005	0.003
16	0.857	0.735	0.544	0.404	0.302	0.227	0.172	0.131	0.114	0.100	0.076	0.059	0.046	0.035	0.031	0.028	0.022	0.017	0.009	0.005	0.003	0.002
17	0.848	0.721	0.523	0.381	0.280	0.207	0.153	0.115	0.099	0.086	0.065	0.049	0.037	0.029	0.025	0.022	0.017	0.013	0.007	0.004	0.002	0.001
18	0.840	0.707	0.503	0.360	0.259	0.188	0.137	0.100	0.086	0.074	0.055	0.041	0.031	0.023	0.020	0.017	0.013	0.010	0.005	0.003	0.001	0.001
19	0.832	0.693	0.483	0.340	0.240	0.171	0.122	0.088	0.075	0.064	0.047	0.034	0.025	0.019	0.016	0.014	0.010	0.008	0.004	0.002	0.001	0.001
20	0.823	0.679	0.465	0.320	0.222	0.155	0.109	0.077	0.065	0.055	0.039	0.028	0.021	0.015	0.013	0.011	0.008	0.006	0.003	0.001	0.001	0.001
21	0.815	0.666	0.447	0.302	0.206	0.141	0.098	0.068	0.057	0.047	0.033	0.024	0.017	0.012	0.010	0.009	0.006	0.005	0.002	0.001		
22	0.807	0.653	0.430	0.285	0.191	0.128	0.087	0.060	0.049	0.041	0.028	0.020	0.014	0.010	0.008	0.007	0.005	0.004	0.002	0.001		
23	0.799	0.640	0.413	0.269	0.176	0.117	0.078	0.052	0.043	0.035	0.024	0.016	0.011	0.008	0.007	0.005	0.004	0.003	0.001	0.001		
24	0.791	0.627	0.397	0.254	0.163	0.106	0.069	0.046	0.037	0.030	0.020	0.014	0.009	0.006	0.005	0.004	0.003	0.002	0.001			
25	0.783	0.615	0.382	0.239	0.151	0.096	0.062	0.040	0.032	0.026	0.017	0.011	0.008	0.005	0.004	0.003	0.002	0.002	0.001			
26	0.776	0.603	0.367	0.226	0.140	0.088	0.055	0.035	0.028	0.023	0.015	0.010	0.006	0.004	0.003	0.003	0.002	0.001				
27	0.768	0.591	0.353	0.213	0.130	0.080	0.049	0.031	0.025	0.019	0.012	0.008	0.005	0.003	0.003	0.002	0.001	0.001				
28	0.760	0.580	0.340	0.201	0.120	0.072	0.044	0.027	0.021	0.017	0.010	0.007	0.004	0.003	0.002	0.002	0.001	0.001				
29	0.753	0.568	0.326	0.190	0.111	0.066	0.039	0.024	0.019	0.014	0.009	0.006	0.003	0.002	0.002	0.001	0.001					
30	0.745	0.557	0.314	0.179	0.103	0.060	0.035	0.021	0.016	0.012	0.008	0.005	0.003	0.002	0.001	0.001	0.001					
40	0.675	0.457	0.212	0.100	0.048	0.023	0.011	0.006	0.004	0.003	0.001	0.001										
50	0.611	0.375	0.143	0.056	0.022	0.009	0.004	0.002	0.001	0.001												

Source: Robert N. Anthony, *Management Accounting: Text and Cases* (rev. ed.; Homewood, Ill.: Richard D. Irwin, Inc., 1960).

TABLE B-6
Present value of $1/12 received monthly for n years

Formula: $\dfrac{1 - (1 + i)^{-n}}{12[(1 + i)^{1/13} - 1]}$ Annual discounting is assumed.

Years (n)	1%	2%	4%	6%	8%	10%	12%	14%	15%	16%	18%	20%	22%	24%	25%	26%	28%	30%	35%	40%	45%	50%
1	0.995	0.989	0.979	0.969	0.959	0.950	0.941	0.932	0.928	0.924	0.915	0.907	0.899	0.892	0.888	0.884	0.877	0.870	0.853	0.837	0.822	0.808
2	1.979	1.959	1.920	1.883	1.848	1.814	1.781	1.750	1.735	1.720	1.691	1.663	1.637	1.611	1.598	1.586	1.562	1.539	1.485	1.435	1.390	1.347
3	2.954	2.910	2.826	2.746	2.670	2.599	2.531	2.467	2.436	2.406	2.348	2.293	2.241	2.191	2.167	2.143	2.098	2.054	1.953	1.863	1.781	1.706
4	3.920	3.843	3.696	3.559	3.432	3.313	3.201	3.096	3.046	2.998	2.905	2.818	2.736	2.658	2.621	2.585	2.516	2.450	2.300	2.168	2.050	1.946
5	4.876	4.757	4.533	4.327	4.137	3.962	3.799	3.648	3.577	3.508	3.377	3.256	3.142	3.036	2.985	2.936	2.842	2.755	2.557	2.386	2.236	2.106
6	5.822	5.653	5.338	5.051	4.790	4.551	4.333	4.132	4.038	3.948	3.778	3.620	3.475	3.340	3.276	3.214	3.098	2.989	2.747	2.541	2.365	2.212
7	6.759	6.531	6.111	5.734	5.395	5.088	4.810	4.557	4.439	4.327	4.117	3.924	3.748	3.585	3.509	3.435	3.297	3.169	2.888	2.653	2.453	2.283
8	7.687	7.392	6.855	6.379	5.954	5.575	5.235	4.929	4.788	4.654	4.404	4.177	3.971	3.783	3.695	3.611	3.453	3.308	2.992	2.732	2.514	2.330
9	8.605	8.237	7.571	6.987	6.473	6.018	5.615	5.256	5.091	4.935	4.647	4.388	4.154	3.942	3.844	3.750	3.575	3.414	3.070	2.789	2.556	2.362
10	9.515	9.065	8.259	7.560	6.953	6.421	5.955	5.543	5.355	5.178	4.854	4.564	4.305	4.071	3.963	3.860	3.670	3.497	3.127	2.829	2.585	2.383
11	10.415	9.876	8.920	8.101	7.397	6.788	6.258	5.794	5.584	5.388	5.029	4.711	4.428	4.175	4.058	3.948	3.744	3.560	3.169	2.858	2.605	2.397
12	11.307	10.672	9.556	8.612	7.809	7.121	6.528	6.015	5.784	5.568	5.177	4.833	4.529	4.259	4.135	4.018	3.802	3.608	3.201	2.879	2.619	2.406
13	12.189	11.452	10.167	9.094	8.190	7.423	6.770	6.208	5.957	5.724	5.302	4.935	4.611	4.326	4.196	4.073	3.847	3.646	3.224	2.894	2.629	2.412
14	13.063	12.217	10.755	9.548	8.542	7.699	6.985	6.378	6.108	5.858	5.409	5.019	4.679	4.380	4.245	4.117	3.883	3.674	3.241	2.904	2.635	2.417
15	13.928	12.967	11.321	9.977	8.869	7.949	7.178	6.527	6.239	5.973	5.499	5.090	4.735	4.424	4.284	4.152	3.911	3.696	3.254	2.912	2.640	2.419
16	14.785	13.702	11.864	10.381	9.171	8.176	7.350	6.658	6.353	6.073	5.576	5.149	4.780	4.460	4.315	4.179	3.932	3.713	3.264	2.917	2.643	2.421
17	15.633	14.422	12.387	10.762	9.451	8.383	7.500	6.772	6.452	6.159	5.640	5.198	4.818	4.488	4.340	4.201	3.949	3.726	3.271	2.921	2.645	2.422
18	16.473	15.129	12.890	11.122	9.711	8.571	7.640	6.873	6.539	6.233	5.695	5.239	4.848	4.511	4.360	4.218	3.962	3.736	3.276	2.924	2.647	2.423
19	17.305	15.822	13.373	11.462	9.951	8.742	7.763	6.961	6.614	6.297	5.742	5.273	4.873	4.530	4.376	4.232	3.973	3.744	3.280	2.926	2.648	2.424
20	18.128	16.501	13.838	11.782	10.173	8.897	7.872	7.038	6.679	6.352	5.781	5.301	4.894	4.545	4.389	4.243	3.981	3.750	3.283	2.927	2.648	2.424
21	18.943	17.167	14.285	12.084	10.379	9.038	7.969	7.106	6.735	6.399	5.815	5.325	4.911	4.557	4.399	4.252	3.987	3.755	3.285	2.928	2.649	2.424
22	19.750	17.819	14.714	12.369	10.570	9.167	8.056	7.165	6.785	6.440	5.843	5.345	4.925	4.567	4.407	4.259	3.992	3.758	3.286	2.929	2.649	2.425
23	20.549	18.459	15.127	12.638	10.746	9.283	8.134	7.218	6.828	6.476	5.867	5.361	4.936	4.574	4.414	4.264	3.996	3.761	3.287	2.929	2.649	2.425
24	21.341	19.087	15.525	12.892	10.909	9.389	8.204	7.263	6.865	6.506	5.887	5.375	4.945	4.581	4.419	4.269	3.999	3.763	3.288	2.930	2.650	2.425
25	22.124	19.702	15.906	13.131	11.061	9.486	8.266	7.304	6.897	6.532	5.904	5.386	4.953	4.586	4.423	4.272	4.001	3.765	3.289	2.930	2.650	2.425
26	22.899	20.305	16.274	13.357	11.201	9.574	8.321	7.339	6.926	6.555	5.919	5.396	4.959	4.590	4.426	4.275	4.003	3.766	3.289	2.930	2.650	2.425
27	23.667	20.896	16.627	13.570	11.331	9.653	8.370	7.370	6.950	6.574	5.931	5.404	4.964	4.593	4.429	4.277	4.004	3.767	3.290	2.930	2.650	2.425
28	24.428	21.476	16.966	13.771	11.451	9.726	8.415	7.397	6.971	6.591	5.942	5.410	4.968	4.596	4.431	4.279	4.005	3.768	3.290	2.930	2.650	2.425
29	25.180	22.044	17.293	13.961	11.562	9.792	8.454	7.421	6.990	6.606	5.951	5.416	4.972	4.598	4.433	4.280	4.006	3.768	3.290	2.930	2.650	2.425
30	25.926	22.601	17.607	14.139	11.665	9.852	8.489	7.441	7.006	6.618	5.958	5.420	4.975	4.600	4.434	4.281	4.007	3.769	3.290	2.930	2.650	2.425
40	32.985	27.605	20.153	15.456	12.256	10.220	8.688	7.550	7.087	6.678	5.992	5.440	4.986	4.606	4.439	4.285	4.009	3.770	3.291	2.931	2.650	2.425
50	39.375	31.711	21.873	16.191	12.676	10.361	8.752	7.580	7.107	6.692	5.999	5.443	4.987	4.607	4.440	4.285	4.009	3.770	3.291	2.931	2.650	2.425

Source: Robert N. Anthony, *Management Accounting: Text and Cases* (rev. ed.; Homewood, Ill.: Richard D. Irwin, 1960).

$6,231. With more frequent compounding the resulting amounts will be somewhat higher for the reason that interest is compounded on interest.

Since in business transactions receipts or payments often occur on a monthly basis, we have also provided (single event) present value factor and repeated event (annuity) present value factor ($P_{n12,r/12}$) tables compounded on a monthly basis in Tables B–5 and B–6, respectively.

Calculations for a series of unequal receipts or payments

In all of the previous illustrations we have assumed that the receipts flowing in or the payments to be made are of equal amounts. This simplifies the calculations. However, if unequal receipts or unequal payments are involved the principles are again the same, but the calculations must be somewhat extended. For example, suppose that the firm makes a foreign investment from which it will receive the following amounts:

Year	Receipts	× Interest factor (15%)	= Present value
1	$100	.870	$ 87.00
2	200	.756	151.20
3	600	.658	394.80
4	300	.572	171.60
		PV of the investment =	$804.60

Using the present value interest table (Table B–2) at an interest rate of 15% we obtain the amounts indicated above. The interest factor is multiplied by the receipts to provide the amounts in the present value column. The amounts for each year are then summed to provide the present value of the investment, which in this example is $804.60. What we are doing in this example is illustrating how an annuity of unequal payments which could not be computed directly from the present value of an annuity table can be handled by breaking the problem into a series of one-year payments received at successively later time periods.

This illustrates a general technique that can be employed in using compound interest relationships. A particular business problem or decision involving the time value of money, no matter how complex, can usually be handled by compound interest methods. The technique is to take a complex problem and to break it into a series of simple ones. Each of the simple problems can be readily handled. Then the results can be combined to arrive at an overall solution. We are confident, therefore, that the reader is now equipped from a computational standpoint to deal with a wide range of complex decisions involving the time value of money.

The determination of the applicable interest rate

A number of sources can be used to determine the applicable interest rate to use in a particular business decision. One broad reference is the general level of interest rates in the economy as a whole. Individual interest rates in the economy generally differ by the maturity (the period of time over which the obligation runs) as well as the degree of risk of the obligation. Short-term U.S. government securities generally bear the lowest rate of interest, while the debt obligations of a small company with an uncertain future usually carry a relatively high rate of interest.

In addition, the levels of interest rates are affected by different business conditions in the economy at a particular time. Interest rates will also be influenced by economic developments in foreign countries. For guidance on interest rate levels in the economy, financial managers may refer to readily available government publications such as the *Survey of Current Business,* published by the United States Department of Commerce; the *Federal Reserve Bulletin,* published by the Board of Governors of the Federal Reserve System; *International Financial Statistics,* published by the International Monetary Fund; and *Economic Indicators,* available from the United States Government Printing Office. All of these publications are available at nominal subscription rates.

Another guide in the determination of what interest rate should be applied in making compound interest decisions is consideration of what the firm could earn if it used the money in some alternative investment opportunity. This is generally referred to as the opportunity cost of an investment. The opportunity cost of investments is the yield on the best alternative use of the funds.

Illustration of the application of Present Value Tables for monthly payments[3]

The Smith Manufacturing Company is contemplating the sale of $20,000 of machinery to a foreign buyer on a two-year basis. The Company's cost of borrowing is 6 percent and it usually charges its customers interest at the rate of 8 percent, its opportunity cost. The firm has the choice of borrowing its own funds, making 24 monthly or 2 annual payments. It is considering asking for a 10 percent down payment and either 24 monthly or 2 annual payments. What decision would be most advantageous to the firm?

1. The firm makes monthly payments and collects from its customer on the same basis.

---

[3] The symbols P^* and A^* represent the use of monthly interest Tables B–5 and B–6.

Amount of sale	$20,000
Down payment, 10%	2,000
Balance	$18,000

Monthly payments from the customer:

Each payment $= 18,000/12(P^*_{2,8\%}) = 1,500/1.848 = \$811.69$

Monthly payments to the lender:

Each payment $= 18,000/12(P^*_{2,6\%}) = 1,500/1.883 = \$796.60$

The present value of the difference between the payments received and the payments made at the firm's opportunity cost is:

$$A^*_{\overline{2}|8} = (\$811.69 - \$796.60)P^*_{2,8\%} = 15.09 \ (1.848)12$$
$$= \$334.63$$

2. The firm makes two annual payments after the down payment to its bank and collects from its customer on the same basis.

Annual payments from customer:

Each payment $= 18,000/P_{2,8\%} = 18,000/1.783 = \$10,095.34$

Annual payments to bank:

Each payment $= 18,000/P_{2,6\%} = 18,000/1.833 = \$9,819.97$

The present value of the difference between the payments received and the payments made at the firm's opportunity cost is:

$$A_{\overline{2}|8} = (10,095.34 - 9,819.97)P_{2,8\%}$$
$$= 275.37 \ (1.783) = \$490.98$$

3. The firm makes 2 annual payments and requests its customer to make 24 monthly payments, each $\frac{1}{12}$ of the annual payment.

The two annual payments of the firm are the same as in (2), namely $9,819.97.

$$\text{Annual payment} = 18,000/1.783 = 10,095.34$$
$$\text{Monthly payments} = 10,095.34/12 = 841.28$$
$$A^*_{\overline{2}|8} = 841.28(12)P^*_{2,8\%} = 841.28(12)1.848 = 18,656.20$$

The present value of the firm's annual payments discounted at the firm's opportunity cost is:

$$A_{\overline{2}|8} = 9,819.97(P_{2,8\%}) = 9,819.97(1.783) = 17,509.01$$
$$\text{Benefit to the firm} = \text{receipts} - \text{costs}$$
$$= 18,656.20 - 17,509.01 = \$1,147.19$$

This represents the net present value to the firm.

Comparison between the three alternative arrangements

This problem makes use of the monthly interest tables and specifically utilizes Table B–6 which represents the present value of an amount received monthly for n years. In (1) the firm makes monthly payments and collects from the customer on the same basis. Since two years are involved, the number 2 line under the appropriate interest rate column provides the rate that applies. The monthly payments from the customer are calculated taking the $18,000, dividing by 12 as the interest table indicates, dividing the resulting $1,500 figure by the interest factor at 8 percent which is 1.848. The result is the monthly payment from the customer, which is $811.69. In a similar fashion the monthly payments that will be required to be paid to the lender by the manufacturer are calculated. This amounts to $796.60. This difference is $334.63.

Under (2), the firm makes two annual payments after the down payment to the bank and collects from its customer on the same basis. The difference in this instance is $490.98. It will be noted that the difference is greater under (2) than under (1). The reason for this is that the sum of the monthly payments is smaller under (1) than the sum of the annual payments under (2). The reason that the sum of the monthly payments is smaller is, since the repayment proceeds more rapidly as payments are being made each month instead of waiting until the end of one complete year before any payment is made, the amount of interest involved is smaller under (1). We make this point because the first reaction of many readers is that anything that involves monthly compounding will involve more interest; but since a repayment is involved, the opposite is true here. It involves less interest.

In (3) the payment by the firm would be the same as it was under (2). However, a new aspect is introduced with regard to the customer. In effect, we are telling the customer that first we want to calculate what your annual payments would be if you were paying in two installments. Then, we will take that amount and divide by 12, as illustrated. This has the effect of enabling us to receive 11/12ths of the annual payments before we pay at the end of the year. Obviously, with this kind of wrinkle the firm will benefit the most. If the customer understood the use of monthly interest tables, he would not have agreed to such an arrangement.

The problem then illustrates some of the practical aspects of the use of the monthly interest tables. We recognize that monthly interest tables are neither generally provided nor generally used. This is one of the reasons why the kind of arrangement under (3) is sometimes encountered. Since only the annual interest tables are generally available, the calculation is made on an annual basis and then divided by 12. It is obviously to the benefit of the seller to proceed in this way. But since the payments are coming in sooner than on an annual basis, the appropriate tables to use, from the standpoint of a person who is making the payments, would be the monthly interest tables.

It is particularly true in connection with international transactions which appear to be complicated anyhow by the possibility of fluctuating exchange rates, etc., that a wrinkle such as the one covering (3) sometimes arises. Notice that while the difference between the results in (1) and (2) are relatively moderate, the difference in the gain to the seller in (3) is more than 100 percent of the amount of gain in either (1) or (2). We suggest that utilization of the monthly interest tables will more than repay the managers' small extra effort to familiarize themselves with the use of the monthly compound interest tables.

APPENDIX C

Risk analysis of business decisions— implications for international financial management*

INTERNATIONAL BUSINESS is a subset of all business. A major problem confronting all business is making decisions under conditions of risk. International business activities are exposed to a wider range of types and degrees of risk than are domestic business activities. Therefore, the methods of considering risk developed for application to business decisions generally are particularly relevant for international financial decisions.

In the analysis of return and risk relationships the most generally used indices are the expected returns and standard deviation of returns. The standard deviation is a measure of the dispersion of returns around their mean or expected return. Thus dispersion of possible returns around their mean is a general measure of the risk of the outcomes resulting from business decisions. In this appendix the concepts of expected return and return dispersion are developed through numerical examples set in the context of the selection of investments under conditions of risk.

Expected returns and return dispersion

For illustration, we shall compare the use of a single figure such as the "most probable" return with an analysis of the probabilities of a range of returns summarized by their average values and their dispersion. The symbols employed are set forth in Table C–1. In Tables C–2 and C–3 analyses are made of the expected returns and their dispersion of a foreign investment and a domestic investment. The prospects for the foreign investment are calculated in Table C–2 and for the domestic investment in Table C–3.

First, the computations for the foreign investment are made. In

---

* Our thanks to Professor Jerome Baesel of York University for valuable contributions in developing this appendix.

column (1) alternative future states of the world are expressed as most probable, optimistic, and pessimistic. These are assumed to be from the standpoint of an investor in the United States. The next column shows the probability factor associated with each state. In column (3) the alternative returns under the three possible states of the world are set forth. A given state of the world may have different implications for different types of investments. The nature of the relationship between the general state of the world and the outcomes for individual investments can be related to underlying economic or business firm characteristics. But the general point here is that the same state of the world

TABLE C–1

Explanation of symbols used in Tables C–2 through C–4

s — alternative future states of the world viewed from the standpoint of the United States

p — the probability assigned to various possible outcomes of an investment

X, Y, M — designation for various investments: X and Y are individual investments; M refers to a broadly diversified investment or the market as a whole

$E(X)$ — the expected return on investment X; this is the weighted average or actuarial return with weights determined by the probabilities

$VAR(X)$ — variance of the returns on investment X from their average; a measure of dispersion

σ — the standard deviation of returns; the square root of variance

may be associated with positive or favorable implications for one investment and negative or unfavorable implications for different types of investments. This is particularly true for business firms that are engaged in business operations on a multinational basis where highly diverse conditions are likely to be encountered at different times and in different parts of the world.

For example, an optimistic future state of the world from the standpoint of a U.S. firm is the kind of event that occurred when, with currency realignment and the removal of the U.S. excise tax, the sale of automobiles in the United States increased. Thus investments in the automobile industry and related industries in the United States would have been favorable. On the other hand, with the higher prices charged for the foreign automobiles in terms of U.S. dollars, their sales and returns on investments in foreign auto companies would become less favorable.

We have thus established a basis for considering alternative future states of the world, their probabilities, and the associated outcomes. In column (4) the probabilities of the alternative state of the world are multiplied times the possible outcomes that were set forth in column (3). By multiplying the probabilities times the values and summing, we obtain an expected return of 10 percent for foreign investment, X.

TABLE C-2

Calculation of the expected return and dispersion of the returns from investment X in a foreign country

(1) Alternative future states of the world	(2) Proba- bility factor p^*	(3) Possible returns from the investment X	(4) Calculation of expected return pX	(5)	(6)	(7)
				Calculation of measures of dispersion		
				$[X - E(X)]$	$[X - E(X)]^2$	$p[X - E(X)]^2$
Optimistic	.3	−.020	−.006	−.120	.0144	.0043
Most probable	.5	.200	.100	.100	.0100	.0050
Pessimistic	.2	.030	.006	−.070	.0049	.0010
			$E(X)$ = .100		$VAR(X)$ = .0103	
$E(X)$ = 10%	σX = 10.2%				σX = .102	

° In this and all of the following examples, the probabilities will always sum to 1, indicating that the total possibilities have been considered.

The corresponding columns in Table C-3 contain similar calculations for the domestic investment for which the expected return is also 10 percent.

The expected return on the domestic investment and on the foreign investment are the same. However, the most probable return for the foreign investment was 20 percent, as compared with the most probable return of only 8 percent for the domestic investment. This result occurs even though the most probable return from the foreign investment is very favorable. The reason for this is the low or even negative return which occurs on the foreign investment if outcomes other than the most probable occur.

We have established that it is the actuarial or expected return that is relevant rather than the return that is "most likely." Consideration of other possibilities requires taking into account the possible dispersion of actual returns from expected returns. This is most generally expressed by various measures of dispersion. One measure is the *range* of possible returns—the difference between the highest and lowest returns. The range is 22 percent for the foreign investment and only 15 percent for

TABLE C-3

Calculation of the expected return and dispersion of the returns from investment Y in the United States

(1) Alternative future states of the world	(2) Probability factor p	(3) Possible returns from the investment Y	(4) Calculation of expected return pY	(5)	(6)	(7)
				Calculation of measures of dispersion		
				$[Y - E(Y)]$	$[Y - E(Y)]^2$	$p[Y - E(Y)]^2$
Optimistic	.3	.18	.054	.080	.0064	.0019
Most probable	.5	.08	.040	−.020	.0004	.0002
Pessimistic	.2	.03	.006	.070	.0049	.0010
			$E(Y)$ = .10		$VAR (Y)$ = .0031	
$E(Y)$ = 10%	σY = 5.6%				σY = .056	

the domestic investment. Two other measures of dispersion, while similar in concept, are sufficiently complex to require systematic calculations. These are shown in Tables C–2 and C–3 for the foreign investment X, and the domestic investment Y, respectively. In column (5) the difference between each possible return and the expected value of the return is set forth. In column (6) these deviations are squared. In column (7) the squared deviations are multiplied by their associated probabilities and the amounts are summed. The weighted sum of the squared deviations is referred to in statistical terminology as the variance. The square root of the variance is called the standard deviation. The standard deviation has several useful statistical properties. For example, a rule of thumb is that the results of future events are likely, with high probabilities, to lie between plus or minus two standard deviations from the expected return. Thus the 10.2 percent standard deviation of the foreign investment could, within a range of high probabilities, either double the expected return or completely wipe it out. Thus, measured by standard deviation, the foreign investment carries much greater risk (10.2 percent) than the domestic investment (5.6 percent).

Efficient diversification of investment

Based on the standard deviation as a measure of risk, the domestic investment, Y, would be clearly superior since it involves the same expected return as the foreign investment but a much smaller degree of risk. But to this point we have been considering individual investments. However, the activities of business firms may also be regarded as a combination of a number of different types of investments. Hence a firm and its investment activities may be analyzed from the standpoint of portfolios.

Before pursuing the implications of viewing the activities of the firm as portfolios, it should be noted that we are here referring to investments in the broad sense. Any activity that involves the allocation or commitment of the resources of the firm represents an investment. Thus an export of goods by an international firm and the resources required to support that activity is a form of investment. Holding cash to avoid risks of loss from committing the funds to another form is itself a form of investment position. Indeed, the form of currency in which the cash or savings account is held reflects some pattern of expectations or judgments about the future values of currencies versus real goods and the future value of currencies of some individual countries as compared with the currencies of other countries. Therefore, the many activities of any individual firm represent components of a portfolio of investments. Hence the decisions of individual firms to engage in one set of activities rather than another set of activities represent the choice of one portfolio of investments as compared with another portfolio of investments.

Viewing the activities of the firm as a portfolio of investments is relevant to any firm—national or multinational. The essential difference between the portfolio considerations of the multinational firm vis-à-vis uninational firm is that the set of opportunities facing the multinational firm is larger and more diverse. That is, all opportunities open to a uninational firm are open to the multinational firm. In addition, the multinational firm is faced with all the international opportunities which are more diverse than the opportunities within a single country.

Thus for the multinational firm decisions must be made with regard to (1) the extent of international activity, (2) the form of international activity, (3) the choices of countries in which sales, purchases, or operations will be carried on and (4) the forms and types of risk to which the firm will be exposed. The international activities of business firms may be regarded as diversification particularly with regard to the geographic locations of activities and the different types of economic influences to which the firm will be exposed as a consequence of its international activities. Thus the international activities of business firms may be regarded as broadening the portfolio opportunities to achieve efficient diversification.

Efficient diversification is minimization of the risk of a business decision or investment for a given expected return. Conversely, efficient diversification can be defined as: for a given level of risk obtaining a higher expected return than from other portfolio combinations.

We have established that the firm may be viewed as a portfolio of investments. A portfolio is a method of achieving diversification. But whether the managers of business firms should attempt to achieve diversification as a leading objective for the firm is another issue. It has been generally agreed that in an economy with well-developed finance markets, investors are better off if management does not attempt to diversify, but focuses on maximizing shareholder wealth as an overriding goal. Individual investors through the financial markets are probably able to diversify more efficiently than the individual firm can diversify. The main reason is that the transactions costs to the individual investor through the financial markets are lower in reversing his investments. An individual company which seeks to diversify by making real asset investments in plant and equipment, or in a sales organization, or in other forms of investments is involved in organization costs and developing an organization to carry on these activities. In addition, substantial costs or losses are involved if the firm seeks to terminate such activities. With the wide range of alternative financial investments available to the individual investor through the securities markets and with the use of a wide variety of information sources available about individual companies and their securities, the consensus is that for investment in domestic activities, the individual investor can diversify efficiently.[1]

However, it may be more appropriate to regard international operations of business firms in the context of portfolio diversification. The individual operating through financial markets is less likely to be able to diversify as efficiently with regard to international investments as for domestic investments. The individual is less knowledgeable about conditions in foreign countries and about foreign firms. In connection with their international activities U.S. firms must familiarize themselves with conditions in the foreign countries in which they will be operating. Thus, U.S. firms in their international activities may provide an efficient form of diversification for individual investors.

It is important to clarify some distinctions between forms of diversification. Portfolio diversification involves combining activities whose returns are less than perfectly positively correlated. This is different from the behavior of a firm which engages in a large number of activities some of which may be dominated by the same underlying economic influences as others. This is not portfolio diversification in any meaningful sense.

On the other hand, business firms have argued at the same time that they are achieving portfolio diversification and synergy as well. For synergy to be achieved there must be some forms of complementarities or some types of economies of scale by combining activities. Where synergy is achieved it is less likely that such investments or projects are subject to different *economic* influences. Since international financial markets for equity positions are not as well-developed as are the markets for equity positions in the major developed economies, the activities of international firms may contribute to more complete markets. For this reason attempts on the part of the firm in its international activities to view its activities as a portfolio and to achieve portfolio diversification can have a greater basis for justification.

What is required for the benefits of portfolio diversification to be achieved is that the activities not be perfectly positively correlated. Therefore, it is possible for a firm to simultaneously achieve synergy and to achieve portfolio diversification at the same time. However, conceptually it is important to keep the two influences separate. It is important for practical reasons as well. If a firm engages in a program of "diversification" by simply engaging in diverse activities, it will achieve neither efficient portfolio diversification nor carryover or synergy. The combining of diverse activities as such does not ensure either portfolio

---

[1] The individual company may achieve economies also from combining diverse but related activities. The activities may be related in a sense that the firm can achieve complementarities or some types of economies of scale by combining the activities.

diversification or synergy. To attempt to achieve either requires careful preplanning and a careful assessment of the underlying economic influences as they will have an impact on the time pattern of returns in relationship to other investments as well as possibilities for achieving economies by combining activities.

We have now justified on both theoretical and practical grounds the bases for treating the firm as a portfolio. Therefore, the individual investments of the firm have to be appraised in the context of their representing components of a portfolio. Therefore, the risk measure attached to the individual investment must be devised from the characteristics of the resulting portfolio rather than the characteristics of the individual investment project. And, therefore, the appropriate risk measure is developed from the characteristics of the portfolio. The concepts can most conveniently be illustrated first by the use of illustrations involving portfolios with only two assets. The relationships can then be generalized.

Risk management by portfolio diversification—concepts

The use of portfolios in achieving efficient diversifications will be illustrated. But some additional background material is required. A new relationship involves the concept of covariance. Covariance is a measure of the extent to which the returns on an individual investment are influenced by (covary with) the more general economic forces and patterns of investment return in an individual country or economy.

The concept of covariance has much practical significance in connection with international financial decisions. Some developments in the world which favor investments in the United States may unfavorably effect foreign activity. Conversely, some developments that may be unfavorable for activities in the United States may favor foreign financial developments. Thus another important aspect of reducing the risk of a group of investments is to analyze their pattern of behavior in relation to possible events that will occur in the world.

A procedure for measuring this aspect of risk is to calculate the covariation of the possible returns from an individual investment with the returns that would be obtained if the firm or investors, in general, were to diversify broadly. The return from a broadly diversified portfolio can be referred to as the "market return." Since the returns on foreign investments are less favorable when returns on investments made in the United States are more favorable (under the assumptions of this illustration), we would expect their covariance with the foreign market to be different from the covariance of domestic investments with U.S. market returns. The symbols COV_{xm} and COV_{ym} will be used to refer to the covariance of the foreign and domestic investments respectively with a general market return.

TABLE C-4

Calculation of the expected return and dispersion of returns from the market average in the United States

(1)	(2)	(3)	(4)	(5)	(6)	(7)
		Possible	Calculation			
Alternative	Probability	returns from	of expected		Calculation of measures of dispersion	
future states	factor	the investment	return			
of the world	p	M	pM	$[M - E(M)]$	$[M - E(M)]^2$	$p[M - E(M)]^2$
Optimistic	.3	.12	.036	.03	.0009	.00027
Most probable	.5	.08	.040	−.01	.0001	.00005
Pessimistic	.2	.07	.014	−.02	.0004	.00008
			$E(M) = .09$		$VAR (M) =$	.00040
					$\sigma_M =$	.02

$E(M) = 9\%$ $\sigma_M = 2\%$

To perform the covariance calculation, the expected returns on the market and the deviation of returns on the market must first be calculated as set forth in Table C-4. In Table C-4 calculations of the expected return and measures of dispersions for the market return are made in a fashion exactly the same as that which is calculated for investments X and Y.

Next in Table C-5 we calculate the variation of the return from the foreign investment with the U.S. market return and the covariation of the return from the U.S. domestic investment with the U.S. market re-

TABLE C-5

Calculation of the covariance of returns from a domestic investment as compared with a foreign investment

Foreign investment

(1)	(2)	(3)	(4)	(5)
	Prob-			
Alternative	ability		Product of	Probability
future states	factor	Deviations	deviations	calculations
of the world	p	$[X - E(X)][M - E(M)]$	$[X - E(X)][M - E(M)]$	$p[[X - E(X)][M - E(M)]]$
Optimistic	.3	$(-.12)\ (.03)$	−.0036	−.00108
Most probable	.5	$(.10)(-.01)$	−.0010	−.00050
Pessimistic	.2	$(-.07)(-.02)$	.0014	.00028
				$COV_{x,m} = -.00130$

Domestic investment

(1)	(2)	(3)	(4)	(5)
	Prob-			
Alternative	ability		Product of	Probability
future states	factor	Deviations	deviations	calculations
of the world	p	$[Y - E(Y)][M - E(M)]$	$[Y - E(Y)][M - E(M)]$	$p[[Y - E(Y)][M - E(M)]]$
Optimistic	.3	$(.08)(.03)$	.0024	.00072
Most probable	.5	$(-.02)(-.01)$	.0002	.00010
Pessimistic	.2	$(-.07)(-.02)$	.0014	.00028
				$COV_{y,m} = .00110$

turn. The calculation procedure involves the following: We begin in column (1) by defining the alternative future states of the world from the standpoint of the U.S. market. Column (2) sets forth the probability factor again. In column (3) the deviation of the returns from the individual investment is multiplied by the deviations of market returns from their expected returns. The product is shown in column (4). In column (5) this product is then multiplied by the associated probabilities. Then these amounts are summed. The resulting figure is the covariance for each of the investments.

Risk reduction by portfolio diversification—illustrative calculations

With the use of the additional concept of covariance we may now proceed to illustrate the use of a portfolio approach in achieving efficient diversification. The symbols that will be employed are set forth in Table C–6. They are generally the concepts that we have already covered with the exception of "correlation" which is related to the concept of covariance.

The relations for use in calculating portfolio return and risk (or mathematical formulas) are:

$$COR_{id} = COV_{id}/\sigma_i\sigma_d \tag{C-1a}$$
$$COV_{id} = COR_{id}\sigma_i\sigma_d \tag{C-1b}$$
$$E(R_p) = xE(R_d) + (1 - x)E(R_i) \tag{C-2}$$
$$\sigma_p = [x^2\sigma^2_d + (1 - x)^2\sigma^2_i + 2x(1 - x)COV_{id}]^{\frac{1}{2}} \tag{C-3}$$
$$x = \frac{\sigma_i(\sigma_i - COR_{id}\sigma_d)}{\sigma^2_i + \sigma^2_d - 2COR_{id}\sigma_i\sigma_d} \tag{C-4}$$

Four basic relations are set forth and will be utilized in the calculations. The concept of correlation coefficient is defined by equation C–1a. It is the covariance divided by the product of the standard deviations of

TABLE C–6

Symbols for analysis of portfolio diversification

$E(R_d)$ = expected return from a domestic investment
$E(R_i)$ = expected return from an international investment
$E(R_p)$ = expected return from the portfolio
σ_d = standard deviation of the returns from a domestic investment
σ_i = standard deviation of the returns from an international investment
σ_p = standard deviation of the returns from a portfolio
COR_{id} = correlation of returns between projects
COV_{id} = covariance of returns between projects
x = proportion of the total portfolio in the domestic investment
$(1 - x)$ = proportion of the total portfolio in the international investment

each of the investments. Alternatively we can write the expression for covariance as the correlation multiplied by the standard deviations of the investments as in equation C–1b.

The equation C–2 sets forth the calculation of the expected return from the portfolio in the two-asset case. It represents the average of the returns on the individual investments weighted by their proportions in the portfolio.

Equation C–3 is the formula for calculating the standard deviation or risk of the portfolio. It is the proportion of each investment squared times its standard deviation squared plus the third term which is two times the product of the two proportions times the covariance between the return from the investments in the portfolio. For the two-asset case, the square root is taken of the sum of these three terms.

The fourth relationship that will be employed is the formula that has been derived for determining the proportion in which investments may appropriately be combined in a portfolio in order to achieve the minimum possible risk by combining investments in a portfolio. The formula set forth is, of course, for the two-asset portfolio.

While we will illustrate the concepts for the two-asset portfolio, the principles are exactly the same for the multi-asset portfolio. For the many investment portfolios, more complex matrices of variance and covariance relationships are involved computationally, but the concepts are exactly the same as those that will be illustrated here.

The illustrative calculations are now presented. We begin with Example 1 in which the basic facts given are first presented. These are the data that will be utilized in the calculations. In Example 1 a correlation of negative one is a critical factor in the computations. The correlation of negative one assumes that when one investment does well the other does poorly and vice versa. The numbers given in the illustration indicate that the foreign investment has a somewhat higher return, but an even greater degree of risk. The two investments are combined equally in the portfolio.

The expected return on the portfolio is seen to be the average of the expected returns from the two individual investments. However, the standard deviation or risk of the portfolio is only 2 percent, which is much below the 6 percent for domestic investments and 10 percent for the international investment.

The example illustrates the power of portfolio diversification. The expected return is the simple average weighted by the proportion of the investments in the portfolio. However, the standard deviation or risk of the portfolio is greatly reduced. This reduction occurs because of the perfect negative correlation between the returns from the two investments. Indeed, with a correlation of negative one the risk or standard deviation of the portfolio can be eliminated (as will be demonstrated below).

Example 1: Correlation of negative one

Given:

$E(R_d) = 10\%$ $\sigma_d = 6\%$ $x = .5$
$E(R_i) = 12\%$ $\sigma_i = 10\%$ $COR_{id} = -1$

Calculations:

$E(R_p) = .5(10) + .5(12) = 11\%$

$$\sigma_p = [(.5)^2(6)^2 + (.5)^2(10)^2 + 2(.5)(.5)(-1)(6)(10)]^{\frac{1}{2}}$$
$$= [.25(36) + .25(100) - .5(60)]^{\frac{1}{2}}$$
$$= [9 + 25 - 30]^{\frac{1}{2}}$$
$$= [4]^{\frac{1}{2}}$$
$$\sigma_p = 2\%$$

It might be difficult in practical circumstances to find an international investment that provides perfect negative correlation with the returns from the domestic investment. An alternative reasonable possibility would be that the correlation between the two investments is zero. This would indicate that they are independent investments. This implies that the economic influences on the two investments stem from independent and unrelated sources or causes. It will be seen that the expected return from the portfolio remains 11 percent since the proportions of the two investments have been unchanged. However, because the correlation between the returns from the two investments is now zero, the standard deviation of the portfolio rises to 5.8 percent, but the risk of the portfolio is still lower than the risk from either of the individual investments.

Example 2: Zero correlation (independent investments)
Same as Example 1 except that $COR_{id} = 0$

$E(R_p) = 11\%$

$$\sigma_p = [9 + 25]^{\frac{1}{2}}$$
$$= [34]^{\frac{1}{2}}$$
$$\sigma_p = 5.8\%$$

Example 3 seeks to illustrate the effects of changing the proportions of the two investments in the portfolio. The calculations are shown. In this example 80 percent of the portfolio is represented by the domestic investment. The expected return on the portfolio is lower than in the previous two examples since greater weight is given to the return from the domestic investment. But since the risk of the domestic investment is lower, the portfolio risk is also reduced below that of Example 2 when the two investments were combined in equal proportions in the portfolio.

Example 3:

Same as Example 2 except that $x = .8$

$E(R_p) = .8(10) + .2(12) = 8 + 2.4 = 10.4\%$

$$\sigma_p = [(.8)^2(6)^2 + (.2)^2(10)^2]^{\frac{1}{2}}$$
$$= [(.64)(36) + .04(100)]^{\frac{1}{2}}$$
$$= [23.04 + 4]^{\frac{1}{2}}$$
$$= [27.04]^{\frac{1}{2}}$$
$$\sigma_p = 5.2\%$$

Example 3 has demonstrated that the proportion in which the investments are combined in a portfolio will influence both the expected return and the portfolio risk. We can now utilize formula C–4 to determine that proportion in which to combine the investments in the portfolio in order to reduce the risk as much as possible. In Example 4 we show that the best proportion for Example 2 where the correlation coefficient was zero is shown to be .735. For Example 1 where the correlation coefficient was a negative one the best proportion would have been .625.

Example 4:

$$COR_{id} = 0 \qquad x = \frac{10(10 - 0)}{(10)^2 + (6)^2} = \frac{100}{100 + 36} = \frac{100}{136} = .735$$

$$x = .735$$
$$(1 - x) = .265$$

$$COR_{id} = -1 \qquad x = \frac{10[10 - (-1)(6)]}{(10)^2 + (6)^2 - 2(-1)(6)(10)} = \frac{10[16]}{100 + 36 + 120}$$

$$= \frac{160}{256} = .625$$

$$x = .625$$
$$(1 - x) = .375$$

We next employ these results in Examples 5 and 6. Example 5 is the same as Example 1 except that the proportion is .735 and the correlation relationship is zero. With a correlation relationship of zero the expected return on the portfolio becomes 10.5 percent reflecting the somewhat greater weight given to the international investment. The risk from the portfolio, however, is reduced to its minimum for the given amount of risk from the individual investments. The risk or the standard of the portfolio returns drops to 5.14 percent. This is lower than in Examples 2 or 3 for which the proportions in the domestic investment were .5 and .8 respectively.

Example 5:

Same as Example 1 except that $x = .735$ and $COR_{id} = 0$

$$E(R_p) = .735(10) + .265(12)$$
$$= 7.35 + 3.18 = 10.53\%$$
$$\sigma_p = [(.735)^2(6)^2 + (.265)^2(10)^2]^{\frac{1}{2}}$$
$$= [.540225(36) + .070225(100)]^{\frac{1}{2}}$$
$$= [19.4481 + 7.0225]^{\frac{1}{2}}$$
$$= [26.47]^{\frac{1}{2}}$$
$$= 5.14\%$$

In Example 6 we have the same facts as in Example 1 except that the proportion of the domestic investment in the portfolio is .625 rather than one half as in Example 1. The expected return is somewhat lower than 11 percent (10.75) since greater weighting is given to the domestic investment as compared with the weighting of one half in Example 1. However, the portfolio risk is completely eliminated. With perfect negative correlation there exists some proportion for combining the investments into a portfolio that will completely eliminate risk. This is because the variation in returns is completely eliminated. When the weighted return from one investment is favorable, the weighted return from the investment that is perfectly negatively correlated will be unfavorable to the same degree.

Example 6:

Same as Example 1 except that $x = .625$

$$E(R_p) = .625(10) + .375(12)$$
$$= 6.25 + 4.5 = 10.75\%$$
$$\sigma_p = [(.625)^2(6)^2 + (.375)^2(10)^2 + 2(.625)(.375)(-1)(6)(10)]^{\frac{1}{2}}$$
$$= [.390625(36) + .140625(100) - 28.125]^{\frac{1}{2}}$$
$$= [14.0625 + 14.0625 - 28.125]^{\frac{1}{2}}$$
$$= 0$$

The concepts of systematic and unsystematic risk

The foregoing examples have demonstrated the power of portfolio diversification in reducing risk. The power of portfolio diversification in achieving risk reduction will be even greater with more than the two assets assumed in the previous examples. What is required for portfolio diversification to reduce risk is that the correlation between the returns from the individual investments be less than positive one. If there is low correlation between the returns from individual components, a portfolio with 15 to 20 assets will approximate the results of "the market as a whole," a broadly diversified portfolio.

But even though a portfolio approximates the risk of a market portfolio this does not mean that the entire risk of the portfolio has been eliminated. The total market itself fluctuates. Thus, if an investment is made in the total market and held for a short period of time the return from such an investment in the market could be either very high or very low. An investment in the entire market which is held for an extended period of time such as 10 to 15 years would yield a return close to the expected return on the market of some 9 percent per annum with a relatively small standard deviation.

The residual risk of total market fluctuation has been referred to as systematic risk.[2] It is the risk of the total market itself. The risk of an individual investment or of a portfolio can be expressed by its covariation with fluctuations in market returns. This is measured by the volatility of the returns to the individual security or to the individual portfolio. Thus, if the return from an individual security or portfolio drops 15 percent when the market return drops 10 percent and when the market return rises 10 percent the return to the individual security or portfolio rises 15 percent, the volatility factor for the individual security or portfolio is 1.5 times that of the market.

Thus, if a security has a volatility of one this means it fluctuates exactly in the same manner as the market. On the other hand, a volatility of 1.5 indicates that the degree of fluctuation for the individual security or portfolio is 50 percent higher than that of the market. Some securities or portfolio could have negative volatilities. This would imply that if the market rose by 10 percent, the return to the individual security or portfolio might drop 10 percent. This would represent a volatility of negative 1. If when the market rose 10 percent the return to the individual security or portfolio dropped 20 percent this would represent a volatility of negative 2.

The concept of volatility is particularly appropriate to analyze the characteristics of international investments. Economic developments that might be favorable to domestic investments in the United States, might be unfavorable to foreign activities and investments and conversely. Thus the concept of volatility describes the behavior of the returns from an individual security or portfolio in relation to those of the market as a whole. By combining the securities or portfolios of different degrees of volatility, the firm or investor can influence the desired level of systematic risk. This will determine how the portfolio moves in relation to fluctuations in the total market. It is in this respect that international investments are of particular interest and value to individual investors and firms. The special characteristics of international investments may enable the firm or investors to achieve portfolio diversification of the kind desired. This then represents another opportunity for international business and international investments generally.

---

[2] The risk that can be reduced or eliminated by portfolio diversification is termed "unsystematic" risk.

THE FORMULATION OF PROBABILITY ESTIMATES

A critical aspect of the foregoing type of analysis involves the formulation of the probability estimates. A number of bases can be used to make these estimates. For example, in formulating the probabilities of repayment on a credit sale, the credit rating of the buyer and his previous payment record are guides. The previous experience of our firm or other firms with investments of the type under analysis can also provide guidance. Sometimes probability judgments may be formulated on the basis of the analysis of qualitative factors influencing the outcomes.

The most pervasive influence on the success or failure of business projects is the general economic climate. Therefore, probabilities are sometimes formulated with respect to forecasts of general economic developments. For example, we might have four probabilities: (1) that the economy will improve slightly, or (2) that it will improve substantially. Another set of possibilities would be (3) that the economy will deteriorate slightly, or (4) that it will deteriorate greatly. We could then assign probabilities on the basis of our evaluation of the economy's outlook. Or, alternatively, we could apply probabilities to prospects for foreign exchange rates. On the basis of the framework set forth in Chapters 2 and 13, we might again have four possibilities: (1) that the balance-of-payments position of the United States would improve slightly, or (2) that it would improve substantially. The other possibilities are (3) that it would worsen slightly, or (4) that it would deteriorate considerably.

Our emphasis is that in a world of new developments, and with continuous changes in economic influences, it is highly unrealistic and impractical to work with what have been referred to as "single-valued estimates." It is simply wrong to work with one number when thinking about uncertain outcomes that will take place sometime in the future. We can be certain only that new developments will occur. It is the task of business managers to assess these changes and become accustomed to thinking of alternative developments that will produce different future states of the world and the investment outcomes associated with them. The manager should then consider what alternative policies and decisions would be best in view of alternate future states of the world.

SUMMARY

International business financial decisions are not basically different from other business decisions. The basic tools used are the same. Only some of the inputs are different. The outcomes of investment are not usually known in advance and decision makers must consider different possible outcomes. This is referred to as risk and can come from new and diverse sources in international situations.

The first step in analyzing an international business investment opportunity would be to consider the different major events we reasonably expect to occur. We would usually first consider basic economic phenomena, such as boom, recession, business as usual, devaluation, etc. These are referred to as "states of the world." Next we make estimates of the probability of each of these "states" occurring. For each state we consider the implication for alternative investment possibilities. We note that one state may have negative implications for one of our investments and positive implications for another.

Next we want to summarize the information we have collected so as to compare different investments opportunities for their benefits and risks. To make this comparison we need summary measures. The two parameters we use are (1) expected return, and (2) standard deviation of return, respectively for benefits and risks. The expected return of an investment opportunity is the weighted average of the returns under all possible states of the world with the probabilities of these states used as the weights. The standard deviation is a measure of the dispersion of the different possible outcomes around the expected return.

In considering investment opportunities with the tools of risk and return, the firm could view its assets as a portfolio, review its existing set of assets, and consider its investment decision in a portfolio context. If a firm does view its investment decisions in a portfolio context, and it uses standard deviation of return as its measure of risk, then the relevant risk considerations of a new investment opportunity becomes not its standard deviation but its covariance with the firm's existing portfolio of assets. The covariance in an index which indicates how the outcomes on the new investment is related to the outcomes of the existing investments.

Although managers could view the firm as a portfolio, should they? In an economy with well-developed equity markets, individuals can diversify for themselves and make their own portfolio decisions by buying different stocks. In this case, they do not need operating business firms to make portfolio decisions for them. In international markets, the firm has the opportunity to gather information and make decisions more cheaply than investors could do it themselves, because international equity markets are not well developed. Thus, managers perform a valuable service to investors by diversifying internationally.

Diversification does not consist merely of engaging in many diverse activities, but in finding those combinations of investments which are efficient: They give maximum return for a given level of risk or have minimum risk for a given level of return. One way of doing this is to seek out international business activities with low or negative covariance with the firms existing assets since this would tend to reduce risk in their resulting portfolio.

When is a portfolio completely diversified? This question has special meaning in an international context. In the domestic market a portfolio is completely diversified when it is perfectly positively correlated with the market portfolio—a broadly diversified set of domestic investment activities. We then use the covariance of an investment's return with the return on the market portfolio as a measure of the investment's non-diversifiable risk. Diversifiable risk is risk of an investment which could, in theory, be diversified away by placing it in a portfolio which was perfectly negatively correlated with it. In practice, most investments have returns which are correlated with the returns on the market portfolio. The correlation of returns with the returns on the market portfolio is risk that cannot be diversified away. Any portfolio which is not completely perfectly correlated with the market has some diversifiable risk in it. Only completely diversified portfolios are efficient.

The basic analysis of business decisions under conditions of risk using the risk and return tools developed here is the same for international business decisions as for purely domestic ones. There are two basic differences for international problems: (1) The set of available investments opportunities is much larger and more diverse, (2) the lack of well-developed equity markets makes it incumbent upon the firm to perform some of the diversification tasks for investors which they would usually perform for themselves or would have done for them by mutual funds. Regardless of these differences, the basic considerations are the same for international investment as for domestic investment.

APPENDIX D

Tables

Compound sum of $1

Present value of $1

Present value of $1 received annually

Sum of an annuity for $1 for n years

Present value of $1/12 received monthly in year n

Present value of $1/12 received monthly for n years

Compound sum of $1 $S_n = P(1 + r)^n$

Year	1%	2%	3%	4%	5%	6%	7%	8%	9%	10%	11%	12%	13%	14%	15%	16%
1	1.010	1.020	1.030	1.040	1.050	1.060	1.070	1.080	1.090	1.100	1.110	1.120	1.130	1.140	1.150	1.160
2	1.020	1.040	1.061	1.082	1.102	1.124	1.145	1.166	1.188	1.210	1.232	1.254	1.277	1.300	1.322	1.346
3	1.030	1.061	1.093	1.125	1.158	1.191	1.225	1.260	1.295	1.331	1.368	1.405	1.443	1.482	1.521	1.561
4	1.041	1.082	1.126	1.170	1.216	1.262	1.311	1.360	1.412	1.464	1.518	1.574	1.631	1.689	1.749	1.811
5	1.051	1.104	1.159	1.217	1.276	1.338	1.403	1.469	1.539	1.611	1.685	1.762	1.842	1.925	2.011	2.100
6	1.062	1.126	1.194	1.265	1.340	1.419	1.501	1.587	1.677	1.772	1.870	1.974	2.082	2.195	2.313	2.436
7	1.072	1.149	1.230	1.316	1.407	1.504	1.606	1.714	1.828	1.949	2.076	2.211	2.353	2.502	2.660	2.826
8	1.083	1.172	1.267	1.369	1.477	1.594	1.718	1.851	1.993	2.144	2.305	2.476	2.658	2.853	3.059	3.278
9	1.094	1.195	1.305	1.423	1.551	1.689	1.838	1.999	2.172	2.358	2.558	2.773	3.004	3.252	3.518	3.803
10	1.105	1.219	1.344	1.480	1.629	1.791	1.967	2.159	2.367	2.594	2.839	3.106	3.395	3.707	4.046	4.411
11	1.116	1.243	1.384	1.539	1.710	1.898	2.105	2.332	2.580	2.853	3.152	3.479	3.836	4.226	4.652	5.117
12	1.127	1.268	1.426	1.601	1.796	2.012	2.252	2.518	2.813	3.138	3.499	3.896	4.335	4.818	5.350	5.936
13	1.138	1.294	1.469	1.665	1.886	2.133	2.410	2.720	3.066	3.452	3.883	4.363	4.898	5.492	6.153	6.886
14	1.149	1.319	1.513	1.732	1.980	2.261	2.579	2.937	3.342	3.797	4.310	4.887	5.535	6.261	7.076	7.988
15	1.161	1.346	1.558	1.801	2.079	2.397	2.759	3.172	3.642	4.177	4.785	5.474	6.254	7.138	8.137	9.266
16	1.173	1.373	1.605	1.873	2.183	2.540	2.952	3.426	3.970	4.595	5.311	6.130	7.067	8.137	9.358	10.748
17	1.184	1.400	1.653	1.948	2.292	2.693	3.159	3.700	4.328	5.054	5.895	6.866	7.986	9.276	10.761	12.468
18	1.196	1.428	1.702	2.026	2.407	2.854	3.380	3.996	4.717	5.560	6.544	7.690	9.024	10.575	12.375	14.463
19	1.208	1.457	1.754	2.107	2.527	3.026	3.617	4.316	5.142	6.116	7.263	8.613	10.197	12.056	14.232	16.777
20	1.220	1.486	1.806	2.191	2.653	3.207	3.870	4.661	5.604	6.728	8.062	9.646	11.523	13.743	16.367	19.461

Source: Adapted from Jerome Bracken and Charles J. Christenson, *Tables for Use in Analyzing Business Decisions* (Homewood, Ill.: Richard D. Irwin, Inc., 1965).

Present value of $1

$$P = S_n(1 + r)^{-n}$$

Years Hence	1%	2%	4%	6%	8%	10%	12%	14%	15%	16%	18%	20%	22%	24%	25%	26%	28%	30%	35%	40%	45%	50%
1	0.990	0.980	0.962	0.943	0.926	0.909	0.893	0.877	0.870	0.862	0.847	0.833	0.820	0.806	0.800	0.794	0.781	0.769	0.741	0.714	0.690	0.667
2	0.980	0.961	0.925	0.890	0.857	0.826	0.797	0.769	0.756	0.743	0.718	0.694	0.672	0.650	0.640	0.630	0.610	0.592	0.549	0.510	0.476	0.444
3	0.971	0.942	0.889	0.840	0.794	0.751	0.712	0.675	0.658	0.641	0.609	0.579	0.551	0.524	0.512	0.500	0.477	0.455	0.406	0.364	0.328	0.296
4	0.961	0.924	0.855	0.792	0.735	0.683	0.636	0.592	0.572	0.552	0.516	0.482	0.451	0.423	0.410	0.397	0.373	0.350	0.301	0.260	0.226	0.198
5	0.951	0.906	0.822	0.747	0.681	0.621	0.567	0.519	0.497	0.476	0.437	0.402	0.370	0.341	0.328	0.315	0.291	0.269	0.223	0.186	0.156	0.132
6	0.942	0.888	0.790	0.705	0.630	0.564	0.507	0.456	0.432	0.410	0.370	0.335	0.303	0.275	0.262	0.250	0.227	0.207	0.165	0.133	0.108	0.088
7	0.933	0.871	0.760	0.665	0.583	0.513	0.452	0.400	0.376	0.354	0.314	0.279	0.249	0.222	0.210	0.198	0.178	0.159	0.122	0.095	0.074	0.059
8	0.923	0.853	0.731	0.627	0.540	0.467	0.404	0.351	0.327	0.305	0.266	0.233	0.204	0.179	0.168	0.157	0.139	0.123	0.091	0.068	0.051	0.039
9	0.914	0.837	0.703	0.592	0.500	0.424	0.361	0.308	0.284	0.263	0.225	0.194	0.167	0.144	0.134	0.125	0.108	0.094	0.067	0.048	0.035	0.026
10	0.905	0.820	0.676	0.558	0.463	0.386	0.322	0.270	0.247	0.227	0.191	0.162	0.137	0.116	0.107	0.099	0.085	0.073	0.050	0.035	0.024	0.017
11	0.896	0.804	0.650	0.527	0.429	0.350	0.287	0.237	0.215	0.195	0.162	0.135	0.112	0.094	0.086	0.079	0.066	0.056	0.037	0.025	0.017	0.012
12	0.887	0.788	0.625	0.497	0.397	0.319	0.257	0.208	0.187	0.168	0.137	0.112	0.092	0.076	0.069	0.062	0.052	0.043	0.027	0.018	0.012	0.008
13	0.879	0.773	0.601	0.469	0.368	0.290	0.229	0.182	0.163	0.145	0.116	0.093	0.075	0.061	0.055	0.050	0.040	0.033	0.020	0.013	0.008	0.005
14	0.870	0.758	0.577	0.442	0.340	0.263	0.205	0.160	0.141	0.125	0.099	0.078	0.062	0.049	0.044	0.039	0.032	0.025	0.015	0.009	0.006	0.003
15	0.861	0.743	0.555	0.417	0.315	0.239	0.183	0.140	0.123	0.108	0.084	0.065	0.051	0.040	0.035	0.031	0.025	0.020	0.011	0.006	0.004	0.002
16	0.853	0.728	0.534	0.394	0.292	0.218	0.163	0.123	0.107	0.093	0.071	0.054	0.042	0.032	0.028	0.025	0.019	0.015	0.008	0.005	0.003	0.002
17	0.844	0.714	0.513	0.371	0.270	0.198	0.146	0.108	0.093	0.080	0.060	0.045	0.034	0.026	0.023	0.020	0.015	0.012	0.006	0.003	0.002	0.001
18	0.836	0.700	0.494	0.350	0.250	0.180	0.130	0.095	0.081	0.069	0.051	0.038	0.028	0.021	0.018	0.016	0.012	0.009	0.005	0.002	0.001	0.001
19	0.828	0.686	0.475	0.331	0.232	0.164	0.116	0.083	0.070	0.060	0.043	0.031	0.023	0.017	0.014	0.012	0.009	0.007	0.003	0.002	0.001	
20	0.820	0.673	0.456	0.312	0.215	0.149	0.104	0.073	0.061	0.051	0.037	0.026	0.019	0.014	0.012	0.010	0.007	0.005	0.002	0.001		
21	0.811	0.660	0.439	0.294	0.199	0.135	0.093	0.064	0.053	0.044	0.031	0.022	0.015	0.011	0.009	0.008	0.006	0.004	0.002	0.001		
22	0.803	0.647	0.422	0.278	0.184	0.123	0.083	0.056	0.046	0.038	0.026	0.018	0.013	0.009	0.007	0.006	0.004	0.003	0.001	0.001		
23	0.795	0.634	0.406	0.262	0.170	0.112	0.074	0.049	0.040	0.033	0.022	0.015	0.010	0.007	0.006	0.005	0.003	0.002	0.001			
24	0.788	0.622	0.390	0.247	0.158	0.102	0.066	0.043	0.035	0.028	0.019	0.013	0.008	0.006	0.005	0.004	0.003	0.002	0.001			
25	0.780	0.610	0.375	0.233	0.146	0.092	0.059	0.038	0.030	0.024	0.016	0.010	0.007	0.005	0.004	0.003	0.002	0.001	0.001			
26	0.772	0.598	0.361	0.220	0.135	0.084	0.053	0.033	0.026	0.021	0.014	0.009	0.006	0.004	0.003	0.002	0.002	0.001				
27	0.764	0.586	0.347	0.207	0.125	0.076	0.047	0.029	0.023	0.018	0.011	0.007	0.005	0.003	0.002	0.002	0.001	0.001				
28	0.757	0.574	0.333	0.196	0.116	0.069	0.042	0.026	0.020	0.016	0.010	0.006	0.004	0.002	0.002	0.001	0.001	0.001				
29	0.749	0.563	0.321	0.185	0.107	0.063	0.037	0.022	0.017	0.014	0.008	0.005	0.003	0.002	0.002	0.001	0.001	0.001				
30	0.742	0.552	0.308	0.174	0.099	0.057	0.033	0.020	0.015	0.012	0.007	0.004	0.003	0.002	0.001	0.001	0.001					
40	0.672	0.453	0.208	0.097	0.046	0.022	0.011	0.005	0.004	0.003	0.001	0.001										
50	0.608	0.372	0.141	0.054	0.021	0.009	0.003	0.001	0.001	0.001												

Source: Adapted from Jerome Bracken and Charles J. Christenson, *Tables for Use in Analyzing Business Decisions* (Homewood, Ill.: Richard D. Irwin, Inc., 1965).

Present value of $1 received annually

$$A_{\overline{n}|r} = \$1\left[\frac{1-(1+r)^{-n}}{r}\right] = \$1P_{n,r}$$

Years (n)	1%	2%	4%	6%	8%	10%	12%	14%	15%	16%	18%	20%	22%	24%	25%	26%	28%	30%	35%	40%	45%	50%
1	0.990	0.980	0.962	0.943	0.926	0.909	0.893	0.877	0.870	0.862	0.847	0.833	0.820	0.806	0.800	0.794	0.781	0.769	0.741	0.714	0.690	0.667
2	1.970	1.942	1.886	1.833	1.783	1.736	1.690	1.647	1.626	1.605	1.566	1.528	1.492	1.457	1.440	1.424	1.392	1.361	1.289	1.224	1.165	1.111
3	2.941	2.884	2.775	2.673	2.577	2.487	2.402	2.322	2.283	2.246	2.174	2.106	2.042	1.981	1.952	1.923	1.868	1.816	1.696	1.589	1.493	1.407
4	3.902	3.808	3.630	3.465	3.312	3.170	3.037	2.914	2.855	2.798	2.690	2.589	2.494	2.404	2.362	2.320	2.241	2.166	1.997	1.849	1.720	1.605
5	4.853	4.713	4.452	4.212	3.993	3.791	3.605	3.433	3.352	3.274	3.127	2.991	2.864	2.745	2.689	2.635	2.532	2.436	2.220	2.035	1.876	1.737
6	5.795	5.601	5.242	4.917	4.623	4.355	4.111	3.889	3.784	3.685	3.498	3.326	3.167	3.020	2.951	2.885	2.759	2.643	2.385	2.168	1.983	1.824
7	6.728	6.472	6.002	5.582	5.206	4.868	4.564	4.288	4.160	4.039	3.812	3.605	3.416	3.242	3.161	3.083	2.937	2.802	2.508	2.263	2.057	1.883
8	7.652	7.325	6.733	6.210	5.747	5.335	4.968	4.639	4.487	4.344	4.078	3.837	3.619	3.421	3.329	3.241	3.076	2.925	2.598	2.331	2.108	1.922
9	8.566	8.162	7.435	6.802	6.247	5.759	5.328	4.946	4.772	4.607	4.303	4.031	3.786	3.566	3.463	3.366	3.184	3.019	2.665	2.379	2.144	1.948
10	9.471	8.983	8.111	7.360	6.710	6.145	5.650	5.216	5.019	4.833	4.494	4.192	3.923	3.682	3.571	3.465	3.269	3.092	2.715	2.414	2.168	1.965
11	10.368	9.787	8.760	7.887	7.139	6.495	5.937	5.453	5.234	5.029	4.656	4.327	4.035	3.776	3.656	3.544	3.335	3.147	2.752	2.438	2.185	1.977
12	11.255	10.575	9.385	8.384	7.536	6.814	6.194	5.660	5.421	5.197	4.793	4.439	4.127	3.851	3.725	3.606	3.387	3.190	2.779	2.456	2.196	1.985
13	12.134	11.343	9.986	8.853	7.904	7.103	6.424	5.842	5.583	5.342	4.910	4.533	4.203	3.912	3.780	3.656	3.427	3.223	2.799	2.468	2.204	1.990
14	13.004	12.106	10.563	9.295	8.244	7.367	6.628	6.002	5.724	5.468	5.008	4.611	4.265	3.962	3.824	3.695	3.459	3.249	2.814	2.477	2.210	1.993
15	13.865	12.849	11.118	9.712	8.559	7.606	6.811	6.142	5.847	5.575	5.092	4.675	4.315	4.001	3.859	3.726	3.483	3.268	2.825	2.484	2.214	1.995
16	14.718	13.578	11.652	10.106	8.851	7.824	6.974	6.265	5.954	5.669	5.162	4.730	4.357	4.033	3.887	3.751	3.503	3.283	2.834	2.489	2.216	1.997
17	15.562	14.292	12.166	10.477	9.122	8.022	7.120	6.373	6.047	5.749	5.222	4.775	4.391	4.059	3.910	3.771	3.518	3.295	2.840	2.492	2.218	1.998
18	16.398	14.992	12.659	10.828	9.372	8.201	7.250	6.467	6.128	5.818	5.273	4.812	4.419	4.080	3.928	3.786	3.529	3.304	2.844	2.494	2.219	1.999
19	17.226	15.678	13.134	11.158	9.604	8.365	7.366	6.550	6.198	5.877	5.316	4.844	4.442	4.097	3.942	3.799	3.539	3.311	2.848	2.496	2.220	1.999
20	18.046	16.351	13.590	11.470	9.818	8.514	7.469	6.623	6.259	5.929	5.353	4.870	4.460	4.110	3.954	3.808	3.546	3.316	2.850	2.497	2.221	1.999
21	18.857	17.011	14.029	11.764	10.017	8.649	7.562	6.687	6.312	5.973	5.384	4.891	4.476	4.121	3.963	3.816	3.551	3.320	2.852	2.498	2.221	2.000
22	19.660	17.658	14.451	12.042	10.201	8.772	7.645	6.743	6.359	6.011	5.410	4.909	4.488	4.130	3.970	3.822	3.556	3.323	2.853	2.498	2.222	2.000
23	20.456	18.292	14.857	12.303	10.371	8.883	7.718	6.792	6.399	6.044	5.432	4.925	4.499	4.137	3.976	3.827	3.559	3.325	2.854	2.499	2.222	2.000
24	21.243	18.914	15.247	12.550	10.529	8.985	7.784	6.835	6.434	6.073	5.451	4.937	4.507	4.143	3.981	3.831	3.562	3.327	2.855	2.499	2.222	2.000
25	22.023	19.523	15.622	12.783	10.675	9.077	7.843	6.873	6.464	6.097	5.467	4.948	4.514	4.147	3.985	3.834	3.564	3.329	2.856	2.499	2.222	2.000
26	22.795	20.121	15.983	13.003	10.810	9.161	7.896	6.906	6.491	6.118	5.480	4.956	4.520	4.151	3.988	3.837	3.566	3.330	2.856	2.500	2.222	2.000
27	23.560	20.707	16.330	13.211	10.935	9.237	7.943	6.935	6.514	6.136	5.492	4.964	4.524	4.154	3.990	3.839	3.567	3.331	2.856	2.500	2.222	2.000
28	24.316	21.281	16.663	13.406	11.051	9.307	7.984	6.961	6.534	6.152	5.502	4.970	4.528	4.157	3.992	3.840	3.568	3.331	2.857	2.500	2.222	2.000
29	25.066	21.844	16.984	13.591	11.158	9.370	8.022	6.983	6.551	6.166	5.510	4.975	4.531	4.159	3.994	3.841	3.569	3.332	2.857	2.500	2.222	2.000
30	25.808	22.396	17.292	13.765	11.258	9.427	8.055	7.003	6.566	6.177	5.517	4.979	4.534	4.160	3.995	3.842	3.569	3.332	2.857	2.500	2.222	2.000
40	32.835	27.355	19.793	15.046	11.925	9.779	8.244	7.105	6.642	6.234	5.548	4.997	4.544	4.166	3.999	3.846	3.571	3.333	2.857	2.500	2.222	2.000
50	39.196	31.424	21.482	15.762	12.234	9.915	8.304	7.133	6.661	6.246	5.554	4.999	4.545	4.167	4.000	3.846	3.571	3.333	2.857	2.500	2.222	2.000

Source: Adapted from Jerome Bracken and Charles J. Christenson, *Tables for Use in Analyzing Business Decisions* (Homewood, Ill.: Richard D. Irwin, Inc., 1965).

Sum of an annuity for $1 for n years $S_{\overline{n}|r} = \$1 \left[\dfrac{(1+r)^n - 1}{r} \right] = \$1C_{n,r}$

Year	1%	2%	3%	4%	5%	6%	7%	8%	9%	10%	11%	12%	13%	14%	15%	16%
1.....	1.000	1.000	1.000	1.000	1.000	1.000	1.000	1.000	1.000	1.000	1.000	1.000	1.000	1.000	1.000	1.000
2.....	2.010	2.020	2.030	2.040	2.050	2.060	2.070	2.080	2.090	2.100	2.110	2.120	2.130	2.140	2.150	2.160
3.....	3.030	3.060	3.091	3.122	3.152	3.184	3.215	3.246	3.278	3.310	3.342	3.374	3.407	3.440	3.473	3.506
4.....	4.060	4.122	4.184	4.246	4.310	4.375	4.440	4.506	4.573	4.641	4.710	4.779	4.850	4.921	4.993	5.066
5.....	5.101	5.204	5.309	5.416	5.526	5.637	5.751	5.867	5.985	6.105	6.228	6.353	6.480	6.610	6.742	6.877
6.....	6.152	6.308	6.468	6.633	6.802	6.975	7.153	7.336	7.523	7.716	7.913	8.115	8.323	8.536	8.754	8.977
7.....	7.214	7.434	7.662	7.898	8.142	8.394	8.654	8.923	9.200	9.487	9.783	10.089	10.405	10.730	11.067	11.414
8.....	8.286	8.583	8.892	9.214	9.549	9.897	10.260	10.637	11.028	11.436	11.859	12.300	12.757	13.233	13.727	14.240
9.....	9.369	9.755	10.159	10.583	11.027	11.491	11.978	12.488	13.021	13.579	14.164	14.776	15.416	16.085	16.786	17.518
10.....	10.462	10.950	11.464	12.006	12.578	13.181	13.816	14.487	15.193	15.937	16.722	17.549	18.420	19.337	20.304	21.321
11.....	11.567	12.169	12.808	13.486	14.207	14.972	15.784	16.645	17.560	18.531	19.561	20.655	21.814	23.044	24.349	25.733
12.....	12.683	13.412	14.192	15.026	15.917	16.870	17.888	18.977	20.141	21.384	22.713	24.133	25.650	27.271	29.002	30.850
13.....	13.809	14.680	15.618	16.627	17.713	18.882	20.141	21.495	22.953	24.523	26.212	28.029	29.985	32.089	34.352	36.786
14.....	14.947	15.974	17.086	18.292	19.599	21.051	22.550	24.215	26.019	27.975	30.095	32.393	34.883	37.581	40.505	43.672
15.....	16.097	17.293	18.599	20.024	21.579	23.276	25.129	27.152	29.361	31.772	34.405	37.280	40.417	43.842	47.580	51.659

Source: Adapted from Jerome Bracken and Charles J. Christenson, *Tables for Use in Analyzing Business Decisions* (Homewood, Ill.: Richard D. Irwin, Inc., 1965).

Present value of $1/12 received monthly in year n

Year (n)	1%	2%	4%	6%	8%	10%	12%	14%	15%	16%	18%	20%	22%	24%	25%	26%	28%	30%	35%	40%	45%	50%
1	0.995	0.989	0.979	0.969	0.959	0.950	0.941	0.932	0.928	0.924	0.915	0.907	0.899	0.892	0.888	0.884	0.877	0.870	0.853	0.837	0.822	0.808
2	0.985	0.970	0.941	0.914	0.888	0.864	0.840	0.818	0.807	0.796	0.776	0.756	0.737	0.719	0.710	0.702	0.685	0.669	0.632	0.598	0.567	0.539
3	0.975	0.951	0.905	0.862	0.823	0.785	0.750	0.717	0.702	0.686	0.657	0.630	0.604	0.580	0.568	0.557	0.535	0.515	0.468	0.427	0.391	0.359
4	0.965	0.932	0.870	0.814	0.762	0.714	0.670	0.629	0.610	0.592	0.557	0.525	0.495	0.468	0.455	0.442	0.418	0.396	0.347	0.305	0.270	0.239
5	0.956	0.914	0.837	0.768	0.705	0.649	0.598	0.552	0.531	0.510	0.472	0.438	0.406	0.377	0.364	0.351	0.327	0.305	0.257	0.218	0.186	0.160
6	0.946	0.896	0.805	0.724	0.653	0.590	0.534	0.484	0.461	0.440	0.400	0.365	0.333	0.304	0.291	0.278	0.255	0.234	0.190	0.156	0.128	0.106
7	0.937	0.879	0.774	0.683	0.605	0.536	0.477	0.425	0.401	0.379	0.339	0.304	0.273	0.245	0.233	0.221	0.199	0.180	0.141	0.111	0.088	0.071
8	0.928	0.861	0.744	0.644	0.560	0.488	0.426	0.373	0.349	0.327	0.287	0.253	0.224	0.198	0.186	0.175	0.156	0.139	0.104	0.079	0.061	0.047
9	0.919	0.844	0.715	0.608	0.518	0.443	0.380	0.327	0.303	0.282	0.244	0.211	0.183	0.160	0.149	0.139	0.122	0.107	0.077	0.057	0.042	0.032
10	0.909	0.828	0.688	0.574	0.480	0.403	0.339	0.287	0.264	0.243	0.206	0.176	0.150	0.129	0.119	0.110	0.095	0.082	0.057	0.041	0.029	0.021
11	0.900	0.812	0.661	0.541	0.444	0.366	0.303	0.251	0.229	0.209	0.175	0.147	0.123	0.104	0.095	0.088	0.074	0.063	0.042	0.029	0.020	0.014
12	0.892	0.796	0.636	0.510	0.411	0.323	0.271	0.221	0.199	0.180	0.148	0.122	0.101	0.084	0.076	0.070	0.058	0.049	0.031	0.021	0.014	0.009
13	0.883	0.780	0.612	0.482	0.381	0.303	0.242	0.193	0.173	0.156	0.126	0.102	0.083	0.067	0.061	0.055	0.045	0.037	0.023	0.015	0.010	0.006
14	0.874	0.765	0.588	0.454	0.353	0.275	0.216	0.170	0.151	0.134	0.106	0.085	0.068	0.054	0.049	0.044	0.035	0.029	0.017	0.011	0.007	0.004
15	0.865	0.750	0.565	0.429	0.327	0.250	0.193	0.149	0.131	0.116	0.090	0.071	0.056	0.044	0.039	0.035	0.028	0.022	0.013	0.008	0.005	0.003
16	0.857	0.735	0.544	0.404	0.302	0.227	0.172	0.131	0.114	0.100	0.076	0.059	0.046	0.035	0.031	0.028	0.022	0.017	0.009	0.005	0.003	0.002
17	0.848	0.721	0.523	0.381	0.280	0.207	0.153	0.115	0.099	0.086	0.065	0.049	0.037	0.029	0.025	0.022	0.017	0.013	0.007	0.004	0.002	0.001
18	0.840	0.707	0.503	0.360	0.259	0.188	0.137	0.100	0.086	0.074	0.055	0.041	0.031	0.023	0.020	0.017	0.013	0.010	0.005	0.003	0.001	0.001
19	0.832	0.693	0.483	0.340	0.240	0.171	0.122	0.088	0.075	0.064	0.047	0.034	0.025	0.019	0.016	0.014	0.010	0.008	0.004	0.002	0.001	0.001
20	0.823	0.679	0.465	0.320	0.222	0.155	0.109	0.077	0.065	0.055	0.039	0.028	0.021	0.015	0.013	0.011	0.008	0.006	0.003	0.001	0.001	0.001
21	0.815	0.666	0.447	0.302	0.206	0.141	0.098	0.068	0.057	0.047	0.033	0.024	0.017	0.012	0.010	0.009	0.006	0.005	0.002	0.001		
22	0.807	0.653	0.430	0.285	0.191	0.128	0.087	0.060	0.049	0.041	0.028	0.020	0.014	0.010	0.008	0.007	0.005	0.004	0.002	0.001		
23	0.799	0.640	0.413	0.269	0.176	0.117	0.078	0.052	0.043	0.035	0.024	0.016	0.011	0.008	0.007	0.005	0.004	0.003	0.001	0.001		
24	0.791	0.627	0.397	0.254	0.163	0.106	0.069	0.046	0.037	0.030	0.020	0.014	0.009	0.006	0.005	0.004	0.003	0.002	0.001			
25	0.783	0.615	0.382	0.239	0.151	0.096	0.062	0.040	0.032	0.026	0.017	0.011	0.008	0.005	0.004	0.003	0.002	0.002	0.001			
26	0.776	0.603	0.367	0.226	0.140	0.088	0.055	0.035	0.028	0.023	0.015	0.010	0.006	0.004	0.003	0.003	0.002	0.001				
27	0.768	0.591	0.353	0.213	0.130	0.080	0.049	0.031	0.025	0.019	0.012	0.008	0.005	0.003	0.003	0.002	0.001	0.001				
28	0.760	0.580	0.340	0.201	0.120	0.072	0.044	0.027	0.021	0.017	0.010	0.007	0.004	0.003	0.002	0.002	0.001	0.001				
29	0.753	0.568	0.326	0.190	0.111	0.066	0.039	0.024	0.019	0.014	0.009	0.006	0.003	0.002	0.002	0.001	0.001	0.001				
30	0.745	0.557	0.314	0.179	0.103	0.060	0.035	0.021	0.016	0.012	0.008	0.005	0.003	0.002	0.001	0.001	0.001					
40	0.675	0.457	0.212	0.100	0.048	0.023	0.011	0.006	0.004	0.003	0.001	0.001										
50	0.611	0.375	0.143	0.056	0.022	0.009	0.004	0.002	0.001	0.001												

Source: Robert N. Anthony, Management Accounting: Text and Cases (rev. ed.; Homewood, Ill.: Richard D. Irwin, Inc., 1960).

Present value of $1/12 received monthly for n years

Formula: $\dfrac{1 - (1 + i')^{-n}}{12[(1 + i)^{1/13} - 1]}$ Annual discounting is assumed.

Years n	1%	2%	4%	6%	8%	10%	12%	14%	15%	16%	18%	20%	22%	24%	25%	26%	28%	30%	35%	40%	45%	50%
1	0.995	0.989	0.979	0.969	0.959	0.950	0.941	0.932	0.928	0.924	0.915	0.907	0.899	0.892	0.888	0.884	0.877	0.870	0.853	0.837	0.822	0.808
2	1.979	1.959	1.920	1.883	1.848	1.814	1.781	1.750	1.735	1.720	1.691	1.663	1.637	1.611	1.598	1.586	1.562	1.539	1.485	1.435	1.390	1.347
3	2.954	2.910	2.826	2.746	2.670	2.599	2.531	2.467	2.436	2.406	2.348	2.293	2.241	2.191	2.167	2.143	2.098	2.054	1.953	1.863	1.781	1.706
4	3.920	3.843	3.696	3.559	3.432	3.313	3.201	3.096	3.046	2.998	2.905	2.818	2.736	2.658	2.621	2.585	2.516	2.450	2.300	2.168	2.050	1.946
5	4.876	4.757	4.533	4.327	4.137	3.962	3.799	3.648	3.577	3.508	3.377	3.256	3.142	3.036	2.985	2.936	2.842	2.755	2.557	2.386	2.236	2.106
6	5.822	5.653	5.338	5.051	4.790	4.551	4.333	4.132	4.038	3.948	3.778	3.620	3.475	3.340	3.276	3.214	3.098	2.989	2.747	2.541	2.365	2.212
7	6.759	6.531	6.111	5.734	5.395	5.088	4.810	4.557	4.439	4.327	4.117	3.924	3.748	3.585	3.509	3.435	3.297	3.169	2.888	2.653	2.453	2.283
8	7.687	7.392	6.855	6.379	5.954	5.575	5.235	4.929	4.788	4.654	4.404	4.177	3.971	3.783	3.695	3.611	3.453	3.308	2.992	2.732	2.514	2.330
9	8.605	8.237	7.571	6.987	6.473	6.018	5.615	5.256	5.091	4.935	4.647	4.388	4.154	3.942	3.844	3.750	3.575	3.414	3.070	2.789	2.556	2.362
10	9.515	9.065	8.259	7.560	6.953	6.421	5.955	5.543	5.355	5.178	4.854	4.564	4.305	4.071	3.963	3.860	3.670	3.497	3.127	2.829	2.585	2.383
11	10.415	9.876	8.920	8.101	7.397	6.788	6.258	5.794	5.584	5.388	5.029	4.711	4.428	4.175	4.058	3.948	3.744	3.560	3.169	2.858	2.605	2.397
12	11.307	10.672	9.556	8.612	7.809	7.121	6.528	6.015	5.784	5.568	5.177	4.833	4.529	4.259	4.135	4.018	3.802	3.608	3.201	2.879	2.619	2.406
13	12.189	11.452	10.167	9.094	8.190	7.423	6.770	6.208	5.957	5.724	5.302	4.935	4.611	4.326	4.196	4.073	3.847	3.646	3.224	2.894	2.629	2.412
14	13.063	12.217	10.755	9.548	8.542	7.699	6.985	6.378	6.108	5.858	5.409	5.019	4.679	4.380	4.245	4.117	3.883	3.674	3.241	2.904	2.635	2.417
15	13.928	12.967	11.321	9.977	8.869	7.949	7.178	6.527	6.239	5.973	5.499	5.090	4.735	4.424	4.284	4.152	3.911	3.696	3.254	2.912	2.640	2.419
16	14.785	13.702	11.864	10.381	9.171	8.176	7.350	6.658	6.353	6.073	5.576	5.149	4.780	4.460	4.315	4.179	3.932	3.713	3.264	2.917	2.643	2.421
17	15.633	14.422	12.387	10.762	9.451	8.383	7.503	6.772	6.452	6.159	5.640	5.198	4.818	4.488	4.340	4.201	3.949	3.726	3.271	2.921	2.645	2.422
18	16.473	15.129	12.890	11.122	9.711	8.571	7.640	6.873	6.539	6.233	5.742	5.239	4.848	4.511	4.360	4.218	3.962	3.736	3.276	2.924	2.647	2.423
19	17.305	15.822	13.373	11.462	9.951	8.742	7.763	6.961	6.614	6.297	5.742	5.273	4.873	4.530	4.376	4.232	3.973	3.744	3.280	2.926	2.648	2.424
20	18.128	16.501	13.838	11.782	10.173	8.897	7.872	7.038	6.679	6.352	5.781	5.301	4.894	4.545	4.389	4.243	3.981	3.750	3.283	2.927	2.648	2.424
21	18.943	17.167	14.285	12.084	10.379	9.038	7.969	7.106	6.735	6.399	5.815	5.325	4.911	4.557	4.399	4.252	3.987	3.755	3.285	2.928	2.649	2.424
22	19.750	17.819	14.714	12.369	10.570	9.167	8.056	7.165	6.785	6.440	5.843	5.345	4.925	4.567	4.407	4.259	3.992	3.758	3.286	2.929	2.649	2.425
23	20.549	18.459	15.127	12.638	10.746	9.283	8.134	7.218	6.828	6.476	5.867	5.361	4.936	4.574	4.414	4.264	3.996	3.761	3.287	2.929	2.649	2.425
24	21.341	19.087	15.525	12.892	10.909	9.389	8.204	7.263	6.865	6.506	5.887	5.375	4.945	4.581	4.419	4.269	3.999	3.763	3.288	2.930	2.650	2.425
25	22.124	19.702	15.906	13.131	11.061	9.486	8.266	7.304	6.897	6.532	5.904	5.386	4.953	4.586	4.423	4.272	4.001	3.765	3.289	2.930	2.650	2.425
26	22.899	20.305	16.274	13.357	11.201	9.574	8.321	7.339	6.926	6.555	5.919	5.396	4.959	4.590	4.426	4.275	4.003	3.766	3.289	2.930	2.650	2.425
27	23.667	20.896	16.627	13.570	11.331	9.653	8.370	7.370	6.950	6.574	5.931	5.404	4.964	4.593	4.429	4.277	4.004	3.767	3.290	2.930	2.650	2.425
28	24.428	21.476	16.966	13.771	11.451	9.726	8.415	7.397	6.971	6.591	5.942	5.410	4.968	4.596	4.431	4.279	4.005	3.768	3.290	2.930	2.650	2.425
29	25.180	22.044	17.293	13.961	11.562	9.792	8.454	7.421	6.990	6.606	5.951	5.416	4.972	4.598	4.433	4.280	4.006	3.768	3.290	2.930	2.650	2.425
30	25.926	22.601	17.607	14.139	11.665	9.852	8.489	7.441	7.006	6.618	5.958	5.420	4.975	4.600	4.434	4.281	4.007	3.769	3.290	2.930	2.650	2.425
40	32.985	27.605	20.153	15.456	12.456	10.220	8.688	7.550	7.087	6.678	5.992	5.440	4.986	4.606	4.439	4.285	4.009	3.770	3.291	2.931	2.650	2.425
50	39.375	31.711	21.873	16.191	12.676	10.361	8.752	7.580	7.107	6.692	5.999	5.443	4.987	4.607	4.440	4.285	4.009	3.770	3.291	2.931	2.650	2.425

Source: Robert N. Anthony, Management Accounting: Text and Cases (rev. ed.; Homewood, Ill.: Richard D. Irwin, 1960).

index

Index